THE HOLY LAND
IN THE ERA OF THE
CRUSADES

THE HOLY LAND IN THE ERA OF THE CRUSADES

Kingdoms at the Crossroads of Civilizations, 1100–1300

Helena P. Schrader

AN IMPRINT OF PEN & SWORD BOOKS LTD.
YORKSHIRE – PHILADELPHIA

First published in Great Britain in 2022 by
PEN AND SWORD HISTORY
An imprint of
Pen & Sword Books Ltd
Yorkshire – Philadelphia

Copyright © Helena P. Schrader, 2022

ISBN 978 1 52678 759 0

The right of Helena P. Schrader to be identified as Author of this work has been asserted by her in accordance with the Copyright, Designs and Patents Act 1988.

A CIP catalogue record for this book is available from the British Library.

All rights reserved. No part of this book may be reproduced or transmitted in any form or by any means, electronic or mechanical including photocopying, recording or by any information storage and retrieval system, without permission from the Publisher in writing.

Typeset in Times New Roman 11.5/14 by
SJmagic DESIGN SERVICES, India.
Printed and bound in England by CPI Group (UK) Ltd., Croydon.

Pen & Sword Books Limited incorporates the imprints of Atlas, Archaeology, Aviation, Discovery, Family History, Fiction, History, Maritime, Military, Military Classics, Politics, Select, Transport, True Crime, Air World, Frontline Publishing, Leo Cooper, Remember When, Seaforth Publishing, The Praetorian Press, Wharncliffe Local History, Wharncliffe Transport, Wharncliffe True Crime and White Owl.

For a complete list of Pen & Sword titles please contact
PEN & SWORD BOOKS LIMITED
47 Church Street, Barnsley, South Yorkshire, S70 2AS, England
E-mail: enquiries@pen-and-sword.co.uk
Website: www.pen-and-sword.co.uk

Or
PEN AND SWORD BOOKS
1950 Lawrence Rd, Havertown, PA 19083, USA
E-mail: Uspen-and-sword@casematepublishers.com
Website: www.penandswordbooks.com

Contents

Chronology viii
Introduction xxxiv

PART I: A SHORT HISTORY OF THE CRUSADER STATES

Chapter 1 Genesis of the Crusader States 2
    The Dar al-Islam, Jihad and the Near East Before
      the Crusades 2
    Christianity, Just War and the Call of the Crusade 7
    The 'Peoples' Crusade' 9
    The First Crusade, 1197–1199 11

Chapter 2 The First Kingdom 22
    Years of Expansion, 1100–1174 22
    On the Defensive, 1174–1185 40
    Catastrophe and Collapse, 1185–1187 57

**Chapter 3 The Third Crusade and the Restructuring of the
    Crusader States** 67
    The Third Crusade, 1187–1192 67
    Re-Establishment of the Kingdom of Jerusalem,
      1192–1195 75
    Establishment of the Kingdom of Cyprus, 1192–1197 77

**Chapter 4 The Second Kingdom or the Kingdom of Acre,
    1192–1291** 83
    A Resurgent Frankish Presence, 1192–1225 83
    The Fifth Crusade, 1216–1221 87
    The Sixth Crusade, 1225–1229 90
    Civil War, 1229–1243 93

The 'Barons' Crusade', 1239–1241   101
Dangerous Entanglements: The Ayyubid Alliance
   and La Forbie, 1239–1244   103
Saint Louis and the Seventh Crusade, 1248–1254   105
Mongols and Mamluks: The Changing Face of
   the Middle East   108
The Loss of Latin Syria, 1265–1291   113

Conclusion   118

PART II: A DESCRIPTION OF THE CRUSADER STATES

Chapter 5   A Mediterranean Melting Pot: The Diverse Population of Outremer   122
Demography of the Holy Land in the Era of
   the Crusades   122
The Native Population in the Holy Land   125
The Franks of the Holy Land   134
Frankish Rule in Cyprus   143

Chapter 6   The 'Ideal Feudal State': Institutions of Government, Justice, Finance, Defence and Religion   149
Feudal Superstructure: Kings, Barons and
   the High Court   149
Courts of All Kinds: The Complex Judicial
   System of the Crusader States   157
Administrative Apparatus of Outremer   160
Defence of the Realm   166
Religious Institutions   176

Chapter 7   Foreign Affairs of the Crusader States: 183
Diplomatic Affairs with the Latin West   183
Diplomatic Relations with Byzantium   186
Diplomatic Relations with Muslim Powers   191

Contents

Chapter 8	**The Economy of the Crusader States: Diversity, Prosperity and Technology Transfer**	197
	Introduction and Overview	197
	Agriculture	200
	Religious Tourism and Financial Services	206
	Industry and Manufacturing	209
	Trade	215
	Technological and Intellectual Exchange	220
Chapter 9	**Life and Lifestyle in the Crusader States**	225
	Urban Landscapes, Infrastructure and Architecture	225
	Frankish Art	241
	Language, Literacy and Intellectual Life	247
	Hospitals and Social Welfare	254
	Food and Fashion	261
Chapter 10	**The Ibelins: An Archetypical Frankish Family**	267
	Obscure Origins 1110–1150	268
	The Second Generation 1150–1200	269
	The Third Generation 1190–1240	279
	The Fourth Generation 1225–1266	288
	Swansong of the House of Ibelin 1250–1374	300
Analysis and Conclusions		302
Recommended Reading		306
Endnotes		313
Index		325

PLATES

Maps: The Crusader States 1100-1180, The Crusader States 1190-1240, The Baronies of the Kingdom of Jerusalem in the 12th C.

City Plans: Jerusalem in the 12th C, Acre in the 13th C.

Genealogy Tables: Rulers of Jerusalem, House of Lusignan in Outremer, House of Ibelin

Illustrations: A Rural Village, Acre Harbor, The Great Hall of the Ibelin Palace in Beirut

Chronology

Year	Month	Event
ca. 33	Passover	Jesus of Nazareth crucified in Jerusalem; start of Christian veneration of the sites of his crucifixion and burial in Jerusalem.
70		Destruction of the Second Temple.
135–136		Expulsion of the Jewish and Christian population from Jerusalem; Jerusalem renamed Aelia Capitolina and paganised; a temple to Venus is built on the site of the crucifixion and resurrection.
326		Empress Helena, mother of Constantine the Great, finds what is believed to be the tomb of Christ.
335		Construction of a great basilica to mark the site of Christ's tomb begins; this church is henceforth known as the Church of the Holy Sepulchre.
613		Muhammed begins teaching his new religion in Mecca on the Arabian Peninsula.
614		A Persian army besieges Jerusalem, which falls after twenty-one days; slaughter of 26,500 Christians and enslavement of ca. 35,000 more; Church of the Holy Sepulchre utterly destroyed.
629		Emperor Herakleios regains control of Jerusalem; resettlement and reconstruction of the Church of the Holy Sepulchre begins; Muhammed, after defeating his enemies in armed conflict, returns on 11 December with his army from Medina where he was in exile.
632	June	Muhammed dies.

Chronology

Year	Month	Event
634–644		Muslim conquests of Egypt, Libya, Persia and Syria.
637		Muslim forces under Caliph Umar the Great lay siege to Jerusalem; the city falls after a year.
649		First Arab attacks on Cyprus.
655		Muslims destroy the Byzantine fleet in a naval engagement.
656–661		War breaks out between Muslim factions resulting in the split of Islam into Shia and Sunni divisions.
678		First Muslim siege of Constantinople.
688		Muslim troops withdrawn from Cyprus and the island is required to pay tribute to both Constantinople and the caliphate in Baghdad.
698		Christian city of Carthage falls to Muslim forces.
711–713		Muslim conquest of much of the Iberian Peninsula.
713		Corsica falls to Muslim forces.
717		Second Muslim siege of Constantinople.
732	10 October	Invading Muslim forces are defeated by the Franks under Charles Martel at the Battle of Tours.
746		Byzantine forces regain control of Armenia and Syria.
768–814		Reign of Charlemagne in Europe.
ca. 825		Muslim conquest of Crete.
827–902		Muslim conquest of Sicily.
837		Muslim forces raid the Italian peninsula.
846		Muslim raiders sack Rome, including St Peter's Cathedral.
853		Byzantine raids in Egypt.
878		Egyptian forces under Shia leader Ahmad ibn Tulun capture Jerusalem from the Abbasid caliphate.
888		Muslims establish a base in Provence for raiding throughout the region.

The Holy Land in the Era of the Crusades

Year	Month	Event
904		Sunni Abbasids regain control of Jerusalem.
961		Byzantines regain control of Crete.
969		Fatimids (Shia Muslims) conquer Jerusalem from the Abbasids a second time; establish Fatimid caliphate in Cairo.
965		Byzantines re-establish a presence on Cyprus.
997		Muslim raiders pillage the Cathedral of Santiago de Compostela in Northern Spain.
1009		Fatimid caliph al-Hakim orders the destruction of all churches and synagogues in his realm; destruction includes the Church of the Holy Sepulchre.
1030		Fatimid caliph Ali az-Zahir authorises the rebuilding of a church on the site of Christ's tomb; the second Church of the Holy Sepulchre is built with funding from Byzantium.
1034		Pisans launch a raid against Muslim North Africa.
1061		Norman conquest of Sicily begins.
1066	14 October	Battle of Hastings; Normans establish their rule in England.
1071	26 August	Seljuks, recent converts to Islam, decisively defeat the Byzantines at the Battle of Manzikert; Normans end Byzantine rule in Italy with the capture of Bari.
1073		Seljuks under Emir Atsiz ibn Uvaq capture Jerusalem from the Fatimids.
1074		Pope Gregory VII proposes a campaign to liberate Jerusalem and assist the Eastern Roman Empire against the Turks.
1077		Jerusalem rebels against Emir Atsiz while he is fighting in Egypt; on his return he massacres the population.
1081		Norman invasion of Greece.
1085		Alfonso VI, King of Castile, expels the Muslims from Toledo.

Chronology

Year	Month	Event
1086		Christian Antioch falls to the Seljuks.
1087		Joint Pisan, Genoese, Roman and Amalfi forces destroy one of the main bases for Arab raiding and piracy in what is now Tunisia.
1095	November	Council of Clermont: Pope Urban II calls for fighting men from the West to go to the assistance of the beleaguered Eastern Roman Empire and liberate Jerusalem from Muslim rule.
1096		Crusading enthusiasm results in massacres of Jews in many cities;
	Spring	The 'Peoples' Crusade' departs from Western Europe;
	August	Main crusade under the papal legate Adhemar departs Western Europe for Constantinople; 'Peoples' Crusade' crosses the Bosphorus and enters Turkish-held territory;
	September-October	Turks obliterate the 'Peoples' Crusade' led by Peter the Hermit;
		Contingents of the main crusade begin arriving in Constantinople.
1097	19 June	Crusaders in cooperation with the Byzantines recapture Nicaea;
	1 July	Crusaders defeat Turks at the Battle of Dorylaeum;
	21 October	Crusaders begin siege of Muslim-controlled Antioch.
1098	March	Baldwin of Boulogne becomes Count of Edessa;
	3 June	Antioch falls to the Crusaders;
	August	The Fatimids recapture Jerusalem.
1099	15 July	Crusaders capture Jerusalem;
	22 July	Godfrey de Bouillon elected 'Protector of the Holy Sepulcher';
	August	Crusaders defeat an Egyptian army at Ascalon.

The Holy Land in the Era of the Crusades

Year	Month	Event
1100	18 July	Death of Godfrey de Bouillon;
	20 August	Franks capture Haifa with Venetian assistance;
	25 December	Baldwin de Boulogne crowned king of Jerusalem in the Church of the Nativity, Bethlehem.
1101	29 April	Arsuf surrenders to Franks and Genoese; population spared;
	17 May	Franks capture Caesarea with Genoese support; population slaughtered;
	August-7 September	Second wave of crusaders wiped out by Turks in Asia Minor;
		Baldwin I defeats the invading Egyptian army at the Battle of Ramla.
1102	April	Raymond of Toulouse defeats Muslim forces from Damascus and Homs near Tortosa;
	27 May	Baldwin defeats Egyptians at Jaffa;
		Franks capture Tortosa and Jubail with Genoese assistance.
1104	7-8 May	Defeat of combined Frankish army at the Battle of Harran;
	26 May	Capture of Acre by Frankish forces with Genoese assistance.
1105	28 February	Raymond de Toulouse dies while besieging Tripoli;
	27 August	Franks defeat another Egyptian army at the second Battle of Ramla.
1108	September	Prince Bohemond of Antioch acknowledges Byzantine suzerainty over Antioch.
1109	26 June	Tripoli surrenders to the Franks; Genoese and Provencal support decisive; population spared;
		County of Tripoli established.

Chronology

Year	Month	Event
1110	13 May	Beirut falls to the Franks with Genoese and Pisan support;
	5 December	Sidon surrenders to the Franks, the latter supported by a Norwegian fleet under King Sigurd; population spared.
1113	15 February	The Hospitallers established as an independent order by pope;
		Frankish expansion to the Jordan halted by defeat of Baldwin II at Sinnabra.
1114		Earliest date for the founding of the Knights Templar.
1118	2 April	Death of Baldwin I;
	14 April	Consecration of Baldwin de Bourcq as Baldwin II;
	25 December	Coronation of Baldwin and his Armenian wife Morphia as king and queen of Jerusalem.
1119	28 June	Defeat of Frankish army under the prince of Antioch at the 'Field of Blood'.
1123	18 April	Baldwin II captured by Balak in Edessa;
	May	Venetian fleet (120 strong) destroys the Fatimid navy; Franks defeat Egyptian army assault on Jaffa;
		Venetians then join the siege of Tyre, providing a blockade by sea.
1124	7 July	Surrender of Tyre to the Franks/Venetians, population spared;
	24 August	Release of Baldwin II;
	October	Baldwin lays siege to Aleppo.
1125	January	Siege of Aleppo abandoned;
	11 June	King Baldwin defeats a coalition of Turkish forces at Battle of Azaz.
1127	September	Imad al-Din Zengi appointed governor of Mosul.

The Holy Land in the Era of the Crusades

Year	Month	Event
1128	June	Zengi takes over Aleppo.
1129	January	Papal recognition of the Templars; Templar rule drawn up at the Council of Troyes (Champagne);
	2 June	Marriage of Fulk d'Anjou to Melisende of Jerusalem;
	November-December	Baldwin II and Fulk besiege but fail to capture Damascus.
1131	21 August	Death of Baldwin II;
		King Fulk and Queen Melisende ascend to the throne, ruling jointly.
1132	11 December	City and castle of Banyas falls to Zengi's forces.
1136	Spring	Princess Constance of Antioch marries Raymond de Poitiers.
1137	July	Louis VII marries Eleanor of Aquitaine;
	1 August	Louis VII becomes king of France;
	August	Zengi defeats Fulk at Montferrand and captures town.
1138	June	Zengi seizes Homs.
1140	12 June	Joint Frankish/Damascene army recaptures Banyas.
1142		Castle of Kerak constructed.
1143	8 April	Manuel I Comnenus becomes Byzantine emperor;
	10 November	King Fulk dies in a hunting accident;
	23 December	Melisende and her son Baldwin crowned jointly; Baldwin rules as Baldwin III.
1144	23-24 December	Zengi captures Edessa; a massacre of the population ensues; all captive Franks executed.
1145	1 December	Pope Eugenius II proclaims the Second Crusade.
1146	14 September	Bernard of Clairvaux preaches the Second Crusade;
	November-December	Zengi dies; Count of Edessa briefly recaptures Edessa before being driven out by Zengi's son Nur ad-Din.

Chronology

Year	Month	Event
1147	May	Unsuccessful invasion of Hauran by Baldwin III;
	mid-May	Second Crusade: departure of German crusaders under Conrad III;
	11 June	Second Crusade: departure of French under King Louis VII;
	17 October	Second Crusade: Iberian crusaders capture Almeria;
	24 October	Second Crusade: Portuguese with Flemish/English support capture Lisbon;
	25 October	Second Crusade: Seljuks obliterate most of Conrad's army at the Second Battle of Dorylaeum.
1148	6 January	Second Crusade: Louis VII ambushed and suffers heavy losses;
	March	Second Crusade: Louis VII abandons what is left of his army at Adalia and sails for Antioch with his clergy, household and wife, Eleanor of Aquitaine; fights with Raymond of Poitiers and continues to Jerusalem;
	April-June	Second Crusade: arrival of the remnants of the Second Crusade under Conrad III and Louis VII;
	24-28 July	Second Crusade: Unsuccessful siege of Damascus;
1149	29 June	Nur ad-Din defeats and kills Raymond de Poitiers at the Battle of Inab;
	15 July	Consecration of the renovated Church of the Holy Sepulchre;
	by year end	Second Crusade: Iberian crusaders drive the Muslims out of Catalonia.
1150	May	Capture of Joscelin II, Count of Edessa;
		Evacuation of the remaining regions of County of Edessa of all Latins and as many native (mostly Armenian) Christians as wished to join.
1151	March	Temporary division of the Kingdom of Jerusalem due to conflict between Queen Melisende and King Baldwin III.

The Holy Land in the Era of the Crusades

Year	Month	Event
1152	March	Frederick I ('Barbarossa') elected king of the Germans;
	April	Baldwin III attacks his mother, forcing her to withdraw to Nablus; unity of the kingdom is restored;
	May	Raymond II of Tripoli murdered by Assassins.
1153	Spring	Reynald de Chatillon marries Constance, heiress of Antioch and becomes prince of Antioch;
	18 May	Henry Plantagenet marries Eleanor of Aquitaine after the dissolution of her marriage to the French king;
	22 August	Franks capture Ascalon; population spared.
1154	25 April	Nur ad-Din gains full control in Damascus;
	25 October	Death of King Stephen of England; Henry Plantagenet becomes king.
1155	2 January	Frederick Barbarossa crowned Holy Roman emperor;
		Nur ad-Din captures Ba'albek, unifying all of Muslim Syria;
		Reynald de Chatillon attacks Byzantine Cyprus.
1157	April	Nur ad-Din briefly gains control of Banyas, instituting a massacre among the population and destroying much of the infrastructure.
	19 June	Nur ad-Din defeats Baldwin III at Jacob's Ford;
		Almohads recapture Almeria and open new Muslim offensive in Iberia lasting to 1212.
1158	September	Marriage of Baldwin III to Theodora Comnena, niece of Emperor Manuel I Comnenus;
	December	Chatillon submits to Emperor Manuel.
1159	April	Ceremonial entry of Emperor Manuel in Antioch.
1161	11 September	Death of Queen Melisende;
	November	Reynald de Chatillon captured by Nur ad-Din.

Chronology

Year	Month	Event
1163	10 February	Death of Baldwin III;
	18 February	Coronation of Amalric;
1163	Spring	Nur ad-Din suffers a resounding defeat at Krak de Chevaliers;
	September	First invasion of Egypt.
1164	April-October	Second invasion of Egypt;
	10 August	Nur ad-Din defeats a combined Frankish-Byzantine army at the Battle of Artah, taking Bohemond III of Antioch, Raymond III of Tripoli, Byzantine dux Coloman and Hugh VIII of Lusignan captive;
	Oct.	Nur ad-Din captures Banyas from a weak garrison, ending Frankish control of the city.
1167	January-August	Third invasion of Egypt; occupation of Alexandria; Nur ad-Din raids into the county of Tripoli, taking advantage of the absence of troops and leaders in Egypt.
	29 August	Marriage of Amalric and Maria Comnena.
1168–1169	October-January	Fourth invasion of Egypt.
1169	March	Saladin becomes vizier of Egypt;
	October-December	Amalric's fifth invasion of Egypt.
1170	December	Saladin's first invasion of the Kingdom of Jerusalem; sack of Darum and siege of Gaza;
	29 December	Murder of Thomas Becket in Canterbury.
1171	Spring	Amalric visits Constantinople;
	10 September	Saladin ends Fatimid caliphate; Egypt submits to Abbasid caliphate.
1174	15 May	Death of Nur ad-Din;
	June	Sicilian fleet besieges Alexandria;

The Holy Land in the Era of the Crusades

Year	Month	Event
1174 (cont.)	11 July	Death of Amalric;
	15 July	Coronation of Baldwin IV;
	28 October	Saladin seizes control of Damascus.
1176	July	Baldwin IV leads raids in the vicinity of Damascus and defeats Saracen forces under Saladin's brother Turan Shah at Ayn al Jarr; release of Raynald de Chatillon;
	17 September	Seljuk Turks defeat Byzantine army under Emperor Manuel I at the Battle of Myriocephalon;
	October or November	Marriage of Princess Sibylla to William 'Longsword' de Montferrat.
1177	June	Death of William Longsword, possibly from malaria;
	August	Arrival of Philip, Count of Flanders, with large crusading force;
	25 November	Baldwin IV decisively defeats Saladin at the Battle of Montgisard following Saladin's first invasion of the Kingdom of Jerusalem.
1178		Baldwin IV orders the construction of a castle at Jacob's Ford.
1179	10 June	Saladin defeats Baldwin IV at the Battle on the Litani/Marj Ayun;
	24-29 August	Saladin destroys the unfinished castle at Jacob's Ford.
1180	April	Marriage of Princess Sibylla to Guy de Lusignan;
	May	Truce between Baldwin IV and Saladin;
	18 September	Philip (Augustus) II becomes king of France;
	24 September	Death of Emperor Manuel I Comnenus.
1181		Maronites unite with the Roman Catholic Church.
1182	May	Outbreak of anti-Latin riots in Constantinople; Andronicus I deposes Alexus II as Byzantine emperor;

Chronology

Year	Month	Event
1182 (cont.)	5 July	Baldwin IV defeats Saladin at the Battle of le Forbelet, ending Saladin's second invasion of the Kingdom of Jerusalem;
	August-September	Franks repulse an attempt by Saladin to seize Beirut;
	November	Reynald de Chatillon launches ships in the Red Sea that prey on pilgrims and attack the Red Sea coast.
1183	February	Chatillon's ships are destroyed and his men killed or captured;
	11 June September	Aleppo surrenders to Saladin; Henry the 'Young King', eldest son of Henry II and Eleanor of Aquitaine dies;
		Guy de Lusignan named Baillie of Jerusalem; Baldwin IV retains crown but retires from government;
	29 September-8 October	Saladin's third invasion of the Kingdom of Jerusalem ends in a stalemate;
	1-2 November	Saladin lays siege to the castle of Kerak;
	20 November	Lusignan relieved of his office of baillie; Baldwin V crowned co-king to his uncle Baldwin IV;
	3-4 December	Saladin lifts siege of Kerak because of the approach of a relieving army commanded by Baldwin IV; Nablus and other cities in Galilee are sacked during his withdrawal.
1184	July	Patriarch of Jerusalem and the masters of the Temple and Hospital depart on an embassy to the West;
	August-September	Saladin again lays siege to Kerak and is forced to withdraw.
1185	ca. 15 April	Baldwin IV dies; Raymond de Tripoli named baillie;
		Raymond signs a four-year truce with Saladin;

The Holy Land in the Era of the Crusades

Year	Month	Event
1185 (cont.)	June	Emperor Andronicus proposes offensive alliance to Saladin, which includes a joint attack on the crusader states;
	Summer	Saladin besieges but fails to take Mosul; alliance negotiated.
1186	August	Death of Baldwin V; Sibylla usurps the throne and crowns Guy king-consort;
	September	Emperor Andronicus murdered by a mob; Isaac II Angelus becomes emperor of Constantinople;
	Autumn	Baldwin de Ramla departs the kingdom; Raymond de Tripoli refuses homage to Guy and signs separate peace with Saladin.
1187	1 May	Saracen reconnaissance-in-force destroys a small force of Templars, Hospitallers and secular knights at the Springs of Cresson;
	May	Tripoli reconciles with Lusignan;
	27 June	Saladin begins his fourth invasion of the Kingdom of Jerusalem;
	3-4 July	Saladin decisively defeats the army of the kingdom at the Battle of Hattin;
	8-10 July	Saladin captures Acre; citizens spared;
	14 July	Arrival of Conrad de Montferrat in Tyre;
	ca. 20 July	Al-Adil captures Jaffa followed by sack, slaughter and enslavement;
	29 July	Sidon surrenders to Saladin; citizens spared;
	6 August	Beirut captured by Saladin; slaughter and plunder follow;
	4 September	Saladin captures Ascalon;
	20 September- 2 October	Siege of Jerusalem; surrender on 2 October followed by forty days to pay ransoms;

Chronology

Year	Month	Event
1187 (cont.)	October	Pope calls for the Third Crusade;
	November-December	Richard of Poitiers, later King Richard of England, takes the cross;
		Saladin unsuccessfully besieges Tyre.
1188	January	Pope Clement III preaches the Third Crusade;
	July	Timely arrival of the Sicilian fleet prevents the fall of Tripoli; Saladin ends his siege;
	August	Saladin and Byzantine emperor Isaac Angelus renew alliance against the crusader states; Byzantium promises to prevent crusades crossing its territory;
	August-September	Saladin systematically invades Antioch, taking Tortosa, Jabala and Latakia, as well as major strongholds before signing eight-month truce with Prince Bohemond.
1189	11 May	Third Crusade: Frederick Barbarossa officially sets out on crusade, traveling overland;
	6 July	Death of Henry II; Richard of Poitiers, son of Eleanor of Aquitaine and Henry II becomes king of England, crowned September 3;
	28 August	Guy de Lusignan commences siege of Muslim-held Acre with Pisan crusader fleet.
1190	22 April	Surrender of Beaufort to Saladin;
	18 May	Third Crusade: Frederick Barbarossa defeats the Seljuk Turks at the Battle of Iconium; capital of the Sultanate of Rum falls to the crusaders;
	10 June	Third Crusade: Frederick Barbarossa drowns in the river Saleph; his army starts to disintegrate;
	4 July	Third Crusade: Richard I and Philip II depart jointly on crusade;
	22 September	Third Crusade: Richard arrives in Sicily; prepares to winter there;
	7 October	Third Crusade: arrival of Frederick of Swabia with remnants of German crusade at siege camp of Acre;

The Holy Land in the Era of the Crusades

Year	Month	Event
1190 (cont.)	ca. 10 October	Queen Sibylla and both her daughters die in siege camp at Acre;
	24 November	Queen Isabella marries Conrad de Montferrat; recognised as queen by barons of Jerusalem.
1191	30 March	Third Crusade: Philip II departs Sicily for Acre;
	10 April	Third Crusade: Richard I departs Sicily; runs into storms; fleet disperses across the Mediterranean;
	20 April	Third Crusade: Philip II's army arrives at Acre;
	6 May-5 June	Third Crusade: Richard I of England captures Cyprus from Isaac Comnenus;
	8 June	Third Crusade: Richard I arrives at Acre with English/Angevin crusaders;
	12 July	Third Crusade: Acre surrenders to the French and English kings; Philip of France leaves for the West via Tyre;
	20 August	Third Crusade: massacre of Muslim hostages by Richard;
	22 August	Third Crusade: crusaders leave Acre and advance down the coast;
	7 September	Third Crusade: crusaders defeat Saladin at the Battle of Arsuf;
	10 September	Third Crusade: crusaders reach Jaffa;
	December	Third Crusade: crusaders approach Jerusalem, but stall.
1192	6 January	Third Crusade: crusaders abandon attempt to take Jerusalem; withdraw to the coast;
	28 April	Conrad de Montferrat killed by assassins in Tyre;
	ca. 2 May	Henri de Champagne elected king of Jerusalem;
	5 May	Henri de Champagne marries Queen Isabella;

Chronology

Year	Month	Event
1192 (cont.)	7-11 June	Third Crusade: crusaders make a second attempt to capture Jerusalem and again withdraw without a siege or assault;
	27-30 July	Third Crusade: Saladin attacks and captures the city of Jaffa; citadel holds out;
	1 August	Third Crusade: Richard comes to relief of Jaffa; retakes the city;
	5 August	Third Crusade: Richard defeats Saladin's army outside of Jaffa;
	2 September	Third Crusade: three-year truce signed between Richard and Saladin; Treaty of Ramla;
	September-October	Guy de Lusignan goes to Cyprus;
	9 October	Richard departs the Holy Land.
1193	4 March	Saladin dies.
1194		Unification of the Holy Roman Empire and the Kingdom of Sicily under Henry VI of Hohenstaufen;
		Death of Guy de Lusignan; his brother Aimery becomes lord of Cyprus.
1196	April	Isaac II deposed; Alexius III becomes emperor of Constantinople;
	18 May September	Aimery de Lusignan does homage to the Holy Roman emperor; Cyprus becomes a kingdom, with Aimery its first king.
1197	Summer	Jaffa falls to Sultan al-Adil;
	September	'German Crusade' arrives in Outremer;
	October	Sultan al-Adil assaults Acre unsuccessfully; Jaffa falls to al-Adil;
	October	Death of Henri de Champagne; Germans recapture Beirut for the Franks;
	December	Marriage of Aimery de Lusignan to Isabella of Jerusalem.

Year	Month	Event
1198	July	King Aimery signs a six-year truce with al-Adil;
		Pope Innocent III calls for another crusade;
		German Hospital of St Mary in Acre transformed into a military order, the Deutsche Orden or Teutonic Knights.
1199	6 April	Richard I dies of wounds in France; succeeded by his brother John as king of England.
1200		Sultan al-Adil, Saladin's brother, wins the succession struggles that have been ongoing since Saladin's death; becomes sultan of Syria and Egypt.
1202		Crusaders, unable to pay Venice for transport already built, are persuaded to become Venetian mercenaries and attack Zara.
1203		Mercenary army (former crusaders) and Venetian fleet successfully restore Alexius IV to the Byzantine throne.
1204	8 February	Alexius IV murdered; succeeded by anti-Latin Alexius V Ducas;
	12 April	Latins capture Constantinople and establish a Latin Empire in Greece;
	Exact date unknown	Al-Adil and Aimery agree on the restoration of Jaffa to Frankish control by diplomatic means.
1205	1 April	King Aimery of Cyprus and Jerusalem dies; Walter de Montbelliard named regent of Cyprus for underaged heir Hugh;
	May	Queen Isabella of Jerusalem dies; John d'Ibelin named regent for underaged heir Marie de Montferrat.
1208	December	Frederick II Hohenstaufen comes of age (14) and takes control of his Kingdom of Sicily.
1210	September	Hugh de Lusignan comes of age; accuses Montbelliard of malfeasance; Marie de Montferrat marries John de Brienne;

Chronology

Year	Month	Event
1210 (cont.)	October	Marie and John crowned Queen and King-consort of Jerusalem.
1212	November	Queen Marie dies giving birth to a daughter, 'Yolanda'; Brienne rules alone.
1213	April	Pope Innocent III calls for a new crusade ('Fifth Crusade').
1215	15 June	Magna Carta signed by King John in England;
	25 July	Frederick II crowned King of the Germans in Aachen.
1217	July	King Andrew II of Hungary is first to embark on the new crusade;
	9 October	In Cyprus, King Andrew joins forces with King Hugh of Cyprus, King John of Jerusalem and Prince Bohemond of Antioch;
	10 November	Crusaders defeat army of al-Adil decisively at Bethsaida.
1218	10 January	Hugh I of Cyprus dies while on crusade; Philip d'Ibelin elected baillie by the High Court of Cyprus;
	February	King Andrew of Hungary, ill, retires back to Hungary;
	July	New wave of crusaders arrives and sets siege to Damietta on the Nile, with John of Jerusalem dominant commander;
	Autumn	Death of Sultan al-Adil; his empire is split between his sons: al-Kamil becoming sultan of Egypt and al-Mu'azzam, sultan of Syria;
		Pope Honorius III sends a legate, Pelagius, to lead Fifth the Crusade, undermining unity of command.
1219	August–September	Principality of Antioch and County of Tripoli come into dynastic union under Bohemond IV;
	4-5 November	St Francis of Assissi arrives and visits the sultan of Cairo;
		Damietta finally surrenders to the crusaders.

Year	Month	Event
1220	March	Al-Muazzam, sultan of Damascus, sacks Caesarea, revealing weakness of Jerusalem's defences during the crusade in Egypt;
	April	John de Brienne abandons Fifth the Crusade and returns to defend his kingdom;
	22 November	Frederick II Hohenstaufen crowned Holy Roman emperor.
1221	July	Fifth Crusade: attempt to march up the Nile to Cairo and meet with defeat;
	September	Fifth Crusade: ends with a treaty swapping Damietta for the release of the captive crusaders and an eight-year truce.
1225	Spring	Henry I (aged 7) crowned King of Cyprus;
	9 November	Frederick II and Yolanda of Jerusalem married in Brindisi.
1226		Frederick II concludes a treaty with sultan of Cairo al-Kamil aimed at his brother al-Mu'assam, Sultan of Damascus; Al-Kamil promises Jerusalem as a reward.
1227	August	Frederick II sets out on crusade but returns due to illness;
	September	Pope Gregory IX excommunicates Frederick II;
	November–December	Philip d'Ibelin dies; John d'Ibelin elected baillie of Cyprus.
1228	25 April	Yolanda gives birth to a son, Conrad, now King of Jerusalem;
	5 May	Yolanda dies;
	25 June	Frederick II sails from Brindisi with a small force;
	21 July	Frederick II arrives in Limassol;
	3 September	Frederick II departs Cyprus for Syria, with King Henry and Cypriot barons now in his army.

Chronology

Year	Month	Event
1229	18 February	Frederick II signs ten-year truce with al-Kamil partially restoring Christian control of Jerusalem for the duration of the truce;
	18 March	Frederick II wears the imperial crown in the Church of the Holy Sepulchre;
	April	Frederick II lays siege to Templar headquarters in Acre;
	1 May	Frederick II departs Acre, never to return; Balian de Sidon and Werner von Egesheim named baillies in his absence;
	May	Frederick II leaves Henry de Lusignan on Cyprus; sells his bailliage to five local barons; Henry married by proxy to Alix de Montferrat; baillies begin a reign of terror against Ibelins and their allies;
	June	Ibelins and supporters land at Gastria, calling for the restoration of their expropriated lands, due process and an end to intimidation of their families;
	14 July	Battle of Nicosia; Ibelin victory; baillies take refuge in mountain castles, which are besieged by the Ibelins; King Henry held captive by the baillies at St Hilarion.
1230	April	Baillies at St Hilarion surrender on the condition of a full pardon.
1231	Summer	John de Brienne, former king of Jerusalem becomes emperor of Constantinople;
	Autumn	Frederick II appoints imperial marshal Riccardo Filangieri his baillie in Jerusalem;
		Filangieri brings a powerful fleet and armed force to Outremer; denied landing at Cyprus;
		Seizes city of Beirut and besieges citadel; presents credentials in Acre, but is met with skepticism;
		Filangieri establishes his base in Tyre;
		Commune of Acre formed to resist imperial breaches of the constitution.

The Holy Land in the Era of the Crusades

Year	Month	Event
1232	February March	King of Cyprus brings his army to Syria in support of Ibelin; Cypriot/Ibelin army attempts unsuccessfully to relieve Citadel of Beirut;
	April-May	Cypriots loyal to the emperor seize control of Cyprus; imperial forces lift siege of Beirut citadel;
	3 May	Imperial forces surprise Cypriot army at Casal Imbert and deliver a humiliating defeat; Henry of Cyprus comes of age;
	mid-May	Filangieri lands on Cyprus; begins a reign of terror;
	late May	King Henry and Ibelins seize imperial ships and sail for Cyprus;
	15 June	Battle of Agridi; decisive Cypriot/Ibelin victory of the imperial army; Filangieri and other imperial knights seek refuge in Kyrenia; siege of Kyrenia begins.
1233	July-August	Kyrenia surrenders to the royal/Ibelin forces; prisoners exchanged.
1235	July	Isabella Plantagenet, sister of Henry III, marries Frederick II;
	August	Papal legate places Acre under interdict for failing to support the emperor;
	October	Pope rescinds interdict because residents are turning to the Orthodox churches;
	Winter	Combined Bulgarian and Nicaean attack on Latin Constantinople defeated.
1236	ca. March	John d'Ibelin, Lord of Beirut, dies of the effects of a riding accident; succeeded by his son Balian of Beirut.
1237	23 March	Death of John de Brienne in Constantinople.
1238		Death of al-Kamil; Ayyubid empire split between his sons.

Chronology

Year	Month	Event
1239	1 September	Arrival of king of Navarra with 1,500 knights; start of the 'Barons' Crusade'.
	13 November	A portion of this army badly defeated at Gaza, with many important lords taken captive;
	7 December	Frederick II's truce expires; Jerusalem, being defenceless, surrenders to Muslim forces from Kerak und al-Nasr.
1240	Spring	Taking advantage of infighting between the Ayyubids, Navarra negotiates a treaty that restores Jerusalem, Bethlehem, Nazareth, Galilee and key castles;
	September	Navarre departs from Acre; Simon de Montfort arrives;
	8 October	Richard, Earl of Cornwall and brother of Henry III, arrives in Acre; completes negotiations with Ayyubids;
	6 December	Kiev falls to the Mongols.
1241	8 February	Cornwall signs truce with the sultan of Egypt;
	9 April	Mongols obliterate a German army at Leignitz;
	23 April	Cornwall obtains release of key prisoners;
	3 May	English crusaders under Cornwall depart the Holy Land;
	June	Ibelin faction propose Simon de Montfort as a compromise candidate to Filangieri as baillie of Jerusalem; Frederick II rejects the proposal.
1243	26 June	Mongols crush a Seljuk army at the Battle of Kosedag; establish control of Muslim Anatolia, Armenia and Georgia;
	Summer	Ibelin faction capture the last imperial stronghold, Tyre, ending Hohenstaufen rule in the Kingdom of Jerusalem.

The Holy Land in the Era of the Crusades

Year	Month	Event
1244	11 July	Khwarazmians seize Jerusalem, slaughtering tens of thousands and desecrating churches; Tower of David falls August 23;
	17 October	Combined Christian/Syrian force crushed at the Battle of La Forbie with heavy losses by an Egyptian/Khwarazmian coalition;
	December	Louis IX vows to recover Jerusalem.
1245	2 October	Al-Salih takes Damascus.
1246	date unknown	Pope absolves the king of Cyprus of all oaths to the Holy Roman emperor, making Cyprus an independent kingdom;
	March	Khwarazmians turn on al-Salih and besiege Damascus;
	May	Ayyubids destroy the Khwarazmians.
1247		Ascalon falls to the Muslims.
1248	25 August	Louis IX's fleet sets sail from Aigues-Mortes for Cyprus, which has been pre-provisioned.
1249	5 June	Seventh Crusade under Louis IX arrives in Egypt; quickly captures Damietta;
	November	Death of Sultan al-Salih.
1250	8-9 February	Louis IX suffers a devastating defeat at the Battle of Mansourah in Egpyt;
	April	Cut off from supplies and trying to retreat, crusading army disintegrates; Louis himself is taken captive along with the survivors of his host;
	2 May	Mamluks murder the Ayyubid sultan of Egypt and seize control;
	late May	Queen of France negotiates a ransom for King Louis; Louis and leading nobles released; bulk of the army remains in captivity pending payment of more money;
	13 December	Frederick II dies; succeeded by his son Conrad.

Chronology

Year	Month	Event
1253		Death of Henry I of Cyprus; succeeded by Hugh II.
1254	Spring	King Louis departs the Kingdom of Jerusalem for France;
	May 21	Death of Conrad Hohenstaufen, titular king of Jerusalem;
		Start of the War of St Sabas between the Venetians and Genoese.
1256		Mongols destroy the Assassins;
		End of hostilities between Venetians and Genoese.
1258	10 February	Mongols capture Baghdad, execute Abbasid caliph; end of the Abbasid caliphate;
	10 June	Oxford Provisions adopted in England.
1260	25 January	Mongols capture and sack Aleppo;
	2 March	Mongols capture and sack Damascus;
	3 September	Mamluks defeat the Mongols at the Battle of Ain Jalut;
	24 October	Baybars murders Sultan Qutuz and assume his place as ruler of the Mamluk empire.
1261	13 June	Baybars re-establishes the Abbasid caliphate at Cairo;
	25 July	Greeks recover Constantinople.
1264	14 May	Battle of Lewes; victory of Simon de Montfort over Henry III.
1265		Mamluks capture Caesarea, Haifa and Arsuf, thus cutting the Kingdom of Jerusalem in half;
	January-March	Simon de Montfort's Parliament held in England;
	4 August	Simon de Montfort defeated and killed at the Battle of Evesham.
1266		Charles d'Anjou, brother of King Louis IX, defeats Manfred of Hohenstaufen and is crowned king of Sicily;
		Mumluks expel Franks from Galilee and capture Templar fortress of Safed.

The Holy Land in the Era of the Crusades

Year	Month	Event
1267	24 March	Louis IX again takes the cross;
	November	Death of Hugh II of Cyprus; succeeded by Hugh III of Antioch-Lusignan.
1268	7 March	Jaffa falls to Baybars, city is sacked and population slaughtered;
	18 May	Antioch falls to Baybars, population slaughtered; this sack is widely recognised as the worst massacre of the entire crusading era;
	29 October	Death of Conradin Hohenstaufen, last titular king of Jerusalem in the Hohenstaufen line.
1269		Hugh III of Cyprus claims Crown of Jerusalem.
1270	25 August	Louis IX sets out on his second crusade (the eighth of the conventionally numbered crusades); dies at the siege of Tunis.
1271	9 May	Prince Edward of England arrives in Acre.
1272	April	Prince Edward signs ten-year truce with Mamluks.
1277		Charles d'Anjou buys Crown of Jerusalem from Marie d'Antioch; this divides kingdom between supporters of Kings of Sicily and Cyprus;
	1 July	Death of Sultan Baybars.
1279	November	Sultan Qalawun emerges victorious from vicious infighting as new Mamluk sultan.
1281	29 October	Qalawun defeats Mongols at Homs.
1285	7 January	Death of Charles d'Anjou; Sicilian claim to crown of Jerusalem extinguished.
1286	15 August	Henry II of Cyprus recognised and crowned king of Jerusalem, uniting Kingdoms of Cyprus and Jerusalem.
1287		Qalawun captures Antiochene port of Latakia.
1289	27 April	Despite truce, Qalawun attacks and captures Tripoli.
1290	10 November	Death of Sultan Qalawun, succeeded by his son al-Ashraf Khalil.

Chronology

Year	Month	Event
1291	6 April	Mamluk siege of Acre begins;
	18 May	Acre falls;
	June	Sidon falls to Mamluks;
	31 July	Beirut surrenders to the Mamluks;
	3 and 14 August	Templars withdraw from their last holdings in the Levant, Tartus and Athlit (Castle Pilgrim).
1307	13 October	Philip II of France arrests Templars on false charges.
1314		Templars dissolved by papal order.

Introduction

The 'crusades' have become a synonym for brutality and bigotry, justifying atrocities on the one hand and inspiring racism on the other. Yet, recent scholarship based on archaeology, data mining and native chronicles has revolutionized our understanding of the Latin East. While historians of past centuries portrayed the Latin Christians living in these states as a tiny, urban elite afraid to venture into the countryside out of fear of their subjects, there is a growing consensus among the scholars of the twenty-first century that the majority of the population was Christian, not Muslim, and that the degree of intermingling and tolerance between Latin and Orthodox Christians was much higher than had been assumed.

The states established by the crusaders in the Middle East were home to a diverse population of Orthodox and Latin Christians, Jews, Samaritans, and Muslims living in harmony more often than in conflict. Not only were churches and monasteries built, but the Kingdom of Jerusalem was also a centre for Talmudic studies, while Muslims lived under Sharia Law. While Western immigrants intermarried with the local population, adopted many local customs and learned to speak Arabic, the native population responded to crusader rule with an astonishing degree of loyalty. There is not one recorded incident of revolt or unrest on the part of Muslims, while the native Christians served in the administration and armies of the newly established states in impressive numbers, often playing a decisive role in military engagements.

Furthermore, for most of the nearly 200 years of their existence, these states were at peace, not war, with their neighbours. Indeed, some historians have argued that they enjoyed *more* peace than almost any European country in this period. This is particularly true if we focus on the two crusader kingdoms, the Kingdom of Jerusalem and the Kingdom of Cyprus, rather than the smaller and more vulnerable Principality of Antioch and the Counties of Edessa and Tripoli.

Introduction

This peace was not a function of an impenetrable wall of hostility similar to the Iron Curtain of the Cold War, but a by-product of open borders, which enabled and encouraged a constant flow of merchants, tradesmen, tourists and pilgrims across the region. These transitory residents amplified the diversity of the native population. In this environment, where no group was dominant, tolerance took root and friendship across ethnic and religious borders became possible. Thus, despite the rise of anti-Semitism in Europe, the crusader states accommodated waves of Jewish immigration. Likewise, during the Mongol advance into Mesopotamia, Muslims fled to – and were given refuge in – the crusader states.

Significantly, trade flourished, reaching new heights and crossing religious borders even during periods of conflict. Nor was it merchandise alone that passed between the diverse cultures of the Near East. Ideas and technology spread, as well. Thriving economic centres at the gateway to the East encouraged the development of maritime powers that dominated the Mediterranean for centuries to come. The existence of Christian powers capable of providing infrastructure and security encouraged tens of thousands of pilgrims to travel from Europe to the Holy Land each year. Those pilgrims returned home altered by their encounters with the East, while the residents of the crusader states were astonishingly well-informed about personalities and politics in their Muslim neighbours.

In short, the crusader states represent a positive example of harmonious coexistence between peoples of highly diverse ethnic and religious affiliation. They were a 'melting pot' society more than half a millennium before the founding of the United States of America. To the extent that we value tolerance and cross-cultural dialogue, the study of the crusader states is a valuable and rewarding subject of investigation.

We are fortunate that records from and about these unique political entities survived in various languages, not just Latin and Arabic, but in French, German, Armenian, Greek, Turkish and Syriac, as well. Equally important to our understanding of the crusader states are the material remains – the ruins of churches and castles, shops and farmhouses, the sculptures, frescos, icons and other works of art, as well as remnants of everyday life from pottery to shoes. Over the last half-century, scholars from a wide range of disciplines, including archaeology, art history and medicine, have increasingly shed light on diverse aspects of life in the crusader states. Their findings have been published predominantly in academic journals and presses. Much of the information is highly specialised and written for fellow academics rather than to inform the general public.

This book is designed to provide hobby historians with an easy-to-read, affordable overview of the crusader states based on the academic research of recent decades. It will debunk many popular myths, such as the 'genocidal' nature of the crusades and the proto-colonial character of the crusader states. It does not, however, purport to break new ground with original research. Instead, it seeks to collect in a coherent and accessible format existing scholarly research on a range of topics in order to create a comprehensive description. It is organised in three parts: (1) a chronological history of the crusader states that enables readers to understand their place in history; (2) a description of the crusader states organised around the topics: demography, state institutions, foreign policy, economy and lifestyle of the people who lived in the crusader states; and (3) a chapter on the rise and fall of the House of Ibelin, which gives the story of these states a human face.

Before embarking on this journey 'beyond the sea' – as contemporaries called the crusader states – it is useful to put them into perspective. First, while we place these states 'in the Middle East', contemporary Europeans did not. They might have been 'beyond the sea', yet they remained in the very heart of Europe because they contained, defended and represented the heart and soul of Christianity: The Holy Land. Although they had independent political institutions and most of their inhabitants had been born in these geopolitical entities, the Kingdom of Jerusalem belonged emotionally to *all* Christians. That was both an asset and a burden to those living in and defending the kingdom.

Geographically, at their largest, the mainland crusader states occupied roughly the same amount of territory as England. These states sat on the coast of the Levant, stretching roughly 967km (600 miles) from Syria through modern Lebanon and Israel to Gaza. Inland, they touched the western flank of the Mt Lebanon range, reached across the Jordan River and, briefly, extended to the northern tip of the Red Sea. Yet it is misleading to think of these political entities as states with fixed borders, even in times of stability. There was no GPS, no engineering surveys, no precisely-scaled maps and no border posts. Borders of this period depended less on features of the landscape than on the ability and political will of the local powers to defend a specific region. Like the

Introduction

borders of ancient Sparta, they stretched as far as the spears and lances of the state could reach. Yet for territory to be *held*, the inhabitants had to recognise and identify with the rulers. In other words, the shape and extent of the crusader states were ultimately defined as much by psychology as topography.

Last but not least, some notes on terminology in this book:

- As noted above, the contemporary collective name for the crusader states was simply 'Beyond the Sea' – in French, 'Outremer'.
- The Western Europeans who had founded, settled in, fought for or simply visited the crusader states were known by the generic term of 'Franks' – regardless of their actual place of origin. Thus, whether Norwegian, Italian, French, Hungarian or Irish at home, they were all 'Franks' in Outremer; 'Ifranj', 'Franj' or 'Faranj' in Arabic. What they shared was their adherence to the Church of Rome or Latin Christianity. Although contemporaries did *not* make this distinction, I have chosen to use the term Franks more narrowly, namely to use it to distinguish the Latin Christian residents of the crusader states from the transient Latin Christians – the pilgrims and crusaders, who came to visit or fight for the Holy Land but did not remain there.
- Likewise, because of the vast diversity of ethnic groups that made up the Dar al-Islam (the House/Abode of Islam) in the region at the time, the term Saracen is used to collectively describe the Muslim opponents and neighbours of the crusader states. The term is *not* derogatory; it is simply a convenient collective that applies equally well to Turks, Kurds, Arabs, Bedouins, Egyptians and Berbers, etc.
- The Eastern Roman Empire, which in the period of this book had existed uninterrupted since the fifth century AD, considered itself the 'New Rome' and its inhabitants called themselves 'Romans'. Western Europeans, however, viewed Rome as the city in Italy where the pope had his residence and referred to those in and ruled by Constantinople as 'Greeks'. To further complicate things, the Eastern Roman Empire included the Balkans and (at times) much of modern Turkey; it was ethnically diverse. For the sake of clarity, this book uses the anachronistic yet convenient and common designation 'Byzantium' or 'Byzantine Empire' when referring to the Eastern Roman Empire.

- Another anachronism consciously employed in this book is the term 'crusades' and 'crusaders'. During the era of the crusades, people who took vows to go to the Holy Land were called 'those who took the cross', 'cross-bearers' or any number of similar terms in different languages, all of which express the same thing as the modern term 'crusader' – only in more complicated ways.
- The numbering of crusades is a historical convention that started in the eighteenth century and was completely unknown in the era of the crusades. Furthermore, the numbers are quite misleading. There were many 'crusades' – like the German Crusade of 1195 or the Baron's Crusade of 1239, not to mention the Baltic Crusades, Albigensian Crusade or the Reconquista – which were not numbered. On the other hand, some of the numbered crusades – like the Fourth Crusade and the Sixth Crusade – were *not* considered legitimate when they occurred because they lacked papal sanction. Nevertheless, these terms are now so widespread and familiar that the books likewise refers to the major expeditions to the Holy Land by the conventional numbered designations.

Now, join me on a journey beyond the sea to the kingdoms of the crusaders.

PART I

A Short History of the Crusader States

Chapter 1

Genesis of the Crusader States

The Dar al-Islam, Jihad and the Near East Before the Crusades

In May 614 AD, Jerusalem fell after a twenty-one-day siege. In accordance with the rules of war applied since the age of the *Iliad*, the civilian population was 'put to the sword'. An estimated 26,500 inhabitants, mostly men, were slaughtered. Roughly 35,000 women and children were enslaved by the victorious Persians. It was not the first time Jerusalem had been captured, sacked and soaked in the blood of its inhabitants – and it would not be the last.

At the time of the Persian invasion, Jerusalem had been part of the Roman Empire for nearly 700 years, since 63 BC. In 33 AD, it had been the venue of Christ's crucifixion and burial. Although the Romans built a temple over these sites to discourage Christian pilgrimage and to humiliate the forbidden Christian sect, in the mid-fourth century AD at the instigation of Empress Helena, mother of Emperor Constantine the Great, a Christian basilica had been built on the reputed site of Christ's tomb. When the Persians captured Jerusalem in 614, they completely destroyed this church, known as the Church of the Holy Sepulchre, along with virtually every other church or monastery in the surrounding region.

It was fifteen years (629 AD) before the Byzantine emperor Herakleios drove the Persians out of Palestine and regained control of Jerusalem. Reconstruction of the Church of the Holy Sepulchre started almost at once, but it was not so easy to replace the 70,000 people slaughtered or carried away as slaves. It was obvious to all that recovery would be slow, but it was largely unnoticed in both Jerusalem and Constantinople that at the end of this same year, a certain Muhammad Ibn 'Abd Allāh Ibn returned victorious to Medina.

Three years later, Muhammad was dead, but his followers immediately began to spread the religion he had taught – by the sword.

The justification for their aggressive territorial expansion was a doctrine called 'jihad'. Although undoubtedly a complex concept which includes the inner struggle against sin, many Islamic scholars and leaders then – as now – interpreted 'jihad' as war against non-believers. Tellingly, Islamic doctrine divided the world into two camps or houses: the House of Islam (Dar al-Islam) and the House of War (Dar al-Harb.) Muslims leaders felt justified, indeed obliged, to conquer the Dar al-Harb not only to expand the Dar al-Islam but also with the goal of bringing peace to the entire world by eliminating the House of War.

Fired with passion for their new religion and justified in their aggression by the theory of 'jihad', Islamic rule expanded rapidly. In the decade 634–644 AD, Muslim armies conquered Egypt, Libya, Persia and Syria. Jerusalem fell after a year-long siege in April 637 AD. Despite the 656 AD split of Islam into Shia and Sunni factions that caused an enduring conflict within the Dar al-Islam, by 678 AD, Muslim forces were at the gates of Constantinople. The 'Queen of Cities' withstood the siege, and the Byzantine Empire was briefly able to roll back some of the Muslim gains in Asia Minor – but only briefly.

By the end of the seventh century, Islam was once again expanding by force of arms. The Christian city of Carthage fell to Muslim armies in 698 AD, and the Muslim conquest of the Iberian Peninsula began in 711 AD. Within just two years, most of Spain and Portugal had been conquered. Likewise, Armenia came under Muslim rule. In the summer of 717 AD, Constantinople was again besieged by land and sea. The Byzantine capital was rescued by a Bulgar relief army, which attacked the Saracens from the rear, causing the Muslims to withdraw on 15 August 718 AD. In the following century and a half, the Byzantine Empire regained control of Armenia and northern Syria, but not Jerusalem.

The expansion of Islam also suffered a significant defeat in Western Europe in 732 AD, when a Muslim army that had advanced almost to the Loire River in France was decisively defeated by a Frankish army under Charles Martel at the Battle of Tours. This ended the Muslim threat to Europe north of the Pyrenees, but Muslim conquests continued in the Mediterranean. The conquest of Crete was completed by 825 AD, and the conquest of Sicily began immediately, although it was not complete until 902 AD. Meanwhile, Muslim raids on the Italian mainland began. In 846 AD, Saracen raiders sacked Rome, including St Peter's Cathedral.

Yet, the establishment of Muslim regimes from Syria to Spain did not mean that the inhabitants of these regions converted to Islam. On the contrary, the majority of inhabitants initially retained their former religions. Muslim rulers, therefore, evolved policies for dealing with their non-Muslim subjects. Jews and Christians were allotted a 'protected' status because Mohammed recognised the prophets of the Old Testament and Jesus as spokesmen of God. According to Mohammed, however, Jews and Christians misunderstood or distorted the word of God, something that Mohammad had been directed by God to correct. Until they accepted Islam, they remained obstinately misinformed and could not enjoy the same status as Muslims.

Like the papal 'protection' of Jews in Europe, the recipients of this protection were not free of persecution, humiliation, exploitation or slaughter. At the best of times, Christian and Jewish elites pursued their professions and were employed in the bureaucracies of the Muslim states, while the peasants were left in comparative peace. At the worst of times, Christians and Jews were harassed, exploited, attacked and slaughtered, their land and livestock was expropriated, and the burden of taxes and forced labor drove people to mass flight. There are many recorded incidents of oppression; here are only a few well-documented cases. Roughly 700 Jews were forced to dig their own graves before being beheaded in Medina under Mohammed's personal direction. Christians were burned alive in their churches in Armenia in 705 and Palestine in 796. In the early ninth century, there were a series of 'popular' attacks on monasteries and convents in which the monks and nuns were murdered and raped and the churches destroyed. In 1009, the caliph al-Hakim ordered the destruction of all churches and synagogues in his domains, including the Church of the Holy Sepulchre. In 1032–1033 more than 6,000 Jews were massacred in Morocco. Under these circumstances, some people were prepared to abandon their faith and convert to Islam, but the process was much slower than is widely assumed. At least 50 per cent of the population of the Holy Land was still Christian when the first crusaders arrived.

In the intervening centuries, the situation in Holy Land had been aggravated by the bitter struggle between Shia and Sunni powers for control of the Levant. In 878, Jerusalem, controlled by Sunni Muslims since 637, was captured by Shia Egypt. In 904, Sunni forces loyal to the Abbasid caliphate regained control of the city. In 969, the Fatimid

Genesis of the Crusader States

caliphate again conquered Jerusalem. In 1073, the Sunni Seljuks captured Jerusalem from the Fatimids, and in 1077, following a rebellion by the inhabitants of Jerusalem, the population was massacred on the orders of the Seljuk governor. In 1098 the Fatimids retook Jerusalem once again.

Another key development in the period before the First Crusade was the arrival in the region of the Seljuks. The Seljuks asserted their mastery over the region by extreme violence, even by the standards of the day. Their conquests were characterised by massacres, rape, wanton destruction and what one commentator called the 'saturation of the slave markets'. The Seljuks were essentially a Turkish/Kurdish military government dependent on an Arab bureaucratic and religious elite and a Christian working and peasant class. They maintained power by terrorising the indigenous rural population with their foreign troops and buying the loyalty of the Muslim elites.

The latter was achieved by posing as the defenders of Sunni orthodoxy. In its name, they imposed theological uniformity that muzzled debate and suppressed political and religious dissent. They also diverted attention from internal discontent by declaring 'jihad' against the Shia. The Shia returned the compliment and declared 'jihad' against the Seljuks. For both, the elimination of heresy was the goal, and the capture of Jerusalem in the course of this struggle was purely incidental.

Indeed, Jerusalem was only of moderate and secondary importance to Islam throughout this period. Jerusalem is not mentioned anywhere in the Quran. Thus, although nowadays it is popular to claim that Jerusalem was the venue of Mohammed's 'Night Journey', early Muslim scholars disputed this association. Likewise, the notion that Mohammed ascended to heaven from Jerusalem appears to date from the twelfth century, that is, after the Christian conquest, not before. The significance of Jerusalem in the pre-crusader period was primarily its association with the Day of Judgement, and secondarily, its association with the prophets, including Jesus.

The construction of the Dome of the Rock under the Umayyads (661–750) was part of an overall building programme intended to glorify the new conquerors. The Islamic face given to Jerusalem was consciously intended to demean the unenlightened Jews and Christians. Thus, the most prominent of Muslim monuments were placed precisely on the most sacred of Jewish sites – the Temple Mount. Despite the Muslim imprint, however, many contemporary Muslim scholars advised Muslim pilgrims to avoid Jerusalem because it was too 'contaminated' by Christianity and Judaism. The local authorities, fearing revenue losses without religious tourism, countered by emphasising Jerusalem's ties to Islam.

Meanwhile, after a period of respite in the tenth century, during which the Byzantines had regained control of Crete and Cyprus, the Byzantine Empire came under intense pressure from the Suljuks. They suffered a decisive defeat at the Battle of Manzikert on 26 August 1071. The establishment of the Seljuk Sultanate of Rum in what is modern-day Turkey placed Constantinople under renewed threat from 1077 onwards. The situation deteriorated further when the Seljuks captured the mighty Christian city of Antioch in 1086.

The palpable fear of the Seljuks was exacerbated by domestic weakness inside the Byzantine Empire. The interests of the urban civil service and the rural aristocracy increasingly diverged. By the mid-eleventh century, the traditional means of raising troops had collapsed, and the empire had become heavily dependent on mercenaries. Furthermore, between 1025 and 1081, there had been no less than thirteen emperors, five of whom were deposed, one forced to abdicate and another murdered. It is hardly surprising that a sense of crisis prevailed. Against this backdrop of profound unease, the new Byzantine emperor Alexius I Comnenus (1081–1118) looked to the West for possible support.

The Byzantine Empire had long relied on Western mercenaries to help fight various enemies from the Balkans to Syria. Indeed, the elite Varangian Guard that served as the emperor's bodyguard was composed primarily of Scandinavian and Anglo-Saxon mercenaries. In a letter to the pope in 1095, Emperor Alexius requested military assistance from the West to counter the Seljuk threat. His appeal coincided, more by chance than design, with an abrupt weakening of the Dar al-Islam in the Near East. In 1092, the Seljuk vizier, who had been the power behind the throne of the Seljuk sultans, died. Although not immediately apparent, the Seljuk empire was about to fragment into a mosaic of weak and fragile states as various Seljuk princes and pretenders squabbled with one another. What had once seemed invincible was suddenly vulnerable.

Christianity, Just War and the Call of the Crusade

For many people nowadays, any war, especially one that is not clearly defensive, appears incompatible with Christianity. This was not the case at the end of the eleventh century. In the fifth century, St Augustine had first articulated the concept of 'just war', a theological defence of wars declared by Christian leaders to oppose aggression and oppression. St Augustine was explicit in condemning wars of religious conversion and prohibited the use of excessive force, but that was theory. In practice, medieval Christians viewed wars against pagans as legitimate. This included the wars against the Vikings in Britain and Ireland, those of Charlemagne against the Saxons, and, of course, the war of the Visigoths against the Moors (Muslims) in Spain. These wars were perceived as defensive and, specifically, as a defence of Christendom. Thus, by the eleventh century, Western Europe had a tradition that honoured, glorified and even sanctified Christian fighting men who fought non-Christians.

When Pope Urban II, in response to the request from Emperor Alexis, appealed to knights under his jurisdiction (knights of the Church of Rome) to go East to liberate Jerusalem, he built upon these traditions. His appeal stressed the fundamental elements of 'just war' (fighting oppression and aggression) by drawing attention to the suffering of fellow Christians in the Muslim-occupied Near East and stressing the threat posed by the 'pagan' Seljuks to the New Rome, Constantinople. Yet, Pope Urban expanded on this familiar theme by adding to his appeal the need to liberate Jerusalem.

In contrast to Jerusalem's peripheral place in Islam, Jerusalem was at the very centre of Christianity. Islamic scholars might debate theoretical spiritual ties to Jerusalem, yet it is certain that Mohammed never set foot there. Jesus, on the other hand, had lived and died there. More significantly, the defining event of Christianity, Christ's resurrection, occurred in Jerusalem. While the Muslims had Mecca and Medina as their primary and secondary holy sites, for Christians (and Jews), Jerusalem was *the* unquestioned central and paramount sacred site of their respective religions.

It was undoubtedly to inspire men to undertake such an enormously dangerous operation across such vast distances that Pope Urban introduced a startling innovation. He offered spiritual rewards to those who undertook to free Jerusalem from Muslim rule. Contrary to popular myth, Urban did *not* promise the remission of sins – certainly not for 'killing Muslims'. Nor did he sanction genocide or forced conversions. On the contrary, church documents explicitly state that participation in an armed expedition to liberate Jerusalem would replace already assigned penance for confessed sins. Furthermore, the church carefully conferred benefits only on those who undertook the armed pilgrimage out of piety – but not on those who sought honour or wealth.

Yet, regardless of what the theologians thought they were offering, many people undoubtedly believed that the armed expedition to Jerusalem would bring them spiritual salvation. Spiritual benefits, not material gains, were the dominant motive for participation in what became known as the First Crusade. Popular theories of the nineteenth and twentieth centuries that postulate most crusaders were landless, younger sons out to snatch land or make a fortune in loot have been discredited by more recent research. Data mining of charters and wills revealed that the vast majority of knightly crusaders were *not* landless and disinherited younger sons, nor the victims of primogeniture as prominent historians of the last century alleged. Rather, most crusaders were wealthy, fief-holders.

There was a reason for this: crusading was enormously expensive, too expensive for landless, younger sons. Even landholding lords often had to sell properties or borrow money to cover the costs of their expedition to the East. Historians estimate that a knight needed to raise roughly five to six times his annual income to finance an armed expedition to Jerusalem.

Admittedly, we only have documentary evidence for members of the landed class, who formed the heavy cavalry of the expedition. Their costs were higher than that of the infantry, as they needed to bring multiple mounts, grooms and servants. We cannot know the motives of the more humble crusaders, but we can assume that they too made substantial financial sacrifices and faced even greater uncertainties than those who could afford to bring a small entourage and cash to pay for food and other necessities along the way.

Furthermore, the notion that most crusaders were out to grab lands in the East is disproved by the simple fact that – with some notable exceptions – the vast majority of them did not stay in the East. The overwhelming majority of crusaders returned home, leaving the crusader states short of defenders. Individuals interested in obtaining land (as opposed to spiritual rewards) had many, less risky options closer to home. Marginal land was being brought under cultivation across Western Europe at this time as new territory was being won in Prussia and Spain. Such land was available without an expensive and dangerous expedition across enemy-held territory to a strange land 'beyond the sea'.

Yet, in addition to the spiritual motives, feudal values were also at play. Under feudal law, a vassal was obliged to come to the assistance of his lord if the latter were attacked or his lands overrun. In this period, Christ was viewed as 'king of kings and lord of lords', while all churches were considered the home of the lord. The preachers of the first crusade described the destruction of churches and their conversion into mosques and drew a parallel to the capture of a lord's castle by a hostile power. In short, the 'king of kings' homeland was occupied by his enemies, and all his vassals – all Christians – were honour-bound to deliver it.

Last but not least, given the twenty-first century tendency to cite the crusades as examples of 'genocide' and 'racism', it is important to stress that twelfth-century crusading letters, chronicles and literature was devoid of cultural, ethnic and religious chauvinism. The emphasis was on the *opportunity* offered by a benevolent God to obtain grace without renouncing the profession of arms, something that appealed to the feudal elites, who were otherwise under constant threat of damnation because of their martial activities. Most crusaders set out for the East for the sake of their personal salvation, and all were – at least theoretically – volunteers. What astonished contemporaries including Pope Urban II – and flat-out terrified Emperor Alexius – was the huge response that the pope's appeal for volunteers provoked. No one in their wildest dreams had foreseen what would come.

The 'Peoples' Crusade'

What the Byzantine emperor had in mind when he requested aid from the West had been several hundred, at most 1,000, trained knights to serve in the Byzantine army. In other words: mercenaries. The emperor planned and expected to place these trained fighting men under the command and control of Byzantine military leaders. Instead, tens of thousands of undisciplined armed pilgrims arrived in the Eastern Roman Empire. The Byzantine government and people felt overwhelmed, baffled and ultimately frightened of the monster they had created.

Likewise, while Pope Urban II may have envisaged something grander than Alexius, he too sought to raise a force of trained fighting men under the leadership of experienced noblemen. When his highly-organised and systematic preaching campaign produced instead tens of thousands of pilgrims, many of whom were non-combatants, he back-pedaled frantically. He prohibited monks from leaving their monasteries. He told priests to absolve the unfit, infirm, destitute and women of crusading vows. He wrote to the rulers of states confronting the Moors to assure them their job (and that of their subjects) was to continue *that* fight, not join the expedition to the east. But the genie was out of the bottle.

Long before the agreed departure date set for the assembly of organised contingents, an armed pilgrimage under the leadership of a charismatic preacher known as 'Peter the Hermit' set off to liberate Jerusalem. The majority of those following Peter had little to lose and no understanding of the risks. Many appear to have believed their devotion alone would induce an all-powerful Christ to sweep aside the heathens. This mass pilgrimage to Jerusalem was more a messianic movement than an armed expedition. It has gone down in history as 'the People's Crusade'.

Historians estimate that as many as 20,000 men and women took part. Although there were some knights among them, the majority were armed with household and farm implements. Expecting God to provide for them, they had no means to pay for provisions. Instead, they felt entitled to steal from the inhabitants of the Christian kingdoms through which they passed, provoking clashes. Only the speed with which the Byzantine emperor made provisions available at his own expense prevented worse incidents. Nevertheless, a mob of pilgrims pillaged the suburbs of Constantinople after reaching the city in July 1096. Meanwhile, in their wake, a second wave of pilgrims undertook a series of violent attacks directed at Jewish communities, notably in Speyer, Worms, Mainz, Trier and Cologne. Peter the Hermit might have inspired his followers with his preaching, but he could not control them.

It is hardly surprising that the Byzantines viewed this mob with horror. The Byzantine emperor had requested military aid; he had not invited the destitute and deluded. He had expected trained and battle-hardened fighting men like the familiar Varangians, not peasants and shopkeepers armed with hoes and hammers. Particularly shocking was the sizeable number of women and children.

Byzantine contempt for this hoard was only magnified when, against the advice of the emperor, these masses of pilgrims insisted on continuing their march. The emperor provided transportation across the Bosporus and the 'Peoples' Crusade' entered Turkish-held territory in August 1096. By the end of October, they were all dead or enslaved. The stragglers, those recruited in Germany and responsible for the attacks on Jews, followed in their footsteps and were wiped out in the spring of 1097.

The First Crusade, 1097–1099

The loss of 20,000 pilgrims engaged in a popular attempt to liberate Jerusalem more by faith than force of arms would have been a sad but largely forgotten footnote to history if it had not been followed by a far more substantial and better organised force that became known as the First Crusade. This second wave of armed pilgrims was remarkably well-prepared, given conditions in Western Europe at the end of the eleventh century, yet it was anything but a disciplined army. Rather, it was a vast collection of hundreds of independent contingents of fighting men, often accompanied by confessors, wives and servants. At the base were individual knights and sergeants, most of whom attached themselves temporarily to a wealthier knight or lord. In exchange for the military service, they received pay and provisions. There was no overall commander, and no one was bound by discipline or duty. These men were volunteers in search of salvation together.

The recruits came predominantly from France, Normandy, Toulouse and Italy, and they formed uneven and loose units headed by the most powerful and reputable lords who had 'taken the cross', or taken an oath to try to liberate the Holy Sepulchre from pagan occupation. The movement of these contingents from their base region to Constantinople was loosely coordinated. The different components travelled by different routes at staggered times to avoid overburdening the Christian territories they transited. The plan called for all contingents to meet up in Constantinople, where the Western leaders expected to be integrated into a larger army commanded by the Byzantine emperor.

As the various companies arrived in Constantinople, the emperor wined and dined the leading noblemen and awed them with his power and wealth. He flattered them and gave them magnificent gifts, yet required them to pay for all provisions needed for themselves and their men. Alexius hinted that he might take the cross himself, but meanwhile tenaciously demanded oaths from the Western noblemen that they would recognise Byzantine suzerainty over all territories they liberated from the Saracens. By the time the last of the Western leaders arrived, the emperor's wiles had aroused the crusaders' suspicions. Count Raymond of Toulouse made his oath of fealty conditional on Alexius' leadership in the coming expedition; the emperor officially excused himself, saying 'regrettably' he had to remain in Constantinople.

It might all have ended there. Baffled and bewildered about the emperor's intentions, the individual crusaders might have simply returned home, sought service with the Byzantines or continued to Jerusalem in small groups as pilgrims rather than liberators. Instead, the leaders decided to proceed with their mission. They had taken vows to liberate Jerusalem, not fight for the Byzantine emperor in whatever way he found convenient, and that was what they would attempt to do.

From this point forward, one can say the crusade was improvised. It also became a wholly Latin or 'Frankish' affair. Although Emperor Alexis provided transportation across the Bosporus and sent two Byzantine generals as military advisors, the Western leaders made the decisions, and the marching, fighting and dying was done by the crusaders, not the Byzantines.

Due to the lack of unified command, however, decisions had to be made collectively at each stage. This was not just a matter of the leading nobles agreeing among themselves; it entailed convincing the common soldiers – all volunteers – of a course of action. Throughout the crusade, assemblies of the participants were called to discuss next steps. These were not empty charades. The will of the common crusaders significantly shaped the course of the crusade.

Nor was it only at such assemblies that the 'ordinary crusader' exerted influence on events. Although the more powerful lords had a solid core of relatives and vassals tied to them by blood or oaths, all other men were volunteers who owed allegiance and obedience to no man. The crusaders tended to cluster in groups based on language or shared cultural ties, under respected or familiar leaders, e.g. men from the same village under the local lord, knights of the same family under the most senior of them. Yet, all remained free to take their swords elsewhere if they could find a richer or more congenial paymaster. This meant an incompetent, disagreeable or stingy lord could lose followers, while a generous, respected or lucky lord could gain adherents – regardless of his official rank and title. The result was an unstructured and fluid collection of units that changed size and character as men died, fell ill, deserted or simply changed affiliation. None of the leaders was sufficiently strong to dominate the others, and the balance of power between them changed constantly.

Altogether, between 50,000 and 60,000 people took part in this expedition, including some non-combatants. Of that number, roughly one-tenth, or 5,000 of the crusaders, were knights. The most important leaders were:

- Robert, Count of Flanders
- Raymond, Count of Toulouse
- Robert, Duke of Normandy (and eldest son of William the Conqueror)
- Stephan, Count of Blois, Robert's brother-in-law
- Hugh of Vermandois, the brother of the king of France
- Eustace, Count of Boulogne
- Baldwin of Boulogne (his brother)
- Godfrey of Bouillon, Duke of Lower Lorraine and brother of Eustace and Baldwin
- Bohemond, Duke of Taranto, a Sicilian Norman
- Tancred, his nephew
- And, perhaps most essential of all, the papal legate, Adhemar, Bishop of Le Puy.

Of these men, only Bishop Adhemar commanded the full respect of all the others.

These men led their large but unstructured host into Turkish territory in May 1097 with the objective (probably suggested by Alexius or his generals) of capturing the capital of the Seljuk Sultanate of Rum: Nicaea. The city, previously Byzantine, had strong walls, was partially defended by a lake and had a powerful Turkish garrison. The city's population, however, was predominantly Christian, former subjects of Constantinople that still identified themselves as 'Roman'. Furthermore, the city was close enough to Constantinople to enable the emperor to provide naval support. The combination of the crusader land army and

Byzantine navy on the lake convinced the Turkish garrison the situation was hopeless. They surrendered to the Byzantines – not the crusaders – on 19 June. This spared the city from assault and the inhabitants from violence and plunder. Emperor Alexius surely congratulated himself; he had just regained a major Byzantine city intact – at no cost to himself. The crusaders, on the other hand, were far from their goal of Jerusalem. The main Turkish army under Sultan Kilij Arslan had not been engaged, and so remained intact, awaiting an opportunity to obliterate this army just as it had the 'Peoples' Crusade'.

The crusaders set out across Anatolia in the height of summer, heading for Antioch. No friendly markets to buy provisions lined the route; they were dependent on foraging in territory that was arid, rugged and controlled by hostile forces. The crusaders advanced in two divisions: a small advance guard under the dukes of Taranto and Normandy and the count of Flanders, followed by the main force under the count of Toulouse and the other lords. Roughly a half-day's march separated the two divisions.

This proved fortuitous when Kilij Arslan brought up his full army and ambushed the advance guard on 1 July. It was at this engagement near Dorylaeum that Western admiration for Turkish mounted archers – and Turkish respect for 'Frankish' knights – was born. For roughly six hours, the crusaders withstood continuous attacks by what appeared to be endless hordes of mounted archers. Bohemond of Taranto took command and, to his credit, rapidly recognised that the best he could do was hold his position and await the arrival of the main force. The knights were ordered to dismount and defend the baggage train and the camp's non-combatants behind a shield wall. As the Turks grew short of arrows – or became frustrated by the lack of results —they attempted to break through this defence. In some places they briefly succeeded, only to be driven back in close combat at which the knights excelled. Meanwhile, hundreds of the non-combatants and poorer infantry without armour were killed by the Turkish arrows. Finally, sometime in the afternoon, contingents of the main crusading force began to arrive. The knights of these divisions left their infantry behind and mounted a massive charge that shattered the Turkish army. The Saracen survivors fled in all directions.

Strikingly and incomprehensibly, the sultan failed to regroup. Except for one last short confrontation quickly won by the crusaders in mid-September, the Turks opted not to confront the crusaders again. Instead, they turned the land itself into the crusader's enemy. As the crusaders advanced deeper into Asia Minor, reclaiming (for the Byzantine emperor) one city after another, they found themselves in territory that had been emptied, picked clean or even burned by the retreating Turks. Water and provisions became desperately short, and progress slowed to an average of 12.5km (8 miles) a day. Thousands died of hunger, thirst, heatstroke and other diseases, while an estimated four of every five horses perished during the march across Anatolia.

The army split up to increase the chances of obtaining the necessary food and fodder. While the main body took the northern route, Tancred and Baldwin de Boulogne, operating independently of one another, took their contingents south into Cilician Armenia. Here, the predominately Christian population welcomed them and assisted them in taking one city after another from the hated Turkish garrisons. Indeed, Baldwin soon left the main crusading host altogether and set off for Edessa with just sixty knights. There, he emerged as an independent ruler in what became the first of the crusader states, the County of Edessa.

The vast majority of the crusaders, however, came to the plains around Antioch. This distinguished city, founded by one of Alexander the Great's generals, was home to one of the four patriarchies of the church and closely associated with Saint Peter. It had long been considered one of the most important cities in Christendom but had fallen to Muslim armies in 637, shortly after Jerusalem. The Byzantine Empire had re-established control of the city in 969, and its conquest by the Seljuks more than 100 years later in 1086 had sent shock waves to Constantinople, triggering the appeal to the West for aid. When the crusaders arrived, Antioch housed a population of roughly 40,000 still predominantly Christian inhabitants. Defended by massive walls reinforced by 400 towers and a large Seljuk garrison, it was far too substantial for the crusaders to completely invest.

Furthermore, despite horrendous attrition during the march, there were still roughly 30,000 crusaders. The need to provide food for so great a host resulted in the establishment of foraging centres as much as 80km (50 miles) away. The resources of most knights and minor lords were nearly exhausted. When winter came, bitter cold aggravated the hunger and exhaustion. Just when the crusaders were at their weakest, Seljuk relief armies attacked, first in late December 1097 and again, in early February 1098. The attacks were beaten off, yet illness, exhaustion, malnutrition, hunger and intense cold continued to eat away at the crusaders' numbers and morale.

The arrival of an estimated 10,000 reinforcements by sea failed to alter the situation. Many men began to desert the crusade. Some sailed away on the ships that had brought reinforcements, while others returned by the land route that was, by their own action, cleared of hostile forces. The most prominent of those who left the siege camp, although his motives remain unclear, was Stephen of Blois; he removed himself to the liberated city of Iskenderum, possibly to recover from illness. The Byzantine advisors likewise departed, perhaps in an attempt to persuade the emperor to send military aid, since a new and bigger Muslim army under the Atabeg Kerbogha of Mosul was approaching.

Fortunately for the crusaders, disaffection was growing *inside* the besieged city as well as outside. Bohemond of Taranto got wind of it but kept the knowledge to himself until he had persuaded his comrades to agree to let him keep Antioch on two conditions: that he captured it and that the Byzantine emperor did not appear in person to claim it. Once they had agreed, Bohemond produced a plan based on the betrayal of one section of the wall by the Armenian captain commanding it. On the night of 2-3 June, a small body of Bohemond's knights scaled the wall without opposition in the sector held by the Armenian. Once inside the city, they opened one of the main gates, enabling the rest of the crusaders to flood in. The Muslim garrison fled to the citadel. The crusaders gained control of the entire city with its mighty fortifications, all without attacks on the civilian population. There was no bloodbath.

It was not a moment too soon. Shortly (by some accounts, only hours) afterwards, Kerbogha's massive coalition army arrived on the scene. It was composed of units recruited across Syria, Iraq and Anatolia. The crusaders were trapped inside the very city they had themselves besieged for nine months. Supplies were desperately short; starvation still haunted the crusaders. Meanwhile, emboldened by the arrival of Kerbogha, the Seljuk garrison sallied out of the citadel to attack the crusaders from the rear. Although beaten off, a crusader sortie against Kerbogha on 10 June also failed.

Panic gripped the crusaders. So many wanted to desert the enterprise that the leaders had to lock the gates at night. Yet some deserters escaped and reached Stephan of Blois. In turn, he made his way West and intercepted Emperor Alexius, who was slowly advancing with a Byzantine army to restore Byzantine control over the territories liberated by the crusaders. Blois either convinced Alexius that the situation in Antioch was hopeless or provided him with a welcome excuse for not attempting a relief effort. This fateful decision was to poison Latin-Byzantine relations for the next sixty years.

Meanwhile, in Antioch, a series of panic-induced hallucinations or cynically orchestrated false visions started to galvanise the crusaders. The most famous was the discovery of a rusty Roman spearhead, which a priest's visionary dream identified as the spear that had pierced Christ's side at his crucifixion. Despite the skepticism of the papal legate, the masses were mesmerised. The leadership sagely recognised that the psychological moment to risk battle had come. On 28 June 1098, the crusaders marched out – almost all on foot because there were so few horses – and attacked Kerbogha's much larger army. The ragtag, half-starved and numerically inferior crusaders put the celebrated Seljuk army to flight, and the Seljuk garrison immediately surrendered the citadel. As one of the leading contemporary historians of the crusades said: 'This extraordinary victory has never been explained.'[1]

This victory was dramatically – and significantly – celebrated by a religious procession composed of the entire Christian community of Antioch – Armenians, Syrians and Latins. The procession wound its way through the city streets to end at the cathedral where the Greek Orthodox patriarch, John V, was re-enthroned. This act's symbolic importance needs highlighting in the face of the persistent allegations that the Franks oppressed the indigenous churches. This ceremonial act in Antioch on 28 June 1098 affirmed the authority of a *Greek Orthodox cleric* over *all* Christians in the city – the Latins no less than the Orthodox. This spontaneous expression of Christian solidarity should not be forgotten, despite the later, persistent squabbles between Latin and Orthodox clergy that punctuate the history of the crusader states.

What followed this astonishing victory was one of the great anticlimaxes of the entire crusade, namely, nothing. The initial reason was undoubtedly sheer exhaustion and the need to recover and regroup. Another factor, however, was evidently genuine confusion about what to do next. The crusaders sent a letter to Emperor Alexius, inviting him to come to Antioch to assert his authority over the city and lead the crusade to its final destination, Jerusalem.

Alexius was not interested. He felt the vows of the crusade's leaders had been sufficiently explicit to secure the restoration of Antioch to Byzantine control without his personal presence, and his interest in Jerusalem was marginal. He prevaricated, telling the crusaders to wait for him and suggesting he would come the following June.

Aside from the fact that the emperor's answer did not reach the crusaders until the following April, sentiment in the crusader camp towards Constantinople had already soured. Most felt doubly betrayed. From their point of view, Alexius had called for the crusade and then failed to lead it when they had come to Constantinople at considerable expense to themselves. Yet more damning still, he had failed to help them in their hour of greatest need, during the nine-month siege of Antioch with inadequate supplies and shelter. The bulk of crusaders were increasingly sympathetic to Bohemond's argument that any oaths taken to the emperor were null and void because, by failing to come to their rescue, the emperor had failed to fulfil his obligations as a feudal lord to a vassal in need. The fact that Alexius did not view the oaths given him as binding, two-way oaths of vassalage was immaterial in the eyes of most crusaders.

The situation was undoubtedly aggravated by the death of the papal legate Adhemar of Le Puy. Adhemar had been a voice of reason, universally respected, and he had represented the unifying authority of the pope. Without him, the secular leaders felt unsure of their mandate. Their uncertainty was manifest by a request to the pope that he come to Antioch to take possession of it – although it is hard to imagine they seriously expected him to appear.

Bohemond's option won almost by default. He was already in possession of Antioch and undertook a series of forays into the surrounding countryside to secure and shore-up 'his' city. He thereby laid the foundations of the second crusader state: the Principality of Antioch. Yet, his actions were controversial. Raymond of Toulouse objected and argued the Byzantine emperor's case. With the wisdom of hindsight, Toulouse appears to have been more jealous than outraged. He soon started to lead expeditions against cities still in Saracen hands with the transparent goal of carving out a new state for himself. It is the actions of these three lords (Baldwin of Boulogne, Bohemond of Taranto and Raymond of Tripoli) that foster the impression that the crusaders were cynical and greedy conquerors.

Yet the bulk of the crusaders balked. By mid-November, when the weather was ideal for campaigning, neither too hot nor too wet, they became furiously vocal in their demands for the completion of their mission. They threatened to elect new leaders to take them to Jerusalem. They had not taken the cross nor suffered so much and come so far to make Raymond of Toulouse prince of some obscure city in Syria. When in January, Toulouse's troops dismantled the walls of a city he had conquered, Raymond reluctantly agreed to resume the march on Jerusalem. In Antioch, too, at an assembly on 2 February 1099, the rank-and-file vociferously protested the inactivity and greed of their leaders. Godfrey de Bouillon sympathised with the rank-and-file, and the other leaders caved in. The crusaders agreed to muster on 1 March at Latakia to commence the march down the coast.

The Fatimids had recaptured the coast of the Levant from the Abbasids only the year before. Their hold on it was tenuous at best. Rather than halting the crusader advance, the captains of the various garrisons made separate treaties that enabled the crusaders to advance unmolested towards their goal. Some cities offered to provide the crusaders with provisions in exchange for not attacking or damaging the surrounding suburbs. These agreements were honoured by both sides, enabling the crusaders to bypass Beirut, Sidon, Tyre, Acre, Haifa and Caesarea without bloodshed – belying the standard depiction of crusaders as genocidal, bigoted and blindly destructive.

North of Jaffa, the crusaders turned inland towards Jerusalem, reaching Ramla on 3 June. Here they learned that the Fatimids were mustering a large army to defend the city. On 6 June, Tancred's cavalry reached the undefended and completely Christian town of Bethlehem. The crusaders were welcomed as liberators. The following day, the crusaders caught their first glimpse of Jerusalem from a hill that became known as Montjoie – the 'Mount of Joy'.

The siege that followed was remarkably short, and the crusader victory nearly as astonishing as at Antioch. The walls and towers of Jerusalem were first-rate and manned by a powerful Egyptian garrison. To ensure no repeat of the treachery that led to the fall of Antioch, the Egyptian garrison commander expelled all Christians from the city. He also took the precaution of poisoning the wells around Jerusalem, forcing the crusaders to transport water from the River Jordan. Most important, however, an Egyptian relief army was already on the way and could be expected within three months. All the Fatimid commander had to do was hold off the ragtag collection of invaders for a month or two.

The crusaders knew about the approaching Fatimid army and this made them determined not to be trapped and crushed between the city walls and the enemy's army. Furthermore, they were so few that they could not surround and seal off the city. Only about 10,000 of the original 50,000 crusaders had made it this far. Of these, at most 1,200 were knights. Assault appeared the only option, and a first attempt was made on 13 June. It failed miserably. Fortuitously, a small fleet of Genoese and English ships sailed into Jaffa harbour and found it abandoned by the Fatimid garrison; the crusaders were able to cannibalize these ships to build siege engines.

On the night of 13-14 July, the siege engines went into position, but throughout 14 July, the Egyptian defenders prevented the crusaders from setting foot on the walls. Early on the morning of 15 July 1099, men from the siege tower under the command of Godfrey de Bouillon gained a foothold on the wall and then broke into the city. They opened one of the gates, and the crusaders flooded in.

What followed was the crusader sack of Jerusalem. This one act of unquestioned brutality is the incident most frequently cited by critics of the crusades – or anyone who wants to highlight atrocities committed by Christians throughout the centuries. Modern commentators forget that the pillage of a city taken by storm was the norm for this period, and many are happy to repeat exaggerations from medieval sources. Ironically, it was the Christian sources, making conscious comparisons to biblical references in order to glorify the significance of the event, that leave an impression of excessive violence. Both the Arab and the Jewish sources treat the sack of Jerusalem for what it was —yet another brutal conquest of a city that had changed hands violently eight times in the last 500 years and three times in the previous quarter-century. From Jewish sources, we know that many Jews survived the crusader capture of Jerusalem and were ransomed. Likewise, many Muslims survived; some were ransomed, some enslaved, some escaped and others were simply banished into the surrounding countryside. Orthodox Christians were not victims as they had already been expelled from the city by the Fatimid garrison. According to modern estimates, between 3,000 and 5,000 people died in the crusader assault and sack. The Persian plunder of the city in 614, remember, had cost 26,500 lives and sent 35,000 women and children into slavery.

Furthermore, the crusaders rapidly came to their senses. They remembered where they were, and in a frenzy of piety descended on the Church of the Holy Sepulchre and the other holy sites to pray, sing hymns and confess their sins.

Yet they hardly had time to indulge in this orgy of faith before the next challenge faced them: the Fatimid army was still advancing and, as at Antioch, they faced losing all they had gained. The crusaders met yet again in an attempt to select a unified commander. They elected Godfrey de Bouillon.

Under his leadership, they marched out of Jerusalem and advanced to face the Fatimids in the field. This was a courageous – not to say audacious – decision, presumably dictated by the belief that, given their resources, they could not defend Jerusalem. The gamble paid off. At dawn on 12 August 1099, the crusader army fell upon a Fatimid army that was still half asleep and caught completely off guard. The crusaders routed the Egyptians.

The crusaders' mission was accomplished. They had liberated Jerusalem.

But now what?

While the immediate threat had been eliminated, Jerusalem remained surrounded by enemies. If the sacrifices of the three-year campaign across 3,200km (2,000 miles) were not to be in vain, the Christian control of Jerusalem needed to be institutionalised. Yet none of the men who had fought their way to Jerusalem by their own strength on their own resources and watched four out of every five of their comrades die were prepared to hand the Holy City over to the Byzantine emperor. And so was born the idea of an independent state – not yet called a kingdom – that would defend Jerusalem for Christendom.

Chapter 2

The First Kingdom

The Years of Expansion 1100–1174

Establishment of a Viable Kingdom
The bulk of the men who survived the First Crusade returned whence they had come, their vows absolved by the restoration of Jerusalem to Christian rule. Contemporaries claim the surrounding cities each had more Saracen troops in their garrison than the Franks had altogether. Fulcher of Chartres, chaplain to Baldwin of Boulogne and a witness of both the crusade and the early years of the crusader states, claims that in 1101, the Kingdom of Jerusalem could muster only 300 knights and an equal number of foot soldiers. If these numbers are correct, only 6 per cent of the knights who joined the First Crusade and less than one-third of those who had survived to capture Jerusalem were still living in the East at the start of the twelfth century.

On the other hand, land grants to Western settlers in twenty-one villages north of Jerusalem in 1099 suggest that substantially more commoners remained in the East. Since the poor were more likely to lack the resources to return home, this is not surprising. An estimated 2,000 common crusaders, or roughly 4 per cent of all those who set out but 20 per cent of those who made it to Jerusalem, settled in the Levant at the end of the First Crusade.

Clearly, 300 knights and 2,000 foot soldiers did not constitute a military force adequate for the defence of Jerusalem against an enemy assault or siege. However, the situation of these remaining Franks was far less precarious than it may seem. Data mining and archaeological surveys conducted at the end of the twentieth century have demonstrated that Jerusalem's hinterland was overwhelmingly Christian. Thus, these few Franks were not trying to rule over a population of resentful Muslims but instead were surrounded and supported by the native Christian population, a pattern recorded across Armenia and in Bethlehem.

The First Kingdom

Control of Jerusalem and its surrounding countryside, on the other hand, was insufficient to secure the Holy City for Christendom in the long run. Jerusalem needed at least one secure port through which pilgrims and reinforcements could pass, and it needed sufficient fighting men to withstand a determined attack by the Fatimids or Seljuks. The fact that the second wave of crusaders, nearly as numerous as the First Crusade, disintegrated after various defeats while crossing Asia Minor in 1100–1101 underlined the severe difficulty of reinforcing the Frankish outpost in Jerusalem by land. If Jerusalem were to remain under Frankish control, it had to have troops of its own. Yet the backbone of Christian armies in the early twelfth century consisted of vassals who gave military service in exchange for land – and land was precisely what the Frankish leadership in Jerusalem at the start of the twelfth century did not have.

Furthermore, the raison d'être of the new political entity was the defence of the most important shrines of Christendom. This was reflected by the fact that Godfrey de Bouillon refused the title of 'king' on the grounds that it would be inappropriate for a mere man to 'wear a crown of gold where Christ had worn a crown of thorns'. Godfrey chose the title 'Protector of the Holy Sepulchre' instead. Yet while the Holy Sepulchre was, without doubt, the most cherished of Christian shrines, it was not the only significant religious site in the region. Because Christ had been born and lived and died in the region, almost every town in Palestine, starting with Bethlehem and Nazareth, could claim a connection to some event in the New Testament. For this reason, the entire region was known to Christians simply as 'the Holy Land'.

This posed four major problems for the few Franks left in possession of this sacred legacy. First, many of the principal sites were still under Muslim control and were 'crying out' – at least in the eyes of the crusaders – for liberation. Second, even the sites now in the hands of the Franks had been neglected, if not actively damaged, during the long years of Muslim rule. Many churches and monasteries were in ruins or in desperate need of repairs and renovation. These places needed massive investment to ensure physical and spiritual integrity, the latter in the form of clerics. Yet neither money nor clergy was available in 1100. Third, pilgrims from across Christendom could be expected to flood to these sites, and the few Franks remaining had to create the infrastructure and secure the environment to receive them. Finally, Jerusalem was so holy that many churchmen believed it should not be subject to secular authority but rather remain an ecclesiastical state.

The last issue proved the most pressing. Had the respected papal legate Adhemar still been alive at the capture of Jerusalem, he might have succeeded in asserting church authority over the inchoate political entity in the making. Certainly, when a new legate, Daimbert, Archbishop of Pisa, arrived to take Ademar's place in late 1099, he attempted to assert church authority. He obtained promises from Godfrey about a position of dominance in the future. Godfrey's untimely death on 18 July 1100, however, dramatically altered the political landscape. Godfrey's knights seized control of the citadel of Jerusalem, the Tower of David, and held it in the name of Godfrey's younger brother Baldwin de Boulogne until the latter could arrive. Their action foiled Daimbert's attempt to establish himself as the ruler of the emerging state – and underlined the brutal reality that Jerusalem belonged not to the holy but to those best able to defend it.

As for Baldwin de Boulogne, he had separated himself from the First Crusade before it reached Antioch to follow a local warlord's invitation to assist in Edessa's defence. Edessa, a city nearly equal in size and wealth to Antioch and Aleppo, was at that time in the hands of a Greek Christian warlord, the most recent strongman in a long line of short-lived warlords who came to power by murder or popular acclaim – only to lose favour and be murdered or flee. This man, Thoros, fearing the fate of his predecessors, had (perhaps understandably) confused the crusaders with Frankish/Norman mercenaries. When he invited Baldwin de Boulogne to come fight his battles for him, he never imagined he was inviting in his successor. Baldwin, however, manipulated Thoros into formally adopting him in a ceremony using Armenian relics and customs. Then within a month of Baldwin's adoption, the mob turned on Thoros, mercilessly murdering him, his wife and his children. Once Thoros was dead, the citizens jubilantly proclaimed his 'son' (Baldwin) 'doux' – a Greek title that usually implied subordination to the emperor in Constantinople.

Despite the title awarded him, Baldwin de Boulogne was no vassal of Constantinople, yet he was hardly a conqueror in control of conquered territory either. He still had only sixty Frankish knights, and he owed his elevation to the local, predominantly Armenian population. From the

The First Kingdom

point of view of the Edessans, they had not established a 'Frankish', 'Latin' or 'crusader' state at all; they had simply replaced one 'strong man with vague Byzantine ties' with another.[1]

Furthermore, Baldwin's career would have been as short-lived and forgettable as that of Edessa's previous half-dozen rulers had he not proved astonishingly adept at building alliances with surrounding warlords, nobles and elites. That process started with the simple expedient of leaving the Armenian administration of the city undisturbed. Baldwin also adopted Armenian symbols and rituals, and he rapidly married into the Armenian aristocracy. Yet he had hardly established himself before he was called to take up his brother's mantle in Jerusalem. So great was the prestige of the Holy City that he abandoned his comparatively secure and wealthy adopted home in Edessa to take up the burden of the precarious and still isolated city-state of Jerusalem.

Baldwin, however, was not prepared to be a mere 'Protector of the Holy Sepulchre'; he wanted a crown – of gold. On Christmas Day 1100, Daimbert crowned Baldwin king of Jerusalem in the Church of the Nativity in Bethlehem, and with this act, the Kingdom of Jerusalem came into being. Baldwin's new kingdom, however, still consisted only of Jerusalem and its hinterland, including Bethlehem, along with a narrow, insecure corridor to the coast at Jaffa. It also still had only about 300 knights and at most 2,000 Frankish soldiers to defend it.

When Baldwin I died eighteen years later, he bequeathed a kingdom that stretched across the Jordan and from Beirut to Gaza, with only Tyre and Ascalon still in Muslim hands. In the north, it bordered not a Muslim state but the newly established crusader county of Tripoli. Much of this expansion was made possible by the support of the Italian maritime powers, who repeatedly sent fleets to the Eastern Mediterranean, which aided in capturing the coastal cities in exchange for trading privileges with the newly acquired territories.

The Kingdom of Jerusalem captured Arsuf and Caesarea in 1101 and Tortosa and Jubail in 1102, all with Genoese support. Two years later, the Genoese enabled Baldwin to take the critical coastal city of Acre. The following year, the siege of Tripoli commenced with Genoese and Provencal maritime support; the city fell four years later (1109). Both the Pisans and Genoese assisted in the capture of Beirut in 1110, while Sidon fell to King Baldwin I, aided by a Norwegian fleet under the command of King Sigurd. Notably, at Arsuf, Acre and Tripoli, the cities surrendered on terms and the Saracen inhabitants were allowed to withdraw unmolested. Meanwhile, Galilee and Samaria were conquered and occupied by the Franks, pushing the borders of Frankish control across the River Jordan and south along the western shore of the Dead Sea.

Fundamental as these offensive victories were, equally vital was King Baldwin's successful defence of his kingdom against persistent attempts by Saracen powers to destroy it. The Egyptians sent a second army to regain Jerusalem in September 1101. At Ramla on 7 September, despite mustering only 260 knights and less than 1,000 infantry, Baldwin was able to put the Egyptians to flight – at the cost of eighty knights and many more infantry. The following year Baldwin again defeated the Egyptians, this time at Jaffa in May. Almost simultaneously, on 14 April, the count of Toulouse routed a Seljuk army from Homs and Damascus near Tortosa, while tenaciously seeking to establish what would become the County of Tripoli. In 1105 when the Fatimids sent a fourth army to drive the Franks out of Jerusalem, Baldwin met them with a force of 500 knights and 2,000 infantry supported for the first time by mounted archers (native cavalry) in unspecified numbers. With this force, Baldwin decisively defeated the Egyptians on 27 August 1105 in what became known as the Second Battle of Ramla. A Frankish defeat at any of these battles would almost certainly have ended in the obliteration of the still nascent Kingdom of Jerusalem.

How then were these victories and the related expansion possible? Where did the replacements for the dead of the First Battle of Ramla come from? How could Baldwin field almost twice as many knights in 1105 as in 1101?

The key was settlement. Baldwin actively encouraged Christian settlement in any territory he wrested from Muslim control. Significantly, this included inviting Syrian Christians to relocate from Muslim-controlled to Christian-controlled territory as well as welcoming Christian settlers from Western Europe. Vitally important to the viability of the kingdom, Baldwin established baronies that could be parceled out as fiefs to maintain a feudal army of knights and sergeants. Even lands granted to, for example, the canons of the Holy Sepulchre, were fiefs owing sergeants to the king's army. What this means is that the land was tilled by free tenants who owed feudal service as sergeants, while the profits of the agricultural activity were split between the tenant and the ecclesiastical landlord.

It was also during Baldwin I's reign that both the Knights Templar and the Knights Hospitaller were established in the Kingdom of Jerusalem. At the time of Baldwin's death in 1118, both institutions were too small to play a significant role in the defence of the realm, but seeds had been planted that would soon bear extremely valuable military fruit.

Baldwin I died on 2 April 1118 without issue. He left behind a kingdom (not just a city) that was economically viable due to the conquest of both coastal ports and inland areas. It was a kingdom with sufficient land to create fiefs and assure fundamental self-sufficiency in foodstuffs such as grains, wine and oil.

Nevertheless, the situation was still precarious. Letters to the West from this period stress that civilians, mainly unarmed clerics, were afraid to travel between cities without an escort. Many pilgrims still fell victim to Saracen ambushes. This was the backdrop against which the Knights Templar were founded as a band of knights dedicated to the protection of pilgrims. The Israeli historian Ronnie Ellenblum characterised this as a period in which the 'threat was continuous', adding the crucial point 'and mutual'.[2] The crusader kingdom-in-the-making was *both* vulnerable and aggressive. The smaller, Saracen coastal city-states and inland garrisons were as threatened and unsettled by the Frankish presence as the Franks were about the larger Muslim powers in Aleppo, Damascus and Cairo.

At Baldwin de Boulogne's death, the throne of Jerusalem passed to Baldwin de Bourcq. The latter was crowned as Baldwin II, alongside his Armenian wife Morphia, on Christmas Day 1118 at the Church of the Nativity in Bethlehem. During Baldwin II's reign, the vital coastal city of Tyre surrendered to the Franks after a five-month siege aided by a large Venetian fleet. The latter had first intercepted and destroyed the Fatimid navy at sea. The Muslim population of Tyre was granted the right to withdraw with their moveable possessions, but the Venetians ran riot and, against the terms of the surrender, engaged in acts of violence. Baldwin II also successfully defeated a coalition of Turkish forces at the Battle of Azaz on 11 June 1125.

Equally noteworthy, during Baldwin II's reign, the Franks began to systematically build their own castles rather than merely occupy existing fortifications as they had done up to this point. Counter-intuitively, most of these castles were built in the parts of the kingdom that were already secure. They were not constructed in areas threatened by Muslim raids and incursions but in regions of substantial agricultural production near concentrations of Christian inhabitants or Christian shrines and pilgrim destinations. The obvious conclusion from this pattern of building was that these castles were not part of a defensive perimeter nor primarily defensive in nature. Instead, these castles were an expression of growing administrative sophistication and control. The exception to this rule was the great castle of Montreal, which was built as an intimidating stronghold controlling the lands beyond the Jordan (the Barony of Transjordan) and threatening – or at least watching – the lines of communication between Egypt and Damascus.

Baldwin II was also responsible for the first codification of laws for the kingdom at an ad hoc 'Council' at Nablus, attended by secular and ecclesiastical lords. He continued his predecessor's policy of encouraging settlement, appealing to the monastic orders to establish houses in his kingdom. The importance of monastic presence was that the religious orders enjoyed huge patronage in the West and brought these enormous financial resources to bear when they established houses in the East. In short, the religious orders could tap the resources needed to rebuild and renovate the Christian churches and convents left in ruins by 400 years of Muslim occupation. The religious orders of this period were known for the sophistication of their administration and for fostering the introduction of modern agricultural techniques. Monasteries across Europe were bringing marginal land under cultivation and increasing yields by constructing expensive infrastructure such as terracing, water mills and irrigation.

Although we know little about the details, under Baldwin II, the Kingdom of Jerusalem evolved efficient administrative, financial and legal structures. These were sufficiently robust to function even in the absence of the king. Taxes and duties were collected regularly, properly recorded and allocated to important building programmes and vital military operations. The construction of castles and cathedrals required quarries, roads, harbours and other forms of infrastructure, which suggests that the economic base of the country was growing rapidly. Likewise, the population and the number of pilgrims were quickly increasing.

These combined factors enabled Baldwin II to take the offensive against two of the most threatening Seljuk power centres: Aleppo

(1124) and Damascus (1129). The latter siege, in particular, was a major operation that appears to have been defeated more by bad weather than enemy action. Furthermore, the sultan was sufficiently unsettled by the Frankish threat to agree to an annual tribute of 20,000 dinars to be left in peace. This latter point underlines the degree to which the Seljuks and the Fatimids viewed the Franks as dangerous opponents. At his death on 21 August 1131, Baldwin II left behind a kingdom stronger than ever. Yet his reign was overshadowed by severe setbacks in the northern Crusader states.

Trouble in the North and the Second Crusade

In 1112, the Principality of Antioch passed to a minor heir still resident in the West, and the regency was given to Roger of Solerno, the brother-in-law of King Baldwin II. Antioch had been under sustained attack from the Seljuks since its inception, with incursions of varying strength recorded almost yearly. Subscribing to the philosophy that the 'best defence is a good offence', Roger attacked at the first opportunity. His success in capturing a number of key cities around Aleppo by 1119, however, provoked two powerful Seljuk leaders, Tughtigin of Damascus and Il-Ghazim, the ruler of Mardin, to form an alliance aimed at his destruction.

The two Seljuk leaders fielded a combined army estimated at 40,000 men. In response, Roger called up all of his troops, which included many native Armenians, and sent word to Jerusalem that he was under threat. Thinking his force of 700 knights, 500 turcopoles and 3,000 to 10,000 infantry was sufficient, he opted not to await reinforcements from Jerusalem. On 28 June 1119, Roger confronted his enemies only to suffer a devastating defeat. The Frankish casualties were so high, the battle went down in history simply as 'the Field of Blood'. Among the dead were Roger himself and almost all of his barons. In addition, Il-Ghazi slaughtered 500 prisoners the day after the battle, increasing Frankish losses. Il-Ghazi then began laying waste to the entire area with impunity. Only the city of Antioch, with its massive walls and 400 towers, was comparatively safe.

King Baldwin hurried north to try to stabilise the situation. He personally assumed the regency of the principality for the 9-year-old prince and prepared to confront Il-Ghazi with troops from the remaining crusader states. This unified Frankish force, however, failed to deliver a decisive knock-out blow. Although Il-Ghazi became more circumspect, his army was still intact when Baldwin returned to Jerusalem, leaving the defence of Antioch in the hands of the neighbouring count of Edessa.

Three years later, Joscelyn of Edessa blundered into a Saracen ambush and was taken captive along with other leading nobles, leaving both Edessa and Antioch in a precarious situation. Baldwin II again rushed north to defend the flank of his kingdom, only to be promptly taken captive himself on 18 April 1123. It was more than a year before he could negotiate a ransom. After his release, he remained preoccupied with the insecurity of the northern crusader states, although his absence from his kingdom caused growing resentment among the barons of Jerusalem. Baldwin II ended up spending roughly 40 per cent of his reign in Antioch and Edessa rather than Jerusalem – without solving the problems there.

The north remained the Achilles heel of the crusader kingdoms for two reasons. First, the Byzantines had never been reconciled to the loss of Antioch, which had been an important part of their empire until only twelve years before the crusader capture of the city. This culminated in a Byzantine attempt to seize the city by force in 1138. The then-prince of Antioch, Raymond of Poitiers, only averted disaster by doing homage to Constantinople for Antioch and agreeing to hold the city as a vassal rather than an independent ruler. Second and more dangerously, the north was threatened by the increasingly powerful Seljuk ruler, Imad al-Din Zengi of Mosul.

Zengi was an exceptionally brutal and ambitious ruler who spent most of his career attacking his fellow Muslims, which perhaps explains why Muslim chroniclers readily describe him as ruthless and merciless. He seized Aleppo in 1128, took Homs in 1138 and repeatedly laid siege to Damascus. To save himself from Zengi, the sultan of Damascus turned to the Franks for support, and the Franks obliged. Yet, while this tactical alliance between Jerusalem and Damascus prevented the latter's fall to Zengi, it gave Zengi an excuse (if he needed one) to attack the Franks.

In 1144, taking advantage of Joscelyn II's temporary absence, Zengi assaulted Edessa. His army broke into the city on Christmas Eve and took the citadel two days later. After the death of Zengi in September 1146, Count Joscelyn briefly retook his city, only to be trapped between the citadel, still in Seljuk hands, and a new army brought up by Zengi's son, Nur al-Din. The result was a massacre of appalling proportions.

The First Kingdom

Significantly, according to a contemporary Syrian Christian account, those who fell into the hands of the Seljuks alive were not merely killed but humiliated – forced to strip naked – and then tortured before being killed. This was not simply the application of the 'rules of war', but a vindictive and cruel act, shocking to both Muslim and Christian contemporaries. Altogether, 30,000 Christians lost their lives in the Seljuk capture of Edessa, while another 16,000 ended up in slavery. Furthermore, the bodies of the slain were left to rot, the wells poisoned, the defences destroyed and the city abandoned altogether. This tactic of not just killing and carrying off the inhabitants but rendering a city indefensible and uninhabitable for the foreseeable future foreshadows the tactics of the Mamluks more than a century later. Yet it was exceptional and hugely shocking at the time.

The loss of Edessa shook Europe. The First Crusade had already become legendary, and very few in the West had any idea of how vulnerable the crusader states had been in the intervening forty-five years. Indeed, Europeans were largely unaware of the frequent setbacks suffered, the high cost (in blood) of the victories, or the continuing threats faced by the Franks in the East. To most Europeans, it appeared that God had granted the Holy Land to the Christians, and all was well with the world – at least the world 'Beyond the Sea'. As a result, the loss of Edessa shattered their world view and triggered a new crusading frenzy that culminated in what is known as the Second Crusade.

From the start, the character of the Second Crusade differed fundamentally from the First. There was no longer any need to 'ransom Christ' or 'liberate' his city or his people from oppression. Instead, a new and dangerous precedent was set of offering spiritual benefits merely for *fighting* for Christ in *any* expedition called for by the pope. Henceforth, a 'crusade' might entail fighting anywhere that the pope viewed as useful. It could be against the Wends on the Elbe or the Moors in Spain, or by the thirteenth century, against heretics or the political enemies of the Holy See.

The Second Crusade also set a precedent by encompassing three divergent theatres of conflict: a campaign led by the Danes and Saxons against the pagans of northeastern Europe, an offensive against the Moors led by Alfonso VII of Castile and Alfonso Henriques of Portugal, and an expedition against the Saracens in the Near East. The crusade to the Near East was divided into two main components: a German crusade under Conrad III and a French crusade under Louis VII.

The Germans first attacked the Jews at home before crossing Byzantine territory in an undisciplined fashion, leading to many clashes with the local authorities and population. They crossed into Turkish territory without awaiting the arrival of the French and promptly walked into a Turkish ambush near Dorylaeum. Here, the bulk of the German crusaders were annihilated.

The French followed in a more disciplined fashion. Although suffering one serious defeat in which King Louis was unhorsed and came close to being captured, they avoided annihilation. Despite remaining in Byzantine-controlled territory thereafter, they found markets rare and insufficient, the terrain inhospitable and the weather cold and wet. To add insult to injury, the Byzantine garrisons largely remained behind their walls, leaving the crusaders vulnerable to lightning strikes by Turkish light cavalry. Even without a major battle, the near-continuous Turkish harassment resulted in steady attrition. Worn down by these tactics, the weather and terrain, the French arrived in the Byzantine port of Adalia on 20 January 1148 in a sorry and dispirited state. Louis VII promptly abandoned his infantry and set sail for Antioch with his wife, Eleanor of Aquitaine. They were accompanied by a small number of knights and nobles. Most of Louis' infantry died of hunger, exhaustion, wounds and disease or accepted slavery in exchange for their lives.

As a result of the disastrous performance of both commanders, few crusaders who came overland made it to the Holy Land. On the other hand, a large contingent of northern Europeans, including many English, arrived by ship, swelling the number of combatants available in the Holy Land to an unprecedented number. Consequently, on 24 June 1148, a council of crusade leaders and local barons convened to discuss what to do with the available troops. The recapture of Edessa was no longer viewed as a serious option. Not only had the destruction been too complete, but Edessa also lacked emotional appeal and religious significance. The argument that the recapture of Edessa was vital to the defence of Antioch fell on deaf ears because the prince of Antioch had done homage to the Byzantine emperor a decade earlier; from the point of view of the Western leaders, that made Antioch's defence the emperor's problem, not theirs. The options narrowed down to an attack on Damascus or an attempt to capture Ascalon, the only remaining port on the coast of the Levant still in Saracen hands.

Historians can only speculate why Damascus, technically still an ally of Jerusalem, became the target of the Second Crusade. Possibly the absence of a significant fleet made a siege of Ascalon impractical. Nevertheless, Damascus was far from an easy target. Crusader forces were insufficient to surround the city and cut it off from supplies and reinforcement. The 'siege' lasted only five days. The mere approach of Zengi's relieving army sent the crusaders scampering back to Jerusalem. The only positive feature of this miserable performance was few casualties; the losses of the crusade came during the march to Jerusalem rather than from this disgraceful military (in)action.

Accounts of what happened in the 'siege' are contradictory and marred by untenable accusations of treachery levelled at practically everyone. Christian sources speak of an inexplicable and unjustified move from a good to a bad position, but Muslim sources record no such redeployment. Conrad III blamed the barons of Jerusalem for giving bad advice. However, the king of Jerusalem (a minor) and the ruling queen both opposed the attack on Damascus and the latter was absent from the siege; the queen could hardly be blamed for the failure of an army doing something she had advised against. Given the history of alliance with Damascus, it is far more likely that the crusaders – always shocked by the readiness of local lords to cooperate with Muslims – ignored the advice of Jerusalem's barons not to attack Damascus in the first place.

Other commentators blamed the militant orders for accepting bribes yet admit that no money passed hands – a fact they explained away citing Saracen duplicity. William of Tyre indirectly blamed Louis VII, saying he promised Damascus to the count of Flanders, thereby offending and demotivating everyone else. Michael the Syrian, a native Christian chronicler, believed the Damascenes tricked Baldwin III into believing Conrad III would depose him and set himself up as king of Jerusalem if the crusaders succeeded in taking Damascus, a complicated conspiracy theory.

The consequences of the ignominious failure of a crusade led by two crowned heads of Europe and advocated by the most important clerics of the age were more profound than the loss of Edessa that had triggered it. For one thing, the sense of 'manifest destiny' that had inspired European confidence in its right to control the Holy Land was shaken. Naturally, clerics attempted to blame the crusaders themselves, suggesting their motives had not been pure enough or that they had sinned too greatly. God, they warned, had sent defeat to punish them. Alternatively, they argued that the loss was a gift of God to 'give brave men an opportunity to show courage and win immorality' in the future.[3]

Human nature being what it is, however, it was much easier to blame someone else. The obvious scapegoats were the Byzantines, who had failed to provide sufficient support and protection during the long march through territory they nominally controlled, and the Franks living in the East, (the so-called 'Poulains'), because they had 'given bad advice', 'taken bribes' or been 'too greedy for titles'. Whatever happened, it further poisoned relations between the West and Constantinople while casting aspersions on the reliability of the Franks living in Outremer. Mistrust of 'the Greeks' and the 'Poulains' became a recurring subplot of all future crusades.

Furthermore, in the immediate aftermath of the failed crusade, Saracen confidence surged, triggering a new attack on Antioch. Prince Raymond, the consort of the heiress Constance and younger brother of Duke William of Aquitaine, rushed out to confront Nur al-Din in the field. Like his predecessor, he did so without awaiting reinforcements from Tripoli or Jerusalem. He was encircled on the night of 28 June 1149 and his army was slaughtered. Raymond was found among the dead. Nur al-Din ordered his head and right arm hacked off his corpse, and they were sent as trophies to the caliph in Baghdad. Meanwhile, with the Frankish military force destroyed, Nur al-Din seized the remains of the County of Edessa.

When the relief force from Tripoli and Jerusalem arrived, there was nothing left to salvage. All the Frankish leaders could do was protect any civilians who wished to evacuate the former County of Edessa and relocate in the remaining crusader states. The Franks ceded all territorial claims to the Byzantine emperor, while Frankish troops escorted the column of refugees south. They had to withstand repeated assaults from the forces of Nur al-Din. It is noteworthy that thousands of Armenians preferred Frankish to Saracen rule and abandoned their homes to seek refuge in Jerusalem. These refugees flooded the Holy City, briefly overwhelming the capacity of charitable institutions.

With the benefit of hindsight, historians often depict the capture of Edessa as the beginning of the end for the crusader states. In fact, Edessa had never been an objective of the crusade. It was not home to a single pilgrimage site. The population remained predominantly Armenian. Edessa might have been a useful buffer, but it was in no way essential to the raison d'être, economy or security of the crusader states.

Consolidation and Cooperation with Constantinople

Despite the loss of Edessa, the heartland of the crusader states was remarkably robust and resilient throughout this period. Baldwin II, who had no sons, was succeeded after his death in 1131 by his eldest daughter Melisende without controversy. She had married Fulk d'Anjou in 1129, and he was crowned co-regent with her in the Church of the Holy Sepulchre. As the hereditary count of Anjou, Fulk had taken the cross and served as a temporary associate member of the Templars in the Holy Land in 1119-1121. After his heir, Geoffrey, had married the daughter of King Henry I of England, Fulk abdicated Anjou in favour of his son and proceeded to the Holy Land to marry Melisende.

Jerusalem experienced and weathered its first serious constitutional crisis when Fulk tried to sideline his wife and co-regent Queen Melisende. The barons of Jerusalem suspected him of wanting to alienate the crown for a younger son from his first marriage and solidly backed Queen Melisende. Likewise, the ecclesiastical lords remained staunchly loyal to the queen. Insinuations of infidelity failed to undermine her position because the rumors were (rightly) dismissed as an attempt by her husband to discredit her. In the end, Fulk, a man famed for his ability to bring rebellious vassals to heel, was forced to respect his wife's position of equal power. So much so that William of Tyre wrote that: 'from that day forward, the king became so uxorious that, whereas he had formerly aroused [his wife's] wrath, he now calmed it, and not even in insignificant cases did he take any measures without her knowledge and assistance'.[4]

Furthermore, once a working relationship had been established between the co-monarchs, they worked together as an effective team. A natural division of labour evolved in which King Fulk focused on military and foreign affairs while Queen Melisende managed the kingdom's domestic administration. Due to Melisende's status as ruling monarch (not merely queen-consort), there was no disruption in government when King Fulk died in a hunting accident on 10 November 1143. Melisende continued to rule, now jointly, with her son Baldwin III, who was only 13 at the time of his father's death. Although the kingdom was briefly roiled in 1152 when Baldwin resolved to push his mother aside and take sole control of the government, the crisis was rapidly resolved without international or security repercussions. Baldwin III reigned until 1163 when he died childless and was succeeded by his brother Amalric. Amalric was required to set aside his wife Agnes de

Courtenay before the High Court would recognise him as king, but once he complied with this requirement, his succession was seamless and rapid. The kingdom remained stable.

Throughout this period, from 1131 when Melisende and Fulk were crowned until the death of Amalric in 1174, the Kingdom of Jerusalem enjoyed a period of peace and prosperity characterised by economic growth and development, the expansion of trade, the evolution of sophisticated judicial and financial systems and decisive military superiority. It has been calculated that Muslims attacked twelve times less often during this period than in the first fifteen years of the kingdom's existence. Furthermore, most major battles were 'waged on Muslim ground in proximity to centres of Muslim population, and most ended in a decisive victory for the Franks'.[5] Frankish superiority on the battlefield was so great that the Saracens tried to avoid battle altogether for most of this period. They preferred surprise raids on what today we would call 'soft' targets. Furthermore, the Frankish army could muster and deploy so rapidly that if Saracen raids ran into resistance, they broke off the attack before the kingdom's military might could be brought to bear. The warfare of this period was, therefore, characterised by short raids of limited scope.

The exception to this was the Frankish capture of Ascalon in 1153 after an eight-month siege. This represented a significant defeat for the Fatimids, who had invested heavily in holding the city. Ascalon was a base for the Egyptian fleet, and as soon as it was lost to them, all the Frankish cities to the north became more secure, as did merchant shipping in the Eastern Mediterranean. Furthermore, Ascalon had been a base for lightning raids into the interior of the kingdom, reaching as far as Hebron. To protect the surrounding region against these raids, in the early 1140s, King Fulk ordered the construction of four castles: Gaza, Blanchegarde, Bethgibelin and Ibelin. At the same time (1142), the baron of Transjordan built on Roman foundations the mighty castle of Kerak southeast of the Dead Sea. These castles, far from being indications of weakness and fear, demonstrated the growing self-confidence of the Franks. They were bastions for projecting power.

The growing importance and viability of the Kingdom of Jerusalem were also reflected in a shift in Byzantine foreign policy. Up to this time, Constantinople's relations with the crusader states consisted primarily of demands for submission to Byzantine suzerainty. While these claims were nominal in the case of Jerusalem itself, Byzantine pressure to regain control of Antioch had forced Antioch's Frankish princes to recognise Byzantine overlordship. Then, in 1155, the new prince of Antioch, Reynald de Châtillon, provoked the just ire of Constantinople by raiding the Byzantine island of Cyprus and engaging in an orgy of savagery including the mutilation of prisoners, extortion, rape, pillage and destruction. Although Châtillon was condemned by the Latin Church and Baldwin III of Jerusalem, his behaviour reinforced Byzantine prejudices against the Latin Christians as 'barbarians'. Yet his savagery also provoked a change in Byzantine policy.

While Emperor Manuel I collected a large army to march against Châtillon, Baldwin III signaled agreement with the need to teach the violent prince of Antioch a lesson. Châtillon rapidly recognised that he was trapped and friendless. In a dramatic gesture, Châtillon appeared before the Byzantine host barefoot and bareheaded with a noose around his neck to indicate his complete surrender to the Byzantine emperor. After this incident, Manuel concluded that Baldwin III was worth cultivating. A series of strategic alliances symbolised by royal weddings followed. Two of Manuel's nieces married successive kings of Jerusalem (Theodora married Baldwin III in 1158 and Maria married Amalric I in 1167), and Manuel himself married Maria, the daughter of the prince of Antioch in 1161.

These marriages represented a conscious attempt to civilise and subtly influence policy in Western courts. But Manuel was also willing to ransom prominent crusader lords languishing in Muslim captivity. Rescuing prominent prisoners created ties of gratitude while also serving as public relations gestures that earned respect and admiration from the public at large. Thus, Manuel ransomed even his archenemy Reynald de Châtillon as well as Bohemond III of Antioch, and he paid a king's ransom (literally) for Baldwin d'Ibelin, the baron of Ramla and Mirabel. Yet, without doubt, the most important feature of Manuel's new policy toward the crusader states were a series of joint military operations. These included action against Nur al-Din in 1158–59, an invasion of Egypt in 1167–68 and a joint siege of Damietta in 1169.

The Frankish-Byzantine invasion of Egypt in 1167–68 was only one in a series of five military interventions in Egypt undertaken by King Amalric between 1163 and his death in 1174. The key characteristics of these operations were their opportunistic and geopolitical character.

Amalric's interventions in Egypt had nothing whatsoever to do with 'crusading'. Nor were they in any way racist or religious, much less genocidal. Amalric was operating exactly like his Muslim and Christian neighbours in these campaigns as he sought geopolitical and economic benefits. Ideology, not to mention idealism, was completely lacking.

Since the capture of Ascalon in 1153, the Fatimids had been paying 'tribute' to the kings of Jerusalem. Meanwhile, the Fatimid state was rotting from the inside as two competing viziers, Dirgham and Shawar, plotted against one another for power. Inevitably, the tribute owed to Jerusalem disappeared into someone's purse or was used for other purposes, providing a pretext for a Frankish invasion in 1163. Amalric's army came within 56km (35 miles) of Cairo before the acting vizier Dirgham panicked, agreeing to an even larger 'tribute', and Amalric withdrew. Unfortunately, the success of this campaign appears to have whet Amalric's appetite for more. Egypt was fabulously wealthy, and the ruling Shia elite was not particularly popular with the majority Sunni population or the Coptic Christians, who still formed a significant minority. Amalric smelled blood.

Meanwhile, however, Dirgham's rival Shawar had fled to Damascus and appealed to Nur al-Din for assistance. Nur al-Din sent one of his most reliable emirs, a Kurd named Asad al-Din Shirkuh. Despite initial setbacks, Seljuk-backed Shawar was able to kill Frankish-backed Dirgham, only for Shewar to discover that his 'protector' (Shirkuh) was intent on replacing him. Shawar immediately turned to the Franks for help. He offered Amalric payments larger than what Dirgham had paid to keep the Franks out, if the Franks would come in to fight his battles for him. In April 1164, Amalric obliged by returning to Egypt with an army. He rapidly put Shirkuh on the defensive, besieging him at Bilbies. But Nur al-Din countered by attacking Antioch. In the Battle of Artah on 10 August 1164, Nur al-Din decisively defeated a combined Frankish-Byzantine army, taking Bohemond III of Antioch, Raymond III of Tripoli, the Byzantine Dux Coloman and Hugh VIII de Lusignan captive – effectively decapitating the entire Christian leadership in the northern crusader states. Once again, a catastrophe in the north undermined the success of the Kingdom of Jerusalem. Amalric was forced to negotiate a truce in Egypt in order to address the situation in the north. Both the Franks and the Damascenes withdrew from Egypt, restoring the status quo ante.

The First Kingdom

Three years later, Nur al-Din made a renewed attempt to seize control of Egypt, and Shawar again turned to the Franks. Amalric initially enjoyed astonishing successes, aided by an Egyptian population that blamed the invading Turks/Kurds for their misery. He succeeded in capturing Alexandria, briefly taking Shirkuh's nephew Salah al-Din – better known in the West as Saladin – captive, but he then accepted terms. The Turks withdrew, and the Egyptians agreed to pay an even larger annual tribute (100,000 gold dinars) for Frankish 'protection'.

Amalric, however, let his threefold success delude him into thinking more was possible. He appears to have envisaged a powerful kingdom controlling the Nile as well as the Eastern Mediterranean. It was an alluring illusion. The capture of Egypt would have made the Kingdom of Jerusalem a major Mediterranean power – and a majority Muslim state. No king of Jerusalem *and* Egypt could have retained the mantle of 'Protector of the Holy Sepulchre', and a Christian ruling elite in Egypt would sooner or later have become as unpopular as the Shia Fatimids.

However, Amalric, the Hospitallers and the Italian city-states were mesmerised by the wealth of Egypt. While Manuel I of Constantinople was probably more realistic, he had little to lose and much to gain if Christian control could be extended. After all, Egypt had once been a part of the Eastern Roman Empire. Therefore, Manuel sent a substantial fleet, including impressive horse transports.

In Jerusalem, however, significant opposition to yet another invasion of Egypt surfaced. An attack constituted a violation of the agreement with Shawar. The Templars warned King Amalric not to make the mistake of the Second Crusade: attacking an ally and creating a new enemy. They refused to take part in the invasion of 1168. Other clerics also warned a violation of the treaty with Shawar would displease God. Yet the militants triumphed, and the invasion went ahead.

The Franks met with initial successes, taking Bilbais in three days and engaging in an orgy of plunder and murder without discriminating between Muslims or Coptic Christians; this atrocity turned the Copts against the Franks for years to come. Meanwhile, betrayed by his former friends the Franks, Shawar turned to his old enemy Nur al-Din. As the Franks advanced on Cairo, Shawar set fire to the old city to stop the Frankish advance and then started offering Amalric bribes. Then Shirkuh arrived with his Kurdish/Turkish Sunni army, and threatened Amalric's rear. The Franks chose to withdraw – all the way to Jerusalem.

The Byzantine fleet likewise headed for home, only to run into storms that destroyed much of it. The campaign had turned into a fiasco.

Yet, far more fateful, this blatant violation of international law triggered a regime change in Cairo. Shirkuh had rescued Shawar from the Franks, but Shawar had no credibility left. Within days of his arrival, the Kurdish emir had the Egyptian vizier murdered. The Sunni Shirkuh made himself vizier of Shia Egypt. Two months later, Shirkuh, too, was dead, apparently of overeating. His successor was his nephew Saladin, and the Kingdom of Jerusalem would never be the same.

On the Defensive, 1174–1185

The Revival of Jihad

Ironically, just when the crusader states started acting like secular powers with no particular religious raison d'être, holy war or 'jihad' enjoyed a revival among the Muslim powers of the Middle East. At times, Zengi had employed the language of 'jihad' to justify his conquests, but contemporaries and historians agree that Zengi was not motivated by religious zeal. Rather, he cynically used calls for 'jihad' to motivate the masses. His son Nur al-Din, in contrast, did not merely trot out jingoistic slogans against 'polytheists' and 'pigs'; he systematically supported Sunni orthodoxy. This included support for religious institutions, mainly madrasas, which were colleges of higher education dedicated to the study of Islamic theology and law. Madrasas proliferated in Nur al-Din's domain and provided much of the intellectual underpinning for his wars against the 'heretical' Shia and Christians. The madrasas fostered a generation of Islamic scholars dedicated to 'jihad' and capable of providing the military elites with beautifully-worded and meticulously argued religious justifications for the aggression they wished to undertake.

Nur al-Din was adept, indeed masterful, in employing every conceivable media for jihadist rhetoric – whether in personal letters, sermons, inscriptions on tombs and buildings or poetry. By all these means, Nur al-Din beat the drum of 'jihad', calling on his subjects to push the infidel into the sea and 'restore' Muslim control of Palestine, particularly Jerusalem. It is hardly incidental that this propaganda also emphasised the need for religious and political unity as a prerequisite of success. 'Jihad' could be used to justify the suppression of dissent

The First Kingdom

within Islam, the eradication of domestic political opponents and war against rival Muslim powers. Thus, the pursuit of jihadist goals justified both external aggression and internal oppression.

To be fair, Nur al-Din did not just preach 'jihad'; he also lived according to Islamic principles. As a ruler, he founded and sponsored hospitals, orphanages, bathhouses and mosques while also placing great emphasis on ruling justly. As an individual, he prayed, listened to readings of the Quran, abstained from alcohol, and forbade music and dancing in his court and camp. William, Archbishop of Tyre called Nur al-Din 'a mighty persecutor of the Christian name and faith' but acknowledged his fundamental piety by noting he 'was a just prince, valiant and wise, and, according to the traditions of his race, a religious man'.[6] Indeed, according to the Jacobite patriarch of Antioch (Michael I Rabo, 1166–1199), Nur al-Din 'considered himself like Muhammed, and was waiting for the Lord to speak to him as he had to Moses'.[7] Nur al-Din's death was allegedly welcomed by many of his subordinates who resented his puritanical Islam and disliked that prayer had banished music, dance and wine. His death was also welcomed by Saladin, albeit for very different reasons.

Saladin had come to power in Egypt without the approval of his sultan, and he was in trouble. Nur al-Din had, to be sure, sent his trusted Kurdish emir Shirkuh to Cairo, and Shirkuh's murder of the Fatimid vizier Shawar had been in Nur al-Din's interest. Shirkuh's coup enabled a Sunni to seize control of the Fatimid state, making it only a matter of time before the Shia caliph also disappeared. Saladin's coup on the death of his uncle Shirkuh, on the other hand, was not sanctioned by Nur al-Din. Saladin had been elected by the emirs in Egypt, a majority of whom were Kurds, without consulting the sultan's wishes. They did so because the election took place in the midst of a nascent crisis. Despite Shirkuh's coup, the Egyptian bureaucracy and military remained intact, and many of these men were still loyal to the Fatimids. The Frankish threat also remained real after five successive invasions, several of which had come close to taking Cairo. Both factors made the rapid election of a new vizier essential. Sending to Nur al-Din in Damascus for his advice or approval did not seem practical. Saladin proved to be the candidate on whom everyone could agree, although by no means enthusiastically.

Saladin's rule was far from secure. He had to ruthlessly suppress a revolt by the Nubian troops, burning their families alive, to force them

41

to withdraw from Cairo in exchange for their lives – only to betray them and slaughter them anyway. He then billeted his troops in their former barracks for his own safety. The situation remained volatile until another timely death came to Saladin's rescue: the Fatimid caliph died. This enabled Saladin, officially the caliph's chief officer and protector, to simply end the 'heretical' caliphate. Saladin announced to the caliph's son and should-be successor that his father 'had not made a bequest that recognised him as his successor'.[8] Indeed, Saladin had not even waited for the critically ill caliph to die. He had ordered the imams in the mosques of Cairo to substitute the Sunni caliph for the Fatimid one in their Friday prayers a week before the caliph's death. The Egyptian people, tired of war, acquiesced to the change of religion as well as the change of ruler.

On the other hand, while Nur al-Din welcomed the extermination of the Fatimid caliphate, he was alarmed by Saladin's increasingly independent behaviour. He rightly suspected that Saladin no longer viewed himself as the sultan's slave, but rather as his equal and rival. To reassert his authority, Nur al-Din ordered Saladin to assist in a campaign against the Frankish castle of Kerak.

Saladin feared that if he showed up, he would be arrested or otherwise removed from his lucrative position in Cairo. So, he told Nur al-Din there were rumors of Shia plots against him, and, if he left Cairo, it would fall back into the hands of the 'heretics'. While undoubtedly a convenient excuse, Saladin may not have been fabricating these rumors. A plot was uncovered, hatched by pro-Fatimid elites, who hoped to drive Saladin and his Kurdish/Turkish troops out of Egypt with the help of the Sicilians and Franks. A traitor in their ranks foiled the plot, and Saladin had the rebels arrested and crucified. Despite this action against the known dissendents, Saladin remained sufficiently insecure and dismissed all the Jews and Coptic Christians from his bureaucracy.

Yet no matter how real the threats, Nur al-Din did not trust Saladin. By early 1174, Nur al-Din's patience had run out. He prepared an invasion of Egypt to bring Saladin to heel. Saladin, however, was saved yet again by a timely death. Nur al-Din fell mortally ill before he could embark on his campaign and died on 15 May 1174. He left behind a 9-year-old boy, al-Salih, as his heir.

The competition between the various Seljuk princes for control of Nur al-Din's empire began at once. Saladin was only one of several contenders, and at this time, he gave no indication of being more moral or religious than any of the others. Indeed, from this point forward until shortly before his death, Saladin was predominantly preoccupied with fighting his Sunni Muslim rivals. Furthermore, throughout his career, Saladin relied heavily on nepotism. He consistently appointed family members to positions that controlled fiscal and military resources, an indication of fundamental insecurity. Although he gained control of Damascus bloodlessly in October 1174, al-Salih took refuge in Aleppo, and he remained a rallying point for dissatisfied subjects and emirs from throughout his father's domains. Saladin did not gain control of Aleppo until al-Salih died in 1183. Thereafter, he continued to face serious opposition from Mosul, which remained in the hands of the Zengid dynasty.

As seen from Jerusalem, however, Saladin was the greatest threat to the kingdom since its inception. Hostility between Shia Egypt and Sunni Damascus represented a fracture in Dar al-Islam of the Middle East that the Franks had been able to exploit. To have Cairo's vast financial resources controlled by the same hostile power that held nearby Damascus was inherently threatening. What made the situation even more dangerous was that Saladin continued Nur al-Din's policy of publicly and ardently expounding 'jihad'.

Whether Saladin pursued 'jihad' from conviction or expediency is controversial. Was 'jihad' only a means to distract his subjects from his usurpation of power and his Kurdish extraction? Christopher Tyreman argues that Saladin was 'a conquering parvenue with no legitimacy', who 'needed to demonstrate his religious credentials ... through overt performance of Koranic models [including] dedication to the culture of jihad'. He contends that 'regardless of Saladin's private beliefs', his political situation required him to behave like a model Islamic leader.[9] Other historians go even further, suggesting that the promotion of 'jihad' by Saladin's regime did not originate with him at all but was rather the work of his sophisticated bureaucracy, manned by the graduates of Nur al-Din's madrasas. Contemporary Muslim critics of Saladin such as al-Wahrani depict Saladin's court in Egypt as wanton and rife with drunkenness and homosexuality in 1177. Then again, accusations of sexual misconduct, intemperance and hedonism were standard, almost interchangeable charges routinely used to discredit Muslim and Christian rulers alike, particularly by their respective clerical opponents. Finally, many have pointed out that if Saladin had died in 1185, before the conquest of the Kingdom of Jerusalem, he would be remembered as nothing more than one of countless petty Middle Eastern despots, struggling to establish a dynastic empire by means of bribery, murder and warfare.

We may never know Saladin's motives, but without a doubt, he used the language of 'jihad' to unite and motivate his subjects. Furthermore, in the last fifteen years of his life, he sought to live in accordance with Sharia law. There is evidence that Saladin experienced a religious epiphany after an attempt on his life in 1176, and possibly a reaffirmation of his religious convictions in 1185. Like Nur al-Din before him, he built mosques, libraries and madrasas. He gave generously to pious causes and charities. He abolished unlawful taxes, even when it reduced his own revenue. He reformed his personal life to conform with Sunni orthodoxy – and he embraced 'jihad'.

His secretary and biographer, Baha al-Din, who knew Saladin intimately, claims: 'Saladin was very diligent and zealous for jihad… . [H]is love and passion for it, had taken a mighty hold on his heart and all his being… . In his love for the jihad on the path of God he shunned his womenfolk, his children, his homeland and all his pleasures.'[10] Baha al-Din claims that Saladin told him directly: 'When God grants me victory over the rest of Palestine I shall divide my territories, make a will stating my wishes, then set sail for their far-off lands and pursue the Franks there, so as to free the earth of anyone who does not believe in God, or die in the attempt.'[11]

The 'Leper King'
Saladin had not yet formed such a vision at the time of Nur al-Din's death, and his rise to power occupied roughly the same period as the reign of the next king of Jerusalem, Baldwin IV. King Amalric of Jerusalem died unexpectedly two months after Nur al-Din. He was only 38 years old, and like Nur al-Din, Amalric left a minor heir, a youth who had just turned 13. Unlike Nur al-Din's death, Amalric's did not trigger a power struggle. None of Amalric's vassals marched an army to his capital city; none of his barons staged a coup that sent his legitimate heir fleeing to the frontiers. Although Jerusalem's constitution gave the High Court the authority to elect kings – almost inviting rivalries and factionalism – consensus coalesced immediately around Amalric's only son, Baldwin. The youth was crowned Baldwin IV four days after his father's death.

The First Kingdom

Yet there was a problem. Roughly four years earlier, Baldwin had lost the feeling in his lower right arm. Although many doctors, including Arab doctors, had been consulted, no one found a cure. The possibility that Baldwin was suffering from leprosy was recognised but not fully acknowledged when he ascended the throne. This may be because he was not severely disfigured or handicapped at the time of his father's death; his face was untouched by the disease. Furthermore, he had been tutored by one of the leading scholars of the kingdom and received special riding instruction to control his horse with his legs alone. In short, his outward appearance was normal.

Even as his condition deteriorated and its name could no longer be denied, Baldwin IV was neither isolated nor forced to abdicate. The fact that the Christian barons, bishops and commons were prepared to submit to a leper astonished the Muslim world, while many today, familiar with horror stories about lepers being ostracised and reviled, are baffled by Baldwin IV's ability to retain his crown. The explanation lies in the fact that the crusader kingdom, with its dominant Orthodox population, was heavily influenced by Byzantine traditions. In the Orthodox tradition, leprosy was not viewed as a sign of sin and divine punishment but rather as a sign of grace. By the fourth century AD, the sufferings of Job were associated with leprosy, and leading theologians reminded the Christian community that lepers too had been made in God's image and were likewise redeemed by Christ. Legends in which Christ appeared on earth as a leper were popular and the disease was referred to as 'the Holy Disease'. This was the context in which Baldwin IV reigned.

While these attitudes explain why Baldwin was never repudiated, Baldwin nevertheless deserves credit for earning and retaining the loyalty of his subjects. Throughout his reign, even as his capabilities and appearance deteriorated, Baldwin never faced rebellion or insubordination. Nor was his reign characterised by exceptional factionalism, as popular literature is prone to suggest. Nevertheless, the combination of his dwindling health and the need to find a suitable consort for his female heir, his sister Sibylla, eventually brought his kingdom to its knees.

During most of Baldwin's minority, the regency was held by his closest male relative on his father's side, Raymond, Count of Tripoli. Tripoli was an able administrator who sought consensus and enjoyed excellent relations with his fellow barons, the church and the military orders. He conscientiously negotiated a marriage for Sibylla with

William 'Longsword' de Montferrat, an eminently suitable Western lord with close ties to the Holy Roman emperor. Tripoli was cautious in foreign and military affairs, rapidly concluding a truce with Saladin that lasted a year.

On 15 July 1176, Baldwin IV took the reins of government into his own hands. He was just 15 and, perhaps due to his youth, proved far less circumspect than Tripoli. He immediately chose a course of confrontation with Saladin. Taking advantage of the fact that Saladin was attacking Aleppo, Baldwin personally led a raid into Damascene territory within two weeks of coming of age and defeated forces under Saladin's brother, Turanshah. Baldwin also quickly renewed ties with Constantinople, sending an ambassador there in the fall of 1176. Behind his keen interest in a Byzantine alliance lay Baldwin's desire to pursue his father's dream of conquering Egypt. To further these ambitions, Baldwin IV accepted Byzantine suzerainty on the same nominal terms as his father and accepted the appointment of an Orthodox patriarch of Jerusalem. The impending arrival of a substantial crusading army under the count of Flanders seemed the perfect opportunity for the Kingdom of Jerusalem to take the offensive again. With Saladin not yet firmly entrenched, prospects of success should not be dismissed.

Before anything could be undertaken, however, both Baldwin and his brother-in-law independently of one another became ill. William de Montferrat died in June 1177, leaving behind a pregnant widow, and Baldwin had not yet recovered when Count Philip of Flanders arrived in Acre two months later. Indeed, Baldwin was so ill that he offered Flanders the regency of his kingdom. (Flanders, like Henry II of England, was Baldwin's first cousin through a daughter of Fulk d'Anjou, by his first wife.)

Astonishingly, Flanders refused the regency of Jerusalem. Since Baldwin was still too ill to command his army, the focus turned towards finding an interim commander-in-chief capable of leading the joint forces of Jerusalem, Byzantium and the crusaders with Flanders into Egypt. Baldwin chose the infamous Reynald de Châtillon, who had since married the heiress of Transjordan. However, Count Philip of Flanders again made problems because he expected to become king of whatever territory was conquered in Egypt. King Baldwin, however, had already agreed with the Byzantine emperor that they would divide any conquered territories between them. Mistrust of Flanders and his intentions led the Byzantines to withdraw their fleet of seventy ships. Flanders promptly abandoned the Egyptian campaign and took his troops to the Principality of Antioch in a huff. With him went the master and knights of the Hospital, the knights of the County of Tripoli and roughly 100 knights from the Kingdom of Jerusalem.

Saladin, who had been gathering troops on his northern border to face a combined Byzantine/Frankish/Flemish invasion, found himself facing an infidel kingdom nearly denuded of troops and led by a bedridden, teenage king. No ruler in his right mind would have squandered such an opportunity. Saladin crossed into the Kingdom of Jerusalem with an army estimated at 26,000 Turkish light cavalry that included 1,000 Mamluks of Saladin's bodyguard. Saladin's intentions were unclear. Was this just a powerful raid intended to destroy, harass and terrify? Or did the sultan hope to strike at Jerusalem itself and possibly put an end to the Christian kingdom?

The inhabitants of Jerusalem were thrown into a panic. Many sought refuge in the Tower of David because the walls of the city had been neglected in the decades of Frankish military superiority. Saladin's first target, however, was Ascalon – the great bastion of Fatimid Egypt that had fallen into Frankish hands only a quarter-century earlier.

King Baldwin, who weeks earlier had been willing to appoint a deputy (Reynald de Châtillon, Lord of Transjordan) to command his army for the invasion of Egypt, rose from his bed and assembled every knight he could. The bishop of Bethlehem brought out the 'True Cross', a relic believed to be a fragment of the cross on which Jesus Christ was crucified. Riding at the head of this small force, Baldwin dashed to Ascalon, arriving only hours before Saladin's advance guard, on or about 20 November 1177.

Here, Baldwin apparently issued the *arrière ban* – the call to arms for every able-bodied man of the kingdom. With Saladin's army surrounding Ascalon, however, it was unclear where they should muster. The 357 knights Baldwin had already collected did not impress Saladin. Concluding that he could keep the king and his paltry force bottled up in Ascalon with only a fraction of his forces, Saladin, along with the main body of his troops, proceeded north to Ramla on November 22 or 23. His advance units had already spread out, looting, raping and burning Ramla, Lydda and Hebron. From Ramla, the main road lay wide open to the defenceless Jerusalem.

Behind Saladin, however, Baldwin sallied out of Ascalon. Rather than making a dash via Hebron to Jerusalem to defend his capital, the Frankish king chose to shadow Saladin's army. With Saladin's main force in Ramla, Baldwin mustered his army in Ibelin roughly 16kms (10 miles) to the south. Either here or previously, he rendezvoused with the Templar master at the head of eighty Templar Knights and, one presumes, roughly equal numbers of sergeants and turcopoles. The Templars had rushed south to defend their castle at Gaza only for Saladin to bypass it. At Ibelin, too, the commoners responding to the 'arrière ban' flooded in.

What Baldwin did next was not just courageous; it was tactically sophisticated: he marched his army onto a secondary road to Jerusalem as if trying to slip past Saladin's force at Ramla. Saladin took the bait and pursued it. In his detailed analysis of the battle based on both Frankish and Arab sources, Michael Ehrlich argues that, by this feint, Baldwin succeeded in maneuvering Saladin onto marshy ground beside a small river at the foot of a hill known as Montgisard. Here, as the Saracens crossed over the river, the Franks reversed their direction and fell upon their 'pursuers'. Ehrlich notes that: 'In these conditions numerical superiority became a burden rather than an advantage. It demanded additional efforts to maneuver the trapped army, which fell into total chaos.'[12]

What followed was a complete victory for the Franks. The sultan's army was routed and fled in disorder. Saladin's troops were slaughtered by pursuing Franks or local villagers set on revenge for the rape and pillage of Saladin's marauding troops. Some of the fleeing Saracens made it as far as the desert only to be captured and sold into slavery by the Bedouins, who also took advantage of Saladin's defeat to plunder his baggage train left at his base camp of al-Arish. Saladin barely escaped with his life, fleeing on a pack camel and arriving in Cairo without his army or baggage. Not until his victory at Hattin did Saladin feel he had wiped out the shame of Montgisard. The cost to the Franks may have been as high as 1,100 dead and 750 wounded, but these numbers have been questioned and certainly were not corroborated by other sources. Certainly, no nobles were killed and very few, if any, knights.

Modern historians following Arab sources give Reynald de Châtillon credit for this astonishing victory. The Arabs, however, did not have a clue who was commanding at Montgisard, much less who had devised the strategy. Historians have also been misled by the fact that Baldwin appointed Châtillon his 'executive regent' while he was so ill that he did not believe he could personally campaign. However, the terms of Châtillon's appointment were that he should command the royal army *in the absence* of the king. Once Baldwin took the field – as he most certainly did at Montgisard – that appointment was null and void.

The two contemporary Christian chronicles of the battle based on eyewitness accounts both identified King Baldwin as the commander of the overall army, while one adds the detail that the baron of Ramla led the vanguard *in accordance with the custom of the kingdom*. The latter point is important as it makes clear that Ramla's prominence was not invented by the chronicler after the fact. According to the custom of the kingdom, command of the vanguard always fell to the baron in whose territory a battle was fought; Montgisard was in the lordship of Ramla. Ehrlich also points out that the entire victory at Montgisard was predicated on superior knowledge of the terrain and the ability to maneuver Saladin into a disadvantageous geographic position. He summarizes: 'Led by a local lord, who certainly knew the terrain better than anybody else on the battlefield, the Frankish army managed to defeat the Muslim army, in spite of its initial superiority.'[13] Regardless of who masterminded the strategy that led to victory, the 17-year-old king, who had appeared on death's door only weeks before, took sound advice, accepted risks, and *rode* with his troops although he could not wield a weapon. Is it any wonder that his subjects loved and trusted him afterwards?

Yet this astonishing and dramatic victory may have gone to Baldwin's head. One year later, in October 1178, he ordered the construction of a major castle at the ford across the Jordan known as 'Jacob's Ford'. This was a vital strategic position, less than a day's ride from Damascus at the gateway to Galilee, but it was also, at least from the Saracen point of view, on Damascene territory. Saladin first tried to bribe Baldwin into stopping work, offering a reported 100,000 dinars for him to dismantle the work already done. When Baldwin refused the bribe, Saladin attacked. Arab sources claim that Saladin was so determined to destroy this castle that 'he tore at the stones with his own hands'.[14] The castle, although garrisoned by the Templars and functional, was not complete. The outer works, the second ring of what should have been a concentric fortress similar to Crak des Chevaliers, was still under construction when attacked. In early September 1179, the castle was undermined, parts of the walls collapsed, and the Templar commander threw himself into the flames as the Saracens broke in. The garrison and the construction workers were slaughtered, and the wells poisoned – too soon it seems. Almost at once, illness overwhelmed Saladin's army, killing ten of his emirs and an unknown number of his troops.

Although the loss of 'Jacob's Ford' has also been called the 'beginning of the end' of the Kingdom of Jerusalem, that judgement seems heavily coloured by hindsight. The destruction of an incomplete castle built on Saracen territory did no more than re-establish the status quo ante. Saladin did not try to occupy and control the castle nor build his own fortress at this location. Furthermore, he agreed to a two-year truce shortly afterwards. Yet there can be no question that for the sultan and king, the gauntlet had been thrown down and picked up; both were bent on hostilities.

Throughout the early 1180s, the Saracens made repeated raids on the borders of the kingdom and the audacity of these raids seemed to increase. In addition to small-scale border raiding, Saladin undertook major campaigns against the Kingdom of Jerusalem in 1182, 1183 and 1184. The campaign of 1182 was a full-scale invasion and the Franks, still commanded by Baldwin IV in person, defeated Saladin's army at a day-long battle in intense heat at Le Forbelet. Although this was not the rout Montgisard had been, it sufficed. Saladin's better showing had more to do with Saladin having learned a lesson at Montgisard than with Frankish weakness.

The following year, Saladin again undertook a full-scale invasion, crossing the Jordan on September 29. The Franks mustered a huge army, allegedly numbering 1,300 knights and 15,000 foot. Saladin successfully raided roundabout, and there were casualties on both sides in various skirmishes, but the decisive confrontation failed to materialise before Saladin was compelled by logistical factors to withdraw across the Jordan. The remaining two Saracen incursions before the campaign that led to the Battle of Hattin were attempts to capture the border fortress of Kerak. In both cases, Saladin broke off his siege as soon as a Frankish field army came to the relief of Kerak.

Yet it would be wrong to picture the Kingdom of Jerusalem as besieged and on the defensive throughout this period. King Baldwin personally led raids into Damascene territory in late 1182. In addition, Reynald de Châtillon twice initiated offensive operations, once striking at Tarbuk (1181–82) and the next year launching ships in the Red Sea.

Bernard Hamilton argues compellingly that both operations – far from being the actions of a 'rogue baron' intent on disrupting the (non-existent) peace for his personal gain – had clear strategic aims. In the first case, the raid prevented Egyptian forces from reinforcing Saladin in his campaign against Aleppo, and in the second case, embarrassed him with his Muslim subjects during his campaign against Sunni Mosul. Baldwin IV had wisely concluded a ten-year alliance with Mosul that included substantial payments to the Franks.

Thus, when we look back on the reign of Baldwin IV (1174–1185), we see that Baldwin won all but one of his confrontations with Saladin. Furthermore, as late as the autumn of 1182, Baldwin was still leading raids into Damascene territory – on horseback. However, between phases of apparent vigor, Baldwin also had bouts of weakness when he was bedridden and seemed on the brink of death. These are recorded in the summers of 1177, 1179 and 1183. These bouts of illness were probably not, or only indirectly, related to his leprosy. Tyre refers to them as fevers, and the cyclical nature of the attacks suggests they may have been malaria. In addition to these periods of debilitating weakness, Baldwin IV was also disintegrating before the eyes of his subjects. He was dying a little more each day. Despite these weaknesses, Baldwin's reign would not appear one of increasing vulnerability were it not for a single fact: the succession had not been adequately resolved. It was the crisis over Baldwin's *successor* that ultimately tore the kingdom apart – and then only after Baldwin himself had found eternal peace.

The Succession Crisis
As soon as Baldwin was diagnosed with leprosy, it was clear he would not marry or sire children. His closest relatives were his sister Sibylla, who was two years older, and his half-sister Isabella, the daughter of King Amalric by his second wife, Maria Comnena. Isabella was only 2 years old at the time her father died and eleven years younger than Baldwin. Although Jerusalem's laws and customs recognised female inheritance, heiresses were required to marry in order to assure that a man could fulfill the military obligations that went with the fief. This applied to the kingdom no less than to a barony or knight's fief. Thus, while Sibylla was recognised as the heir apparent, the issue that preoccupied the High Court was finding a suitable husband who would, as her consort, command Jerusalem's feudal army.

Efforts to find a husband for Sibylla predated the death of Amalric. The archbishop of Tyre was sent to France in 1171–72 and returned with Stephen de Sancerre, a brother-in-law of Louis VII of France. After only a few months in the kingdom, however, Sancerre withdrew. His reasons can only be speculated upon. Given that Sibylla herself was still living in a convent and only 13 years old, it is unlikely his decision had anything to do with her, although she may have felt slighted.

The next candidate, William de Montferrat, arrived in 1176 and married Sibylla in October. Sibylla, then 17, became pregnant almost immediately. Unfortunately, Montferrat died within less than a year. She bore Montferrat a posthumous son in August 1177. This made marrying her less appealing to future candidates, as her next husband would have to accept that Montferrat's son took precedence over his own offspring.

The count of Flanders tried to arrange a marriage for Sibylla during his sojourn in the Holy Land, but his candidates were rejected as unworthy. Next, King Baldwin wrote to Louis VII of France, requesting a suitable consort for Sibylla, and the French king chose Hugh, Duke of Burgundy, probably to get this troublesome nobleman out of France. Burgundy, however, failed to arrive because after the death of Louis VII, he decided his future was in France rather than Jerusalem.

As each foreign candidate failed for one reason or another, sentiment for marrying Sibylla to a local nobleman grew. Such a solution would have ensured that the candidate was already adapted to the kingdom's climate, constitution and circumstances. More than one of Sibylla's barons may have contemplated the advantages of marrying her himself or to his heir, but we know of only one concrete contender: Baldwin d'Ibelin, Baron of Ramla and Mirabel.

Both the *Chronicle of Ernoul* and William of Tyre's history report that Baldwin harboured hopes of marrying Sibylla at the latest by 1179. More astonishing, these rumors were known to both Saladin and the Byzantine emperor. However, by 1180 Sibylla was 21 years old and had other ideas. At Easter, she married – in obvious haste – the third son of a Poitevan nobleman named Guy de Lusignan. Guy's elder brother Aimery had been in the kingdom for nearly a decade and had steadily advanced in royal service. He was competent, likeable and respected. His younger brother Guy, however, arrived under a cloud. According to the biographer of William Marshal, Guy and his older brother Geoffrey attempted to kidnap Eleanor of Aquitaine, who by this time was queen

The First Kingdom

of England. While she escaped, Guy (or his brother) struck down the earl of Salisbury – from behind. Salisbury was allegedly unarmoured at the time and in the act of mounting. It was an unchivalrous act and sharply condemned by contemporaries. Allegedly it made Guy persona non grata in the Plantagenet court. Be that as it may, the younger Lusignan had nothing to recommend him and the fact that the marriage took place in a hurry without pomp during Easter week all suggest a scandal.

William of Tyre attempts to explain the haste of the marriage (which he reports) with suspicions on the part of King Baldwin against the count of Tripoli, Bohemond of Antioch and Baldwin of Ramla. Allegedly, the king feared these men conspired to marry Ramla to Sibylla and make Ramla king in Baldwin's stead. Yet Tyre also reports that the alleged conspirators peacefully attended Easter services and then went their separate ways – astonishing behaviour for would-be usurpers. Furthermore, the 'Chronicle of Ernoul' offers another, far more credible explanation: Guy seduced Sibylla, and the hasty marriage was necessary to cover up the disgrace.

Whatever the reasons for the marriage, Guy was promptly made count of Jaffa and Ascalon, the traditional title of the heir apparent, and in 1183 when Baldwin suffered one of his recurring bouts of incapacitating fever, he named Guy de Lusignan – as his probable successor – regent of the realm. Shortly afterwards, Saladin invaded, and the largest feudal army ever mustered in the history of the kingdom collected at Sephorie – and proceeded to do nothing. While Tyre admits he heard conflicting explanations of why and could not 'fully ascertain the truth of the matter',[15] King Baldwin blamed Guy de Lusignan for the sorry showing. Tyre reports: 'Meanwhile the king realized that in the conduct of affairs [in the recent campaign], the Count of Jaffa ... had shown himself far from wise or valiant. Through his imprudence and general inefficiency, the condition of the kingdom had fallen into an evil state.'[16] Moreover, according to Tyre, 'by the unanimous advice of the barons', he crowned his nephew, Sibylla's son by William de Montferrat, co-monarch. Baldwin then summoned the feudal army and the True Cross and marched out to lift the siege of Kerak, which Saladin had undertaken with great vigor. Saladin withdrew rather than face the Leper King.

On his return to Jerusalem, Baldwin set out to find a means of dissolving his sister's marriage to Lusignan. Sibylla refused to cooperate, and Lusignan remained defiant, going to the extreme of retreating behind

Ascalon's walls and refusing entry to the king. Lusignan next attacked Bedouins under the king's protection. Yet Sibylla remained devoted to Guy, strong evidence that Ernoul's version of her marriage is accurate. To her death, Sibylla remained passionately attached to Lusignan, hardly the behaviour of a girl forced into a political marriage by her panicked brother. The church sided with the 'virtuous' Sibylla, the barons with the king.

Meanwhile, the king's health continued to deteriorate. Baldwin could no longer ride. Indeed, he could no longer use his hands or feet, and he was losing his eyesight. King Baldwin had to be carried in a litter when he led his army to relieve Kerak in 1183 and again when he confronted Lusignan at Ascalon. He called a council at Acre and turned over the rule of his kingdom to the count of Tripoli. It was also agreed that Tripoli would serve as regent for Baldwin V, who was just 6 years old; the boy's maternal uncle, the count of Edessa, was named his guardian. Finally, the barons swore that should Baldwin V die before he came of age, they would ask the kings of England and France, the pope and the Holy Roman emperor, to adjudicate the succession between Amalric's surviving children, the Princesses Sibylla and Isabella. In short, the succession had not been satisfactorily resolved when on or around 15 April 1185, Baldwin IV succumbed to his illness at the age of 23. Just over a year later, in summer 1186, Baldwin V also died, still a child of ten.

Usurpation of the Throne

What happened next amounted to a coup d'etat. The barons of the kingdom had sworn oaths to consult Western leaders on who should succeed Baldwin V. Even in the absence of such an oath, the election of the successor to a deceased monarch had lain with the High Court since the founding of the kingdom. The High Court had *not* always selected strictly based on the principle of primogeniture, and it had successfully imposed conditions on candidates. There was nothing 'pro forma' or 'routine' about the High Court's role in selecting a monarch, and nothing automatic about choosing the elder of two sisters.

Thus, when Sibylla persuaded the patriarch of Jerusalem to crown her queen in the Holy Sepulchre, she consciously acted in violation of the kingdom's constitution. Sibylla was neither selected nor approved by the High Court of Jerusalem. She was a usurper, and she knew it. She acted with the support of her closest relatives – her maternal uncle, the titular count of Edessa; her father-in-law by her first marriage, William Marquise de Montferrat (who was not a baron of the kingdom); her brother-in-law Aimery, and two avowed enemies of the acting regent: the master of the Knights Templar and the lord of Transjordan, Reynald de Châtillon. (No other supporters of Sibylla are known by name.)

Furthermore, some of these and other unnamed supporters demanded that Sibylla divorce her unpopular and distrusted husband, Guy de Lusignan, and take a new husband. Sibylla agreed, on the condition she would be allowed to choose her new husband. As soon as she was crowned, she announced that she had selected Guy de Lusignan as her new husband. In short, Sibylla intentionally deceived her supporters. Indeed, she had to crown Guy herself because the patriarch of Jerusalem was so shocked by her duplicity that he refused to do so.

Meanwhile, the other members of the High Court met in Nablus, having been summoned by the regent to discuss the succession. There was nothing inherently illegal or suspicious about this venue. The High Court had met outside Jerusalem on various other occasions, Nablus belonged to the royal domain, and it was comparatively close to Jerusalem. What happened at Nablus also belies accusations of treason on Tripoli's part. When news reached Nablus that Sibylla had been crowned queen, there was no effort to make Tripoli king in her stead. Rather, the assembled barons, bishops and knights agreed to crown Princess Isabella in Bethlehem. Because she had been selected by the High Court, Isabella would have been the legitimate queen of Jerusalem had she been crowned.

While the idea of two rival queens may sound suicidal in light of the threat posed by Saladin, it may not have been as risky as it sounds. If, as Ernoul claims, the overwhelming majority of barons were at Nablus, they could muster significantly more troops than Sibylla's supporters. In short, they stood a reasonable chance of defeating known military incompetents such as Edessa, the younger Lusignan and the stubborn Templar Master, Gerard Rideford. Furthermore, as horrible as civil war sounds, it might, in fact, have been better than what happened under Sibylla and Guy: the near obliteration of the entire kingdom in less than a year.

However, Isabella's coronation was prevented by her own husband. Isabella had been married since the age of 11 to Humphrey de Toron, a youth little older than herself. Toron is described in the chronicles variously as 'cowardly and effeminate'[17] and 'more like a woman than a man' with 'a gentle manner and a stammer'.[18] Although present in Nablus, once the High Court decided to recognise and crown his wife, he slipped out in the dark of the night and went to Jerusalem, where he did homage to Sibylla and Guy. This act made it impossible for the High Court to crown him king. Fourteen-year-old Isabella, however, could not rule alone; she needed a consort to fulfil the feudal function of commanding the kingdom's armies. Therefore, Humphrey's homage to Sibylla robbed his wife of a throne and the High Court of a viable alternative to Sibylla and Guy. The majority of barons caved in and duly did homage to the usurpers. Two men did not: Baldwin, Baron of Ramla and Mirabel and Raymond, Count of Tripoli.

The baron of Ramla and Mirabel had himself been a contender for Sibylla's hand, which may explain his bitterness and refusal to accept Lusignan as king. In front of his peers, he refused to do homage to Guy, abdicated his entire inheritance in favour of his infant son and left his lands and son in the care of his younger brother Balian before departing the kingdom. Ramla went to Antioch, where he was welcomed and then disappeared from the pages of history. While his action was dramatic, it did not weaken or endanger the kingdom, since his brother was mature and capable of governing his barony and leading its troops.

Tripoli, on the other hand, did not abdicate but rather withdrew to Tiberias on the Sea of Galilee. This was the main city in the Principality of Galilee, which Tripoli held by right of his wife. Guy responded by summoning the feudal army to invade Galilee. Tripoli countered by requesting assistance from Saladin, which the sultan graciously granted.

Although Guy had provided the provocation by threatening an invasion, Tripoli's pact with Saladin was treasonous. The Principality of Galilee was a part of the Kingdom of Jerusalem, and Tripoli had no right to make a separate peace with an avowed enemy to preserve his control over it. Furthermore, Galilee sat on the border with the Sultanate of Damascus and extended inwards almost to Nazareth. His treaty with Saladin gutted the kingdom and made it indefensible, not to mention the removal of the 100 knights of Galilee from the feudal levy. While his refusal to acknowledge Guy as king was understandable and based on sound legal principles, his treaty with Saladin was an action that endangered not only the crown but every man, woman and child in the kingdom. It is not defensible.

Balian d'Ibelin offered to act as a mediator between Lusignan and Tripoli, but Lusignan had meanwhile seized Beirut, another of Tripoli's fiefs, and Tripoli would not negotiate until Beirut was restored to him.

Amidst this stand-off, Reynald de Châtillon broke the existing four-year truce with Saladin by attacking a caravan travelling from Cairo to Damascus. Unlike earlier actions by Châtillon, this does not appear to have had any strategic dimension to justify it. When Lusignan ordered Châtillon to restore the prisoners and plunder to Saladin, Châtillon flatly refused. Tellingly, Châtillon explained his action with the assertion that he was the absolute ruler of Transjordan and did not have to take orders from the king in Jerusalem. This suggests Châtillon had backed Lusignan's usurpation precisely because he viewed him as so weak and ineffectual that he could ignore him altogether. The kingdom that had repeatedly rallied around the Leper King was disintegrating as a direct consequence of the usurpation of Lusignan.

Saladin, smelling blood, was quick to react. With the truce off, he gathered his forces for a full-scale invasion. In advance, he sent a reconnaissance in force into the kingdom. In accordance with the terms of his agreement with Tripoli, he demanded and received a 'safe-conduct' for his men to pass unmolested through Galilee. Near the springs of Cresson, this force encountered a small body of Templars, Hospitallers and secular knights estimated at 120. Although vastly outnumbered, the Templar master ordered an attack. The result was the slaughter of nearly every Frankish knight in the engagement. The sight of Templar heads on the lance tips of the victorious Saracen patrol as it passed back out of Galilee shook Tripoli. He agreed to come to terms with Lusignan. When the two men met, Tripoli went on his knees before Lusignan, and the latter raised him up to embrace him. It was May 1187.

Catastrophe and Collapse, 1185–1187

An Avoidable Defeat

On 27 June 1187, Saladin's army crossed the River Jordan. For his sixth incursion into the Kingdom of Jerusalem, the sultan had mustered a force estimated at 30,000 regular troops augmented by unknown numbers of volunteers motivated by 'jihad'. The Franks fielded their entire feudal army of 1,200 knights, including about 600 knights from the militant orders and fifty knights from Antioch. Notably, this army included the full contingent of troops from Lusignan's erstwhile insubordinate barons of Tripoli and Transjordan. The Frankish knights were supported by an equal or larger number of turcopoles and 18,000 infantry.

The Frankish army mustered at the springs of Sephorie, which provided abundant water for the entire force. Saladin led his army along the west bank of the Sea of Galilee to besiege Tiberias. The city rapidly fell, but the citizens and garrison withdrew into the citadel held by Raymond of Tripoli's wife, Eschiva of Tiberias. She sent word to the feudal army requesting relief.

Lusignan called a council of war, as was customary in medieval armies, to discuss strategy. Although the lady of Tiberias' four adult sons pleaded passionately for the army to lift the siege of Tiberias, the lord of Tripoli recommended caution. He urged the king to send to Antioch for more troops and suggested that the army should withdraw towards Acre. This, he argued, would lure the Saracens deeper into the kingdom and expose them to the frustrations of heat, thirst and living off the land.

Such a strategy was totally at odds with the traditions of the Kingdom of Jerusalem. The Franks had either taken the offensive or drawn up their lines of defence as close to the borders as practical. Tripoli's strategy would have exposed large swaths of the kingdom to enemy action. Unsurprisingly, the suggestion met with outraged rejection, particularly from Tripoli's inveterate opponents Reynald de Châtillon and Templar Master Rideford. They called Tripoli a traitor and claimed his advice was designed to benefit Saladin. Consensus was found around a third option: staying at Sephorie and making Saladin come to them from across the comparatively arid plateau between them and the Sea of Galilee.

During the night, however, the Templar master persuaded Lusignan to overturn the consensus decision and instead strike out across the barren plateau to relieve Tiberias. No chronicler was in the tent with Lusignan and Rideford. We do not and cannot know what was said or why. However, we know Rideford was a rash man who apparently knew only one command: 'attack'. Furthermore, he had stolen money deposited with the Templars by King Henry II of England to hire additional troops. While this initially gave him greater leverage over Lusignan, it also meant he risked the wrath of King Henry. German historian Hans Eberhard Mayer argues: '[The theft] could be justified, and Henry's wrath cooled, only by a spectacular success such as could not be achieved if the army simply sat it out at [Sephorie].'[19] King Guy was receptive to the Templars' advice because he had been severely criticised for failing to seek battle in 1183. He seems to have believed a major victory would bolster his fragile standing with his subjects, while inaction would damage it further.

At dawn on 3 July 1187, Lusignan ordered the army to advance towards Tiberias. They took the old Roman road to the springs of Turan, which they reached before midday. Military historian John France argues that at Turan, the Franks would have been in an 'unassailable position' while still able to cut Saladin off if he tried to move deeper into the kingdom. Had he stopped here, Lusignan would have been acting wisely and within the agreed strategic framework. Instead, he ordered the army to continue onto the plateau.

Saladin thanked Allah. Saladin wrote in a letter: 'Satan incited Guy to do what ran counter to his purpose.'[20] Saladin rapidly sent light cavalry to cut the Franks off from retreat – and the water at Turan. In addition, mounted archers harassed the rearguard relentlessly, causing it to slow. A gap opened between the main and rear divisions. Tripoli urged Guy to press forward to reach water at Hattin, six miles away. Guy, possibly influenced by the fact that Rideford was with the rearguard, opted to camp where he was – without water anywhere at hand.

During the night, the rearguard caught up to the main force, but no one had any water. Furthermore, they were now surrounded by the enemy. The latter lit fires so that smoke tormented the Franks. By morning, morale was breaking, and there were some desertions, but the bulk of the army resumed the march. Saladin's army blocked their way to water, whether at Hattin to the north, the Sea of Galilee to the East or Turan to the West. Wisely, the sultan refrained from attacking until his enemies were further weakened by heat and thirst as the sun climbed higher.

The Franks needed to break through the Saracen encirclement to reach water, but all accounts agree Lusignan had no coherent plan for doing so. We know from Arab sources that the Franks undertook multiple charges, several of which were viewed as extremely dangerous and one of which came close to reaching Saladin. A charge led by the count of Tripoli, possibly on orders from Guy, managed to tear open the Saracen ranks. However, only the count and a few of his knights escaped before the Saracens reclosed the gap, keeping the bulk of the army trapped. Another charge led by Ibelin enabled the escape of an estimated 200 knights and maybe 3,000 infantry of the rearguard. Yet, none of these apparently uncoordinated Frankish attacks were sufficient to allow the entire army to escape. Eventually, the Christian infantry broke and sought refuge on the slopes of the hills. The bulk of the knights were forced to follow up the incline – a hopeless position without water. Here, they were overwhelmed. The gruelling battle had lasted many hours in the burning heat of a Palestinian summer and had been hard-fought, but Saladin's victory was ultimately crushing.

The king and most of the barons of Jerusalem were taken prisoner, along with the emotionally and symbolically important relic of the True Cross. There were so many common prisoners that the price of slaves plummeted from Damascus to Cairo. The Christian dead were left to rot on the field and were so numerous that years later, the field of bones still awed visitors. Yet, the salient point about Hattin is that defeat was not inevitable. Nor was it caused by factionalism or treason. All the barons mustered and fought at Hattin. They gave their views in council, but they followed Lusignan's orders. Once they engaged, a massive charge was the only viable option. The Franks made several. It was not 'treasonous' when Tripoli and Ibelin partially succeeded, but 'heroic' when Châtillon and others failed.

Yet the consequences of this defeat were catastrophic. Because the entire feudal army had followed Guy's summons, the castles and cities of the kingdom were denuded of troops. Left behind were the elderly, women, children, invalids and clerics. These had no chance of defending cities, and the rules of war were clear: defiance justified slaughter, surrender enabled survival.

Saladin wasted no time in following up on his victory. His army moved immediately for Acre, thereby cutting the kingdom in two. He obtained Acre's surrender just four days after Hattin. Saladin then split his army in two, sending his brother south with half his forces and turned north himself. He bypassed Tyre as too hard a nut to crack quickly but obtained the surrender of Sidon on 29 July. Beirut resisted and was put to the sword on 6 August.

Meanwhile, in the south, Saladin's brother al-Adil captured Jaffa on 20 July after resistance, and the citizens were slaughtered or enslaved. Gaza, Hebron, Nazareth, Sebasta, Nablus, Bethlehem, Ramla and Ibelin fell in swift succession. By 4 September, Saladin had joined his brother before Ascalon, and the city surrendered to him on terms. Only the great castles in Transjordan and the northern bastions of Belvoir and Safad held out, while just two cities remained in Frankish hands: Tyre and Jerusalem.

The First Kingdom

Siege and Surrender of Jerusalem 1187

Jerusalem was flooded with refugees from the surrounding countryside and other parts of the kingdom. As many as 60,000 people are believed to have taken refuge there in the weeks following Hattin, bringing the total population to approximately 80,000. Accounts speak of people having to camp in the streets because there were no available lodgings. According to eyewitness accounts, there were fifty women and children for every man and only two knights in the entire city.

While still outside Ascalon, Saladin asked Jerusalem to send a delegation to discuss surrender. Significantly, this delegation was composed of burgesses and represented the people of Jerusalem, not the government or nobles. Noting that 'Jerusalem was the house of God', Saladin offered extremely generous terms: if no reinforcements arrived by Pentecost of the following year, the burgesses were to surrender the city in exchange for being allowed to depart with all of their movable goods. The burgesses rejected these terms, saying: 'they would never surrender that city where God had shed His blood for them'.[21] Infuriated by their intransigence, Saladin vowed to initiate a bloodbath when he took the city.

Among those in the city were Queen Sibylla and the dowager Queen Maria Comnena. The latter was Balian d'Ibelin's wife, and the baron obtained safe conduct from Saladin to escort her and their four young children out of the city. The terms of the safe conduct required that he go unarmed and remain only a single night. On his arrival, however, Ibelin was besieged by the population, who begged him to remain in the city to organise the defence. The patriarch absolved Ibelin of his oath to Saladin, and Ibelin informed the sultan of his situation. Saladin had no interest in seeing a Byzantine princess caught up in what promised to be a bitter siege and sent some of his Mamluks to escort Maria Comnena from Jerusalem to Frankish-held Tripoli. Saladin also allowed Queen Sibylla to join her captive husband at Nablus. With no thought for her kingdom, her subjects or her God, Sibylla rushed to her husband's side, putting the ruling queen of Jerusalem voluntarily in Saracen hands. This is perhaps the best evidence that her marriage to Guy was one of passion, not political convenience.

On 20 September 1187, Saladin's army encamped around Jerusalem. For the next four days, the fighting was so bitter that the Arab chronicler Imad al-Din fabricated '70,000 Frankish troops, both swordsmen and archers'[22] to justify the failure of Saladin's forces to overwhelm the defenders. The more reliable historian Ibn al-Athir makes no claims about the number of defenders but acknowledges: 'Then began the fiercest struggle imaginable; each side looked on the fight as an absolute religious obligation'.[23] He also reports that the Frankish knights made sorties in which they inflicted serious casualties. Another account claims that at least one such sortie drove the attackers back to their camp.

On 25 September, Saladin redeployed his army against the northwest corner of the city. He employed sappers to undermine the walls, protecting them with artillery and cavalry so they could work unhindered. On 29 September, a segment of the wall roughly 30 metres long collapsed. At this point, the city was no longer defensible, although one last sortie out of the Golden Gate appears to have been aimed at capturing or killing Saladin, who was camped on the Mount of Olives. This sortie was rapidly driven back into the city.

On the following day, Ibelin sought terms. Saladin dismissed the proposal out of hand; one did not surrender a city already held. Ibelin countered that if he and his men had no hope of surrender, they would kill all the Muslim prisoners, the women and children, and then destroy the Holy Sites of all religions before sallying forth to seek a martyr's death. Saladin was undoubtedly moved by the threat to the holy sites, which he had tried to protect by offering generous terms before the start of the siege. He agreed to consult with his emirs about the offer, and after lengthy negotiations, Ibelin secured a surrender. This gave those trapped in the city forty days to raise a ransom to buy their release.

The ransom was set at 10 dinars per man, five per woman, and two per child. While this was 'peanuts' to the wealthy, such a ransom was simply impossible for the poor and the masses of refugees who had already lost everything. Wages in this period ranged from between 2 and 38 dinars *per year*.[24] How was a widow with several children supposed to find 9, 11 or 13 dinars? Ibelin had recognised the problem immediately and haggling over a lump-sum payment for the poor had drawn out the negotiations. Ibelin ultimately negotiated Saladin down from a demand of 100,000 dinar for the entire population to a lump sum of 30,000 dinars for 8,000 paupers, while the rest paid their own ransoms.

Ibelin had miscalculated. When the forty days were up, there were still roughly 24,000 inhabitants unable to make the payment. Only 8,000 were covered by the 30,000 dinars Ibelin had promised – funds paid, incidentally, by the Knights Hospitaller from money deposited with them by Henry II of England. This left 16,000 paupers with no ransom. Ibelin and the patriarch offered to stand surety, while an effort was made to raise the necessary ransoms from abroad. Saladin turned them down, although as a gift, he released 1,000 of the poor without a ransom. Nevertheless, roughly 15,000 Christians could not be ransomed and went into slavery. Their fate is best described by Imad al-Din in the following chilling passage:

> Women and children ... were quickly divided up among us, bringing a smile to Muslim faces at their lamentations. How many well-guarded women were profaned, how many queens were ruled, and miserly women forced to yield themselves, and women who had been kept hidden stripped of their modesty, and serious women made ridiculous, and women kept private now set in public, and free women occupied, and precious ones used for hard work, and pretty things put to the test, and virgins dishonoured and proud women deflowered ... and untamed ones tamed, and happy ones made to weep![25]

Survival and Defiance
Saladin's focus turned to the last city in the former Kingdom of Jerusalem still in Frankish hands: Tyre. Many of the survivors of Hattin were concentrated here under the command of the dynamic Conrad de Montferrat. A brother of Queen Sibylla's first husband, Montferrat had arrived off Acre shortly after it surrendered to Saladin. Although oblivious of the catastrophe that had befallen the kingdom, he learned of it from the pilot who met his ship. Rather than landing in Arab-held Acre, he sailed for Tyre. Here he found the garrison demoralised and contemplating surrender. He rallied the citizens and defied Saladin, who moved on to easier pickings. After the surrender of Jerusalem in October 1187, Ibelin led the surviving fighting men who had survived the siege of Jerusalem here. Saladin followed on his heels and laid siege to Tyre.

The city was located on an island connected to the mainland by a narrow causeway on which there were three successively higher walls. It was unassailable by sea because of rocks in the surrounding waters. Despite several attempts to force a surrender, Tyre held. By the end of December, Saladin's army had been in the field for eight months. Sated with conquests and loot but cold, wet and homesick, it started to disintegrate. After a Christian ruse lured Saracen ships into the harbour and their capture, Saladin withdrew, leaving Tyre in Frankish hands at the start of 1188.

At the start of the next campaign season, Saladin turned his attention to the two remaining crusader states: Tripoli and Antioch. Tripoli was saved by the timely arrival of a fleet of sixty Sicilian ships loaded with crusaders. Saladin had no desire to tangle with such a large, fresh and motivated force and continued up the coast. He destroyed Tortosa on 3 July 1188 and subsequently took Valania, Jabala, Latakia and the castles of Saone, Darbsak and Baghras. Panicked, Prince Bohemond offered Saladin an eight-month truce, including a clause to surrender Antioch if no assistance arrived within that time. Saladin, who had no desire to waste time and troops on besieging a city as formidable as Antioch, agreed.

If Saladin thought the Franks were beaten, however, he was wrong. On 3 June 1189, Frankish troops from Tyre took to the field to retake Sidon. If successful, the operation would have extended Frankish control in the direction of the County of Tripoli and would have enabled Sidon to be used as a base for recapturing the more important port of Beirut. Regaining control of Sidon and Beirut would have re-established continuous Frankish control of the coastline of the northern Levant. In addition, firm Frankish control of the region between Tyre and Sidon would have enabled cultivation of the coastal plain. This was important to support the population of Tyre, which was flooded with refugees from the rest of the kingdom. Within ten days, however, it was evident that the balance of forces still overwhelmingly favoured the Saracens, and the Franks withdrew to Tyre. Although not a success, the incident is evidence of the fighting spirit of the men of Outremer.

Meanwhile, Saladin had released Guy de Lusignan after the latter swore never to take up arms against Muslims again and promised to go 'across the sea'. Instead of keeping his word, Lusignan went to Antioch and, in the summer of 1189, returned to his lost kingdom with a force of approximately 700 knights and 9,000 infantry. After being refused admittance to Tyre by Conrad de Montferrat, who argued Guy had lost his crown when he lost his kingdom, Guy's small army continued down the coast to lay siege to Acre.

The First Kingdom

This port had once been the economic heart of the kingdom, but the Christian population had been expelled after surrendering to Saladin in July 1187. It was now heavily garrisoned with Egyptian troops fiercely loyal to Saladin. Because Acre was located deep inside Saracen-held territory, a Frankish siege of Acre required continuous provisions and reinforcements by sea. Furthermore, Saladin quickly brought up troops to besiege the besiegers.

The ensuing siege lasted two full years and cost tens of thousands of Christian lives. According to the *Itinerarium Peregrinorum et Gesta Regis Ricardi*, one of the most important contemporary accounts, the siege cost Christendom the patriarch of Jerusalem, six archbishops, twelve bishops, forty counts and 500 barons. While there are no reliable sources for the number of commoners lost, one contemporary observer claimed 75 per cent of the participants died, another that 'more than half' never went home. In either case, tens of thousands of ordinary people – fighting men, clergy and camp followers – were lost in the siege of Acre.

Furthermore, although both sides repeatedly launched assaults against the other, all were ultimately defeated at a high cost. Between these major battles, small-scale skirmishing occurred on an almost daily basis, causing continuous attrition. Nevertheless, disease, deprivation and unsanitary conditions accounted for the lion's share of the casualties. In short, the history of the siege of Acre is a grim tale of stalemate, reminiscent of the horrible trench warfare of the First World War and just as senseless. Except for possibly distracting Saladin from renewed assaults on Tyre, Tripoli and Antioch, it served no military purpose.

The siege also ended the reign and life of Queen Sibylla. She died of an unnamed illness, along with her two surviving children. Since Guy de Lusignan ruled only by right of his wife, Sibylla's death destroyed the last shred of Guy's legitimacy. The barons of Jerusalem promptly recognised Sibylla's sister Isabella as the rightful heir to the throne. Isabella, however, was still married to the man who had betrayed them in 1186: Humphrey de Toron. Under no circumstances were the surviving barons prepared to do homage to Humphrey de Toron. Furthermore, having been tricked once by Sibylla's promises to divorce and remarry, the lords of Outremer insisted on Isabella divorcing Humphrey and marrying *their* candidate, Conrad de Montferrat, *before* they would do homage.

Despite the outraged polemics and histrionic language of some of the chronicles, which speak of an 'abduction' worse than that of Helen of Troy, the facts are remarkably straightforward and undisputed. In mid-November 1190, Isabella was removed against her will from the tent she shared with Humphrey de Toron at the siege camp of Acre. She was not, however, taken and raped by Conrad. Instead, she was sequestered and protected by the senior French cleric, the bishop of Beauvais, while a church court was convened to rule on the validity of her marriage to Humphrey. The case hinged on the theological principle of consent. Humphrey claimed that Isabella had consented to the marriage, but when challenged by a witness to the wedding, he 'said nothing' and backed down. It was further proved that Isabella was only 11 at the time of her marriage to Humphrey, making her below the legal age for consent. This meant the marriage was invalid, whether she had consented as a child or not. The court ruled exactly this, and the marriage was dissolved. Isabella agreed to marry Conrad de Montferrat, and following the wedding ceremony, the barons of Jerusalem did homage to her as their queen.

Chronicles hostile to Montferrat alleged rampant corruption, vile motives on the part of the barons and Isabella's mother, and dismissed 18-year-old Isabella because 'a woman's opinion changes very easily' and girls are 'easily taught to do what is morally wrong'.[26] Modern historians and novelists are apt to focus on the melodrama of a young woman dragged from the bed of 'the man she loved' to marry a man picked by others. The allegations of base motives are utterly unfounded, and the portrayal of Isabella as helpless pawn insulting. Isabella was given a clear and simple choice: she could remarry Humphrey or have the crown of Jerusalem. Isabella chose the crown – despite the fact that her kingdom consisted of only one city and a miserable and beleaguered siege camp on the day she made her choice.

Chapter 3

The Third Crusade and the Restructuring of the Crusader States

The Third Crusade, 1187–1192

The fall of Jerusalem sent shock waves through Europe. Pope Urban III allegedly died of grief on hearing the news. His successor, Gregory VIII, issued a call to crusade just nine days later in a papal bull that blamed the catastrophe on the sins of all Christians and summoned everyone to acts of penance and contrition. One of the first noblemen to 'take the cross' was Richard Plantagenet, Count of Poitou, followed within months by his father King Henry II of England, King Philip II of France and Holy Roman Emperor Frederick 'Barbarossa'.

Due primarily to hostilities between the Plantagenets and Capets, the German crusade got underway first, in May 1189. It was composed of an estimated 12,000 foot and 3,000 knights, most of whom travelled with the emperor overland, although smaller contingents went independently by sea. Barbarossa's army was highly disciplined and prepared to pay for provisions but encountered difficulties as soon as it crossed into Byzantine territory. The new emperor, Isaac II Angelus, had signed an agreement with Saladin, including a promise to obstruct the passage of crusaders headed for the Holy Land. As a result, Barbarossa's force found no markets for provisioning and met with repeated harassment from 'bandits' and 'brigands', probably in the pay of Constantinople. Barbarossa brushed aside the ineffective attempts to stop him, forced Isaac to provide transportation across the Dardanelles, and crossed into Muslim controlled territory on 22 April 1190.

On 18 May, Barbarossa decisively defeated a Turkish army at the Battle of Iconium. The German crusaders then occupied Konya, the capital of the Seljuk Sultanate of Rum, where they replenished supplies and replaced significant equine casualties. The truce negotiated with the

Turks allowed free passage through the rest of the sultanate. On 30 May, the army crossed back into Christian territory, entering Cilician Armenia, where it met with hospitality and support for the first time. One of the most important modern historians of the crusades, Christopher Tyreman, claims that Barbarossa's performance up to this point was 'one of the most remarkable feats of western arms in crusading history'.[1]

Yet it was all undone by a single accident. On 10 June 1190, Frederick Barbarossa drowned while crossing the River Saleph. It is unclear if he had a heart attack while riding through the icy water or if he was caught in a whirlpool, as one account claimed. Whatever happened, his death triggered the almost complete disintegration of his host. Most of the crusaders turned back. Only a small contingent under his son Frederick of Swabia reached Antioch and eventually the siege at Acre, where many of the remaining German crusaders died.

Meanwhile, the death of Henry II on 6 July 1189 paved the way for an uneasy peace between France and England. Philip II was, at best, a reluctant crusader and did not yet have a well-organised and centralised bureaucracy comparable to that of the Plantagenets. Although he attempted to raise extra funding through a special tax, domestic resistance was considerable. Philip proved unwilling or unable to enforce collection and ultimately raised only a modest force. However, a number of his powerful barons (the duke of Burgundy, the counts of Flanders and Champagne) recruited and paid for substantial contingents. In consequence, the French host probably equaled that of Barbarossa, e.g. 15,000 men.

On the other hand, Richard of Poitou, now king of England, was fully dedicated to the crusade. Contemporaries claim that crusading fever swept England, fuelled by what is described as the love of God, hope for remission of sins – and respect for the king. The latter should not be underestimated. Richard also proved remarkably inventive in raising funds to finance his great expedition. In addition to the 'Saladin Tax' – which he vigorously collected, he engaged in practices which are nowadays considered offensive, such as selling offices. In the twelfth century, however, royal offices were instruments of patronage, and payment for them in one form or another was expected, not exceptional. More scandalous in the eyes of his contemporaries was the sale of properties from the royal domain because it diminished royal revenue in the long term. Yet Richard successfully increased exchequer receipts for the year 1190 by two to three times the norm.

The Third Crusade and the Restructuring of the Crusader States

Richard's focus on being well-financed and his organisational talent for raising funds served his soldiers well. For a start, it enabled Richard to build a fleet to transport his army by sea, avoiding the gruelling 3,219km (2,000 mile) march that had depleted crusading armies in the past. Furthermore, this fleet was vital in maintaining lines of supply throughout the entire crusade and enabled two decisive amphibious operations.

After wintering in Sicily, the French (also travelling by sea but in chartered vessels) sailed on 30 March 1191 for Acre, arriving without incident on 20 April. Richard's fleet of 209 ships sailed ten days later and immediately ran into violent storms that scattered it. Richard diverted to Cyprus, which he captured from a self-proclaimed and unpopular despot before proceeding to Acre, which he reached on 8 June.

The arrival of the French and English forces decisively tipped the balance of forces in favour of the besiegers. While French and English fleets blockaded Acre by sea, the kings deployed large siege engines against the city. At last, the crusaders were numerous enough to hold off Saladin's forces while engaging in assaults on the city. The Saracen garrison rapidly recognised that surrender might be unavoidable and opened negotiations. The initial crusader demands for the return of all prisoners and all coastal cities were unrealistic and consequently rejected. Eventually, the Franks were talked down to the terms agreed upon on 12 July 1191, namely (1) restoration of the True Cross, (2) release of 2,700 prisoners and (3) payment of 200,000 dinars. The garrison also provided 2,700 hostages (fighting men, not women and children) to stand surety for the fulfillment of the terms.[2] Significantly, the deal was made with the garrison at Acre, not Saladin. When the sultan learned of them, he was allegedly 'distressed' yet felt honour-bound to uphold them.

At this point, Philip II concluded he had fulfilled his crusading vows and promptly sailed back to France to the shock and scorn of the entire crusading host, including his subjects. French command passed to the duke of Burgundy – the same man who had been betrothed to Sibylla of Jerusalem in 1179–80 but reneged on his promise. Meanwhile, Saladin twice failed to deliver. Richard made the strategic decision to execute all the hostages in plain view of Saladin's army. Although Richard had the right to do what he did by the standards of the day, his action still shocked contemporaries and has blackened his name ever since.

Historians have pointed out that Richard could ill afford to leave sufficient troops in Acre to guard nearly 3,000 prisoners. Others note that he needed to signal strength and determination to Saladin. Often overlooked, the Lyon Continuation of Tyre reports that the principal reason the Franks had agreed to the surrender terms in the first place had been because 'they were keen for the Christians to be released from Saracen captivity'.[3] As a result, when Saladin failed to deliver either the cross or the prisoners, the common troops were outraged and rebellious. Namely, 'when King Richard saw the people weeping and lamenting because Saladin had deceived them, he had great pity and wanted to calm those who were in such great distress'.[4] Read: he feared his own authority could be undermined, and he might lose control of his army. Tragically, it was prisoners on both sides who paid the price of Saladin's neglect and Richard's vengeance. Richard executed the hostages and Saladin killed any Christian prisoners who fell into his hands in the days following this massacre.

On 25 August, the crusader army, estimated at 20,000 men of which 1,200 were knights, set out from Acre along the coastal road heading for Jerusalem via Jaffa. Although the crusaders were marching through what had been the heart of the Kingdom of Jerusalem, the region had been overrun by Saladin's forces four years earlier, and the inhabitants had been slaughtered, enslaved or driven off. No Saracen settlers had been sent to replace them. The fields lay fallow, the gardens left to go to seed, and the vineyards had been broken down. In short, the army was dependent on provisioning by sea. On the other hand, the horses had ample pasturage, and water was plentiful since wells and aqueducts were still functioning. Furthermore, the fleet sailed down the coast, keeping pace with the army, carrying food, fodder, supplies and munitions, as well as offering medical facilities for the wounded.

The latter was important because the sultan's forces controlled the interior and could move and deploy at will. This meant the crusaders had to advance in battle formation, prepared to fight every foot of the way. Richard adopted the standard tactic of the Franks, the 'fighting box', anchoring his formation on the sea, placing his baggage immediately beside the coast, the knights east/left of the baggage and the infantry on the landward flank of the formation, where they could protect the vulnerable horses. The entire formation advanced at the pace of the infantry.

The Third Crusade and the Restructuring of the Crusader States

Richard's objective was to reach Jaffa, where he hoped to establish a defensible stronghold for the assault on Jerusalem. He had no interest in a full-scale battle with Saladin. On the other hand, Saladin needed to avenge the slain of Acre and prevent the Franks from gaining control of another coastal city where they could entrench themselves. He wanted to engage the Franks while they were in the open so he could bring his superior numbers to bear. His reputation was at stake.

Richard maintained rigid discipline throughout the march, and despite daily provocation and harassment by Turkish mounted archers, the army made slow but steady progress down the coast. According to Arab sources, the Franks kept marching despite having as many as ten arrows embedded in their shields or armour. The Franks, furthermore, had enough troops to regularly rotate between the exposed eastern flank and the protected western flank. They passed through the ruins of Caesarea on 1 September 1191 and were a day's march from Arsuf six days later.

On 7 September, however, Saracen forces massed in such numbers that the crusaders knew they were about to face an onslaught. Richard gave strict orders for the knights not to charge the enemy unless he had personally given the order, which was to be communicated by trumpet signals. The sultan, commanding an army roughly twice that of the crusaders, ordered the attack at 9.00 am, after the Franks had marched for several hours in the summer heat. He ordered massed infantry attacks for the first time, which pressed in to engage the crusader infantry, inflicting significant casualties. However, these failed to halt the advance.

By noon, the leading crusader units had reached the well-watered orchards north of Arsuf. The Saracens began focusing their attacks on the rearguard formed by the Hospitallers. Casualties among the horses mounted dangerously, and the master of the Hospital rode forward to Richard requesting permission to attack before all his horses were slaughtered. Richard refused. Returning to the rear, the master found that his men were pressed so hard that they were marching backwards. Again, the master rode forward to beg Richard for permission to launch a counterattack. Richard once again said no.

Before the Hospitaller master could return to the rearguard, the marshal of the Hospital broke out of the line with the cry of 'St George', leading a Hospitaller charge. This was rapidly reinforced by the knights of Champagne, marching immediately beside the Hospitallers. Richard sounded the trumpet signal, and along the entire line, the infantry stepped aside to allow the knights through the infantry screen.

The pro-Richard *Itinerarium* (and many modern commentators) make much of the fact that the attack was not initiated by Richard and suggest it was somehow 'mistimed' as a result. The eyewitness account of Baha al-Din, on the other hand, describes the Frankish charge as 'simultaneous' – showing just how rapidly the Hospitallers had been reinforced. Baha al-Din also described the charge as superbly timed and well-coordinated. Claims that Richard might have won a decisive victory had he charged at a different point in time are misleading. With the Saracens in control of the interior, there was no way to pin them down and annihilate them. The only army that might have been annihilated in this engagement was Richard's; he had his back to the sea.

Significantly, at the moment of the Hospitaller attack, many mounted Turkish archers had dismounted to improve their aim. After two weeks of failing to provoke a charge, they probably assumed the Franks would not charge. Equally important, Richard was with the van. In any battle, there are moments with a junior commander close to the action senses an opportunity that a distant senior commander cannot know about. The fact that the charge was initiated by the experienced and disciplined Hospitaller marshal, not some rash young crusader, suggests it was a rational decision based on calculated risks. The marshal did not have time to send to Richard for permission and did not want to risk another 'no', either. He made a command decision, hoping and expecting to be reinforced. His instincts proved correct.

The Hospitaller charge, rapidly reinforced by the rest of the cavalry, achieved the maximum results possible. While Frankish/crusader casualties were light, the knights inflicted bruising casualties on the enemy that seriously wounded Saracen morale. Ibn Shaddad, who fought in the battle, speaks of a 'complete rout', while Ibn al-Athir says the sultan's forces came close to being destroyed. Most critical, Saladin's aura of invincibility acquired at Hattin was shattered. Respect for Frankish military potency was restored. Although Saladin successfully rallied his troops, the crusaders completed their march to Jaffa without further opposition. Thereafter, Saladin avoided all direct military confrontation with Richard the Lionheart.

At Jaffa, Richard focused on rebuilding the city's broken defensive infrastructure and securing the route to Jerusalem. While this made

The Third Crusade and the Restructuring of the Crusader States

strategic sense and was a testament to Richard's grasp of the essential requirements of a successful campaign, it was slow work. Unsurprisingly, Richard made his first diplomatic overtures to Saladin during this time. Like any good general, Richard recognised that it would be madness to fight if he could obtain his objectives through negotiations.

The political objectives of the Third Crusade were crystal clear: the restoration of Christian rule over the Holy Land. The latter was defined roughly as the land where Christ had lived and died, most especially the site of his execution, burial and resurrection: Jerusalem. Saladin's political objective was to defend the status quo: Muslim control over the territory coveted by the crusaders. There was no common ground between these two positions. As long as both sides believed they could win, the pressure for compromise was insufficient to allow for a diplomatic solution.

Richard's problem was that time was running out. The autumn rains had started, and since Saladin burned and destroyed as he retreated towards Jerusalem, the crusaders were camping out in the open. More important, Saladin was known to have strongly garrisoned Jerusalem, yet still had sufficient resources to maintain a substantial field army. Any attempt to besiege Jerusalem exposed the crusaders to the risk of being trapped between these two forces. Furthermore, victory was nearly as dangerous as defeat because the crusaders did not have enough men to prevent Saladin's army from severing their lines of communication and supply to the sea. Such circumstances induced the Templars, Hospitallers and local barons to advise against an assault or siege of the Holy City. In an assembly of all crusaders, their reasoning persuaded a majority to vote for withdrawal to the coast. Yet this decision shattered the morale and cohesion of the army.

The crusade had been called, and men had taken the cross to recapture Jerusalem. If that goal was unobtainable, why stay? From this point on, the bickering between factions became pronounced. Many men drifted back to 'the flesh pots' of Acre, while the French increasingly refused to recognise Richard's leadership.

With what troops he had, Richard reoccupied Ascalon and rebuilt its defences. By summer, however, popular pressure forced Richard to make a second approach on Jerusalem – with the same result. Meanwhile, Richard had learned that his brother was trying to usurp the English crown with the help of Philip II. Richard realised he must return home.

His objective in the Holy Land switched to leaving the Kingdom of Jerusalem in a defensible state. Richard identified the recapture of Sidon and Beirut to establish continuous Frankish control of the coast from Jaffa to Latakia as the most valuable strategic use of available resources.

Before he could carry out his plan, however, Saladin struck. At the end of July 1192, word reached Richard that Jaffa was under attack. With his household of just fifty-five knights and roughly 2,000 Italian archers, Richard sailed in a half-dozen ships to stiffen garrison morale long enough for a larger force under the command of the king of Jerusalem to advance down the coastal road to Jaffa's relief. On arrival, Saracen banners flew from the towers of the town, and Richard thought he'd come too late – until a swimmer flung himself from the citadel into the water and swam out to inform Richard that the citadel was still in Frankish hands. Richard immediately ordered his ships to beach themselves on the shore, and despite thousands of Saracen troops camped at the base of the city walls, Richard led an amphibious assault. The king of England was the first to go ashore with a weapon in each hand. He fought his way through the Saracens on the beach to an unlocked (!) postern gate and led his small force into the city. Within hours, his men had control of the city; the enemy had been too busy celebrating its victory and sleeping off its excesses to realise what had happened.

The ease of this victory is best explained by the fact that Saladin and most of his cavalry was elsewhere. On learning of Richard's arrival in Jaffa, Saladin returned, and at dawn on 5 August, attacked Richard's meager troops, who were camping in front of the city because no one had yet cleared away the corpses (of both sides) rotting inside. Nearly caught off-guard, Richard's men defended themselves, some of them half-naked, kneeling behind their shields, while the crossbowmen took turns firing. Eventually, a dozen nags were rounded up, and Richard led a 'charge' of twelve knights against the thousands of horsemen in Saladin's army. This astonishing feat is described by the Arab chronicler Baha al-Din based on eyewitness reports. He writes: 'It was reported to me that the King of England took his lance that day and galloped from the far-right wing to the far-left and nobody challenged him. The sultan was enraged, turned his back on the fighting and went to Yazur in high dudgeon.'[5]

Saladin's abortive attempt to retake Jaffa proved to be the diplomatic turning point. Within less than a month, Richard and Saladin signed a three-year eight-month truce on 2 September. Neither side was content with the results, and both remained committed to continuing the fight. Yet the two sides had reached the end of their resources for the moment. Imad al-Din, eloquent as always, puts the following words into the mouth of Saladin's advisors:

> Look too at the state of the country, ruined and trampled underfoot, at your subjects, beaten down and confused, at your armies, exhausted and sick, at your horses, neglected and ruined … . If [the Franks] fail to get their truce they will devote all their energies to strengthening and consolidating their position; they will face death with high courage … and for love of their Faith will refuse to submit to humiliation.… During peacetime we shall prepare for war and shall renew the means of striking a blow with point and blade.[6]

Baha al-Din notes that when the Frankish lords Humphrey of Toron and Balian d'Ibelin went to the sultan's camp to conclude the truce, they were 'received with great honour and respect', adding, 'Both sides were overwhelmed with such joy and delight as only God can measure.'[7]

As pilgrims had always done, the men of the Third Crusade returned to the West. Richard the Lionheart was one of the last to depart, taking ship on 10 October. He left behind a fragile and vulnerable kingdom that hardly seemed likely to survive beyond the end of the truce, yet it lasted ninety-nine years.

Re-Establishment of the Kingdom of Jerusalem, 1192–1195

The foundations of this 'second' Kingdom of Jerusalem were laid by Richard the Lionheart, not only through the territorial gains of his campaign but by his wise decision to allow the barons of Jerusalem to, in accordance with their traditions, select their next king. After initially siding with Guy de Lusignan, the course of the crusade convinced Richard that Guy would never be able to hold the fragile kingdom together. The issue came to a head in April 1192, when Richard received news that his brother John had allied with Philip II, and he was at risk of losing his crown and his empire. He announced his decision to return to the West to confront his domestic enemies and asked each man in the army to decide, according to his own conscience, whether to remain to fight for Jerusalem. The *Itinerarium* describes what happened next:

> When they had discussed this for some time, the wiser of them returned this reply to the royal enquiry: because the country had been devastated by disputes and disagreements, ... the most essential thing was to create a new king whom everyone would obey, to whom the country could be entrusted, who would wage the people's wars and whom the whole army would follow. If this did not happen before King Richard's departure, they declared they would all leave since they were unable to guard the country by themselves.[8]

Richard then asked them who they wished to be their king. 'At once all the people, small and great, went down on their knees and begged and implored him to raise the marquis [Conrad Marquis de Montferrat, Queen Isabella's husband] to be their prince and defender.'[9]

Richard accepted this decision and sent his nephew Henri Count of Champagne to Montferrat in Tyre with the news of his election. With the message delivered, Champagne left Tyre but had only gone as far as Acre when the news overtook him that Conrad had been assassinated. Although attempts were later made to pin the blame on Richard, Saladin and even Humphrey of Toron, the most probable explanation is that Montferrat had offended the violent Shia Muslim sect, the Assassins.

Champagne immediately returned to Tyre, probably to verify the truth of this seemingly incredible rumor. One version of what happened captured the popular imagination and has been repeated uncritically ever since. Allegedly, 'the people' of Tyre welcomed Henri with jubilation and proclaimed him king. This has no basis in historical fact. Kings were not elected by popular acclaim in the Kingdom of Jerusalem, and certainly not by the citizens of a single city. The High Court, composed of the feudal class, barons, knights and bishops, elected kings. The Lyon Continuation of Tyre, which is based largely on material from Outremer, explicitly states that 'on the advice of the barons of the Kingdom of Jerusalem', Richard nominated his nephew, Henri de Champagne, as the next king.

While this is undoubtedly closer to the truth, it still ignores a central point. Queen Isabella had already been recognised by the barons and bishops of Jerusalem as queen; they had done homage to her already.

She was very much alive and, indeed, pregnant. All of this 'proclaiming', 'electing' and 'nominating' actually consisted only of finding a suitable husband for the widowed queen. Champagne was a 26-year-old bachelor who had been campaigning in the Holy Land for more than eighteen months, having come out before the main forces of the Third Crusade. He was a nephew to both the king of England and the king of France, his mother being Eleanor of Aquitaine's daughter by Louis VII. This made him a diplomatic choice, assuring support from both the French and English.

Medieval chronicles agree, however, that Henri de Champagne was initially reluctant to accept the crown. Acceptance meant he would not be able to return home. The kingdom itself existed more in people's hearts than in reality. It was threatened on all sides by the armies of Saladin. The crusading force that had re-established control of the coastline was already disintegrating, and the king of England had announced his intention to return home. Furthermore, if Queen Isabella gave birth to a son, this posthumous child by Montferrat would take precedence over Champagne's offspring. It did not look like a very promising proposition to the young count of Champagne. Yet, Henri changed his mind abruptly, according to the *Itinerarium,* because Queen Isabella persuaded him by her grace and beauty.

Whatever the exact sequence of events, on 5 May 1192 – just eight days after she had been so unexpectedly widowed – Isabella married the count of Champagne. Henri's first act as king of Jerusalem was to persuade his uncle, the king of England, to remain through the campaign season rather than immediately depart for England. This enabled the crusaders to consolidate gains, and with Richard's dramatic victory at Jaffa, to bring Saladin to the negotiating table. When Richard departed in October, he allegedly promised his nephew that he would return with a new crusading army to continue where he left off when the truce expired. Meanwhile, Henri and Isabella set about re-establishing regular government from a 'provisional' capital in Acre. The institutions of government from the High Court down were reconstituted and started to function again.

Establishment of the Kingdom of Cyprus, 1192–1197

It is hard to imagine the survival of this fragile kingdom stretching along the coast from Jaffa to Tyre if Richard the Lionheart had not left another legacy: Frankish control of the island of Cyprus. This former Byzantine province had suffered the first Muslim attacks in 649, and had been fought over and exploited by Constantinople and Cairo in the succeeding centuries until firm Byzantine control was re-established in 965.

In 1185, Isaac, a renegade from the Comnenus family arrived in Cyprus, claiming to have been appointed governor. A year later, after the fall of the Comnenus dynasty, he proclaimed himself the 'true' emperor and began a reign of terror. Contemporary Byzantine chroniclers claim that 'he defiled himself by committing unjustifiable murders ... [and] inflicting, like some instrument of disaster, penalties and punishments that led to death. The hideous and accursed lecher illicitly defiled marriage beds and despoiled virgins.'[10] While we can assume that much of this is exaggeration, Isaac's rule was viewed in Constantinople and by his subjects as illegal and tyrannical. The bulk of the aristocratic elites abandoned the island for the safety of Constantinople, leaving behind a cowed but discontented urban middle class and rural population.

Isaac was also known for preying on Frankish shipping, so it was not surprising that when three of Richard the Lionheart's ships washed up on Cyprus in distress, the crews were captured and the cargoes seized. A fourth ship sought refuge in Limassol harbour, having suffered severe storm damage. Aboard that vessel was Richard's sister Joanna, the widowed queen of Sicily and his bride-to-be, Berengaria of Navarre. Fearing what would happen if they went ashore, the royal women refused Isaac's invitations to disembark.

On 5 May 1191, Richard sailed into Limassol harbour searching for his lost ships, only to find his bride-to-be and sister aboard an unseaworthy vessel running out of drinking water but afraid of being held for ransom or worse if they went ashore. Richard sent an envoy to Isaac Comnenus requesting the release of his shipwrecked men, compensation for the property removed from his wrecks and permission to come ashore for water and provisions. According to all contemporary accounts, Isaac Comnenus returned an extremely rude reply.

Richard responded as could only be expected of the proud Plantagenet: he attacked. The exact sequence of events varies according to which chronicle one follows, but there is no disagreement on the results: Richard seized control of Limassol without notable casualties. Isaac Comnenus' army, however, was still intact. Richard had to eliminate this latent threat, so he offloaded some of his warhorses, exercised them through the night to restore their land legs, and then attacked

The Third Crusade and the Restructuring of the Crusader States

Isaac Comnenus' army at dawn the next day. Richard's early morning attack caused panic among the despot's troops. While Isaac took flight, Richard's men overran the enemy camp, capturing huge quantities of booty – again, without notable casualties.

Richard returned triumphantly to Limassol. On 12 May, he married Berengaria and had her crowned Queen of England. Still in a hurry to get to the Holy Land, however, he granted comparatively mild terms for Isaac's surrender. Isaac agreed to reparations for Richard's ships and treasure and promised to accompany him on crusade with a force of 1,000 men. In his absence, the island's strategic castles were to be held by men appointed by Richard.

While these terms were undoubtedly humiliating for a self-styled emperor, they were a far cry from 'unconditional surrender'. Had Isaac complied with the terms of the agreement, the last crusader kingdom might never have come into being. Isaac, however, was not interested in the crusade and assumed that Richard was in such a hurry to continue his crusade that he would not waste time pursuing a defeated Cypriot despot. Isaac fled during the night.

Perhaps encouraged by the fact that local noblemen, dignitaries and the Italian merchant communities were already doing homage to him, Richard chose to grasp the vast opportunity offered by Isaac's betrayal and seize control of the entire island. This decision to take Cyprus was not a 'diversion' from crusading much less an act of greed. On the contrary, the conquest of Cyprus was Richard's greatest contribution to the crusader cause.

To obtain his goal, Richard divided his army into three parts, and while a small force pursued Isaac over land, the bulk of Richard's army re-embarked on the fleet. Splitting in two and moving in opposite directions, Richard's army systematically secured the surrender of coastal cities and castles. Due to Isaac's unpopularity, this was achieved bloodlessly. At Famagusta, Richard disembarked with his troops and advanced on the capital, Nicosia. Expecting an ambush, Richard personally commanded the rearguard of his army. Isaac obliged, and Richard handily defeated him a third time. Isaac again escaped, this time to the nearly impregnable mountain fortress of Buffavento.

Perched on the top of a steep, rocky corniche so narrow it was not possible to build courtyards or wide halls, the castle could be held by a small garrison as long as supplies lasted. Isaac assumed Richard would not waste time with a siege but continue to Acre instead, leaving Isaac to retake his island at leisure. Unfortunately for Isaac, Richard's fleet had already taken the port and castle of Kyrenia, and with it, Isaac's only child, a daughter. Fortunately for the crusader cause, Isaac's love for this child was so strong that he abjectly surrendered on 1 June. In less than a month and with the loss of only two men, Richard the Lionheart had taken complete control of the rich and strategically important island of Cyprus.

Cyprus is an island encompassing nearly 10,000 square kms (3,800 square miles) of mostly fertile land, including extensive forests. It has ample water resources, significant mineral deposits (notably copper), and a mild Mediterranean climate. The port of Famagusta is only 198kms (123 miles) from Beirut and 295kms (183 miles) from Acre. Furthermore, Cyprus produced grain, sugar, olives, wine and citrus fruits in abundance. Its location made it an ideal staging platform for future crusades and a strong base for ships to interdict any Saracen warships intent on preying on the coast of the Levant. Cyprus was thus both a breadbasket and a military base for the existing crusader states.

That Richard's goal in capturing Cyprus was purely strategic, rather than dynastic, is demonstrated by the fact that he almost immediately sold the island to the Knights Templar for 100,000 pieces of gold. Templar rule of Cyprus, however, was one of the most shameful episodes in the history of the order. Fully engaged in the Third Crusade, the Templars sent only fourteen knights supported by less than 100 other men. They were evidently not the best men and within six months had provoked riots. On 5 April 1192, a violent mob forced the Templars to take refuge inside their commandery in Nicosia. Vastly outnumbered, the Templars offered to surrender the entire island in exchange for safe conduct to the coast. The Greek rebels refused.

The French Continuation of William of Tyre tells what happened next:

> When ... their commander and the brothers realized that the Greeks would have no mercy, they commended themselves to God and were confessed and absolved. Then they armed themselves and went out against the Greeks and fought them. God by His providence gave the victory to the Templars, and many Greeks were killed or taken. [The Templars] immediately came to Acre and explained

what had happened to the master and convent. They took counsel among themselves and agreed that they could no longer hold the island as their property, but ... would return it to King Richard in exchange for the security that they had given him.[11]

The Templar surrender of Cyprus coincided almost exactly with the High Court's election of Conrad de Montferrat as king of Jerusalem. King Richard cleverly offered to sell Cyprus to the deposed king of Jerusalem, Guy de Lusignan. Lusignan accepted the 'consolation prize', although it is doubtful he sailed for Cyprus before the end of the Third Crusade since few knights, sergeants or turcopoles would have been likely to go with him as long as Richard the Lionheart was still in the field. Whatever the exact date of his arrival on Cyprus, Guy was accompanied by a small group of Frankish lords and knights whose lands had been lost to Saladin in 1187–88 and not recaptured in the course of the Third Crusade. Guy arrived on an island that was either still in a state of open rebellion or completely lawless.

Due to the scarcity of sources recording what happened next, most histories repeat a charming story which probably originated in the now lost chronicle of Ernoul. According to this source, as soon as Guy arrived on Cyprus, he sent to his arch-enemy Saladin for advice on how to rule it. What is more, the ever chivalrous and wise sultan graciously responded that 'if he wants the island to be secure he must give it all away'.[12] Allegedly, based on this advice, Guy invited settlers from all the Christian countries of the eastern Mediterranean to settle on Cyprus, offering everyone rich rewards and making them marry the local women. Accordingly, the dispossessed peoples of Syria, both high and low, flooded to Cyprus and were rewarded with rich fiefs, until Guy had just enough land to support twenty household knights.

This is a fairy tale. Guy did not arrive on a deserted island; the population of Cyprus was roughly 100,000. While most inhabitants were apolitical peasants, there were substantial urban and ecclesiastical elites still on the island. These had welcomed Richard the Lionheart to rid themselves of a tyrant, but rapidly proved their mettle in a revolt against Richard's administrators and again, by their successful rebellion against Templar rule. The Knights Templar had abandoned the island because they believed it would be too costly, time-consuming and difficult to pacify.

In short, the large Greek Orthodox population on the island identified themselves as Romans (Byzantines), and were not waiting to welcome 'good King Guy' as their overlord. Indeed, we know the names of two Cypriot patriots who led continued resistance to Latin rule until nearly the end of the century, namely Isaac of Antiochetta and Kanakes.[13] We also have references to abandoned villages and population flight in the accounts of the contemporary Cypriot abbot and later saint Neophytos the Recluse.[14] All of this suggests that a period of unrest and violence preceded the 'happily ever after' ending of the popular fairy tale.

Guy de Lusignan died either in April or towards the end of 1194 and was replaced as lord of Cyprus by his elder brother Aimery. By the end of Aimery de Lusignan's reign in 1205, the island had been pacified and transformed by the steady influx of immigrants from Syria, Antioch and Armenia. Furthermore, Aimery obtained a crown by submitting the island to the Holy Roman emperor and established a Latin church hierarchy on the island. Last but not least, Aimery founded the dynasty that would rule a prosperous and independent Cyprus for the next 200 years.

Chapter 4

The Second Kingdom or the Kingdom of Acre, 1192–1291

A Resurgent Frankish Presence, 1192–1225

With the wisdom of hindsight, the 'second kingdom' of Jerusalem is usually portrayed as fragile, vulnerable and continuously tottering on the brink of collapse. This is a misleading exaggeration that reduces a century of history to a single snapshot taken towards the end of that hundred years. In the half-century between the departure of the Third Crusade and the catastrophic defeat of the Frankish army at La Forbie in 1244, the reconstituted kingdom experienced a period of comparative prosperity, peace and territorial expansion.

Without question, the most important factor enabling this remarkable recovery was the death of Saladin in 1193. His death led to the fragmentation of his empire into bickering principalities based in Cairo, Damascus, Aleppo, al-Jazira, Hama, Homs, Baalbek and the Transjordan. Each of these mini-states was ruled by a different member of the Ayyubid dynasty. Rivalry among the various rulers for dominance over the entire empire was constant. Although punctuated by periods of comparative calm when one or another of the many princes temporarily came out on top, the competition for dominance between the various Ayyubids frequently sparked open warfare.

Probably to bolster his position vis-à-vis his relatives and rivals, Saladin's brother, al-Adil, turned on the crusader states in 1197, attacking Acre in September. Although source material for this campaign is limited, one contemporary source claims al-Adil mustered an army 70,000 strong. Al-Adil was decisively defeated in a day-long battle fought on the plain before Acre by a combined force of native Franks and German crusaders.

The Germans had come to the Holy Land as part of a crusade organised by the Holy Roman Emperor Henry VI, who had taken the cross in 1195. Historians estimate that the numbers of crusaders involved in this crusade equalled or exceeded participation in the Third Crusade, and the leaders included some of the most powerful nobles of the Holy Roman Empire. Contingents started to arrive in the Holy Land in the spring of 1197, and the main force sailed into Acre harbour on 22 September 1197, albeit without the emperor himself.

Trouble began almost at once. The German crusaders behaved so arrogantly towards the local population that tensions erupted. The German leadership wisely intervened and removed their troops from the city to a camp outside. Meanwhile, having failed to seize Acre, al-Adil turned his attention on Jaffa. Henri of Champagne swiftly tried to gather a force to relieve the beleaguered city only to be killed in a bizarre accident. He either accidentally stepped backwards out of a window, or the entire balcony collapsed under him. Either way, this sudden tragedy put an end to the relief efforts, and Jaffa fell to al-Adil. The barons of Jerusalem were compelled to find a new husband for their widowed queen to command the kingdom's armies. Their choice fell on the man who had transformed Cyprus from a hotbed of rebellion into a stable monarchy under Frankish rule: Aimery de Lusignan. In January 1198, Aimery married Queen Isabella and was crowned king of Jerusalem.

Even before his coronation, however, Lusignan brought Cypriot troops to the mainland and took command of the forces of Jerusalem to conduct an offensive campaign in cooperation with the German crusaders. Rather than attempting to confront al-Adil at Jaffa, Aimery led the army north against the poorly garrisoned cities of Sidon, Beirut, Gibelet and Botron, thereby eliminating the Muslim-controlled enclaves that had separated the Kingdom of Jerusalem from the County of Tripoli.

The Germans next laid siege to Toron, but before they succeeded, word reached the Holy Land that Emperor Henry VI had died, leaving behind a 3-year-old son. This news led to the disintegration of the German crusade, as the leading nobles hurried home to deal with the inevitable power struggles that would ensue. It was left to King Aimery to negotiate a truce with al-Adil, which was signed on 1 July 1198.

By 1200, al-Adil had successfully established his dominance over his brother's empire, completely sidelining his brother's seventeen sons. Thereafter, he demonstrated a distinct disinclination to tangle with the Franks. This policy of caution vis-à-vis the crusader states proved a trademark of the entire Ayyubid era (1193–1260).

On the one hand, Ayyubid caution sprang from the lesson learned during the Third Crusade, namely: no matter how complete a victory appeared, there were limitless numbers of fanatical Christians willing to come East to reverse it. According to a leading historian of the Ayyubids, 'the Ayyubids were willing to go to extraordinary lengths in making treaties and conceding territory in order to avoid provoking the arrival of fresh waves of crusaders'.[1]

On the other hand, the Ayyubids had an economic interest in peace. The rulers of Egypt, Syria and Mesopotamia profited immensely from the export of goods through the ports of the Levant to Western Europe. To foster this profitable trade, the Ayyubids were willing to grant Western, predominantly Italian, merchants trading privileges inside their territories. Yet, they also recognised that many more foreign merchants preferred to operate from the Christian-controlled cities along the coast. The Ayyubids therefore had no interest in eliminating these important transshipment points.

Furthermore, nothing was more critical to the maintenance of that trade than peace. Thus, for the sake of revenue that supported their lifestyle – and their wars with their brothers, cousins and other Muslim rulers – the Ayyubid princes were willing to come to terms with the Franks. Throughout the Ayyubid period, relations with the Frankish kingdoms were characterised by truces, alliances and counter-alliances. When circumstances favoured it, these tactical coalitions included active cooperation between Franks and Saracens.

Such policies inevitably drew the censure of the Muslim religious elites who dominated the literate class and recorded history. Through their lens, we are shown the princes of Islam abandoning 'jihad' to pursue pleasures and sport. Yet trade benefitted the population not just the princes – and so did peace. It would be wrong to infer widespread discontent with Ayyubid policies, despite the disapproval of Islamic clerical chroniclers.

The Ayyubid's counterparts in the crusader states were likewise more detached from crusading ideology than ever before. During the thirteenth century, popes had expanded the concept of crusading to include wars against heretics (e.g. the Albigensians), pagans (the Baltic crusades) and political rivals (the 'crusades' against the Hohenstaufens). In addition, the papacy increasingly stressed the penitential nature of crusading, thereby de-emphasising concrete results. The Franks of Outremer, in contrast, were focused on survival and prosperity. For the inhabitants of the crusader kingdoms, recovery of lost territory, including Jerusalem, remained a priority less for emotional and religious reasons than for material benefits. Regaining control of the fertile agricultural hinterland behind the coastal cities was crucial to economic autonomy while re-establishing more defensible, forward borders, such as the Jordan and the Dead Sea, contributed significantly to security. The Franks wanted results, but the Western crusaders, it became clear, were more interested in their own souls (and benefits) than in the Holy Land itself.

In 1204, forces initially raised for a campaign to regain Jerusalem were diverted by Venice to attack commercial rivals. After a complicated series of events, the former crusaders (now Venetian mercenaries) seized Constantinople. While the sack that followed outraged contemporaries from Rome to Mosul, it resulted in the establishment of a Latin 'empire' on the Greek peninsula, straddling the Bosporus and stretching along the northern shore of the Mediterranean. It was flanked by territory still held by Greek Orthodox forces in western Greece and what is now Anatolia.

The impact of this new Frankish entity on the existing crusader states is controversial. Many argue that the existence of a Latin empire based in Constantinople diverted Western resources that might otherwise have flowed to the older crusader states, but such 'lost opportunities' are hard to quantify. Ultimately, the losses may not have been sizeable, simply because the different states attracted different kinds of men. Even during the original campaign, as much as one-third of the crusaders refused to be diverted to Constantinople and continued to the Holy Land. Here, they joined an army under King Aimery that raided into the Galilee, prompting al-Adil to conclude a new six-year truce on terms highly favourable to the Franks. On the other hand, if the Fourth Crusade had gone ahead as planned, these knights would have been engaged in an assault on Egypt with far more dubious benefits for the existing crusader states. Furthermore, the establishment of the Latin Empire of Constantinople gave the Franks near-complete mastery of the Eastern Mediterranean, including the creation of a comparatively stable Frankish state in the Peloponnese. Lastly, a surge in new mercantile activity on the part of the Italian city-states followed the conquest of Constantinople.

Meanwhile, Christian Armenia was also gaining in strength. The Armenian leaders agreed to a (more nominal than substantive) reconciliation with the church in Rome, thereby facilitating closer ties with the crusader states. While intermarriage with the princes of Antioch led to irritating dynastic conflict, the salient point was that Christian-controlled

The Second Kingdom or the Kingdom of Acre, 1192–1291

territory extended from what is now Alanya on the Turkish Mediterranean coast through Antioch down the coast of the Levant to Jaffa.

Nevertheless, bad luck continued to plague the Kingdom of Jerusalem with respect to its dynasty. In late March 1205, the dynamic and competent Aimery de Lusignan died of food poisoning after a meal of bad fish. He was followed within weeks by Queen Isabella. The Kingdom of Cyprus passed to Aimery's 6-year-old son Hugh, while the Kingdom of Jerusalem was inherited by Isabella's oldest surviving child, Marie, her daughter by Conrad de Montferrat, then aged 12 or 13. Both children required regents. In Cyprus, the High Court elected Walter de Montbéliard, husband of Hugh's elder sister Burgundia. In Jerusalem, the High Court chose Isabella's maternal half-brother, John d'Ibelin, Lord of Beirut.

While upholding and renewing truces with the Ayyubids to ensure stability, Beirut's principal task was finding a suitable husband for Queen Marie, who would replace him at the helm of the kingdom. As it had done so often in the past, the High Court turned to the king of France, requesting a suitable candidate. John de Brienne, a minor nobleman from Champagne, was selected in 1208. Before coming east, he sought to raise funds and troops to enable a military offensive upon his arrival. As a result, Brienne did not reach the Holy Land until 1210. He immediately married Marie de Montferrat and was crowned king alongside her in Tyre. He was accompanied by just 300 knights, a force insufficient to alter the balance of power in the Holy Land. Despite raids in Galilee and up the Nile, he enjoyed no important military successes. So, like his predecessors, he sought yet another six-year truce with the Ayyubids.

In November 1212, misfortune struck again: Marie de Montferrat died giving birth to a daughter. She was only 20 years old, and her infant daughter Yolanda (also referred to as Isabella II) became queen of Jerusalem at birth. Brienne was recognised as his infant daughter's regent, and because he was already crowned and anointed, he retained the title of king.

The Fifth Crusade, 1216–1221

Meanwhile, in Western Europe, crusading sentiment was on the rise once again. In 1212, a youth movement to regain Jerusalem by faith alone shamed the pope into issuing a new crusading appeal in 1213.

The youthful king of Sicily and Germany, Frederick II Hohenstaufen, stepped into his grandfather and father's crusading footsteps, taking the cross at his coronation in Aachen on 25 July 1215. Other kings were also recruited, namely the kings of Cyprus, Hungary, and Jerusalem, but Pope Innocent III was determined to retain control of this crusade, which he considered only one strand of a vast and permanent crusading movement. Pope Innocent III envisaged crusading as a permanent state of warfare against the enemies of the church, wherever they were, and whatever form they took (Moors, pagans, Saracens or heretics). Despite Innocent's death in 1216, this crusading vision was adopted and pursued by his successor Honorius III, who appointed a papal legate, Cardinal Pelagius, to represent him on the Fifth Crusade. Because the cardinal embodied papal authority in a campaign without a dominant secular leader – and because he had the largest purse – Pelagius wielded undue influence. This experiment with church leadership of a crusade proved utterly disastrous.

The first contingents of crusaders started arriving in Acre in late 1216. They helped to marginally push back the borders of the Frankish kingdom before sailing in late May 1217 to lay siege to the Egyptian port of Damietta. The goal was to strike a decisive blow against the Ayyubids in their power-base of Egypt in order to force them to surrender not just bits and pieces of territory but everything that had once been part of the Kingdom of Jerusalem. The strategy assumed that an attack on Cairo would threaten the Ayyubids to such an extent that they would concede Jerusalem.

The siege of Damietta lasted nearly two years and was characterised by a lack of unified command as contingents of crusaders came and went independently. While the siege was on-going, the sultan al-Adil died in August 1218, and his empire broke up. The two major pieces, Egypt and Syria, went to his sons al-Kamil and al-Muazzam respectively, while the smaller fragments on the fringes went to other heirs. Shortly after the crusaders captured Damietta in December 1219, al-Kamil persuaded his brother al-Muazzam to attack the crusader states to divert attention from Egypt. The tactic worked only partially. With King John and most of his knights in Egypt, the Saracens were able to strike deep into the heart of the kingdom, overrunning and laying waste to Caesarea. King John and the knights of Jerusalem rushed back to their homeland to restore the situation. This, however, did not seriously alter the situation

The Second Kingdom or the Kingdom of Acre, 1192–1291

in Egypt since the vast majority of the crusaders remained in position and retained possession of Damietta.

Al-Kamil tried a new tactic: diplomacy. He offered to restore all territories that had formerly belonged to the Kingdom of Jerusalem – except for the castles of Transjordan – in exchange for the crusaders evacuating Egypt. All sources agree that King John and the barons of Jerusalem were wholeheartedly in favour of accepting these terms. For them, this was what the crusade was about. The military orders, however, objected to the fact that the castles in Transjordan were not included. The crusaders from the Italian city-states opposed the treaty because they considered Egypt a far more lucrative trading base than inland Palestine. The German crusaders appear to have been reluctant to abort a crusade that their emperor had vowed to join, even if he was still notably absent. The papal legate seems to have seen the offer as a sign of weakness that justified pursuing the crusade with more vigor. For whatever reasons, the offer was rejected, and the crusade continued, meaning the crusaders remained in occupation of Damietta awaiting the arrival of Emperor Frederick II.

He never came. He had excuses. Other items on his agenda, such as subduing a Muslim rebellion in Sicily, took priority.

In July 1221, after rejecting a second offer from al-Kamil with roughly the same terms as before, the crusaders marched out with the goal of capturing Cairo. Instead, the Nile flooded, and the Saracen army used its superior knowledge of the terrain to cut the crusaders off from their supplies and retreat. It was a complete debacle in which Damietta was returned to the sultan, not for Jerusalem, but merely for the lives and freedom of thousands of captives. The survivors went home with their tails between their legs.

In retrospect, the truce offered by al-Kamil looks like it was a good deal, yet this was probably always a mirage. Al-Kamil was giving away his brother's (not his own) territory, and it is doubtful he could have delivered on his promises. Even if al-Muazzam had cooperated, and the fact that he destroyed Jerusalem's fortifications suggests he intended to, the agreement would have been temporary because, from the Muslim perspective, the maximum validity of any truce signed with non-believers was ten years, ten months and ten days. The fact that al-Kamil did not fully comply with the terms of the agreement he *did* sign likewise suggests that the grandiose offer of restoring the Kingdom of Jerusalem to its former borders was a red-herring designed to sow dissent among the crusaders. Nevertheless, considering the outcome of the advance up the Nile, the crusaders might have done better to call the sultan's bluff.

The Sixth Crusade, 1225–1229

Frederick II's singular failure to show up for the Fifth Crusade, despite ceremoniously taking crusader vows in both 1215 and 1220, did not go unnoticed across Christendom; he was widely blamed for the crusade's failure. In 1225, however, Frederick II agreed to marry Queen Yolanda of Jerusalem. Although the terms of the treaty explicitly recognised Yolanda's father as king of Jerusalem until his death, it was widely believed this marriage would motivate the emperor to undertake a crusade to Jerusalem since any child born of Frederick's marriage to Yolanda would inherit the crown. In short, the expansion of the kingdom was now in Frederick's dynastic self-interest. Frederick solemnly promised to lead a new crusade no later than August 1227, accepting the pope's explicit warning that failure to meet this deadline would result in excommunication.

In November 1225, Frederick's marriage to the 13-year-old Yolanda of Jerusalem was celebrated by proxy in Acre, followed by Yolanda's coronation as queen of Jerusalem in Tyre. Yolanda then sailed to Brindisi to marry Frederick in person. As soon as the marriage was celebrated, Frederick titled himself 'King of Jerusalem' and demanded homage from the barons of Jerusalem, who had travelled with his bride to Sicily. This action was a clear violation of the terms of his marriage settlement with John of Brienne, and Brienne immediately protested to the pope. The latter sympathised and gave the deposed king appointments and income but took no action against Frederick; the promised crusade was more important to him than Brienne's crown.

Frederick duly gathered his forces in Apulia in the summer of 1227, only for an epidemic to strike down thousands of men before they could depart. Despite being ill, Frederick put to sea to avoid excommunication. After the Landgraf of Thuringia died at sea, however, Friedrich lost heart and returned to Brindisi. Pope Gregory IX promptly excommunicated him. Under the circumstances, the excommunication was hardly justified. In retrospect, it represented the opening volley in a power struggle between the papacy and the Hohenstaufens that would last for decades.

The Second Kingdom or the Kingdom of Acre, 1192–1291

At the heart of the conflict were differing views of the role of sacred and secular authority, a topic beyond the scope of this work. However, as a result of the excommunication, Frederick's planned expedition to the Holy Land lost papal blessing and could no longer be called a 'crusade'. Indeed, the papacy explicitly characterised it as an 'anti-crusade'.

To make matters worse, in April 1228, 15-year-old Queen Yolanda of Jerusalem died from the complications of childbirth. She left an infant son, Conrad, as heir to her kingdom. With Yolanda's death, Friedrich II lost the right to call himself King of Jerusalem, the title now belonging to his infant son Conrad. The most Frederick could claim was the regency for his son (as John of Brienne had done for Yolanda) until the boy came of age at 15. Characteristically, Frederick ignored the law of Jerusalem and insisted on calling himself 'King of Jerusalem' until the day he died.

Frederick also proceeded with his (anti-)crusade. His reasoning appears that if he succeeded in liberating Jerusalem, this would vindicate his earlier delays and prove that God was on his side in his conflict with the pope. Friedrich had good reason to believe he *would* liberate Jerusalem because he had already been promised the city by al-Kamil. The sultan of Egypt had fallen out with his brother al-Muazzam and was looking for allies. He offered to deliver Jerusalem to the emperor in exchange for the emperor helping him take it away from his brother in the first place. It was rather like the king of France promising to give London to the Holy Roman emperor – just as soon as the latter had captured it for him.

The irony of the deal appears to have been lost on Frederick Hohenstaufen – and many modern commentators. Expecting a rapid diplomatic end to his 'crusade', Frederick took a comparatively small number of fighting men with him, all of whom were drawn exclusively from his domains since knights and nobles from the rest of Europe were not prepared to join an 'anti-crusade' led by an excommunicate. After a stop in Cyprus that will be discussed later, Frederick proceeded to Acre, arriving on 10 September 1228. Shortly after his arrival, he learned that the pope had raised an army to invade the Kingdom of Sicily with the declared intent of deposing him. One of the men leading the pope's forces was the man Frederick had so callously humiliated: his father-in-law, King John of Jerusalem.

The threat to his core kingdom made a rapid conclusion of his Near Eastern expedition imperative. Frederick immediately opened secret negotiations with al-Kamil, reminding him of earlier promises. However, al-Muazzam had meanwhile died, and al-Kamil no longer felt he needed the assistance of a Christian ruler to subdue his much weaker nephew. Frederick was reduced to begging al-Kamil for Jerusalem on almost any terms. On 18 February 1229, after five months of secret negotiations, a personal treaty was signed between Frederick and al-Kamil, which, significantly, did not include commitments by any of the other Ayyubids.

Biographers and admirers of Frederick Hohenstaufen are apt to call Friedrich's preference for diplomacy over warfare 'enlightened' or attribute his 'astonishing success' to greater 'subtlety' and even 'genius'. It has been claimed, for example, that the treaty demonstrated Frederick's 'willingness to compromise and his diplomatic skills'.[2] The fact that the Franks had employed diplomacy for more than 100 years before Frederick's arrival is ignored. Furthermore, the fact that Frederick was vehemently criticised by the patriarch of Jerusalem, the Templars, the Hospitallers and the local barons, as well as the population at large, is attributed blithely to the alleged bigotry of the church and 'bloodthirsty' character of the Franks in Outremer. Such allegations reflect ignorance of the Holy Land, the Franks, the circumstances of the treaty and substance of the objections to Frederick's treaty.

Praise for Frederick's treaty is almost entirely misplaced, given the fact that he did *not* secure Jerusalem. What Frederick II obtained was *temporary* Christian control (ten years, ten months and ten days) of *some* of Jerusalem and a couple of other cities, such as Bethlehem. The treaty explicitly prohibited Christians from setting foot on the Temple Mount and prohibited the Franks from building walls around Jerusalem. Rather than defensible borders, the Christians were granted a narrow corridor connecting Jerusalem to Jaffa. This could so easily be severed that it represented a vulnerability rather than an asset. The truce furthermore left the Saracens in control of key strategic castles such as Kerak and Montreal, while prohibiting the Franks from undertaking military campaigns elsewhere. The truce left Jerusalem so exposed that not one religious institution returned their headquarters to the holiest city in Christendom – it was too obviously doomed.

Furthermore, the superficial success of Frederick's bloodless crusade obscures the fact that the constitution of Jerusalem reserved to the High Court the right to make treaties. Frederick II Hohenstaufen blissfully ignored this constitutional nicety. He negotiated in secret and presented the barons of Jerusalem with a fait accompli. This, as much as the seriously flawed terms of the treaty, outraged the local nobility. The Arab sources, meanwhile, stressed that al-Kamil openly bragged that 'when he had achieved his aim and had the situation in hand, he could purify Jerusalem of the Franks and chase them out'.[3]

The terms of the truce reveal the degree to which Frederick's entire 'crusade' was about his power struggle with the pope rather than Jerusalem or the Holy Land. While leaving the residents of Outremer to deal with the consequences of his worthless truce, he made a great show of wearing the imperial crown in the Church of the Holy Sepulchre. This was his way of thumbing his nose at the pope, yet it was also 'an affront to the laws and traditions of the Kingdom of Jerusalem, a blatantly illegal action bordering on sacrilege. It is no wonder, then, that the Christians in the East saw the crusade of Frederick II as a war aimed not at Muslims but at themselves.'[4]

Having had his day in Jerusalem (and ostentatiously telling the Muslims they should continue their call to prayer, even in his presence), Frederick departed the Holy Land never to return. Despite being titular kings of Jerusalem, neither his son nor his grandson ever set foot in the kingdom. It was left to other kings, such as Louis IX of France, to try to reclaim Christian control of the Holy City and secure the Holy Land. Meanwhile, the common people of Acre expressed their opinion of Frederick's 'anti-crusade' by pelting him with offal and intestines from their rooftops and balconies as he made his way to the harbour to embark on his return voyage. Yet by far, the worst aspect of Frederick II's anti-crusade was the legacy it left behind: civil war.

Civil War, 1229–1243

The opening volley in this war occurred incongruously at a banquet shortly after Frederick's arrival in Cyprus on his way to Acre for the Sixth Crusade. Frederick invited his 'dear uncle', the acting regent of Cyprus and former regent of Jerusalem, the lord of Beirut, to a banquet. The emperor used extremely friendly and flattering language and explicitly requested that Beirut bring 'his children'. Furthermore, the emperor provided robes and insisted that Beirut's eldest sons serve him at table, all gestures designed to simulate the highest affection and respect. Under cover of darkness, however, the emperor brought troops into the venue and hid them. At Frederick's signal, these armed men came out of their hiding places and surrounded the unarmed guests.

Frederick then demanded that Beirut surrender his lordship – without stating a reason much less proving any wrongdoing – and repay the funds he had allegedly embezzled from the Cypriot treasury during his and his brother's tenure as regents. Despite explicit threats of violence, the lord of Beirut responded by saying he held Beirut by right and that neither he nor his brother had ever embezzled a penny of the revenue of Cyprus.

While historians have rightly suggested that the latter is hardly credible, the issue here was not which of the two men was ultimately right but rather the fundamental principle of due process. An eyewitness account written within twenty years of the event put the following words into the lord of Beirut's mouth: 'I will furnish you proofs by the usage and by the court of the Kingdom of Cyprus; but be certain that for fear of death or of prison I will not do more unless the judgement of the good and loyal court requires me to do.'[5] While this is unlikely to be a verbatim quote, it neatly summarises the issues at stake. Beirut was able to walk out of the banquet alive with the bulk of the Cypriot knights and barons at his back, not because his record as regent was impeccable, but because he demanded no more than what his contemporaries viewed as just: the right to a trial before his peers. The emperor's response was to seize hostages and allow them to be mishandled while in his custody.

A temporary compromise was worked out. The emperor agreed to release the hostages and bring the charges against Beirut in the respective High Courts in exchange for Beirut surrendering the castles of Cyprus to the emperor's men and joining his crusade. While Beirut, his adult sons, nephews and vassals were in Syria, however, the emperor sent the count of Cotron to Cyprus to lay waste the lands of Beirut, his family and supporters. Furthermore, Frederick attempted to arbitrarily bestow the lordship and castle of Toron on his clients, the Teutonic Knights, ignoring the claims of the hereditary heirs, thereby alienating another powerful family in Outremer. He likewise attempted to seize control of the Templar castle of Athlit by force. By all these actions, Frederick demonstrated that he had no interest in the laws or constitution of the kingdom, respected no one's rights but his own, and was perfectly willing to use force against his subjects to get his way.

When Frederick departed the Holy Land via Cyprus, he sold the regency for the still underage King Henry of Cyprus to five Cypriot noblemen. They were ordered to ensure Beirut and his supporters never again set foot in the island kingdom. This demonstrated that all his signed promises to bring his charges against Beirut before the High Court were worthless. Frederick then sailed away, never to return.

The 'five baillies' of Cyprus (as they have gone down in history) began a rapacious regime that undermined their popularity. Consequently, when Beirut returned with what must have been a small force, he was able to land at Gastria and advance to the outskirts of Nicosia. The five baillies called up the feudal army of Cyprus and met Beirut's army at the Battle of Nicosia on 14 July 1229. Although the victory went to the Ibelins, all five baillies escaped to the mountain castles. Beirut was forced to besiege both Kantara and St Hilarion. Not until shortly after Easter 1230 did the baillies surrender the last holdout, St Hilarion, in exchange for a full amnesty.

Frederick II, however, had not achieved his objectives. So, in the autumn of 1231, he sent his Imperial Marshal Richard Filangieri with a fleet of thirty-three ships loaded with mercenaries to enforce his rule in the kingdoms of Cyprus and Jerusalem. In the former, Frederick issued orders to King Henry in his capacity as the 'Overlord of Cyprus'. In Jerusalem, Frederick named Filangieri his 'baillie' or deputy.

Filangieri anchored first off Cyprus and sent the bishop of Melfi ashore as Frederick's envoy. In Frederick's name, the bishop ineptly demanded that King Henry of Cyprus expel the lord of Beirut and all his relatives from his realm. Henry blandly pointed out that he could not comply with the emperor's orders because he himself was a relative of Beirut. He further noted that it was a lord's duty to defend his vassals – not hound them out of their fiefs without cause or trial.

Since Beirut had rushed to Cyprus with nearly all his vassals and men, and Beirut's adult sons held the Cypriot ports, the emperor's marshal recognised a landing would be met by armed resistance and made the wise decision not to attempt such a landing. Instead, he sailed by night and struck at the undefended city of Beirut. The town surrendered without a fight, but the citadel – with only a skeletal garrison – held firm for its lord. Leaving the bulk of his forces investing the citadel, Filangieri continued to Acre, where he presented his credentials as Frederick's baillie and was recognised as such by the High Court of Jerusalem. However, the court objected to his seizure of the city Beirut on the grounds there had been no judgement by the court against the lord of Beirut. Filangieri, who had just sworn to uphold the laws and customs of the kingdom, answered that he needed to 'take counsel' with his magnates. He withdrew from Acre, established his household in Tyre, and joined his troops to pursue the siege of the Beirut citadel with increased vigor. In short, Filangieri had no more interest in the laws and customs of the kingdom than did his master Frederick II. The lord of Beirut had been disseized by force without a judgement of the High Court.

Beirut, however, refused to concede defeat. Instead, he made a dramatic appeal to King Henry of Cyprus for aid, and the king responded by personally calling up the entire feudal army of Cyprus. After a dangerous winter crossing, this army landed on the Syrian coast. Here the former imperial baillies and some eighty knights (roughly 20 per cent of the Cypriot feudal elite) defected from King Henry's host and rode for Tripoli. The remaining troops under the lord of Beirut and King Henry advanced down the coast to challenge the imperial army besieging Beirut. When it became clear that the Cypriot army was insufficiently strong to lift the siege, Beirut smuggled roughly 100 fighting men through the sea blockade into the citadel and then withdrew with the rest of the army to Acre in search of additional backing.

Beirut put his case before the High Court. This brought him the direct support of some forty knights, while the High Court sent a high-ranking delegation to Filangieri to advise him to end his siege. Filangieri referred them back to Emperor Frederick. His blunt dismissal of the concerns of the representatives of the High Court swung public opinion in Outremer behind Beirut.

Meanwhile, the latter had crucially won the support of the Genoese – who were already dogged opponents of the Hohenstaufens in Italy. In addition, the 'Commune of Acre' was formed. This ad hoc body with no legal basis or function served as a rallying point for opponents of imperial power from all classes, ethnic groups and religions. The 'commune' elected the lord of Beirut their 'mayor'. With these forces, Beirut felt strong enough to risk an attack on Filangieri's base in Tyre. The threat to Tyre forced Filangieri to lift the siege of Beirut citadel and offer to negotiate. While the lord of Beirut was negotiating with Filangieri's envoys in Acre, however, Filangieri's army overran the Cypriot/Ibelin camp at Casal Imbert, capturing ships, horses, tents, equipment and twenty-four knights. King Henry barely escaped, riding the six miles to Acre to bring word of the fiasco to Beirut in his nightshirt.

In assessments of this incident, too much attention has been paid to the fact that the Cypriots/Ibelins were caught completely off guard and too little to how the defeat significantly increased popular support for the lord of Beirut. For the first time, the two men appointed by Frederick as baillies on his departure from the Holy Land (i.e. the men who represented imperial power from May 1229 until Filangieri's arrival in September 1231) – Balian of Sidon and Eudes de Montbelliard – joined Beirut.

Presumably, they were swayed by the fact that international law prohibited hostilities during negotiations. Thus, not only were the Cypriots/Ibelins fully justified in not expecting an attack, but Filangieri's surprise strike was considered treacherous. Like the banquet for unarmed guests in which Frederick hid soldiers and the count of Cotron's attack in Cyprus while Beirut was loyally serving under Frederick in Syria, this attack struck contemporaries as deceitful and dishonourable.

Meanwhile, thinking the lord of Beirut and the king of Cyprus were effectively knocked out of action by their humiliation at Casal Imbert, Filangieri took his fleet and army to overrun Cyprus. There could be no pretence of acting in the interests of King Henry because the king had come of age. Had Henry previously been coerced into supporting Beirut, he was now free to take revenge. Instead, he requested the papal legate excommunicate Filangieri so he would be justified in seizing imperial war galleys still tied up in Acre harbour. The papal legate demurred but suggested Henry take the ships on his own initiative. He did.

In these ships, the Cypriot/Ibelin army returned to Cyprus. They dramatically wrecked the expropriated ships on a coastal island, crossed over a ford only passable at low tide, and took Famagusta from the rear without resistance as the imperial forces fled in the night. Henry was able to reoccupy his capital without bloodshed. However, Filangieri still commanded a much larger army of imperial mercenaries. He also had the support of the eighty knights who had defected at the start of the year. Most alarming to the king, his sisters were trapped in the castle of St Hilarion, which was besieged by imperial forces, and supplies were running dangerously low.

The latter forced Henry and Beirut to attempt the relief of St Hilarion, thereby risking a confrontation with the imperial forces drawn up on the flank of the mountain ridge separating Nicosia from St Hilarion. The Cypriot/Ibelin army was so small that the imperial knights overconfidently charged down upon it, abandoning their strong position. In the ensuing Battle of Agridi fought on 15 June 1232, the Cypriot/Ibelin force decisively defeated Filangieri's men. The battle is remembered for the role played by the infantry, primarily composed of local troops who came out in support of their king. These reportedly killed unhorsed imperial knights while helping Cypriot/Ibelin knights back into the saddle. Imperial casualties were huge by the standards of the day, namely sixty knights. Nevertheless, Filangieri was able to withdraw with the bulk of his troops to the coastal castle of Kyrenia.

From here, Filangieri appealed to Antioch, Armenia and the emperor for help; he received none. He and those Cypriots who had sided with him sailed away to safety, while a garrison held Kyrenia for almost a year before surrendering to King Henry. Frederick II never again tried to interfere in Cypriot affairs, and in 1246 the pope solemnised the de facto situation by formally absolving King Henry of all oaths of vassalage to the Holy Roman emperor. Thereafter, the Kingdom of Cyprus was fully independent.

However, Frederick's claim to be king of Jerusalem and rule without the High Court's consent had not been resolved. Nor had his determination to humiliate the lord of Beirut waned. While Beirut enjoyed the solid backing of the bulk of the politically active elements in the Kingdom of Jerusalem, including the Knights Templar, the Genoese and the Commune of Acre, the Teutonic Knights were staunchly imperial in their loyalties, and the Hospitallers increasingly sided with the emperor as well. Finally, a minority of knights and burgesses, concentrated in Tyre, remained loyal to the Holy Roman emperor. Thus, the kingdom was divided.

Recognising that the use of force had failed in the short-term, Frederick II put forward a compromise proposal that entailed a general amnesty for everyone who had (in his opinion) committed treason – except the Ibelins. He also recognised the de facto division of the kingdom into two halves, proposing that henceforth the north of the kingdom be ruled from Tyre by his baillie Filangieri, while the south of the kingdom – with the intransigent Acre – be governed by a new baillie who he again appointed without the approval of the High Court. The proposal shows just how little the emperor understood the rebellion. The problem was not one of personnel but principle. The opposition challenged his right to appoint *any* baillie without the consent of the High Court and objected to his attempts to disseize one of their number without a judgement of the High Court.

The Second Kingdom or the Kingdom of Acre, 1192–1291

In April 1234, the pope became involved in seeking a settlement between the emperor and his rebellious subjects in the Holy Land. The terms he proposed amounted to unconditional surrender by the rebels, recognition of the emperor's right to appoint whoever he liked, dissolution of the Commune of Acre and no pardons for the Ibelins. The rebels shrugged and ignored the offer, bringing down papal wrath, which included not only excommunication for the lord of Beirut and his supporters but a papal interdict on the city of Acre. By October, the pope was frantically rescinding the interdict because so many Franks were turning to the Orthodox churches. At last, recognising that one cannot negotiate an agreement by listening only to one side, the pope asked the rebels to send representatives to Rome to discuss terms.

The men sent to Rome appear to have been intimidated and bullied into accepting disadvantageous terms because on their return they were nearly lynched. New envoys were sent back to the pope, arriving in April 1236. Meanwhile, the lord of Beirut had died still in full possession of his fiefs and wealthy enough to dispense largess with both hands on his deathbed. More importantly, however, the pope's relationship with Frederick II was deteriorating again. Pope Gregory IX suddenly discovered that the rebels might have some valid points after all. After that, he made no further attempt to intervene, and the stalemate continued.

In April 1243, the infant boy whose birth had killed Queen Yolanda turned 14. In accordance with the laws of Sicily, he was now 'mature', and Frederick used this fact to announce that Conrad was now appointing his own representatives. This was again a violation of the constitution of Jerusalem; heirs in Jerusalem did not attain majority until the age of 15. Furthermore, Frederick continued to style himself as 'King of Jerusalem' undermining his own claims. The barons of Jerusalem weren't fooled by his ruse. They became even more inventive in finding transparently self-serving legal arguments for non-compliance. The most important of these was a fictitious claim that when a monarch came of age while absent from the kingdom, his/her closest relative *resident in the country* held the regency until the ruler appeared in person to take the homage of vassals. By this ploy, Conrad's great-aunt Alice, the dowager queen of Cyprus, became regent. She demanded the surrender of Tyre to her, and when (as expected) Filangieri refused, Balian of Beirut (John d'Ibelin's eldest son and heir) seized it by force. Filangieri returned to Sicily, where Frederick imprisoned him for his years of loyal service and sent, in his stead, Thomas of Accera. The latter did not dare set foot in the Kingdom of Jerusalem and spent his entire tenure in Antioch instead.

A colourful contemporary account of the conflict written by Philip de Novare, an opponent of the emperor, has disproportionately influenced modern understanding of the conflict, reducing it to nothing more than a personal struggle between Frederick II and the lord of Beirut. This is unfortunate. While Beirut was a highly respected nobleman, he did not enjoy the support of roughly four-fifths of the Cypriot nobility, more than half of the Syrian nobility, the Templars, the Genoese and the Commune of Acre because he was such a nice fellow.

Stripped of personalities and rhetoric, the underlying issue in this conflict between Emperor Frederick and the rebel barons were conflicting views about the nature of monarchy in the Kingdom of Jerusalem. Frederick II was a proponent of absolutism, who viewed himself as emperor and king by the grace of God. He recognised no constraints on his rights to rule – neither laws nor constitutions, institutions nor counsels, nor even his own promises, as he reserved to himself the right to change his mind about anything.

The Kingdom of Jerusalem, on the other hand, was a feudal state par excellence. First and foremost, the nobility of Outremer held to the fundamental feudal concept that government was a contract between the king and his subjects, a reciprocal agreement entailing obligations on both sides. Frederick consistently flouted the laws and customs of the kingdom and especially the High Court. He did so by not recognising that his right to the crown of Jerusalem derived from his wife and extinguished at her death, passing then to his son. He did so by not recognising the role of the High Court in naming regents and baillies. He ignored the High Court again by not bringing his charges against Beirut before it and likewise defied it by not obtaining its advice and consent for his treaty with al-Kamil. What's more, he did all this within four years of his coronation. By the time he departed the Holy Land in May 1228, the emperor had squandered all credibility as a fair and honourable monarch by repeatedly breaking his word and behaving like a despot.

The baronial faction countered by becoming ever more inventive in discovering 'laws' and customs that undermined Hohenstaufen rule. If the barons and their legal scholars were by the end so nimble and creative as to verge on 'a cynical manipulation of law and custom',[6] this was because, from 1232 onwards, the baronial opposition was desperately trying to keep a proven tyrant from gaining greater control of the kingdom. That does not negate the fundamental belief in the rule-of-law as opposed to the rule-by-imperial whim that lay at the core of the baronial opposition to Frederick.

As a tragic footnote to this conflict, on his deathbed in December 1250, Frederick II bequeathed Italy, Germany and Sicily to his son Conrad, his son by Yolanda, but suggested that Conrad give the Kingdom of Jerusalem to his half-brother Henry, the son of his third wife, Isabella of England. This proves that Frederick utterly failed to recognise or accept that the crown of Jerusalem was not his to give away. Because it derived from his wife, it could only pass to her heirs – not to whomever Frederick pleased and only with the consent of the High Court. This attempt to give Jerusalem away to someone with no right to it is like a final insult to the bride Frederick neglected and possibly abused. It also demonstrates that to his last breath, he remained either ignorant of or indifferent to the constitution of the Kingdom of Jerusalem.

The Barons' Crusade, 1239–1241

Meanwhile, after nearly a decade of fraternal fighting, al-Ashraf died in 1237, leaving al-Kamil the victor in the Ayyubid power struggle – until he died one year later. The Ayyubid empire at once disintegrated into warring factions again. Thus, when Frederick II's truce with al-Kamil expired in 1239, the brothers, sons and nephews of al-Kamil were at each other's throats. Since this event had been anticipated for some time, large contingents of crusaders began to arrive to resume hostilities almost at once. These included a substantial army under several prominent French nobles, the most senior of which was Thibaut, Count of Champagne and King of Navarre. The factions within the Kingdom of Jerusalem temporarily overcame their differences and joined forces to confront the Ayyubids. The latter, meanwhile, reoccupied the defenceless Jerusalem in December.

Despite a defeat at Gaza in November (caused by crusaders foolishly ignoring the advice of the masters of the military orders and their senior commanders), Navarre took advantage of infighting among the Ayyubids to obtain a highly advantageous treaty with al-Kamil's brother, al-Salih Ismael. This restored to Christian control the hinterland behind Sidon, the castles of Beaufort, Belvoir and Safad, and the towns and castles of Toron and Tiberias. The Franks also obtained promises of the surrender of Jerusalem, Bethlehem, Nazareth and Galilee to Frankish rule in exchange for Frankish help in defeating Ismael's cousin Daud, who had taken control in Damascus. The crusaders rapidly re-established control in the northern territories and started to raid into Galilee. Daud came under enough pressure to likewise make concessions to the crusaders in exchange for peace. In late summer 1240, he signed an agreement that ceded to the crusaders nearly everything that had belonged to the Kingdom of Jerusalem in 1187, except the predominantly Muslim region around Nablus and the Transjordan. The treaty may, however, have included dangerous clauses about providing assistance to Daud in a war against his cousin Ayyub, who had recently seized power in Egypt.

Meanwhile, in October 1240, an English force composed of 800 knights led by Richard, Duke of Cornwall, sailed into Acre. Cornwall was not only the brother of King Henry III of England, he was also the new brother-in-law of Frederick II since the marriage of his sister Isabella to Frederick in July 1235. He was accompanied by another brother-in-law, the husband of his sister Eleanor, Simon de Montfort, Earl of Leicester. Cornwall rebuilt the citadel at Ascalon and opened the lines of communication to Daud only to discover the latter no longer needed crusader assistance and was not inclined to honour the terms of the agreement he had signed with Navarre. Cornwall promptly switched tack and accepted a deal offered by Ayyub of Egypt that included a prisoner exchange, including prisoners captured at the fiasco at Gaza the previous year. Cornwall demonstratively sided with Frederick II in his conflict with the rebellious barons of Outremer and handed over Ascalon to Frederick's representatives before departing the Holy Land on 3 May 1241 bound for England via Sicily.

Significantly and enigmatically, however, he carried with him a proposal signed by Balian of Beirut and other leading rebel barons, which put forward a plan to end the dispute between the barons and the emperor. The rebel barons laid out conditions for reconciliation as follows: (1) a full pardon for all rebels including the Ibelins, (2) the appointment of a baillie acceptable to them who would hold power in the entire kingdom until Conrad came to the kingdom in person and (3) the promise that the interim baillie would swear to uphold the laws and customs of the kingdom. In exchange, the lords and burgesses of

Jerusalem would swear to obey Frederick's baillie. Most importantly, the letter identified by name the imperial baillie they were willing to accept, namely, Frederick's brother-in-law Simon de Montfort. Frederick ignored the letter, and no more was heard of the proposal.

We can only speculate on what Montfort had done or said to win the support of the rebel barons, but it is undoubtedly noteworthy that he shared a cousin with the most prominent rebel baron, Balian of Beirut. More intriguing, in light of Simon de Montfort's later role as the leader of a baronial revolt in England, it appears that Balian of Beirut and his spirit of rebellion against arbitrary royal authority impressed Simon de Montfort as much as the other way around.

Dangerous Entanglements: The Ayyubid Alliance and La Forbie, 1239–1244

The year 1243 saw not only the expulsion of the last vestiges of Hohenstaufen rule from Outremer but also the reoccupation of Jerusalem and the Temple Mount by the Franks. This was made possible by a new alliance with a different faction of the Ayyubids, namely with as-Salih Ismail (now the ruler of Damascus) and an-Nasir Daud, who controlled Transjordan. These princes offered the Franks substantial concessions in exchange for an offensive alliance directed at their hated rival (and relative) in Cairo: as-Salih Ayyub.

This treaty differed significantly from earlier treaties, particularly the truce with Frederick II. in that it recognised Christianity's higher claim to Jerusalem and the right of the Christians to build fortifications. Furthermore, it gave the Franks the territory around Jerusalem necessary for its defence and viability. In short, it laid the foundation for what could have been a more sustainable Frankish state.

The Egyptians allied themselves with the Kharasmians, a Turkish tribe displaced by the Mongol invasions of 1220. Whether this alliance provoked the Damascene approach to the Franks or was itself a response to the Frankish/Damascene alliance is unclear. In any case, in 1244, the Kharasmians swept into Syria and rapidly took control of the regions of the kingdom recently restored to Frankish rule. In August, they took Jerusalem and engaged in an orgy of destruction that left churches desecrated, the Holy Sepulchre gutted, and at least 5,000 mostly native Christians dead.

The Franks and their Ayyubid allies mustered their armies and prepared for the showdown with Egypt. The Frankish army probably equaled in size the force which had been fielded at Hattin in 1187 with as many as 1,200 knights, but with one striking difference: as many as 1,100 of those knights were members of the military orders rather than civilian knights. Also striking is that the muster took place in Acre, where the Saracen leaders were welcomed and hosted by the Knights Templar. The combined Frankish/Saracen army advanced via Jaffa and Ascalon to Gaza on the border of the kingdom. On 17 October 1244, this army confronted the Egyptian Ayyubid forces and their Kharasmian allies. In a battle lasting two days, the Egyptians and Kharasmians won the upper hand. They shattered the Damascene/Transjordan wing first, setting it to flight, and then ground down the Franks.

Muslim casualties amounted to 25,000 men, while the Franks lost 16,000. These casualties included the master of the Teutonic Knights along with nearly all 400 Teutonic Knights, 312 Templars, 325 Hospitallers and all fighting members of the Knights of St Lazarus. Both the Templar and Hospitaller masters were taken prisoner along with thirty-four other Templars, twenty-six Hospitallers and three Teutonic Knights. Also among the prisoners was the lord of Jaffa, Walter de Brienne, who was tortured in front of Jaffa to persuade the city to surrender. The garrison steadfastly refused to submit, and Brienne died of his injuries in captivity months later.

The sultan of Cairo followed up his victory by conquering his Muslim opponents' territories in Transjordan and Syria, thereby re-establishing the dominance of the sultan of Cairo over the Ayyubid empire. Yet he made no attempt to subdue the Kingdom of Jerusalem. While this sounds astonishing, there were good reasons for restraint. First and foremost, As-Salih Ayyub was not engaged in 'jihad'. He had fought the Franks not because of their religion but because they were allied with his Muslim enemies. His self-interest in continued trade with and through the crusader states remained intact.

Furthermore, he knew that while the losses of the military orders at La Forbie were huge, the secular chivalry had suffered hardly at all. The great lords of Beirut, Sidon, Toron, Caesarea and Arsuf do not appear to have been engaged in the battle. Their fighting capacity remained undiminished, as did the entire feudal host of Cyprus, a significant point since, at this time, King Henry of Cyprus was recognised as the regent of Jerusalem by the local barons. Clearly, in an all-out assault on the heart of the crusader kingdom, the Franks would have been able to put up a tenacious defence. The sultan of Cairo wisely sought to avoid such a confrontation possibly because he was also facing an increasingly dangerous threat from the Mongols in the north.

Finally, the Ayyubid fear of a new crusade sat deep – and not unjustified. In December 1244, a dying young man vowed that if God would grant him a reprieve, he would recapture Jerusalem for Christendom. He experienced a miraculous recovery and was to prove one of the most determined and tenacious of all crusaders: King Louis IX of France.

Saint Louis and the Seventh Crusade, 1248–1254

Practically from the moment of his recovery, King Louis devoted himself to preparing his crusade. This was predominantly a French affair, not only because it was the brainchild of a French king, but also because the struggle between the papacy and the Holy Roman emperor had reached a state of open warfare. The pope had declared Frederick II 'deposed' and called for a 'crusade' to enforce his ruling. This effectively precluded German and Italian participation. Nevertheless, France was so wealthy and Louis' position so strong that with his own resources he was able to launch one of the best organised and financed crusades of the entire era.

Between 15,000 and 18,000 fighting men were involved; of which as many as 2,800 were knights. Louis systematically collected funds and chartered large numbers of ships, including long-distance horse transports and shallow-draught landing craft, the latter contributing decisively to the capture of Damietta. He also pre-positioned supplies of wine and grain in massive dumps on Cyprus. Louis personally took an active and intense interest in every aspect of the preparations for his crusade.

On 25 August 1248, King Louis embarked at Aigues Mortes, accompanied by three of his brothers and his queen. He adopted the same strategy as the Fifth Crusade, namely attacking Egypt, expecting that a decisive victory over the Ayyubids in their powerbase would force concessions in the Holy Land. The crusaders wintered in Cyprus, where they enjoyed the hospitality of King Henry and restored the health of their horses while awaiting additional contingents.

In May 1249, King Louis sailed for Damietta with an army reinforced by numerous Cypriot contingents under the command of the constable and seneschal of Cyprus, Guy and Baldwin d'Ibelin, respectively. After a dangerous storm, the fleet arrived off Damietta on 4 June; the next day, Louis undertook a dangerous amphibious landing against armed opposition. Jean de Joinville, the seneschal of France and participant in this landing, tells the following story in his biography of King Louis:

> When the king heard that the standard of Saint Denis was on shore he ... refused to be parted from the emblem of his sovereignty, and leapt into the sea, where the water came up to his armpits. He went on, with his shield hung from his neck, his helmet on his head, and lance in hand, 'till he had joined his people on the shore... . [Here] he put his lance under his armpit, and holding his shield before him, would have charged right in among [the Saracens] if certain sagacious men who were standing around him had allowed it.[7]

Despite multiple attacks by Saracen cavalry, the crusaders held on to their bridgehead on the sands before the city while their horses were brought up in the second wave of landing ships. As night fell, the crusaders prepared to besiege Damietta as the Fifth Crusade had done for a year-and-a-half. They were astonished to learn the entire city had been deserted. The sultan's troops had retreated upriver, and the garrison and population – feeling abandoned – had fled after them.

This was a stroke of luck that allowed the army to take control of a walled city containing ample food, water and shelter, without casualties. Ironically, because the crusaders had expected a long siege, their attack had been launched while the Nile was still flooded. This meant they could not follow-up their surprise victory because they had to wait for the floodwaters to recede. This had the added benefit of allowing temperatures to drop to more tolerable levels for marching and fighting and enabling reinforcements to arrive under Louis's brother, the count of Poitiers.

In due time, a war council discussed strategy. The majority favoured an attack on Alexandria to facilitate a diplomatic deal benefitting the crusader states. In contrast, Louis' brother, the count of Artois forcefully argued that the way to kill a snake was to crush its head: i.e. an assault

The Second Kingdom or the Kingdom of Acre, 1192–1291

on Cairo. Louis accepted this advice, and on 20 November 1249, led his army out of Damietta to advance up the Nile towards Cairo.

Meanwhile, the sultan al-Sahil Ayyub had died and been succeeded by his son, Turan Shah. Because the latter was not present in Egypt, the sultan's Mamluks assumed temporary command of the Egyptian army. They concentrated at Mansourah while the crusaders made slow but steady progress marching up the Nile. Throughout the march, King Louis' fleet kept his army well supplied and held open the lines of communication to Damietta, where the queen of France remained with a substantial garrison. At Mansourah, a well-fortified town positioned strategically at the junction of two branches of the Nile, progress ground to a halt.

The crusaders could not advance on Cairo without first crossing over one branch of the Nile and taking Mansourah. All attempts to bridge the river failed. Then on 8 February 1250, an Egyptian traitor revealed a ford to the crusaders, and King Louis' army started crossing the Nile. Unfortunately, the advance guard was placed under the command of Louis' impetuous brother Robert, Count of Artois. He rushed ahead against the king's explicit orders. Artois succeeded in overrunning the Saracen camp outside the city walls but foolishly followed the fleeing Saracen troops into the city itself, where the French were trapped in the narrow, irregular streets and set upon by the entire population. Not one of them escaped, and the count of Artois' body was hung from the walls in triumph. With the main body of troops, King Louis was able to withstand a counterattack and fight his way forward to successfully occupy the camp vacated by the Saracens, but the city remained firmly in Saracen hands.

This bloody, indecisive and bitter victory was the turning point in the crusade. While the crusaders remained encamped before Mansourah, the Saracens transported disassembled ships by camel and reassembled them upriver from Damietta. These Saracen warships started to systematically intercept Louis' supply ships. By April, Louis' army was starving and diseased. Both scurvy and dysentery had decimated the ranks. Louis, himself desperately ill, gave the order to retreat. The Saracens harassed the crusaders every step of the way, until Louis, no longer able to ride or stand, surrendered.

The first thing the sultan did was to order the execution of all the sick and wounded among the poor; only those well enough to be enslaved were spared. The nobles were held for ransom, and the bargaining began.

With threats of torture, including showing Louis the instruments of torture to be employed, the sultan attempted to force the king to surrender the formidable castles of the crusader kingdoms still in Frankish hands. Louis replied that the sultan could do with him as he pleased, but he could not surrender the fortresses because he did not control them. The sultan eventually settled for the return of Damietta as the king's ransom and payment of 800,000 bezants for all the other prisoners. Although the sultan was then assassinated by his Mamluks, the terms of the treaty were respected, and Louis and most of the high-ranking nobles were released upon the return of Damietta and payment of half the ransom.

The bulk of those released had had enough crusading and returned home at once, but King Louis sailed for Acre instead. He was determined to remain in the Holy Land until the last of the prisoners had been returned. He also set about strengthening the defences of the Kingdom of Jerusalem. He accomplished the latter by extensively refortifying Acre, Caesarea, Jaffa and Sidon at his own expense. He also arranged for a permanent garrison of 100 French knights at Acre supported by appropriate, if unnamed, numbers of sergeants, archers and support troops, bringing the total commitment close to 1,000 men. Meanwhile, Louis tenaciously and sagely negotiated with the Muslim states, who were again at war with one another and willing to court the Franks.

Ultimately, Louis signed a truce with the new rulers of Egypt, the Mamluks, because they still held thousands of captives. He concluded a treaty with them in 1252 that secured the release of the remaining prisoners and cancelled his outstanding debt of 400,000 bezants. In 1254 he signed a truce with Damascus and Aleppo as well. These treaties secured a comprehensive if temporary peace for the Kingdom of Jerusalem. On 24 April 1254, Louis sailed for home. Despite the tragic end of his crusade, he left the Kingdom of Jerusalem stronger than before. As Thomas Madden put it: 'The contrast between Louis IX and Frederick II could not have been more stark.'[8]

Mongols and Mamluks: The Changing Face of the Middle East

While Louis' diplomatic successes continued the long tradition of securing survival for the crusader states via truces with the fragmented

The Second Kingdom or the Kingdom of Acre, 1192–1291

Saracen states threatening them, the very foundations on which such truces had been built were melting away. A decade before King Louis' surrender, a new Asiatic power had intruded upon the already complex scene: the Mongols. The Mongols were unlike any previous invader in that they flatly rejected compromise and peace, demanding complete and unconditional surrender instead. When the pope asked why they were invading without provocation or grievance, the Mongols replied that they 'did not understand his words' – they conquered because they could and because 'God' had given the entire earth to them.[9] The savagery and brutality of Mongol conquests were unprecedented; they terrified Christians and Muslims alike.

The Mongols invaded and laid waste to the Rus between 1236 and 1242, the climax being the capture and sack of Kiev in 1240. A year later, the Mongols obliterated a German army at the Battle of Leignitz and defeated the Hungarians at the Battle of Mohi. Further expansion into Europe was only prevented by internal rivalries among Mongol leaders, which ultimately resulted in them shifting their focus to Asia Minor and the Middle East. In 1243 they crushed the Seljuks at the Battle of Kosedag, leading to the conquest of Anatolia, Armenia and Georgia. The king of Cilician Armenia and the prince of Antioch surrendered their independence and did homage to the Mongols to avoid destruction. In 1256, after a pause to deal with internal issues, the Mongols advanced again, this time eliminating the stronghold of the Assassins. In 1258, they captured and pillaged Baghdad in one of the most shocking excesses of violence known to history. The savage sack was characterised by wanton destruction that obliterated wealth as well as priceless cultural monuments and treasures, including mosques, palaces, hospitals and no less than thirty-six libraries. The Mongols executed the caliph, allegedly by rolling him into a rug and trampling him with their horses, thereby ending the 500-year-old caliphate. The number of civilians slaughtered is estimated at over 100,000 and possibly twice that, leaving the city a shattered and depopulated ruin for generations afterwards. Two years later, the Mongols captured and sacked first Aleppo and then Damascus. The Ayyubid empire had been destroyed, and many of the survivors fled to the territories controlled by the Franks for safety.

The Mongols, meanwhile, turned their eyes to the rich prize of Egypt. They sent ambassadors demanding submission, but the new rulers of Egypt, the Mamluks, were not inclined to submit. Instead, they sought an alliance with the Franks. The Franks declined to participate in a joint offensive but granted the Mamluks permission to march through Frankish territory to confront the Mongols. On 3 September 1260, the Mamluks met the Mongols southwest of the Sea of Galilee in what had once been part of the Kingdom of Jerusalem at the Battle of Ain Jalut. After hours of fighting, the Mamluks feigned flight and lured the Mongols into a trap. The Mongol army was obliterated, and the Mongol threat receded. Yet in its place was a new, dynamic and triumphant power: the Mamluks.

The Mamluks were slaves, purchased as children and trained rigorously to become elite troops. Ethnically they were predominantly Caucasian, increasingly drawn from the Turcomen tribes inhabiting the region north of the Black Sea, but they were indoctrinated in Islam from the time of their capture. Their education included rigorous religious instruction by Islamic scholars but did not extend much beyond religion. As they grew up, the amount of time spent training for war increased. They were drilled in horsemanship and mounted combat with the lance, sword and bow. They also learned hunting, wrestling, polo and rudimentary veterinary skills. Although freed at maturity, they remained soldiers for life. They made up the bodyguards and elite units of the various Ayyubid princes and emirs for generations. They were famed and feared for their loyalty, devotion to duty and religious orthodoxy. The latter did not stop them from murdering each other as unscrupulously as they broke treaties and broke their word.

The Mamluk regime in Egypt had been established through the assassination of Turan Shah – before the eyes of King Louis and the other French captives. It is described in detail by the eyewitness Joinville:

> [Turan Shah's] bodyguard hacked and slashed … one of these men gave him [the sultan] a lance-thrust in the ribs. He continued his flight with the weapon trailing from the wound … . So they came and killed him, not far from the place where our galley lay … Faress-Eddin-Octay cut him open with his sword and took the heart out of the body. Then, with his hands dripping with blood, he came to our king and said: 'What will you give me now that I have killed your enemy?'[10]

Furthermore, the Mamluks were not a dynasty, rather they were a professional elite. This meant that power belonged to the strongest.

The Second Kingdom or the Kingdom of Acre, 1192–1291

The initial beneficiary of the assassination of Turan Shah was a certain Aybeg, but he was murdered on 10 April 1257. His son briefly ruled, but by 12 November 1259, he had been replaced by the sultan Qutuz. The latter won the battle of Ain Jalut, only to be stabbed to death shortly afterwards by a group of his emirs led by al-Din Baybars.

Baybars managed to retain power for seventeen years from 1260–77. He controlled both Syria and Egypt, but unlike his Ayyubid predecessors, he did not do so as the ruler of a loose coalition of princes and emirs whose loyalty had to be courted, but rather as the commander-in-chief of a highly centralised state dedicated to war. This state depended on the support of the religious elites to keep the government functioning, and it purchased their loyalty with religious bigotry.

Yet there was no question in anyone's minds that the Mamluks were usurpers – and former slaves. To stay in power, they needed to establish new legitimacy, and as soldiers, the most obvious means of doing so was to declare war, or more specifically, 'jihad'. The Mamluks employed 'jihad' to distract their subjects from their illegitimacy and unite them against a 'common enemy'. As a result, the Mamluk period was characterised by increased hostility to non-Muslims inside and outside the territories they controlled. Religious minorities in the Mamluk states, particularly Christians, suffered increasingly harsh discrimination and oppression. Once the Mongol threat was banished, the Mamluks turned their attention to active 'jihad' against the crusader states with the stated intention, as recorded by Baybars' biographer Shafi bin Ali, of 'waging war until no more Franks remain on the surface of the earth'.[11]

Breaking with the Ayyubids and placing religion above economic expediency, Baybar's objective was the absolute destruction of the crusader states, including their economies. He pursued military tactics that explicitly targeted economic assets, destroying crops, orchards, livestock, aqueducts and other infrastructure. He slaughtered or enslaved the population of the territories he conquered, making no distinction between Franks (Latin Christians) and native Christians. When he succeeded in taking cities, as he did in 1265 with the capture of Caesarea, Haifa and Arsuf, he destroyed them so they could not be used as bridgeheads for future crusades – and in so doing, destroyed their economic value to his own state as well as the revenue that derived from them to his people.

Having split the Kingdom of Jerusalem in half with the above conquests, Baybars next attacked the Templar fortress of Safed in 1266.

Despite having promised to spare the inhabitants if they surrendered, he massacred them. In 1268, he captured Jaffa and again brutally sacked and razed the city after slaughtering and enslaving the population. The same year, he took Antioch. He ordered the gates of the city closed while his troops slaughtered every single living thing inside – and then sent a letter bragging about his brutality to the prince of Antioch, who had been absent when the attack and sack occurred. This letter was very long, very detailed and very triumphant in tone. Below is only a tiny excerpt:

> The churches themselves were razed from the face of the earth, every house met with disaster, the dead were piled up on the seashore like islands of corpses … . You would have seen your knights prostrate beneath the horses' hooves … your women sold four at a time and bought for a dinar of your own money … your Muslim enemy trampling on the place where you celebrate mass, cutting the throats of monks, priests and deacons upon the altars … your palace lying unrecognisable. [12]

The scale of destruction shocked the world, including the Muslim world. It was recognised at the time as the worst massacre in crusading history, similar in scope to the sack of Baghdad by the Mongols a decade earlier. It also ended the economic prosperity of the city, turning it into a ghost town for generations to come – indeed, reducing its status to that of a provincial backwater to this day.

In 1271, Baybers captured the illustrious Hospitaller fortress of Crac de Chevaliers and the headquarters of the Teutonic Knights in the Holy Land, Montfort. In 1277, Baybers died of poisoning; whether it was accidental is impossible to know. After two years of vicious infighting among the Mamluk emirs, Qalawun emerged as the new sultan. He had pushed aside two of Baybars' sons to get there and immediately faced a revolt from a fellow Mamluk emir in Damascus, which he put down militarily only to ally himself with his rival to defeat a new Mongol threat. The Mongols were again defeated at the Battle of Homs on 29 October 1281. Thereafter, Qalawun turned his attention to dismantling the remnants of the crusader states with a combination of threats, extortion and outright force.

The Second Kingdom or the Kingdom of Acre, 1192–1291

The Loss of Latin Syria, 1282–1291

The Franks were helpless in the face of the Mamluk onslaught. They simply did not have the resources or the defensible borders necessary to win an military confrontation with armies drawn from the entire region and subject to centralised, professional control. Nor could they win a diplomatic game with a power uninterested in coexistence or even economic self-interest.

It did not help that, except for Cyprus, the crusader states had started to rot away from the inside. The problem was twofold. On the one hand, the increasingly urban character of the state and the growth in commercial activities had resulted in the Italian merchant states with their poisonous rivalries playing a more dominant role. On the other hand, ever since Frederick II had sailed away, the ruling dynasty had been absent from the kingdom and disinterested in its fate.

The unity of the kingdom was shaken when the bitter rivalry between the Venetians and the Genoese erupted into open warfare. Not only did the parties engage in bloodshed on the streets of Acre, but the militant orders took opposite sides, and the barons of the kingdom were divided. Since there was no king present in the country, there was no forceful central authority to enforce a settlement. The war ended with a sea battle between the fleets of the respective rivals in which the Genoese lost half their ships and an estimated 1,700 men. That hardly strengthened the kingdom, even if it ended the immediate bloodshed.

The issue of absentee kings was arguably the single most important factor that undermined the internal viability of the crusader states in the thirteenth century. Even the long drawn out civil war is only imaginable in the absence of the king. Had Frederick II been prepared to stay in the Holy Land or to send his son Conrad to grow up and live there, the rebel barons would not have stood a chance of effectively defying his authority.

After the capture of Tyre, the barons recognised as regent the closest relative of the absent Hohenstaufen monarch living in the Holy Land. This is usually portrayed as a cynical attempt to retain control of affairs, but instead should be seen as an effort to find a ruler with a stake in the kingdom. The first of these regents had been the dowager queen of Cyprus, Alice of Champagne. Alice was followed by her son King Henry I of Cyprus until his death in 1253 and then by his son King Hugh II.

The latter two kings appointed regents of the Kingdom of Jerusalem who resided there and could exercise a modicum of weak power, but they were not comparable to a resident king such as those Jerusalem had had throughout most of the twelfth century. Yet worse was still to come.

In 1268, Conrad of Hohenstaufen died without heirs, and a succession dispute broke out between King Hugh III of Cyprus and Maria of Antioch. With a mercenary disregard for the well-being of the kingdom, Maria of Antioch sold her claim to Charles d'Anjou, the younger brother of King Louis of France. Charles, like the latter Hohenstaufens, never set foot in the kingdom. He merely sent a baillie who successfully exploited self-interest and personal vanity to undermine King Hugh's authority. As a result, the latter abandoned the Kingdom of Jerusalem in disgust and returned to Cyprus. By the time Charles d'Anjou died in 1284, enabling Henry II of Cyprus to be recognised and crowned as undisputed king of Jerusalem, the kingdom existed in name only.

Baybars and Qalawun had been systematically chipping away at the substance of the kingdom, not only by open assault but by cutting deals with individual lords and cities in a classic example of 'divide and conquer'. All these separate treaties were short-sighted as it must have been obvious to all that no one city could withstand the Mamluks on their own. Yet fear and weakness misled individual lords to cling to illusions even as the world unraveled around them. Other lords gave up altogether, selling out to the military orders, which were the only institutions that appeared to have the necessary resources – based on their vast networks in the West – to stand up to the Mamluks.

By 1282 the kingdom had been reduced to nothing but a collection of isolated cities and castles with little connection between them, let alone a common government and policy. It was no longer possible to travel overland between the various cities without a sizeable, armed escort. While the cities became larger with walls enclosing more extensive urban areas, the countryside became first depopulated and then hostile.

In 1285 the Mamluks captured the renowned Hospitaller castle at Marqab. In 1287 the port of Latakia was taken. In 1289, despite a truce then in effect, Qalawun attacked and captured Tripoli. As usual, he slaughtered the men, enslaved the women and children, and then destroyed the harbour, castle and fortifications, as well as the churches and other structures. In 1290 Qalawun died, but he was succeeded by

The Second Kingdom or the Kingdom of Acre, 1192–1291

a son as ruthless as himself, al-Ashraf Khalil, who quashed several rebellions among his own emirs. The assault on the Franks continued.

In April 1291, the siege of Acre began. At this time, Acre had a population of roughly 20,000, and the walls had been reinforced both by King Louis following his first crusade and by Edward of England, who had briefly campaigned indecisively in the Holy Land in 1271–72. The Mamluks held an 11 to 1 manpower advantage and had brought numerous siege engines and engineers to undermine the walls. The outcome was never in doubt. All that was left to the Franks was what Balian d'Ibelin had promised Saladin at Jerusalem in 1187: to die fighting and take as many of the enemy with them as possible.

The Genoese didn't feel like martyrs and withdrew by ship at once. With them went those women, children and other non-combatants who could afford passage. Left behind were predominantly fighting men – the reverse of the 1187 situation in Jerusalem. Those willing to fight and die for the honour of their already dead kingdom were the Venetians, Pisans, Templars, Hospitaller and Teutonic Knights. The Templars and Hospitallers were both commanded by their respective masters. Total forces are estimated at roughly 14,000 fighting men, of which 700 were knights.

The Mamluks opened the siege with their engines and conducted repeated assaults. On the night of 14-15 April, the Templars attempted a night sortie against the Mamluks led by Master William de Beaujeu; the Hospitallers did likewise a few days later. Neither had any significant impact on the enemy. Thereafter, the knights resigned themselves to a defensive battle.

On 4 May, King Henry arrived from Cyprus with several hundred knights and 500 infantry, but these forces were insufficient to alter the balance of forces. Furthermore, the walls had been undermined, and the hammering of the siege engines was taking its toll. King Henry tried to negotiate and received a brusque rejection.

On 18 May, one of the towers collapsed after being mined, forcing the defenders to abandon the large suburb of Montmusard. They retreated to the old city but were unable to hold the onslaught that swept in after them. Fighting became hand-to-hand and street-to-street. The Templar master took a mortal wound in the armpit, and two of his brothers carried him on their shields to the Templar headquarters where he died. The Hospitaller master was also wounded, but not mortally. He was carried to a Hospitaller ship in the harbour, which then put to sea. King Henry likewise took ship and returned to Cyprus with as many of his men as he could collect. The patriarch of Jerusalem tried to depart, but he allowed so many swimmers into his longboat while rowing out to a waiting galley that it capsized and sank.

With so many fleeing for the port, the defence of the city collapsed altogether, and a bloodbath ensued. Those who could sought refuge behind the walls of the Templar citadel, located in the southwest corner of the city, backed up against the sea to the west and the harbour to the south. It is unknown how many people ultimately found refuge here, but it must have been hundreds, if not thousands. For five days, they remained inside while Acre was looted and burned around them.

On 25 May, the Templar marshal negotiated a surrender that would allow those inside to depart unharmed. When the gates were opened, and the Mamluks entered, however, they began molesting the women and children. This was either a misunderstanding, i.e. the Mamluks believed the safe conduct applied only to fighting men, or the emir accepting the surrender did not have control over his troops. The Templars, who were still armed, responded by killing all the Saracens within their headquarters and then defiantly raising the black-and-white Baucent over the ramparts again. As they did so, they must have known that they thereby sacrificed all hopes of surrender.

The sultan sent for the Templar marshal the next day, allegedly to renegotiate. The marshal, either foolish or seeking martyrdom, went to meet his fate and was beheaded within sight of those in the Templar citadel. The Mamluks undermined the walls of the citadel, causing a breach on 28 May. As thousands of Saracens rushed in triumphantly, the entire Temple crashed down, killing defenders and attackers alike.

Meanwhile, Tyre – which had withstood two sieges by Saladin and provided the beachhead for the Third Crusade – was evacuated 19 May. This meant that all that remained of the Kingdom of Jerusalem were Sidon, Beirut and the Templar castles of Tortosa and Athlit (Castle Pilgrim). Sidon fell to assault in June. Beirut surrendered 31 July, and the Templar castles were evacuated 3 and 4 August, respectively.

Unlike 1187, there was no foothold left from which to launch a new crusade, and the loss of Acre did not trigger one. The crusading spirit had become too diffused and weakened over the previous century. Meanwhile, the Mamluk policy of economic destruction ensured that

The Second Kingdom or the Kingdom of Acre, 1192–1291

the trading routes that had once passed through the Levant had shifted north across what is now Turkey or south to Egypt. The once great cities were left in ruins, plundered for stone by the peasants and reclaimed by the dunes, or partially rebuilt as provincial towns. Once a flourishing crossroads of goods, technology and culture, the entire region became a forgotten backwater for centuries to come.

Of the crusader states, Cyprus alone remained in Frankish hands. It took in the refugees of all religions and ethnic groups, and for roughly a century, Famagusta became the commercial heir to Acre.

Conclusion

In retrospect it is clear that La Forbie was only an apparent and not a substantive turning point. The battle was not a clash between Christians and Muslims, but rather between Ayyubid princes, in which the Franks had the misfortune to back the losing side. Notably, the defeat did not result in the Kingdom of Jerusalem being over-run and destroyed – precisely because the victor was not engaged in jihad. Thus, decisive as this battle appears, it was not the cause of subsequent decline. As long as the Ayyubid princes remained in control of the territories surrounding the crusader states, it was possible to 1) make truces with them, and 2) play them off against one another. The Ayyubids were far too interested in profiting from the trade they had with the crusader states to undertake serious jihad. It was not until the rise of the Mamluks that the crusaders faced opponents set on their destruction and eradication.

The Mamluks were not a dynasty, but a cadre of fanatical, orthodox, military leaders willing to sacrifice economic considerations for religious orthodoxy and victory. The Mamluks pursued a ruthless policy of aggression against the crusader states that included routinely breaking truces, breaking the terms of truces, slaughtering prisoners, and engaging in the wanton destruction of economic assets and cultural monuments to render the cities they captured uninhabitable for generations to come. The Mamluks did not pursue wars of conquest in which they hoped to occupy and benefit from the territory they conquered but rather wars of annihilation.

Yet the Mamluks alone were not responsible for the destruction of the crusader states. The rot came from the inside as well. From 1100 to 1225, Jerusalem was ruled by kings resident in the kingdom, who viewed the defense of the Holy Land as their raison d'etre. From Baldwin I to John de Brienne, these kings had been fighting men devoted to the kingdom they inherited, whether by blood or marriage.

In 1225, that changed. The marriage of the heiress of Jerusalem, Yolanda, to the Holy Roman Emperor Frederick II Hohenstaufen, put

Conclusion

the crown – and fate – of Jerusalem into the hands of a man who already possessed a vast empire. As events were to prove, Frederick II never gave more than a tinker's damn about Jerusalem or the kingdom named after it. He spent less than a year in the domain, he ignored its constitution, sought to humiliate and break the local barons, and on his death bed in 1250 tried to alienate it from the legitimate heir. His son and grandson were titular 'Kings of Jerusalem', who never set foot in the kingdom, had no understanding of its laws, people or problems, and exercised no influence there. Their worthless rule was followed by a succession crisis that was not solved until 1284, when the kingdom was already beyond salvage.

In short, between 1225 and 1284, the Kingdom of Jerusalem effectively had no central authority. It is hardly surprising that in the circumstances internal factions formed, and that clashes over policy led to bloodshed. Without central authority, the barons soon resorted to pursuing independent policies that further eroded the state, while the Italian city-states pursued their commercial rivalries without the least regard for the impact on the viability of the Latin East.

None of this was inevitable. The crusader states, backed with the resources of Cyprus, might well have held their own against the Mamluks and Mongols, if they had been led by a strong, determined and militarily capable king. This was effectively what the barons of Jerusalem had sought in 1190, when they rejected the leadership of the ineffectual Guy de Lusignan and chose Conrad de Montferrat as the king-consort of their queen. In the thirteenth century, they would have needed to reject the 'legitimate' Hohenstaufen kings in favour a truly elected king committed to the defence of the Holy Land – say Simon de Montfort. However, the barons of Outremer, despite their 'rebellion', were ultimately too conservative to take that radical leap, necessary though it was for their existence. Yet that assessment, obviously, is the wisdom of hindsight.

PART II

A Description of the Crusader States

Chapter 5

A Mediterranean Melting Pot
The Diverse Population of Outremer

Demography of the Holy Land in the Era of the Crusades

The popular perception of the demography of Holy Land in the era of the crusades is one of a native Muslim population ruled by a tiny, Christian elite. Indeed, leading historians of the last two centuries portrayed the crusader states as 'proto-colonial' in character. However, over the previous quarter-century, this picture has been profoundly altered by new archaeological finds, analysis of neglected sources and data mining of a variety of documents. To understand the demography of the Holy Land in the era of the crusades, it may therefore be useful to forget preconceived notions and begin with the basics.

When Jerusalem fell to Muslim forces in 638, the population was entirely Christian; the Jews had been expelled after supporting the Persian assault on the city a quarter-century earlier. The establishment of a Muslim regime in the region did not result in the instant conversion of the entire population to Islam. On the contrary, the Quran condemns forced conversions, and while they are known to have taken place wherever Muslim regimes were established, conversions were neither wholesale nor instantaneous.[1] The Arab conquests of the seventh, eighth and ninth centuries did not result in the spread of the religion of Islam so much as the spread of regimes ruled by Islamic military elites.

Despite the oppression and humiliation of non-Muslims under Islamic rule throughout the Umayyad period (661–750), non-Muslims still constituted the majority of the population throughout the Arab empire in 1000 AD, including in the Holy Land. The Muslim scholar Ibn al-Arabi, writing at the end of the eleventh century, noted that the countryside around Jerusalem was entirely Christian. Indeed, many towns in Palestine were still overwhelmingly Christian in 1922, nearly 1,300 years after the Muslim conquest of Jerusalem. In other words, although the territory controlled and ruled by Islamic elites expanded dramatically between 634 and 1099, the number of people adhering to Islam grew at a much slower rate.

Furthermore, between the Muslim conquest and the First Crusade, the Holy Land changed hands between Abbasids, Fatimids and Seljuks. To the natives of the Levant, the Arabs and Egyptians were no less 'alien elites' than the Romans and Byzantines, who had ruled the region before 638 AD, and the Turks and Franks, who ruled after 1099 AD. In all cases, the conquerors formed the political, military and, to a lesser extent, the economic elites during their respective period of dominance, but they did not replace the native population. Both Arabs and Turks relied heavily on troops drawn from outside the region (e.g. Turcoman tribesmen) and slave-soldiers (Mamluks), a factor that contributed significantly to their unpopularity.

Levels of oppression measured in terms of expropriations, massacres, deportations, enslavement, suppression of religious establishments, harassment, discrimination, social ostracism, labour conscription, taxation and other financial burdens varied over the centuries depending on the individual ruler. Accounts written by the natives – as opposed to those reported by the Arab/Turkish chroniclers – catalogue the massacres, torture, wholesale enslavement, financial oppression and humiliations that impoverished and demoralised the Christian and Jewish populations, even under allegedly enlightened and tolerant regimes.[2] These methods inevitably led to 'voluntary' conversions, often to escape death, slavery, expropriation or the sale of children to the Muslim state, yet at a much slower rate than was assumed in the eighteenth to twentieth centuries.

Furthermore, the minority Muslim population found in the Holy Land at the time of the First Crusade was less the product of the gradual Islamisation of the native population than a result of immigration. Nomadic Arab tribes had been encouraged to migrate to conquered territories, where land, infrastructure and entire villages had been handed over to them after the slaughter, enslavement and deportation of the native population. This immigration occurred unevenly across the region so that concentrations of Muslim inhabitants were found in some areas but not others.

Although the crusaders did not seek either extermination or mass conversion of the Muslim population, the numbers of Muslims in the Holy Land shrank during the Frankish conquest due to both casualties and voluntary emigration. Thus, while the populace of cities such as Ascalon, Acre and Tyre had been predominantly Muslim before the First Crusade, siege and assault took their toll. Furthermore, terms of surrender enabled Muslim inhabitants to withdraw with their movable property. Most ruling Muslim elites were not interested in remaining in places where they had lost their power and status, and so departed. Left behind were the poor and powerless. After the establishment of Frankish rule, Muslims were prohibited from residing in selected cities such as Jerusalem and Ascalon yet remained a significant minority in other cities such as Acre, Tyre, Beirut and Sidon.

In short, the demographics of the crusader states were highly complex and varied considerably from region to region. Nevertheless, some features are clear. The urban populations of most cities, with the notable exceptions of coastal Antioch (Latakia and Jabala), were predominantly Christian, in some cases with small Jewish and Samaritan minorities. The rural population in Edessa, Antioch and Cyprus was predominantly Orthodox Christian, with Christians accounting for two-thirds of the population in Edessa and Antioch and 95 per cent in Cyprus. Tripoli was probably 50 per cent Christian, while the Kingdom of Jerusalem was the most ethnically and religiously diverse crusader state. Altogether, historians now estimate that when the kingdom was established, native Christians made up more than 50 per cent of the populace, while Muslims formed a sizeable minority and Jewish and Samaritan communities represented smaller minority groups.

During the first half-century of Frankish presence, however, the balance tipped in favour of Christian dominance. An estimated 140,000 predominantly Christian immigrants from Western Europe settled in the region, and their offspring were also Christian. In addition, the kings of Jerusalem pursued a policy of encouraging (Orthodox) Christian immigration from neighbouring Muslim states. Melkite Christians are known to have left the sultanate of Damascus to resettle in Jerusalem and possibly other cities, while Coptic Christians from Egypt settled in Ascalon.

Furthermore, when Nur al-Din's forces overran the County of Edessa between 1144 and 1150, tens of thousands of Armenian refugees fled to the Kingdom of Jerusalem. Here they formed a large, dynamic and loyal community. In 1172, this Armenian community was enlarged when the Armenian patriarch in Egypt relocated to Jerusalem, bringing many of his flock with him. Finally, many Muslims converted to Christianity in this period. Some converts may have been nominal Muslims, men and women who had adopted Islam to avoid being killed, enslaved or impoverished and humiliated as 'dhimmis'. Another motive for conversion was the draconian punishment for interfaith marriage, which put many women under pressure to convert to marry a Christian. Estimating numbers, much less motives, is nearly impossible, yet some sources claim that conversions were 'extensive'.[3]

On the mainland, roughly half of the total population lived in the large urban centres, while on Cyprus, the inhabitants were 90 per cent or more rural. Although urbanisation was greater in the Holy Land than in Western Europe in the same period, the Kingdom of Jerusalem was not a predominantly urban society until the hinterland was lost in the wake of Saladin's conquests.

Altogether, the total native population of the mainland crusader states is estimated at approximately 600,000, of which 450,000 were in the Kingdom of Jerusalem, 100,000 in Antioch and about 25,000 in Edessa and Tripoli each. In Cyprus, the population probably numbered about 100,000. Added to the native people were the 140,000 immigrants from Western Europe. Unaccounted in the above numbers are the Franks born in the Holy Land, predominantly the children of mixed marriages. Given the fact that the Franks were cultivating land that had become depopulated and lost to desertification by building irrigation systems and other infrastructure, it is probable that significant population growth occurred during the Frankish era. While no precise estimate of the population growth is possible, the combined population of the crusader states by 1187 might well have reached 1 million people.

The Native Population in the Holy Land

Orthodox Christians
In the above discussion, all native Christians were treated as a single group. However, the Christians in the Holy Land of the crusader era were extremely diverse. The most numerous Christian populations were Melkites, Armenians, Jacobites and Maronites, but there were also smaller communities of Coptics, Georgians, Nestorians and Ethiopians. Furthermore, the distribution of these groups was uneven across the crusader states. Edessa, for example, was essentially an Armenian state

with a Jacobite minority. Antioch was mostly Melkite (Arabic-speaking Greek Orthodox) with considerable communities of Armenians and Jacobites (a Syrian branch or sect of Orthodox Christianity which adhered to Monophysitism founded by the monk Jacob in the sixth century AD.) The Christian half of the population in the County of Tripoli and the far northern parts of the Kingdom of Jerusalem (what is now part of Lebanon) were predominantly Maronite (the Maronites were another branch or sect of the Syrian Orthodox Church founded by the monk Maron in the fourth century AD). The rest of the Kingdom of Jerusalem, in contrast, was predominantly Melkite. However, it was also home to smaller communities of Greek-speaking Orthodox as well as Armenian, Georgian, Coptic and Ethiopian Christians.

Differences of doctrine separated all these various Christian denominations from one another and the Latin Church, as the Roman Catholic Church was commonly called in this polyglot environment. Confusingly, linguistic differences did not always conform to doctrinal differences. Thus, Melkites and Greek Orthodox shared the same basic doctrines and viewed the patriarch of Constantinople as the head of the church, but the former spoke Syriac or Arabic, while the latter retained the use of Greek in the liturgy. Syriac or Arabic was used by Jacobites, Maronites and Copts, although they differed on doctrine. Serious tensions and frictions existed between the various Orthodox communities dating back to Byzantine rule, when Armenians, Jacobites and Maronites had all been viewed as heretics and persecuted to various degrees by the Greek Orthodox state.

The assumption that the Latin Church likewise viewed these various other Christian denominations as heretics and sought to suppress them, however, is incorrect. Pope Urban II, in his initial appeal, explicitly described the Eastern Christians as 'brothers' and 'sons of the same Christ'.[4] Furthermore, recent research based on Orthodox sources reveals a surprisingly nuanced and tolerant approach to the various Christian groups on the part of the Latins. The patriarch of the Jacobite church writing in the twelfth century noted that the Franks 'never sought a single formula for all the Christian people and languages, but they considered as Christian anyone who worshipped the cross without investigation or examination'.[5]

While it is true that all forms of Orthodox Christianity were viewed with various degrees of skepticism by the Roman Catholic theologians, the crusader states were not theocracies run by religious scholars. They were secular states governed by educated but fundamentally hard-nosed, practical, fighting men. From the very start, Frankish knights, sergeants and settlers mingled with the local population, sharing not only markets and taverns, but churches and confessors – a clear indication that for the average Frank, the common belief in Christ outweighed the theological differences that animated church scholars. Furthermore, with time, the Frankish feudal elite intermarried with the local aristocracy, while farther down the social scale, intermarriage with local Christians came sooner and occurred on a wider scale. The Frankish kings viewed themselves as the protectors of all their subjects, regardless of religious affiliation.

Undoubtedly, in both secular and ecclesiastical spheres, the apex of society was occupied by Franks, who were, by definition, Latin Christians. In the context of the twelfth and thirteenth centuries, this was normal. People of this era unanimously recognised the simple rule: to the victor go the spoils. The Orthodox Christians living in the crusader states did not look at their position through the lens of modern human rights activists or political scientists expecting absolute equality of legal status and opportunity. On the contrary, the native Christians viewed the Franks in comparison to their predecessors.

Much has been written over the last century about the tolerance of Muslim regimes towards Christians and Jews, the so-called 'dhimmis' or non-Muslims sharing the same roots as Islam. Most of what has been written focuses on the theories propounded by Muslim scholars of the golden age and anecdotal evidence of non-Muslims, especially Jews, who rose to positions of privilege and power. In contrast, Egyptian scholar Bat Ye'or in her seminal work, *The Decline of Eastern Christianity under Islam: From Jihad to Dhimmitude*, undertook a comprehensive study of the practice, rather than the theory, of Islamic relations with subject peoples. Based on Arab, Turkish, Armenian, Syriac, Latin and Greek sources, Ye'or demonstrates that Muslim regimes over 1,300 years of history based their policies toward non-Muslim subjects less on the theories of Islamic scholars than on Quranic verse 9:29. She notes that Muslim policy was also heavily influenced by Mohammad's personal example, which included the extermination of the entire Jewish population of Medina.

Conquest in the name of 'jihad', furthermore, meant that all non-Muslim inhabitants of newly-conquered territories were legally prisoners of war, who had to ransom their lives, property and freedom through the payment of tribute – in perpetuity – unless the 'captive' converted to Islam. In the early years of Islamic expansion, the standard treatment of 'prisoners' was massacre and enslavement; the numbers of slaves recorded in conquest after conquest are in the tens of thousands, all of whom were deported to reduce the likelihood of revolt. They were replaced either by Muslim settlers or, more often, (Christian) slaves from somewhere else. While slaughter and enslavement were standard practice throughout the world, other powers such as Persia, Byzantium, or the Vikings, did not justify their treatment of conquered people with religious dogma. The factor that made the Arab conquests of the seventh and eighth centuries unique was that the Muslims based their sense of superiority on religion (Quran 3:106) and believed they were 'fulfilling a religious duty and executing the will of Allah'.[6]

Gradually, however, as regions became pacified, 'the predations ... upon the natives, the only taxable labour force, assumed such catastrophic proportions that the revenue of the Umayyad state diminished considerably'.[7] In consequence of this economic imperative, Islamic jurists developed sophisticated theories on the correct treatment of 'dhimmis', which have charmed modern historians. Indeed, there is evidence that some Christian, Jewish and Zoroastrian elites prospered under Muslim rule. On the one hand, the 'dhimmi' leaders – often the religious leaders of the respective subject faiths – were responsible for collecting and paying the tribute to the Muslim rulers; some of what they gathered found its way into their own pockets. On the other hand, as with the Franks themselves, the Arab and Turkish military elites responsible for conquest needed educated and experienced administrators. Christian and Jewish secretaries, accountants, diplomats, translators, bankers and merchants were too useful to exterminate, so a small class of non-Muslim urban elites enjoyed comparative immunity from the discrimination. This did not, however, end the oppression of their poor, uneducation and rural co-religionists.

The prosperity and privileges of the few should not obscure the misery, impoverishment and denigration of the vast majority. There are countless examples from Muslim, Christian and Jewish sources that demonstrate the discrepancy between the fine theories laid out in Islamic legal texts and the reality on the ground. At best, the legal protection offered dhimmis by Islam resembled the 'protection' provided to the Jews of Western Europe by the pope. There were equally wide discrepancies between the fate of urban elites and the peasant majority.

A Mediterranean Melting Pot

This majority was systematically decimated by massacres, reduced to slavery or – at best – impoverished by taxation (tribute) and arbitrary theft, which destroyed their livelihood during Muslim rule. Oppression was so great in some periods and regions that it resulted in mass exodus, leaving entire villages abandoned. 'The Syro-Palestinian oases cultivated since antiquity, the agricultural and urban centres of the Negev, Jordan, and the Orontes, Tigris and Euphrates valleys ... had disappeared and become ghost towns, abandoned to pasturage, where herds of goats and camels grazed amid the ruins'.[8]

Most Christians and Jews who survived in this oppressive environment had no legal protections because their word was considered worthless in an Islamic court. They were required by Sharia law to live in smaller and more dilapidated homes. They were not allowed to build houses of worship or conduct any religious rite or ceremony in public and were prohibited from wearing symbols of their religion. They were required to wear distinctive clothing and carry proof they had paid their taxes. They were forbidden from riding horses or camels and from bearing arms. The Muslim population was actively encouraged to demonstrate contempt for non-Muslims by shoving them aside or otherwise demeaning them.

Compared to such humiliations, the difference in the status between Orthodox and Latin Christians in the crusader states was negligible. The two centuries of crusader rule constituted a period of economic and religious revival for the Christians of the Levant. Orthodox monasticism experienced a significant expansion under Frankish rule as old monasteries were restored, and new monasteries were built. The Frankish elite also proved generous patrons to Orthodox parish churches, while the Orthodox clergy enjoyed the same privilege of being exempt from the jurisdiction of secular courts as the Latin clergy. The squabbles over titles and sources of income between the senior clergy of the various Christian denominations tend to obscure the fact that, at the parish level, the Orthodox faithful remained under the care and guidance of Orthodox priests and free from interference, much less pressure to convert to Latin rites.

The most lucrative and prestigious ecclesiastical posts did come under the control of the Latin church in the crusader era, but not because of the expulsion of the Orthodox clergy. On the contrary, after capturing Antioch, the authority of the Greek patriarch over both Latins and Melkites was explicitly recognised by the crusaders. However, many Orthodox prelates had fled Muslim persecution prior to the arrival of the crusaders, and these vacant sees were filled by the crusader leadership with Latin bishops. The only instance of a Melkite bishop being ousted from his post had to do with power politics (an attempt by the Greek emperor to impose his authority), rather than church politics. The bottom line is that 'more Melkite bishops could be found throughout Palestine after the crusader conquest then had been there in the previous fifty years'.[9]

Meanwhile, Frankish rule offered opportunities for Orthodox secular elites. The Franks, particularly in the first decades of the First Kingdom, were far too few in number to control their rapidly expanding territories without the active support of the indigenous population. They needed men capable of collecting taxes, customs duties, market fees and other revenue. They needed men to enforce the laws and administer justice to the local communities. They needed a functioning economy, which meant not disrupting agricultural activities or interfering in existing trade patterns. Christopher MacEvitt, in his excellent work, *The Crusades and the Christian World of the East: Rough Tolerance,* demonstrates that many Orthodox Christians became wealthy landowners and merchants throughout the crusader states. Armenian lords were major landowners and vassals. Orthodox knights not only fought with the Franks; in some instances, they commanded Frankish knights and, in one case, rose to the prestigious position of marshal of Jerusalem.

While individuals might be exceptions, there is evidence of more widespread identification between natives and Franks. For example, native Orthodox Christians were patrons of both the Templars and Hospitallers. Chronicles in Syriac express admiration for the piety and charity of the Franks. Perhaps most poignant, two poems written in the late twelfth century by different Syriac authors lament the fall of the Frankish kingdom, revealing complete identification on the part of the native authors with the Franks, by referring to them as 'our people'.[10]

The greatest evidence of native support for the Franks, however, is the fact that the native (Arabic-, Syriac- and Armenian-speaking) population of Syria and Palestine contributed materially to the defence of the crusader kingdoms. On the one hand, Christians living both inside and outside the crusader states contributed to an effective intelligence network. We know anecdotally of native Christians acting as spies and scouts. At least one modern scholar claims 'the Frankish field intelligence was better than the Muslim one'.[11] Exactly what this intelligence network looked like, however, is unclear.

On the other hand, and of far more importance, was the contribution of native Christians to the military forces of the crusader states. This is especially surprising in light of the fact that, except for the Armenians, centuries of 'dhimmi' status had completely demilitarised the native population. Yet, in the period of Frankish rule, the native population formed a substantial portion of urban garrisons and contributed to the infantry of the field army. Steve Tibble in his recent study, *Crusader Armies*, argues that not only were there very few 'genuine crusaders' in the armies that defended Outremer, but that 'even local Franks were in a minority, marching in units with Armenian-speaking comrades, or with other native [Arabic-speaking] Christian soldiers'.[12]

Most significant and startling is the dominance of native Christians in the light cavalry, particularly mounted archers. The latter was an arm of cavalry unknown to the West but militarily essential in the Near East of the crusader period. In his excellent study of Frankish turcopoles, Yuval Harari demonstrates definitively that the term 'turcopole' did *not* refer to Muslim mercenaries, much less to apostate Muslims or the children of 'mixed marriages', as is so frequently alleged in popular literature. On the contrary, the turcopoles of the Frankish armies were predominantly Christians – native Christians. Harari also reveals that these troops made up, on average, 50 per cent of the cavalry of the crusader states in any engagement.[13] In short, native Christians were financially able to support the huge expense of training, equipping and maintaining a cavalryman and his mount, i.e. they were affluent and empowered, and they were in large numbers willing to fight – and die – for the crusader states.

Muslims

As mentioned above, whether Abbasids, Fatimids or Seljuks, the wealthy and educated Muslims who had formed the ruling class during 400 years of Muslim dominance were displaced by the new Frankish rulers. Those Muslim elites who survived the confrontation with the Franks moved to territories still under Muslim control. Left behind were the poor, the poorly educated and the non-political.

These residents were not only poor and powerless; they were fragmented and divided. Although the Muslims of southern Syria and Palestine were predominantly Sunnis, there was a strong Shia presence in northern Palestine and Transjordan (Tiberias, Nablus and Amman).

Shias were also numerous in Tripoli, Sidon and Beirut. Here too, close to the Ismaili stronghold of Alamut in the mountains of Lebanon, were communities of Ismailis. Relations between these different denominations of Islam were neither harmonious nor fraternal.

One might expect – and indeed the Muslims probably did expect – for the Franks to treat their Muslim subjects similarly to 'dhimmis' in Islamic regimes. Certainly, the Muslims in the crusader states were subject to extra taxes. Although not required to wear distinctive clothing, Muslims were prohibited from dressing 'like Franks'. In addition, severe penalties were placed on sexual contact between Christians and Muslims; whether the man was Muslim or Christian, he faced castration, while the woman, Christian or Muslim, had her nose amputated.

Nevertheless, overall the condition of Muslims in the crusader states was noticeably better than that of 'dhimmis' in Muslim countries. Unlike Christians and Jews under Muslim rule, there were no prohibitions on Muslims constructing houses of worship, engaging in religious rituals in public or the wearing of religious symbols. Indeed, functioning mosques are recorded in Tyre, Bethlehem and Acre, and in addition Muslims were allowed to pray in churches that had formerly been mosques. Muslims also enjoyed legal protections, as will be discussed under institutions (Chapter 4). There was no discrimination in housing nor prohibitions against riding horses or carrying arms. There was no institutionalised culture of humiliating and demeaning Muslims, although it is likely that individual Christians, mainly those who had suffered under Muslim rule, may have taken pleasure in the reverse of status.

The cumulative impact of this comparatively mild treatment was a Muslim population that remained remarkably docile throughout the Frankish period. There is not one recorded incident of rebellion or riots after the consolidation of Frankish rule in the 1120s. Even during Saracen invasions of Christian territory, there is no evidence of cooperation and collaboration on the part of Muslim inhabitants with the Saracen invaders, except in Jabala and Latakia, which welcomed Saladin in 1188. Perhaps even more astonishing, archaeological evidence of numerous unfortified farms, manors and rural villages shows the Christian population did not fear the Muslims living in their midst.

Perhaps Ibn Jubayr, a visitor from Muslim Spain in the late twelfth century, accurately assessed the situation of the Muslims in the crusader states when he wrote:

Their hearts have been seduced, for they observe how unlike them in ease and comfort are their brethren in the Muslim regions under their [Muslim] governors. This is one of the misfortunes afflicting the Muslims. The community bewails the injustice of a landlord of its own faith, and applauds the conduct of its opponent and enemy, the Frankish landlord, and is accustomed to justice from him.[14]

Jews and Samaritans

Although never official policy, the crusades unquestionably fostered antisemitism in Western Europe. Long before the first crusaders reached Jerusalem, Jewish communities in the Rhineland were attacked, and many Jews were massacred mercilessly. All subsequent crusades were likewise accompanied by outbreaks of violence against Jews in Western Europe. It may therefore come as a surprise that Jews in the crusader states suffered no persecution. Instead, the Franks mostly treated Jews the same as they treated Muslims, with rough tolerance.

In the early years of conquest, Jews were undoubtedly massacred, but not because of a targeted policy. They were killed alongside the Muslims when cities that resisted the crusaders fell to assault. Likewise, when cities agreed to terms, Jews were allowed to withdraw with their portable goods and chattels on the same terms as their Muslim neighbours. This led to a reduction in the number of Jews living in the Frankish territories in the immediate aftermath of conquest. Famously, Jews were prohibited from resettling in the city of Jerusalem.

Yet there is ample evidence that Jews returned to other cities – or never left at all. Records show large Jewish communities in Tyre and Acre throughout the Frankish era and smaller communities in Ascalon and elsewhere. Furthermore, there were at least two dozen villages occupied entirely by Jews in Galilee, between Tiberias and Nablus.

Like the Muslims, Jews throughout the crusader states were subject to extra taxes – just as they were forced to pay tribute as 'dhimmis' when living under Islamic rule. They were, however, allowed to practise their religion publicly without inhibition and, unlike under Muslim rule, could – and did – build new synagogues, notably in Nablus and near Safed. For the most part, they were also free to govern their own affairs and live in accordance with Jewish laws and customs without interference. There was no ghettoisation and not one recorded incident of communal violence against Jews. Thus, while their status was undoubtedly inferior to that of the Christians, the situation of Jews in the crusader states was markedly superior to the condition of Jews across Western Europe and, as with their Orthodox Christian neighbours, better than their status as 'dhimmis' in Islamic states.[15]

Meanwhile, the First Crusade had sparked a Jewish messianic movement. According to Joshua Prawer, 'in some communities the Jews sold their property and waited for the Messiah who would bring them to Jerusalem'.[16] Certainly, the establishment of the crusader states and regular trade and pilgrimage traffic between the Holy Land and Western Europe allowed European Jews to undertake the pilgrimage to Jerusalem and other sacred places in the Holy Land. The pilgrim traffic to the crusader states included a substantial portion of Jews – and like their Christian counterparts, many of them chose to stay in the Holy Land.

Jewish immigration to the Holy Land in the Frankish period led to a flourishing of Judaic culture. There were rabbinical courts in both Acre and Tyre (and possibly Tiberias), and Palestine was one of only three centres in the world for Talmudic Study. From the second quarter of the thirteenth century until its fall, Acre became a vibrant Jewish centre, a 'cross-section of the different communities of the Diaspora. The leading elements were Jews from Spain and from northern and southern France, in addition to eastern Jews, whether Palestinian-born or from neighbouring Moslem, countries.'[17]

Last but not least, there was still a sizeable Samaritan population. (Note: Samaritans accept only the first five books of the Old Testament as divinely inspired.) Although many Samaritans had been driven into exile across the Middle East, the centre of Samaritan worship and scholarship was in Nablus, which is where the largest Samaritan population was concentrated in the crusader era. A large number of Torah scrolls produced by Samaritans have survived from the crusader era, providing evidence of a flourishing of activities in this period.

The Franks of the Holy Land

Crusaders, Pilgrims, and Militant Monks: The Transient Population

The first Franks in the Holy Land were the participants of the First Crusade, and the vast majority of these returned to the West. In the succeeding

200 years, waves of crusaders periodically swept over the Holy Land. The overwhelming majority of these men likewise returned to their homes after the military campaign ended. In addition to the participants in organised military expeditions, individual fighting men made the journey to the Holy Land as 'armed pilgrims' for reasons of personal penance, sometimes voluntarily and other times imposed by a confessor. These men joined in ongoing military actions or participated in local operations before returning home when their penance was completed. All of these men can be called 'Franks' yet need to be distinguished from the permanent Frankish population of the crusader states because of the transient character of their stay in the Holy Land. While they temporarily swelled the military forces available to the armies of the Frankish states, they retained Western European perspectives and identities.

The same is true of the many unarmed pilgrims who flooded the Holy Land between 1100 and 1291. The numbers of pilgrims who made the long and dangerous journey to the Holy Land in this period are astounding. Just three years after Jerusalem returned to Christian control, more than 1,000 pilgrims were killed in a single storm when twenty-three pilgrim ships were wrecked off Jaffa harbour. Yet that was a period when most pilgrims travelled on cargo ships, which could take no more than fifty passengers. Within a few decades, special pilgrim ships with a passenger capacity of 200 were in operation, and by the thirteenth century, the pilgrim ships could take up to 1,500 passengers. The military orders transported 6,000 pilgrims per year from the port of Marseilles alone. Presumably they transported similar numbers from the Italian ports and Sicily, while the bulk of the pilgrim traffic traveled in commercial vessels. The number of religious tourists to the Holy Land may have been as high as 50,000 annually.

The pilgrim ships left Western Europe in two waves each year, one in the spring and another in the fall. Although ships generally travelled independently, within a few weeks of one another, hundreds of ships brought thousands of pilgrims to the ports of the Levant, predominantly Acre, but also Haifa, Caesarea and Jaffa. Pilgrims also came overland. They came from every Christian country in the world. There were Ethiopians, Egyptians and North Africans, Armenians and Georgians, Norwegians, Scotsmen, Hungarians, and citizens of the semi-independent Italian city-states and all the component parts of the Holy Roman Empire. Unlike the crusaders, who were by definition fighting men, many pilgrims were women. Some women accompanied their husbands, fathers or brothers; others came solo, many as widows and nuns. Male or female, most pilgrims remained in the East only one season, i.e. about six months; very few stayed more than a year. They contributed considerably to the local economy, yet they were visitors, not residents.

Members of the military orders were the last type of transient resident in the crusader states. The military orders were a new form of religious institution that enabled men to be both monks and knights. While members of these orders were expected to renounce all wealth, attend mass multiple times a day, fast, pray and eat in silence, and for the most part live in controlled communities segregated from the secular world (especially women), members were not required to give up the profession of arms. Rather, these orders were designed to capture the religious zeal of the time and funnel the fervor and energy of fighting men into religious channels. This spirit of militant Christianity gave birth to no fewer than seventeen military orders, eight on the Iberian Peninsula, two in what is now Italy, and two in German-speaking Europe in addition to the orders founded in the Holy Land. The most famous and powerful of the militant orders were the Templars, the Hospitallers, the Teutonic Knights and, to a lesser extent, the Knights of St Lazarus, all of which were established in the crusader states.

The individual history of these orders is beyond the scope of this book. The point here is that, although the raison d'être of both the Templars and Hospitallers was to defend the Holy Land and the Christian pilgrims that visited it, they were not subject to local ecclesiastical or secular authority; neither the king nor the patriarch could command the Templars, Hospitallers, or Teutonic Knights. Furthermore, while these orders maintained a standing presence in the Holy Land and garrisoned key castles, the individual members of these orders were drawn from around the world, and their sojourn in the Holy Land was temporary. The affiliation and loyalty of members of the militant orders were to their respective order, not the crusader states.

Italian Communes

As outlined earlier, the Italian maritime powers played a critical role in establishing Frankish rule over the coastal cities of the Levant and contributed materially to the viability of the crusader states. In exchange for

A Mediterranean Melting Pot

their help, these quintessentially commercial states obtained huge economic concessions. The Italian merchant states evinced the rapaciousness so often attributed to all crusaders, and they consistently placed commercial advantage above the interests of both crusading and the crusader states.

As early as 1000, just one year after the capture of Jerusalem, the Venetians obtained a treaty that set a pattern for all future agreements with the maritime cities. This granted to Venice a church, market and one-third of the booty of any city captured by the Franks if captured in the period during which their fleet was present – whether the Venetians participated or not. By 1124, the Venetians had negotiated a church, street, square and oven in every royal and baronial city in the kingdom, as well as the privilege to try all lawsuits involving Venetian citizens before Venetian courts. They had also obtained control of one-third of the cities of Tyre and Ascalon and were exempt from all taxes.

Despite these grandiose privileges and rights, the Italian presence in the early years of the Latin East amounted to little more than trading outposts with communal lodgings and warehouses. The so-called 'palazzos' of the Italian merchant communes consisted of warehouse and shop space on the ground floor (that individual merchants could rent out by the square foot), and lodgings on the upper floors, rented out by the week or month. In between were the offices, courts and reception rooms for the commune's administrative bodies. Rather than grand residences, the 'palazzos' were the practical consolidation of functional space needed by a transient population of merchants, agents, sea-captains and sailors. These men came only briefly to conduct business and returned 'home' – to Pisa, Genoa or Venice – as soon as possible. Their families remained in the home city, and in the 'off-season', the Italian quarters were practically deserted.

Only gradually did some of the less prominent members of this essentially transient community start to linger in the East. Only very exceptionally, such as in the case of the Embriachi family of Genoa, did prominent, aristocratic families establish a permanent presence in Outremer. Yet, men of lesser standing at home sometimes found it advantageous to settle, marry and acquire personal property in Outremer. As a result, by the end of the thirteenth century, there were some members of the Italian communes who were third or fourth-generation residents of Outremer. Despite this fact, they remained legally and emotionally the subjects of their home cities rather than the Kingdom of Jerusalem.

The Italians failed to develop any strong emotional tie to the cause of crusading or the Holy Land, being as happy to attack Christian cities (e.g. Zara and Constantinople) or obtain trading privileges in Muslim ones (e.g. Alexandria). Their primary concern was 'dominating the lines of communication and commerce between the eastern shores of the Mediterranean and Europe'.[18] This set them apart from the other residents, both native and immigrant. Certainly, the Italian communes retained their aloofness from the rest of crusader society. The right to their own courts was fiercely defended, as were their other privileges, particularly immunity from royal taxes and service. They remained enclaves of foreigners, rather like diplomatic or colonial enclaves in later centuries, living by their own laws, speaking their native language – and retaining their rivalries.

Settlers and 'Poulains'

The Franks of the Holy Land were neither the transient Western populations of crusaders, pilgrims and militant monks nor the representatives of Italian commercial empires. Instead, they were men and women of Western origin and Latin faith who made the Holy Land their home. In the beginning, their numbers were tiny. Only an estimated 15 per cent of the surviving crusaders, or as few as 2,000 to 4,000 men, remained in the East at the end of the First Crusade. However, immigration to the Holy Land began almost at once, so that by the end of King Baldwin IV's reign, an estimated 140,000 to 150,000 Western European immigrants had settled in Outremer.

At the apex of Frankish society were the nobles and knights, the feudal elite drawn from the second or third tier of the European nobility, mostly from France, Normandy, and the Holy Roman Empire. Kings, dukes and counts came on crusade, but rarely did they stay in the Holy Land. Their vassals, on the other hand, often did. Some of these men came from landowning families with regional influence and reputation, such as Godfrey de Bouillon, Raymond de Toulouse, Henri de Champagne and John de Brienne. Many others were the younger sons and brothers, or the castellans and stewards and household officials of the hereditary lords. Similarly, the majority of Outremer's knights, i.e. the knights that remained in the East, had not been fief-holders at home but rather household knights or freelancers; men without either land or livery.

Frankish society also had an exceptionally large clerical component. The Latin Church maintained two patriarchs (Jerusalem and Antioch), six archbishops, and twenty-three bishops in the crusader states – all with their respective cannons and clerical support apparatus. These clerics, however, represented only the tip of the iceberg. The Holy Land naturally attracted men with a religious vocation, and all the various monastic orders hastened to establish houses near the important shrines of Christianity. Thus, in addition to the militant orders, there were Augustine, Benedictine, Premonstratensian, Cistercian, Carmelite, Dominican and Franciscan houses operating in Frankish states by the end of the era. Altogether, 121 different monastic sites have been identified in the former Kingdom of Jerusalem. Also, 360 Latin churches have been discovered, roughly evenly divided between rural and urban locations.[19] In the immediate vicinity of Jerusalem, it is believed that approximately 50 per cent of the Frankish population was composed of churchmen.

The rest of the Frankish population, the commoners, were all freemen; there were no serfs in the crusader states – not even among the native populace in rural villages. Outremer's peasant farmers did not owe feudal services but instead paid fixed (and comparatively low) rents. Unlike Europe, where the 'commons' or 'Third Estate' was fractured, merchants and tradesmen consciously viewing themselves as superior to peasants, the non-noble Frankish population of the crusader states appears to have enjoyed a common identity as 'burgesses'. They were recognised as a separate and distinct 'order' as early as 1110. Furthermore, the burgesses, whether urban or rural, were integrated into Frankish society and government to an astonishing degree. Their presence and consent was considered necessary 'not only when the bourgeois were directly concerned'.[20] For example, the coronation ceremony of the Lusignan kings, which was probably modeled on that of the kings of Jerusalem, required the officiating prelate to ask the 'prelates, barons, knights, liegemen, burgesses and representatives of the people who were present for their approval' before anointing the monarch.[21] Prominent burgesses were also included on the witness lists of kings and nobles, something not usual at this time in Western Europe.

The notably higher status for the bourgeois is probably attributable to the fact that the origins of the class lay in the foot soldiers of the First Crusade; they had been the comrades-in-arms of the nobles who founded the crusader states. Those who came later as settlers constituted the yeoman class that contributed sergeants to the Frankish armies. They manned the garrisons of cities and castles and provided archers and pikemen to the feudal host. As will be discussed later under military institutions, the nature of warfare in the Near East in the twelfth century made knights exceptionally dependent on the infantry for survival and success. They could not afford to alienate men who were essential to their military survival and consequently accorded them an exceptional degree of respect.

In the countryside, the Franks founded hundreds of new settlements with distinctive features that distinguished them from the settlements of the natives. The architecture of these rural Frankish settlements was closer to the urban middle-class architecture of the same period in Western Europe. They were mostly multistorey structures constructed of stone, sometimes with undercrofts and staircases, usually with rooftop water collection and cisterns fed by piping, plastered interior walls, and often with chimney fireplaces. These features made them luxurious by European standards of the period and highlighted the affluence and self-esteem of the burgesses of Outremer.

Significantly, rural Frankish settlements were far more common than previously assumed. For more than a century, it was assumed that the Latin settlers were concentrated in the urban centres, predominantly on the coast of the Levant. The traditional nineteenth- and twentieth-century interpretation of Frankish society in the Holy Land hypothesised a decadent urban elite, collecting rents from oppressed native farmers. According to historians of the last century, the Franks were afraid to venture into the hostile environment of the countryside, not only because of an 'ever-present' Saracen threat but also because they were hated by their tenants and subjects. Some historians such as Joshua Prawer did not hesitate to draw parallels between Frankish rule in Palestine/Syria and apartheid in South Africa.

However, in his seminal work, *Frankish Rural Settlement in the Latin Kingdom of Jerusalem*, Professor Ronnie Ellenblum catalogued and collated findings to present a radically different picture. Ellenblum's work has since been complemented by additional studies, surveys and research on the part of a new generation of scholars. Together, this research confirms that the Frankish rural presence was much more widespread than had been previously assumed. More than 700 Frankish towns and villages have been identified, making it impossible to characterise Frankish society in the twelfth century as urban.

Furthermore, the bulk of these smaller towns and villages had no walls or fortifications of any kind, a clear indication that the Franks did not feel threatened. Far from fearing invasions, much less riots or violence on the part of their neighbours, the Franks felt secure enough to make major long-term investments. Alongside the hundreds of parish churches, manors and farmhouses, they built irrigation systems, terracing and roads.

Equally important, contemporary research shows the Frankish settlers did not displace the local inhabitants, expelling them from their land and houses. They did not deprive the native population of their land, livelihood or status. On the contrary, the documentary evidence demonstrates that the Franks were fastidious in recording and respecting the rights of the native inhabitants. Rather than displacing the locals, they built villages and towns in abandoned, previously unsettled areas or, more commonly, beside existing towns. The native pattern of settlement was to locate towns and villages in valleys, whereas the Franks built a castle/manor on hills or heights. Frankish farmers settled at the foot of this administrative centre. The older towns and villages were left intact, along with the ownership of the land cultivated by the native inhabitants. This meant the Frankish settlers were integrated with the native Christian population, often sharing churches as well as markets, ovens, mills and wine and oil presses. This evidence combined with the fact that there is no indication of residential segregation based on nationality or religion in the nineteen large cities in which the Franks lived discredits Prawer's thesis of an apartheid society.

Regarding economic status of the inhabitants of these villages, documents show that a high proportion of the Frankish settlers in these rural areas were skilled tradesmen. This is probably because most peasants (not to mention serfs) felt a strong bond to the land and little interest in emigration. In the Holy Land, the building trades such as carpenters, masons and blacksmiths, appear to be particularly well represented, but the data sample is too small to make sweeping generalisations. In addition to the building trades, silversmiths, bakers, butchers, vintners, drovers and herdsmen, cobblers and (former) servants have been found. Whatever these men had been in the past, in Outremer, they leased out farms and become free peasant farmers, except for those tradesmen such as the baker, butcher and tavern keeper, who supplied services to the local community.

The national origin of the settlers was nearly as diverse as their professions. French settlers, mainly from Southern France but also from Burgundy, Champagne and the Isle de France, were most numerous, and a northern dialect of French became the lingua franca of the mainland crusader states. However, documents show there were also significant numbers of immigrants from Italy and Spain as well as settlers from Scotland, England, Bohemia, Bulgaria and Hungary. Whatever their background, the immigrants to Outremer adopted for themselves the term first used by the Byzantines and Saracens to describe them. That is, 'Frangoi' (Greek) or 'al-Ifranj' (Arabic). The settlers translated these terms into Latin as 'Franci' and into French as 'Franc' and used it to describe themselves.

More modern waves of voluntary emigration to America, Australia and South Africa demonstrate that emigrants who choose to go to a 'new' country usually do so with a psychological willingness to create a new identity. In the case of the settlers in the Holy Land, integration and intermarriage with the local population further contributed to the creation of a new identity at an astonishing rate. Writing no later than 1127, the cleric, Fulcher of Chartres wrote:

> We who were occidentals have now become orientals ... .
> We have already forgotten the places of our birth ... . Some have taken wives not only of their own people but Syrians or Armenians or even Saracens who have obtained the grace of baptism ... . Words of different languages have become common property known to each nationality, and mutual faith unites those who are ignorant of their descent ... . He who was born a stranger is now as one born here; he who was born an alien has become a native.[22]

The children of these settlers, especially the children of mixed marriages, were no longer Europeans or crusaders. They considered themselves Franks. Later generations of crusaders referred to them by the derogatory term 'poulains', which is best translated as 'half-breeds'; it certainly held racist connotations. The racism of the Europeans remained a distinguishing feature of the transient population, yet it was strikingly not a characteristic of the Franks of Outremer.

Frankish Rule in Cyprus

The Greeks

Whereas the crusader states in Syria/Palestine were populated by a patchwork of minorities adhering to various faiths, the Kingdom of Cyprus at the time of the crusader conquest was a homogenous state inhabited almost exclusively by Greeks. There were only comparatively small Armenian, Maronite, Jacobite, Coptic, Ethiopian and other Christian communities. (The Armenian minority in Cyprus had the dubious distinction of being the only element of the Cypriot population that sided with Isaac Comnenus during Richard the Lionheart's campaign.) The Jewish, Samaritan and Muslim population in Cyprus in the twelfth century was insignificant. Greek was the primary language. Most important, Cyprus had never been fully conquered and occupied. As a result, while the population had paid tribute, it had not been subjected to systematic decimation and humiliation in the form of deportations, enslavement and Islamisation. In short, the Greeks of Cyprus had not yet been 'dhimmis'; a fate that did not overtake them until the Ottoman occupation.

As in Syria and Palestine, however, most of the former elites, in this case, the Byzantine aristocratic class, emigrated before the establishment of Frankish rule. The despot Isaac Comnenus had driven most of the Greek landowning class back to Constantinople with excessive taxes, expropriations and tyrannical behaviour before Richard I's conquest. Of those that remained, some left during the period of transition, while a few aristocratic families remained. Initially, the latter retained land and wealth but did not owe military service and were not feudal vassals. By the fifteenth century, however, even this distinction began to blur, and Greeks were enfeoffed.

In the era of the crusades, Cyprus was overwhelmingly agricultural, and rural inhabitants made up about 95 per cent of the population. The peasants of Cyprus were divided into two categories in accordance with Byzantine practice. There were 'paroikoi', unfree peasants tied to the land, similar to serfs in Western Europe, and 'francomati', free tenant farmers. The status of these lower classes was not substantially altered under Lusignan rule. For the most part, the new Frankish landowners employed Greek stewards on their estates. They also drew on the services of Greek 'jurats', who represented the interests of the communities, analogous to the 'rais' that represented the Muslim peasants in the Kingdom of Jerusalem. For the vast majority of peasants, the change of regime was hardly noticeable. While it was no worse than what had gone before, it was also not dramatically better, as in the case of former 'dhimmis' on the mainland. With time, increased prosperity brought benefits and growth in the urban population. This, in turn, increased the prices of agricultural products, benefitting the peasant class as well.

The small Greek middle-class was composed of professionals and bureaucrats who had administered the island for Constantinople ever since the Arabs were expelled in the tenth century. The civil servants were often members of the Orthodox clergy and sometimes belonged to ecclesiastical families with generations of government service. (Greek priests could marry, so a career in the church was often a family tradition). Others were remnants or lesser members of the old aristocracy. Otherwise, the middle class consisted of well-educated secular professionals such as doctors, lawyers, translators, accountants and the like.

All these men were invaluable to the Lusignans, who had the sense not only to employ them but to retain the very institutions that the Byzantines had used to administer the island. Thus, although the language of the Lusignan court was French, the Greek administrative class remained in place, evolving into a new Greek 'aristocracy of the pen'. By the fifteenth century, some members of this wealthy Greek elite had been accepted into the Frankish nobility, although conversion to Latin Christianity was necessary to hold a fief.

As in Latin Syria, the native – in this case, Greek – elites contributed to the defence of the realm by providing the vitally important horse archers of the Cypriot army, misleadingly called 'turcopoles'. These are recorded not only in royal service but in the service of individual lords, an indication of considerable prosperity for at least some rural Greek families. In the civil war against Emperor Frederick II's lieutenants (1229–32) and the Genoese war (1373–74), the Cypriot Greeks sided with the Franks against the outsiders from the Holy Roman Empire and Italy.

Culturally and socially, the Greeks remained dominant. Although a Latin church was established on the island, the Orthodox Church retained its hierarchy and clergy. The Latin Church siphoned off income in the form of land and tithes from the Latin landlords, but the vast majority of the population, including many wealthy patrons, remained Orthodox, enabling the Greek Orthodox Church to prosper throughout Lusignan rule. There was only one incident of persecution of Orthodox clergy in the entire Lusignan era. It was during a civil war in which the ruling king was a minor (and probably not in control) and possibly not present on the island at all.

Furthermore, there was no segregation based on religion or ethnicity. Greeks and Latins lived side-by-side, although the Italian communities voluntarily congregated in the coastal cities. The Latin feudal elite was most heavily concentrated in the capital of Nicosia, while the Italians were present primarily in the ports. Already by the late thirteenth century, the Latin population was commissioning Greek artists to paint icons for personal worship, while in the fourteenth century, the Greek Orthodox were happy to borrow Gothic style elements such as flying buttresses when building a new Orthodox cathedral.

Despite attempts by the pope to prevent intermarriage celebrated according to the Greek rites, by the fourteenth century, such marriages were so common that the Latin archbishop of Nicosia could only attempt to impose some restrictions over them. Likewise, although Latin remained the language of the High Court, Greek was the language of the streets and much diplomatic correspondence. Greeks learned French and Latin to advance their careers in the Lusignan bureaucracy, while the Franks learned Greek to conduct business on their estates, engage in trade and commerce and participate in cultural activities. Over time, a unique Cypriot dialect evolved, which borrowed many words from French and became the language of the island.

The overall satisfaction of the natives with Frankish rule is reflected in the fact that there was not a single uprising after the establishment of the Lusignan dynasty, nor are there any reports of Frankish landlords being murdered or held for ransom. This was not due to 'passivity' on the part of an oppressed population, which had risen twice in the short period between the departure of Richard I and the arrival of the Lusignans. Crete provides an illuminating comparison. Here, there were seven major rebellions against Latin (Venetian) rule in the thirteenth century and another three in the fourteenth century. In contrast to the Venetians, however, Lusignan rule was not designed to exploit a colony for the benefit of a distant power. The Lusignans lived in Cyprus among their people and identified with them.

The Franks

Just as the native population of Cyprus differed in character from the local inhabitants of Syria and Palestine, the Frankish elite that established itself on Cyprus also differed in subtle but significant ways from the elite of the earlier crusading states. Frankish rule was created on Cyprus not by crusaders who had slogged their way across Europe and Asia in a gruelling campaign inspired by religious fervor and characterised by hardship, attrition, and blood, but rather by the disinherited descendants of those first crusaders. The first Frankish lord, Guy de Lusignan, had the dubious honour of being responsible for the loss of the Kingdom of Jerusalem and, with it, the respect of his vassals and subjects. When he arrived in Cyprus in late 1192 with only a few supporters as landless as himself, he was a deposed king, unable to come to terms with his fate and still claiming his lost crown. Fortunately for Cyprus, Guy de Lusignan died within two years of his arrival, and his far more competent elder brother Aimery shaped the future kingdom.

Although not born in Outremer, Aimery had settled there around 1170. He married into one of the established families, the Ibelins, and rose to constable of the Kingdom under Baldwin IV. When Aimery stepped into his brother's shoes as lord of Cyprus in 1194, he was more 'poulain' than crusader. That meant he understood compromise, adaptation and survival in an 'alien' environment. The knights with Aimery were likewise men who had lost their lands in Syria, men who had once held fiefs in Oultrejourdain and Galilee, in Hebron, Bethsan, Nazareth or Ascalon – all the areas of the former Kingdom of Jerusalem that had not been regained in the course of the Third Crusade. They, too, knew that survival in the Near East required more than force of arms; it required cooperation with the native population and exchange with the surrounding states in the form of trade and diplomatic relations.

The Lusignans adopted a conscious policy of encouraging immigration. According to legend, Guy sent word to Armenia, Antioch, Acre and throughout the Latin East, saying he would give land generously to all settlers. Allegedly, Guy offered to reward not only knights but sergeants and burgesses as well, and the response included 'shoemakers, masons and Arabic scribes'.[23] The reference to Arabic scribes is notable as it highlights that Orthodox Christians also resettled in Cyprus after the establishment of Frankish rule. In particular, Maronites, Melkites and Armenians appear to have moved to Cyprus, settling on the coastal

A Mediterranean Melting Pot

plains, principally on the north of the island. These 'Syrian' immigrants were granted special status by the Lusignan kings, who recognised their service and loyalty to the Franks on the mainland and gave them special privileges. Immigrants from the mainland crusader states also continued to provide turcopoles and infantry for the armies of their Frankish lords.

In the second half of the thirteenth century, Cyprus experienced regular waves of refugees from Syria and Palestine as one metropolitan area after another fell to the Mamluks. The waves became a veritable 'flood' of refugees in 1291 when the last vestiges of the crusader states on the mainland collapsed under the Mamluk onslaught. Yet, like emigration to America centuries later, it was rarely the destitute and unskilled who escaped impending disaster. The bulk of the refugees from Latin Syria were noblemen, knights, affluent merchants and administrators, or, at least, skilled burgesses. By the end of the thirteenth century, the Franks and their Syrian allies made up approximately one-quarter of the population of Cyprus, which means they were between 35,000 and 40,000 strong.

Long before that flood, however, Cyprus benefitted from the arrival of the nobility of Outremer: the Bethsans, Gibelets, Montbeliards, Briennes, Montforts and, of course, the Ibelins. These were not landless families like most of the refugees, but powerful lords that retained sizeable landholdings and titles on the mainland. They had resources and interests outside the Kingdom of Cyprus, a fact that proved both advantageous and dangerous. On the one hand, their holdings in Syria enabled them to bring resources and men to Cyprus. On the other hand, their interests in Syria often led them to draw resources away from Cyprus to prop up their holdings on the mainland. Critically, and often overlooked, Cypriot fiefs held from these nobles enabled ordinary knights, who had lost their fiefs on the mainland, to maintain their character and status as landholders. The lack of a Syrian fief did not necessarily mean that a Frankish knight belonged to the landless urban class, living on the handouts from the crown; many knights such as Philip de Novare held land-fiefs from the Syrian barons – on Cyprus.

The kings of Cyprus, on the other hand, were surrounded not by jihadist states but by water. The fiefs they distributed brought their holders income and status without requiring huge investments in the construction, manning and maintenance of expensive fortresses. The nobles of Cyprus had money for the pleasures of life – hunting, hawking, patronage of the arts and church. For the kings, it meant that the nobility was not well-positioned to rebel and far more dependent on royal patronage for status and prestige.

The Cypriot nobles became famous for their wealth and love of pleasure. One visitor in the mid-fourteenth century claimed that the Cypriot knights and nobles were the richest in the world. He noted that the count of Jaffa (a Cypriot, despite the title) had 500 hunting dogs, while others had dozens of falconers and some kept leopards for hunting. They also engaged in frequent tournaments. The Lusignan palace in Nicosia was considered one of the finest in the medieval world, with a great throne room, many golden ornaments, tapestries, paintings, organs, clocks, multiple baths and fountains, gardens and a menagerie.[24] Unfortunately, the Lusignan palaces were destroyed during the Ottoman occupation, and all that remains are fragments now preserved in the museums of Cyprus.

Slaves

No description of medieval Cyprus is complete without reference to slavery. Unlike the Latin Church, the Orthodox Church did not condemn the slavery of fellow Christians. In the crusader states on the mainland, Latin dominance was strong enough to eliminate Christian slavery despite tolerating the enslavement of Muslims, primarily captives. In Cyprus, however, the custom of owning slaves was so widespread among the native elites that the 'tolerance' of the Lusignans shamefully extended to the acceptance of Christian slavery.

Chapter 6

The 'Ideal Feudal State'
Institutions of Government, Justice, Finance, Defence and Religion

Feudal Superstructure: Kings, Barons and the High Court

Confronted with the need to institutionalise their control of conquered territories, the founders of the crusader states recreated familiar Western European structures. The crusader states thus embody the state of European feudalism at the start of the twelfth century. Simplified, this was a hierarchical pyramid based on mutually beneficial agreements between the king and his barons, the barons and their knights and the knights and their peasants. Feudal oaths bound both parties and established duties on the two sides. At this time, the duties of both kings and vassals had become complex, yet kings had not yet started to amass the kind of power that enabled them to become absolute monarchs. While kings in Western Europe centralised and consolidated power in the succeeding two centuries, feudalism in the crusader states remained comparatively stable, more corporate and more diffused. In other words, the feudal law applied in the Kingdom of Jerusalem represented a developed but not yet decadent form of feudalism.

More astonishing, the feudal laws of Jerusalem were codified. After the near loss of the kingdom in the aftermath of Hattin, the political-legal leadership of the early thirteenth century sought to reconstruct institutions by capturing and recording the collective memory of a generation. To that end, scores of educated noblemen undertook to write down and comment on the laws and the customs which had formed the legal basis for governing the pre-Hattin Kingdom of Jerusalem. While not the same thing as a formal collection of laws, these works combined provide a remarkably detailed description of feudal law and practice in the twelfth- and thirteenth-century crusader states. Based on these documents, historians have described the Kingdom of Jerusalem as an 'ideal' feudal state. Yet, while the state was a feudal state 'par excellence', it was also unique with many unique features unknown to feudal kingdoms of Western Europe.

First Among Equals: the 'Elected' Kings of Jerusalem

Perhaps the most obvious curiosity of the Kingdom of Jerusalem was that the kings were 'elected' rather than succeeding strictly on the basis of hereditary right. A legal scholar writing in the kingdom in the thirteenth century claimed unequivocally: 'When this land was conquered it was by no chief lord, but by … the movement of pilgrims … They made a lord by agreement and by election and they gave him the lordship of the kingdom.'[1] The terminology 'lordship of the kingdom' is significant because it implies a position less than that of a sovereign. The king of Jerusalem was viewed by his subjects as no more than 'first among equals', and – critically – as such, was no less subject to the law than they.

'The Law', however, was still inchoate and evolving. In Godfrey's short reign, the consuming priority was defending the territory captured. With few men and no financial resources to hire huge mercenary armies, Godfrey adopted the familiar European practice of granting fiefs to men in return for military support; it was effectively a revival of the primitive feudalism of the early Middle Ages. Godfrey gave away land – often land he had not yet conquered – to those men willing and able to recruit enough fighting men to secure said territory. The men to whom Godfrey gave land recruited their armies by promising land in fief to themselves, creating the traditional pyramid of feudal obligations. For the first few decades, however, the military situation remained so precarious that many fiefs fell vacant, reverting to the crown. These were granted to new lords – often more than once. It was not until the middle of the twelfth century that lordships had stabilised and became largely hereditary among a small number of resident families.

Nevertheless, the vulnerability of the kingdom in those early decades established other precedents that shaped the balance of power between kings and lords. The kings enjoyed the prestige of being kings, the highest-ranking noble in the kingdom and held extensive royal domains around Jerusalem, as well as directly controlling the cities of Acre and Tyre, and (intermittently) Jaffa and Ascalon, Nablus (Samaria) and Hebron, the latter three in personal union with the crown. These great royal fiefs gave the kings of Jerusalem financial resources far beyond that of any individual vassal, and with these, the ability to create money-fiefs or hire mercenaries. Furthermore, the king summoned and commanded the feudal armies of the kingdom. He summoned parliament and other assemblies. Lastly, he controlled church and state appointments, thereby retaining the ability to obtain clients through patronage.

However, from the very inception of the realm, the kings of Jerusalem were extraordinarily dependent upon the cooperation, approval and counsel of their vassals. The geopolitical situation necessitated powerful marcher baronies as the first line of defence for the religious heartland around Jerusalem. These, in turn, needed mighty castles with sizeable garrisons of sergeant-archers and mobile defence forces composed of knights and turcopoles. These baronial armies, while essential to the defence of the realm, could also be turned against the king if their lords became disaffected. As a result, the kings of Jerusalem always had to tread warily not to alienate or offend the important magnates. Those that did, such as Fulk and Frederick II, soon found they had a civil war on their hands. The situation was, as one English scholar summarised it, 'one which the English barons tried to establish when they forced Magna Carta on their reluctant monarch'.[2]

In short, the kings of Jerusalem had less power than contemporary European monarchs such as Philip II of France or Henry II, Richard I or Edward I of England. For example, they could only enter the territory of their vassals in times of war or for assemblies. They did not have the guardianship of minor heirs and heiresses, which means they could not use them as tools of patronage. They did not receive 'relief' (a feudal payment) on the succession of heirs to a fief. They did not have a monopoly on minting money or collecting salvage.

Yet, without doubt, the most exceptional baronial privilege was that Jerusalem's constitution recognised a vassal's legal right to withdraw service, i.e. to rebel, if the king failed to fulfil his feudal obligations. In theory, the process entailed a vassal bringing charges against the king before the High Court (discussed below), and – should the king fail to abide by a judgement of that court in the vassal's favour —the right to withdraw feudal service to the crown. While this right is implicit in other feudal states, what made Jerusalem exceptional was the vassal's right to call upon his peers to support him. That is, the king's failure to respect a judgement of the High Court could trigger a collective feudal 'strike'.

Historians have pointed out that this rarely worked in practice because solidarity among vassals on any issue was rarely sufficient to make collective action possible. Even where there was a strong consensus, powerful monarchs could employ mercenaries to circumvent the impact of their vassals' refusal to render service. This is precisely what happened during the war between the barons and Frederick II in the early thirteenth century. Yet there are several instances in the history of the kingdom when the barons acting together forced Jerusalem's kings to alter their policies – without civil war. Baldwin I, for example, was forced to repudiate Adelaide of Sicily. Likewise, it was the refusal of the knights and nobles to crown Agnes de Courtenay that forced Amalric to renounce her. Another case in point was the collective refusal of Jerusalem's knights and nobles to tolerate Guy de Lusignan as regent in late 1183. Baldwin IV was forced to dismiss Guy, resume personal governance and physically lead the feudal host to the relief of Kerak. Indeed, even Frederick II was ultimately brought to his knees by the opposition of his barons, despite the deployment of mercenaries.

The position of the kings of Cyprus was entirely different. The conquest of Cyprus was carried out under the unified command of the king of England. He sold his conquest to Guy de Lusignan, who bequeathed it to his closest male heir in strict accordance with the principles of French primogeniture. Thereafter, the kingdom remained a dynastic possession of the Lusignans. The traditions of Jerusalem found only a faint symbolic echo in the coronation ceremony of the Cypriot kings; before the coronation, the officiating cleric asked the assembled clergy, nobles, knights and commons for their approval of the monarch.

Barons, Knights and the High Court: The Powerful Vassals of Outremer

In the crusader states, there were a variety of different kinds of fiefs. There were land fiefs ('fié en terre') familiar from Western Europe where a knight received one or more rural villages (casal), producing sufficient income to finance the maintenance of one or more knights (i.e. the knight[s], including their squires, horses, arms and armour). In the crusader states, however, there were also several money fiefs ('fié en besans'). These likewise ensured that a knight had sufficient income to maintain himself, horses, equipment and status, but the income was derived from royal revenue. This could be a stipend directly paid from the king's treasury, similar to a retainer for household knights, but in this case, hereditary. Or it might be something more exotic, such as the tribute owed by the Bedouins, or the revenue collected from markets or bazaars, or a portion of the income from economic monopolies such as salt extraction. It was common across the crusader states for individual knights to have mixed fiefs, that is, to draw income from both land and money fiefs, a practice that suggests knights sought to diversify revenue streams for their financial security. Such diversification was also applied geographically after the conquest of Cyprus. Nearly all lords (and probably many knights) held fiefs on the mainland and Cyprus.

Another unique feature of fiefs in the Holy Land was that there were many 'sergeantries', that is, fiefs owing not knights' service, but rather service of a sergeant. Many of the 'sergeantries' were held by non-immigrant and non-Latin tenants. Finally, the laws of the crusader states distinguished between traditional fiefs granted or inherited and fiefs of conquest ('fié de conquest'). While the former had to be bequeathed to the rightful heirs in accordance with the laws of the land, fiefs of conquest could be disposed of at will, bypassing legal heirs. One generation later, however, they were no longer viewed as fiefs of conquest and had to pass to the legal heirs.

The inheritance laws in the crusader states were shaped by the overriding imperative to ensure an adequate military force for the defence of the realm. To prevent the concentration of fiefs in one pair of hands with the effect of denying the kingdom needed fighting men, the inheritance of more than one fief was initially prohibited. However, the laws were soon modified to allow a man to inherit and hold more than one fief, on the condition he could meet all feudal obligations by financing knights for the fiefs he did not represent in-person. This could be done through sub-enfeoffing, i.e. creating 'rear vassals' or retaining knights (hiring knights for wages). It was common practice for a knight holding multiple fiefs to divide them among his heirs at his death, but this was not a legal requirement. An alternative was for the knight to designate his eldest son as his heir and for the heir to enfeoff his siblings as rear-tenants. Significantly, however, an heir who was physically or mentally incapable of rendering military service could be passed over in favour of a sibling.

Surprisingly for states so dependent upon feudal service for defence, female inheritance was recognised and rigorously upheld.

The explanation is likely the exceptionally high mortality rate among men, which often made women the standard-bearers of their families. However, an heiress between the ages of 12 and 60 was required to have a husband capable of performing military service. If not already married, heiresses 12 and older were summoned by their lord and given a choice between three candidates of comparable rank. Refusal to marry one of these candidates theoretically resulted in the loss of the fief for one year and a day, after which the process was repeated. In practice, some heiresses, such as Constance of Antioch, got away with rejecting candidates without forfeiting their fiefs.

The duties of vassals in Outremer were first and foremost military service, and unlike in England, military service could not be commuted to a monetary payment (scutage). Furthermore, fief-holders were required to be physically present in the kingdom; absence of more than one year resulted in forfeiture – again to ensure they would meet feudal obligations. Military service in the Holy Land could be commanded for up to one year, a length of service far in excess of the usual forty days familiar from England and France. Military service included garrison duty for castles and cities and mustering with the feudal army for mobile operations.

Non-military feudal obligations included maintaining law and order within the realm by participating in inquiries into crimes, delivering summonses and providing counsel to pleaders and defendants before the lower courts. Last but not least, vassals holding knight's fiefs (but not sergeantries) were required to participate in the government of the realm by sitting on the High Court, which is significant and unique to the crusader kingdoms. In most kingdoms, only selected or elected representatives of the knightly class sat in parliament. In the Kingdoms of Jerusalem and Cyprus, on the other hand, the number of knights was sufficiently small for all to be required to give council via the High Court. Thus, the thirteenth-century jurist Geoffrey Le Tor wrote:

> All liege-knights of the king ... are peers, whoever they are, high or low, poor or rich ... they protect one another in their rights and maintain one another in law and also as they are called upon to act as counsel, to give judgements and issue recorts. And the speech of one carries as much force as that of any of the others.[3]

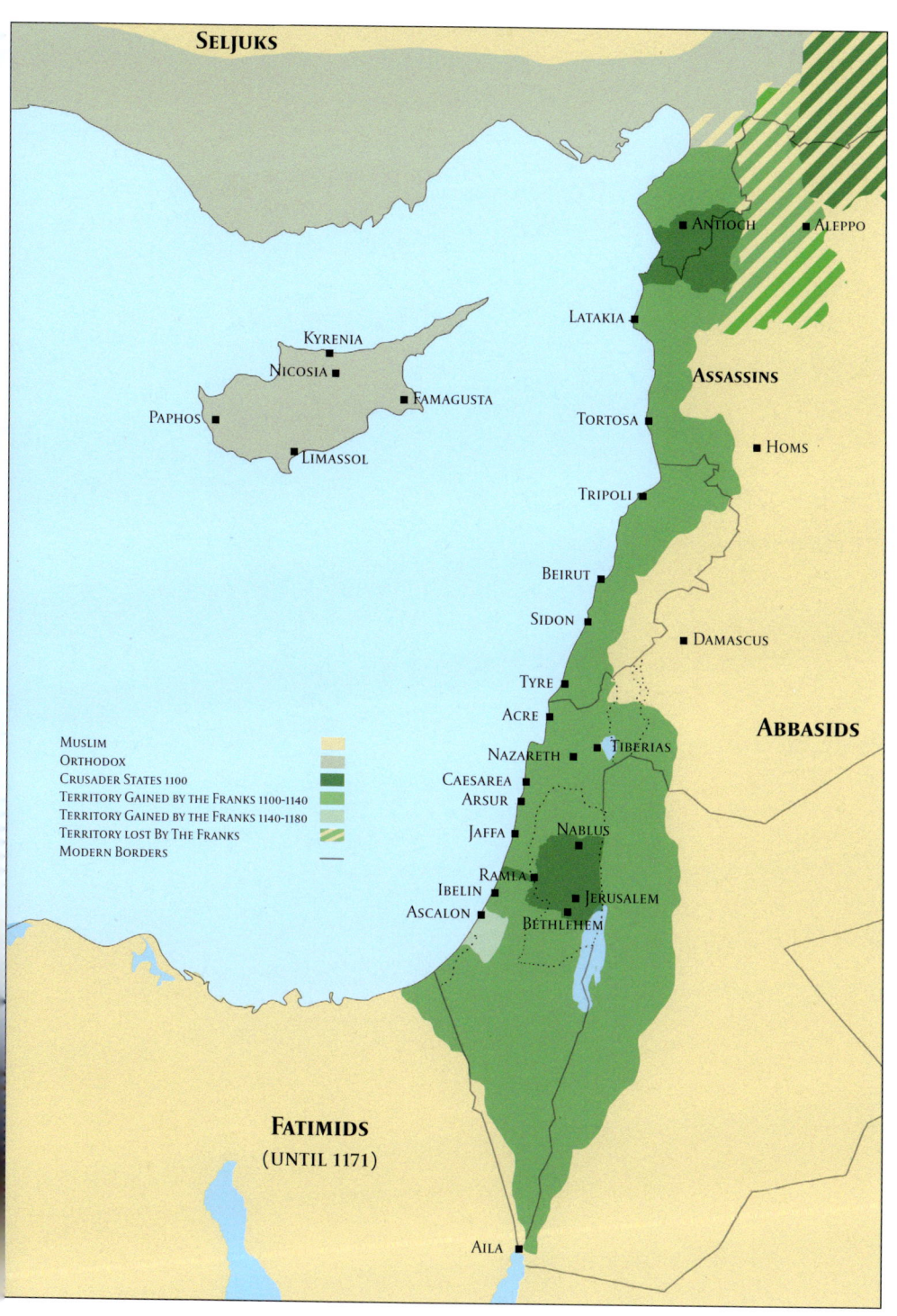

The Crusader States 1100–1180.

The Crusader States 1190–1240.

The Baronies of the Kingdom of Jerusalem in the Twelfth Century.

Knights owed to the Feudal Army 1180

Barons: 514
Beirut: 21
Sidon: 50
Toron: 18
Galilee: 100
Caymont: 6
Caesarea: 25
Bethsan: 25
Sebaste: 24
Nablus: 85
Jaffa: 25
Ascalon: 25
Ramla & Mirabel: 40
Ibelin: 10
Transjordan: 40
Hebron: 20

Bishops: 16
Nazareth: 6
Lydda: 10

Royal Domain: 149
Jerusalem: 41
Acre: 80
Tyre: 28

TOTAL: 679*

*Source: John of Jaffa's Le Livre des Assises, Chapter XII. As noted by Peter Edbury, some discrepancies occur in the original, e.g. the knights of neither Arsuf nor Scandaleon are listed, but the baronies existed based on other data. In short, this represents only an approximation of the knights of the feudal army.

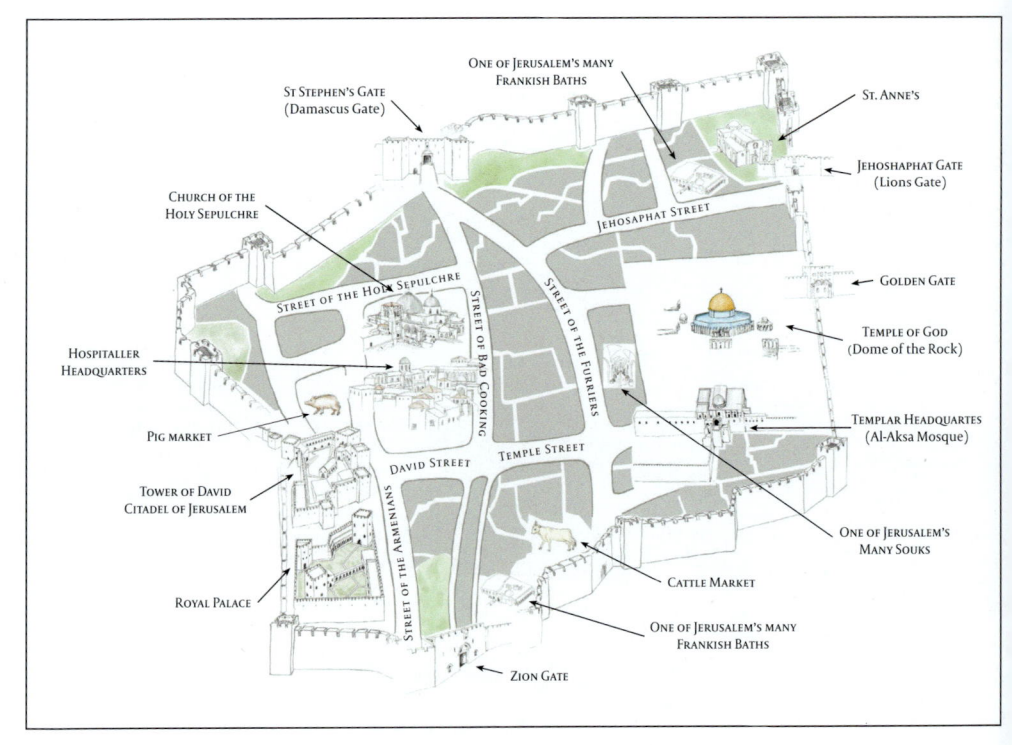

Jerusalem City Map Twelfth Century.

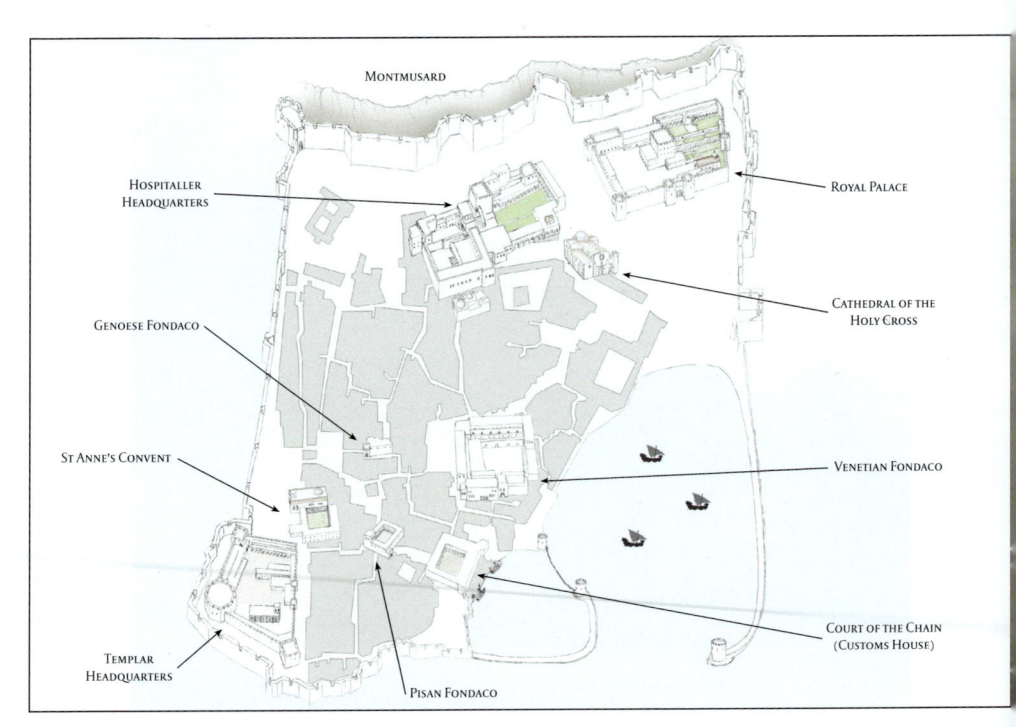

Acre City Map Thirteenth Century.

Rulers of Jerusalem in the Twelfth Century

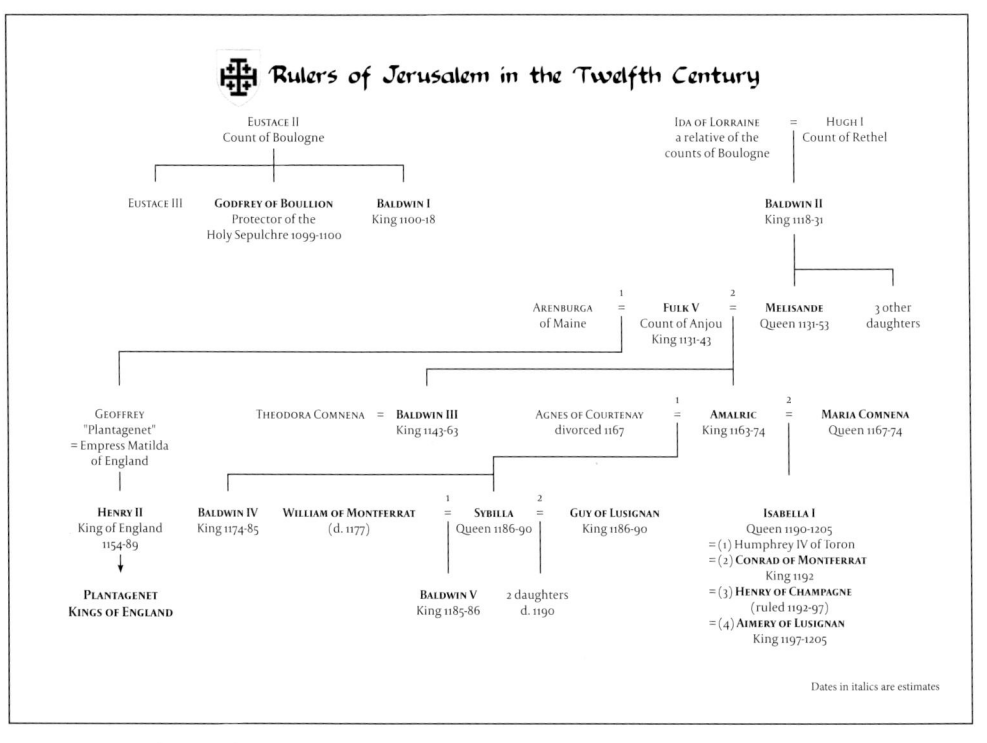

- **Eustace II**, Count of Boulogne
  - Eustace III
  - **Godfrey of Bouillon**, Protector of the Holy Sepulchre 1099-1100
  - **Baldwin I**, King 1100-18

- **Ida of Lorraine**, a relative of the counts of Boulogne = **Hugh I**, Count of Rethel
  - **Baldwin II**, King 1118-31
    - (1) **Arenburga** of Maine = **Fulk V**, Count of Anjou, King 1131-43 = (2) **Melisande**, Queen 1131-53
    - 3 other daughters

- **Geoffrey "Plantagenet"** = Empress Matilda of England
  - **Henry II**, King of England 1154-89
  - **Plantagenet Kings of England**

- **Theodora Comnena** = **Baldwin III**, King 1143-63

- **Agnes of Courtenay** divorced 1167 = (1) **Amalric**, King 1163-74 = (2) **Maria Comnena**, Queen 1167-74
  - **Baldwin IV**, King 1174-85
  - (1) **William of Montferrat** (d. 1177) = **Sybilla**, Queen 1186-90 = (2) **Guy of Lusignan**, King 1186-90
    - **Baldwin V**, King 1185-86
    - 2 daughters d. 1190
  - **Isabella I**, Queen 1190-1205
    - = (1) Humphrey IV of Toron
    - = (2) **Conrad of Montferrat**, King 1192
    - = (3) **Henry of Champagne** (ruled 1192-97)
    - = (4) **Aimery of Lusignan**, King 1197-1205

Dates in italics are estimates

House of Jerusalem Twelfth Century.

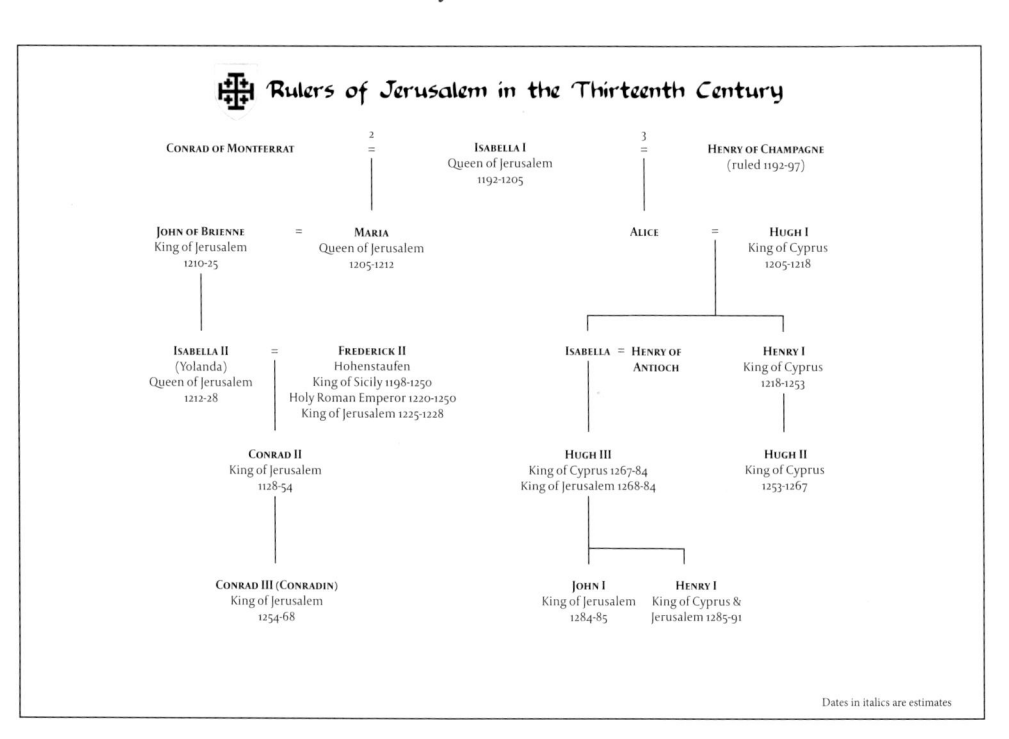

Rulers of Jerusalem in the Thirteenth Century

- **Conrad of Montferrat** = (2) **Isabella I**, Queen of Jerusalem 1192-1205 = (3) **Henry of Champagne** (ruled 1192-97)

- **John of Brienne**, King of Jerusalem 1210-25 = **Maria**, Queen of Jerusalem 1205-1212

- **Alice** = **Hugh I**, King of Cyprus 1205-1218

- **Isabella II (Yolanda)**, Queen of Jerusalem 1212-28 = **Frederick II** Hohenstaufen, King of Sicily 1198-1250, Holy Roman Emperor 1220-1250, King of Jerusalem 1225-1228
  - **Conrad II**, King of Jerusalem 1128-54
    - **Conrad III (Conradin)**, King of Jerusalem 1254-68

- **Isabella** = **Henry of Antioch**
  - **Hugh III**, King of Cyprus 1267-84, King of Jerusalem 1268-84
    - **John I**, King of Jerusalem 1284-85
    - **Henry I**, King of Cyprus & Jerusalem 1285-91

- **Henry I**, King of Cyprus 1218-1253
  - **Hugh II**, King of Cyprus 1253-1267

Dates in italics are estimates

House of Jerusalem Thirteenth Century.

House of Cusignan in Outremer to 1267

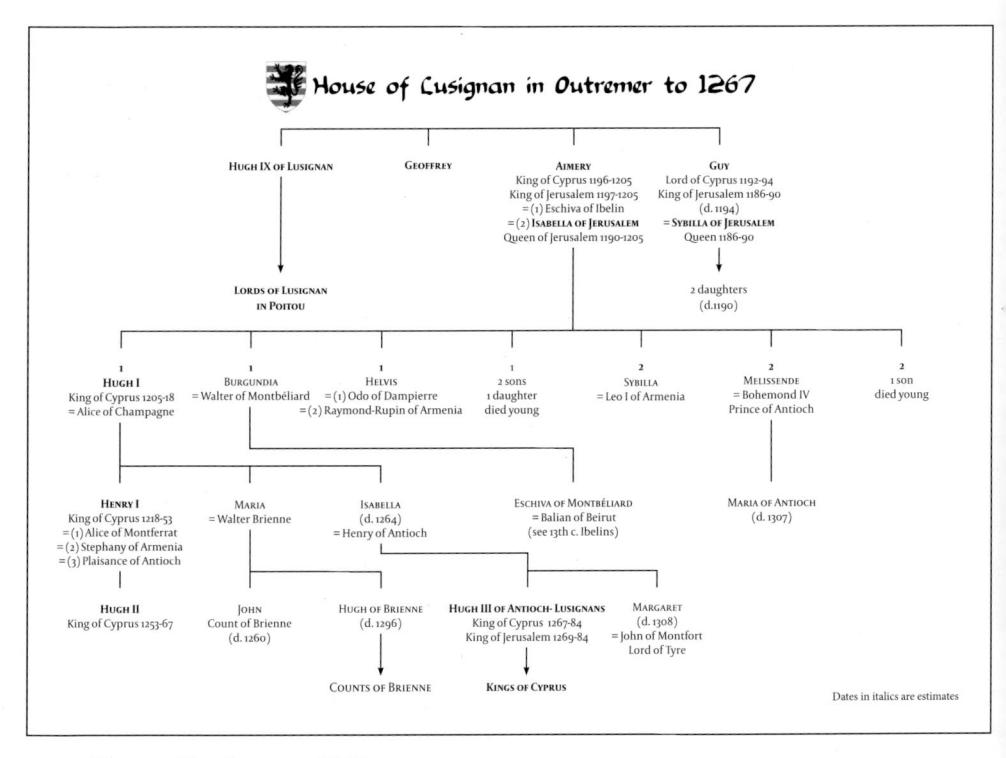

- **HUGH IX OF LUSIGNAN**
  - ↓
  - **LORDS OF LUSIGNAN IN POITOU**

- **GEOFFREY**

- **AIMERY**
  King of Cyprus 1196-1205
  King of Jerusalem 1197-1205
  = (1) Eschiva of Ibelin
  = (2) **ISABELLA OF JERUSALEM**
  Queen of Jerusalem 1190-1205

- **GUY**
  Lord of Cyprus 1192-94
  King of Jerusalem 1186-90
  (d. 1194)
  = **SYBILLA OF JERUSALEM**
  Queen 1186-90

Children of Aimery (1) and Guy (2):

1 HUGH I	1 BURGUNDIA	1 HELVIS	1 2 sons 1 daughter died young	SYBILLA	2 MELISSENDE	2 1 son died young
King of Cyprus 1205-18 = Alice of Champagne	= Walter of Montbéliard	= (1) Odo of Dampierre = (2) Raymond-Rupin of Armenia		= Leo I of Armenia	= Bohemond IV Prince of Antioch	

2 daughters (d. 1190) — children of Guy

Next generation:

- **HENRY I** King of Cyprus 1218-53
  = (1) Alice of Montferrat
  = (2) Stephany of Armenia
  = (3) Plaisance of Antioch
- **MARIA** = Walter Brienne
- **ISABELLA** (d. 1264) = Henry of Antioch
- **ESCHIVA OF MONTBÉLIARD** = Balian of Beirut (see 13th c. Ibelins)
- **MARIA OF ANTIOCH** (d. 1307)

Next generation:

- **HUGH II** King of Cyprus 1253-67
- **JOHN** Count of Brienne (d. 1260)
- **HUGH OF BRIENNE** (d. 1296) → COUNTS OF BRIENNE
- **HUGH III OF ANTIOCH-LUSIGNANS** King of Cyprus 1267-84 King of Jerusalem 1269-84 → KINGS OF CYPRUS
- **MARGARET** (d. 1308) = John of Montfort Lord of Tyre

Dates in italics are estimates

House of Lusignan to 1267.

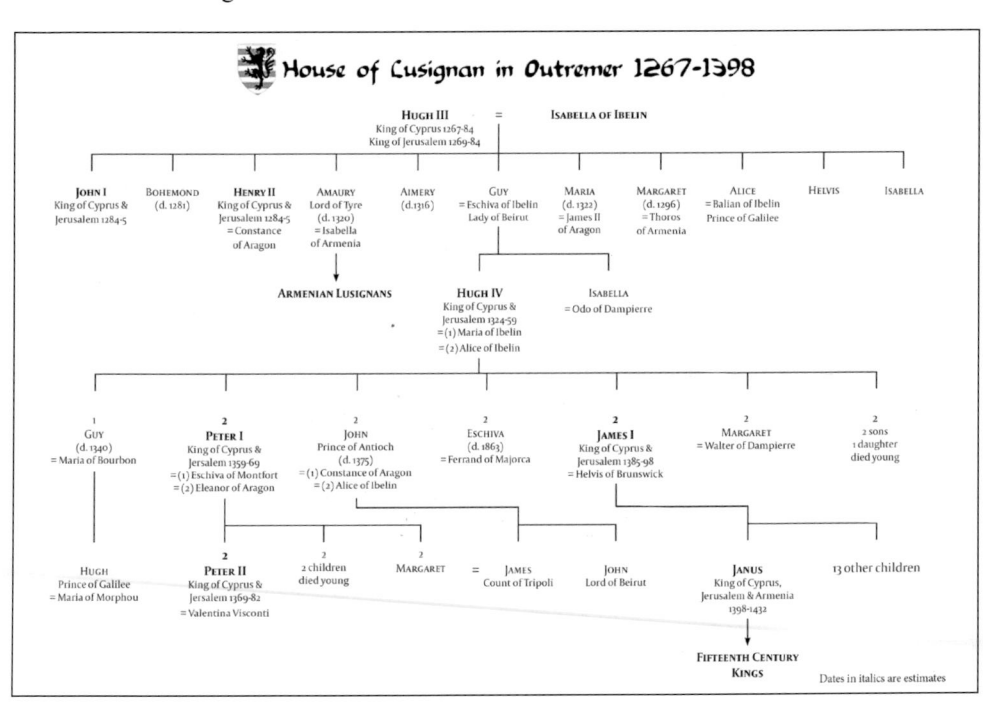

House of Cusignan in Outremer 1267-1398

HUGH III = **ISABELLA OF IBELIN**
King of Cyprus 1267-84
King of Jerusalem 1269-84

Children:

- **JOHN I** King of Cyprus & Jerusalem 1284-5
- **BOHEMOND** (d. 1281)
- **HENRY II** King of Cyprus & Jerusalem 1284-5 = Constance of Aragon
- **AMAURY** Lord of Tyre (d. 1320) = Isabella of Armenia → ARMENIAN LUSIGNANS
- **AIMERY** (d. 1316)
- **GUY** = Eschiva of Ibelin Lady of Beirut
- **MARIA** (d. 1322) = James II of Aragon
- **MARGARET** (d. 1296) = Thoros of Armenia
- **ALICE** = Balian of Ibelin Prince of Galilee
- **HELVIS**
- **ISABELLA**

Children of Guy:
- **HUGH IV** King of Cyprus & Jerusalem 1324-59
  = (1) Maria of Ibelin
  = (2) Alice of Ibelin
- **ISABELLA** = Odo of Dampierre

Children of Hugh IV:

| 1 GUY (d. 1340) = Maria of Bourbon | 2 PETER I King of Cyprus & Jerusalem 1359-69 = (1) Eschiva of Montfort = (2) Eleanor of Aragon | 2 JOHN Prince of Antioch (d. 1375) = (1) Constance of Aragon = (2) Alice of Ibelin | 2 ESCHIVA (d. 1363) = Ferrand of Majorca | 2 JAMES I King of Cyprus & Jerusalem 1385-98 = Helvis of Brunswick | 2 MARGARET = Walter of Dampierre | 2 2 sons 1 daughter died young |

Next generation:

- **HUGH** Prince of Galilee = Maria of Morphou
- 2 **PETER II** King of Cyprus & Jerusalem 1369-82 = Valentina Visconti
- 2 2 children died young
- 2 **MARGARET** = **JAMES** Count of Tripoli
- **JOHN** Lord of Beirut
- **JANUS** King of Cyprus, Jerusalem & Armenia 1398-1432 → FIFTEENTH CENTURY KINGS
- 13 other children

Dates in italics are estimates

House of Lusignan post-1267.

House of Ibelin in the Twelfth Century

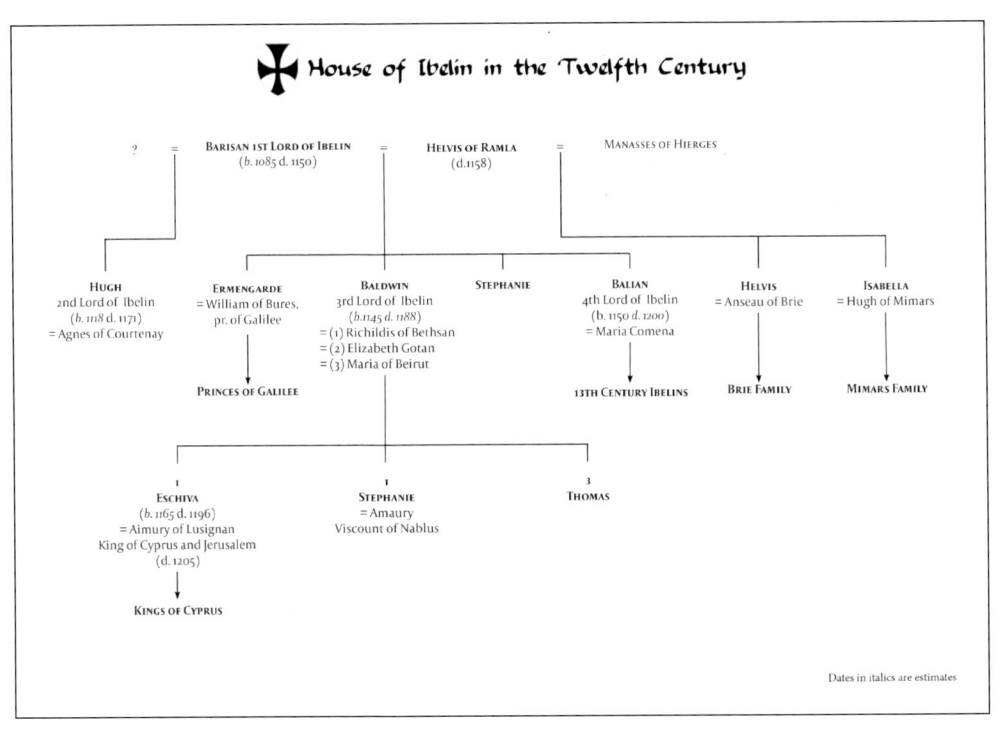

- ? = **BARISAN 1ST LORD OF IBELIN** (b. 1085 d. 1150) = **HELVIS OF RAMLA** (d. 1158) = **MANASSES OF HIERGES**

Children:
- **HUGH**, 2nd Lord of Ibelin (b. 1118 d. 1171) = Agnes of Courtenay
- **ERMENGARDE** = William of Bures, pr. of Galilee → PRINCES OF GALILEE
- **BALDWIN**, 3rd Lord of Ibelin (b. 1145 d. 1188) = (1) Richildis of Bethsan = (2) Elizabeth Gotan = (3) Maria of Beirut
- **STEPHANIE**
- **BALIAN**, 4th Lord of Ibelin (b. 1150 d. 1200) = Maria Comena → 13TH CENTURY IBELINS
- **HELVIS** = Anseau of Brie → BRIE FAMILY
- **ISABELLA** = Hugh of Mimars → MIMARS FAMILY

Children of Baldwin:
- (1) **ESCHIVA** (b. 1165 d. 1196) = Aimury of Lusignan, King of Cyprus and Jerusalem (d. 1205) → KINGS OF CYPRUS
- (1) **STEPHANIE** = Amaury, Viscount of Nablus
- (3) **THOMAS**

Dates in italics are estimates

House of Ibelin Twelfth Century.

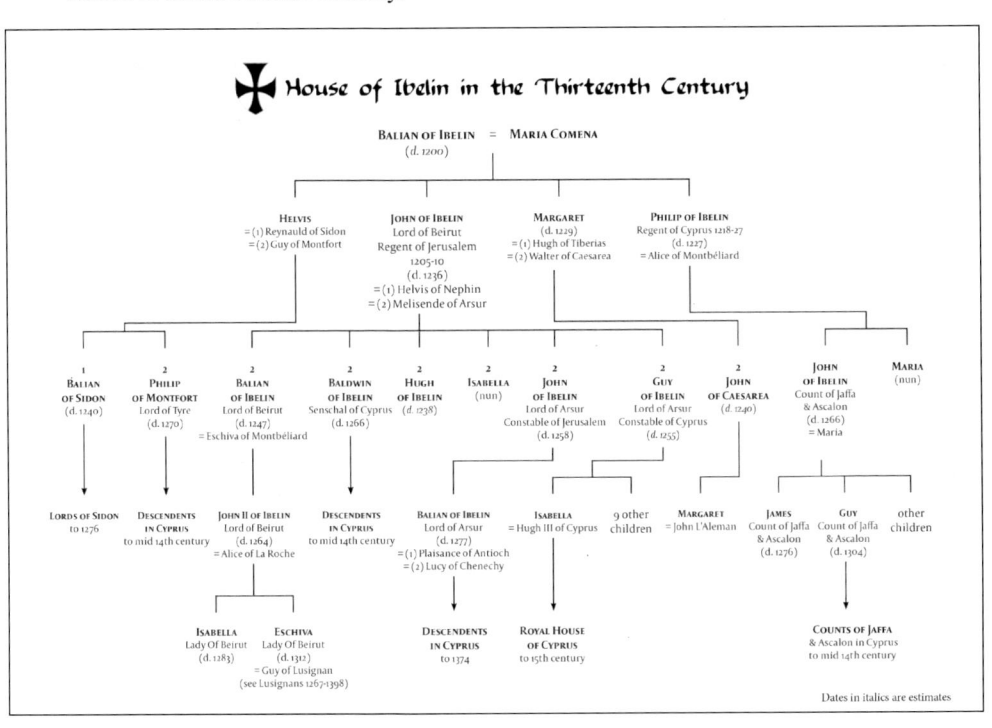

House of Ibelin in the Thirteenth Century

BALIAN OF IBELIN (d. 1200) = **MARIA COMENA**

Children:
- **HELVIS** = (1) Reynauld of Sidon = (2) Guy of Montfort
- **JOHN OF IBELIN**, Lord of Beirut, Regent of Jerusalem 1205-10 (d. 1236) = (1) Helvis of Nephin = (2) Melisende of Arsur
- **MARGARET** (d. 1229) = (1) Hugh of Tiberias = (2) Walter of Caesarea
- **PHILIP OF IBELIN**, Regent of Cyprus 1218-27 (d. 1227) = Alice of Montbéliard

Grandchildren:
- (1) **BALIAN OF SIDON** (d. 1240) → LORDS OF SIDON to 1276
- (2) **PHILIP OF MONTFORT**, Lord of Tyre (d. 1270) → DESCENDENTS IN CYPRUS to mid 14th century
- (2) **BALIAN OF IBELIN**, Lord of Beirut (d. 1247) = Eschiva of Montbéliard
- (2) **BALDWIN OF IBELIN**, Senschal of Cyprus (d. 1266) → DESCENDENTS IN CYPRUS to mid 14th century
- (2) **HUGH OF IBELIN** (d. 1238)
- (2) **ISABELLA** (nun)
- (2) **JOHN OF IBELIN**, Lord of Arsur, Constable of Jerusalem (d. 1258)
- (2) **GUY OF IBELIN**, Lord of Arsur, Constable of Cyprus (d. 1255)
- (2) **JOHN OF CAESAREA** (d. 1240)
- **JOHN OF IBELIN**, Count of Jaffa & Ascalon (d. 1266) = Maria
- **MARIA** (nun)

Next generation:
- **JOHN II OF IBELIN**, Lord of Beirut (d. 1264) = Alice of La Roche
  - **ISABELLA**, Lady Of Beirut (d. 1283)
  - **ESCHIVA**, Lady Of Beirut (d. 1312) = Guy of Lusignan (see Lusignans 1267-1398)
- **BALIAN OF IBELIN**, Lord of Arsur (d. 1277) = (1) Plaisance of Antioch = (2) Lucy of Chenechy → DESCENDENTS IN CYPRUS to 1374
- **ISABELLA** = Hugh III of Cyprus → ROYAL HOUSE OF CYPRUS to 15th century
- 9 other children
- **MARGARET** = John L'Aleman
- **JAMES**, Count of Jaffa & Ascalon (d. 1276)
- **GUY**, Count of Jaffa & Ascalon (d. 1304) → COUNTS OF JAFFA & Ascalon in Cyprus to mid 14th century
- other children

Dates in italics are estimates

House of Ibelin Thirteenth Century.

Rural Village in the Kingdom of Jerusalem Twelfth Century.

Acre Harbour in the Thirteenth Century.

Interior of Beirut Palace.

The 'Ideal Feudal State'

The concept of all knights being equal can be traced back to the reign of Amalric I. In a move to increase royal power over the magnates, King Amalric I introduced the 'Assise sur la ligece', which required the so-called rear vassals, the vassals of the prominent 'tenants-in-chief', to do 'liege-homage' to the king in addition to the homage they gave to their direct overlord. 'Assise sur la ligece' also gave the king the right to demand fealty from the rear vassals and effectively force them to abandon their direct overlord in the event of disputes between the king and his great vassals. However, it also had the collateral effect of making rear vassals peers of the realm, entitled to sit on the High Court and raise issues directly before the king.

Legal scholars agree that the High Courts of Jerusalem and later Cyprus were more powerful than the parliament in England during this period. La Monte summarised the High Court's powers as follows:

> It included within its sphere of activity the modern departments of executive, legislative, and judiciary. Its word was law ... and the king who endeavored to act without the advice of, or contrary to the decisions of, his High Court found himself confronted with a legalized rebellion on the part of his subjects.[4]

Specifically, the High Court elected the kings, determined the regents of minors and selected the consort of heiresses to the crown. Furthermore, the High Court controlled the 'purse strings' because its approval was required for levying taxes. Likewise, no treaty was valid without the High Court's consent. It oversaw the registration and transfer of all feudal property and – curiously – horses. It settled disputes concerning the forfeiture and inheritance of fiefs. It served as the jury in cases indicting any member of the court (i.e. any fief-holder in the kingdom, including the king) for criminal offensives such as murder, rape and assault, and in cases of feudal law, such as the default of service or homage. Last but not least, it tried all cases of high treason.

Strikingly, under the leadership of the rebel barons, Balian of Beirut and his cousin Philip de Montfort (the latter a cousin of Simon de Montfort, the English parliamentary reformer), non-nobles were invited to attend a session of the High Court in June 1242. Thereafter, the military orders, Italian communes and other confraternities took part in more than a half-dozen political assemblies with a quasi-parliamentary character.

Despite this trend towards expanding the franchise in the formal structure of the High Court, political reality made some vassals a little more equal than others. In the hands of powerful lords, the prominent frontier baronies were virtually free of royal control. They administered justice within their territories, they minted their own coins, and most importantly, they conducted independent foreign policy. This happened in 1186 when the count of Tripoli and prince of Galilee (by right of his wife) made a separate truce with Saladin. It explains why Reynald de Châtillon refused to compensate the crown for violating a truce signed by King Guy, with words to the effect that he was lord of his land just as Lusignan was lord of his.[5] Possibly, Lusignan's attempt to curb the autonomy of his great magnates led to their intense hostility to him. The problem re-emerged in the thirteenth century when Mamluk pressure mounted, and royal authority decayed under the absentee Hohenstaufen and Angevin kings. Once again, the barons began to make separate treaties with their enemies, disregarding the interests of the kingdom as a whole.

Finally, a last note on the High Court of Jerusalem: while much has been made of the fact that non-Franks could not bring charges against the feudal elite in the High Court, this was not a discriminatory privilege but rather the consistent application of the fundamental concept of judgement by one's peers. Those outside the feudal elite *could* bring charges against vassals before the *Cour de Bourgeois*. If the jury here found the evidence of wrongdoing sufficient to indict a member of the feudal elite, the case was then referred to the High Court, where the defendant had to answer the charges and submit to a judgement by his/her peers.[6]

In Cyprus, in contrast, the power of vassals was greatly reduced. Surrounded by water rather than hostile states, there was no need for marcher baronies, massive fortifications, or large garrisons and feudal armies. To be sure, vassals owed feudal service, but in practice, it was rarely required, so even the most celebrated magnates had no independent armies with which to defy the king. Yet there was one anomaly about the barons of Cyprus: most of them held titles derived from lordships they had once held on the mainland. For example, the lord of Beirut was one of the foremost landowners in Cyprus. The same is true for the lords of Caesarea and Arsur, the count of Jaffa and others. However, it appears their Cypriot fiefs, rather than being geographically consolidated, were scattered across the island, similar to the situation in England after the Norman conquest. Without a territorial base, disaffected barons were in no position to either rebel or conduct independent foreign policies.

Courts of All Kinds: The Complex Judiciary System of the Crusader States

Arguably the most fundamental function of any state is the administration of justice. When a government fails to deliver justice, it loses its legitimacy and either becomes tyrannical or disintegrates into anarchy. This is why the study of legal systems is so essential to an understanding and assessment of the legitimacy and efficacy of any government. The legal system in the Kingdom of Jerusalem is no exception.

Fundamental to any effective system of justice is acceptance and recognition of the legitimacy of the legal authorities by the population. This is notoriously difficult when the administrators of justice speak a different language, have a different faith, or follow different legal traditions from the legal system's subjects. As a result, the imposition of law by an invading force is inherently challenging, and wise conquerors have usually been cautious about replacing local law and custom with a new system.

The Kingdom of Jerusalem faced an especially daunting challenge since, from its inception, it was a multi-ethnic, multi-lingual and religiously diverse state. The rulers of the crusader states responded to the challenge by allowing a network of partially overlapping local or 'manorial' courts to continue while adding a superstructure of additional courts. These were the High Court (see above) for the feudal elite, the Court of the Bourgeois for the burgesses (sergeants), and two courts for cross-cultural civil cases: the commercial court ('cour de la fonde') and the maritime court ('cour de la chaine'). In addition, the Italian communes had legal jurisdiction over their members, who were subject to the laws and customs of their home cities. Of course, clerics of any religion were tried before their respective religious courts.

The Lesser Courts
In all these courts, the overriding principle was judgement by one's peers, supplemented by two corollary principles: (1) in disputes between

individuals from different strata of society, the case should be tried before peers of the weaker (lower) person, and (2) In cases between individuals from various ethnic groups of the same strata, the case should be brought before the defendant's peers.

The practical outcome of this theoretical approach was that in virtually all matters of family and religious law, the residents of the crusader states sought resolution from the religious authorities of their respective faiths. In rural areas, civil and criminal cases not involving Franks were tried before local native judges following the laws and customs predating the First Crusade.

In urban areas, however, the intermingling of peoples was too great to allow for such a simple rule, so a commercial court was created to deal with commercial cases between different ethnic and religious groups, and a maritime court handled maritime disputes regardless of the religious or national affiliation of the parties. In each, a representative of the local lord presided over the court as 'baillie' but did not pass judgement. Rather, the case was tried by six jurors drawn from the same class as the parties to the dispute. So, in the maritime court, for example, the jurors had to be sailors or merchants. Of these, two were Franks and four natives, a ratio that clearly favoured the Franks on a national scale but may have roughly reflected the composition of the population engaged in maritime activities.

The significance of these courts, particularly for the Muslim population, was that all social and religious disputes were handled by the local imam. In matters concerning the local feudal lord, Muslims were still usually represented by a Muslim 'ra'is' appointed by a Muslim council of elders. Finally, in commercial disputes with non-Muslims, they could turn to the commercial court, where they enjoyed the same rights as all other litigants. This is a sharp contrast to the legal status of 'dhimmis' in Muslim states. 'Dhimmis' were brought before the Qadi, or Islamic judge, who did not recognise the validity of an oath given by a non-Muslim.

Court of the Bourgeois

Other than the Italians, Latin immigrants to the Holy Land who were not members of the feudal elite received justice from the thirty-seven Courts of the Bourgeois. These courts, also referred to as the Lower Courts (as opposed to the High Court), were created to address disputes involving non-noble Franks that did not fall within the jurisdiction of the commercial or maritime courts and were primarily criminal cases.

Cases before the Courts of the Bourgeois were tried before a viscount (see below) appointed by the local lord (e.g. the king in royal domains, the prince of Galilee in Galilee, etc.) and twelve jurors. Like the baillies of the other courts, the viscount established neither the verdict nor the sentence. Instead, he was charged with ensuring due process, maintaining order in the courtroom and enforcing the sentence pronounced by the jurors. Litigants had the right to request 'counsel' from the court. If requested (and it was highly recommended by the medieval commentators!), the court appointed one of the jurors, who thereafter did not sit in judgement of the case but became an advocate, much like a court-appointed lawyer today. Furthermore, although there was not yet a profession known as 'lawyers', men who gained a reputation for understanding the law were revered and repeatedly appointed as either jurors or advocates. There was, however, no such thing as the 'prosecution'. The state had not yet assumed the role of pursuing justice and punishing crime in its own name. For a case to come to trial, an individual had to bring charges against someone else for violating the law. The Courts of the Bourgeois met more frequently than the High Court, presumably because they had more business to conduct given the larger numbers of burgesses.

Medieval Cyprus followed a similar pattern. For the most part, the Lusignans granted the Greeks and other groups judicial autonomy. One exception to this was that serfs came under the jurisdiction of their respective landlords. In practice, however, the law applied was the 'custom of the manor', which was usually inherited from before the Frankish invasion. Furthermore, judgement was by the defendant's peers – other Greek serfs. As on the mainland, social and religious issues were usually solved by the clergy of the respective religious community, but in Cyprus, this authority was expanded to a de facto comprehensive judicial system for all civil cases between Greeks, i.e. the vast majority of the population. Cyprus also adopted Courts of the Bourgeois for handling commercial and criminal disputes between ethnic groups, while the Cypriot High Court dealt with all disputes between members of the feudal elite. In Cyprus, criminal courts were royal courts.

Administrative Apparatus of the Outremer

In addition to the defence of the realm and the administration of justice, every kingdom required an administrative apparatus to ensure the smooth functioning of the state in both peace and war. These are the professional bureaucrats and diplomats of the modern state. In medieval times, before the evolution of professional cadres of civil servants, states depended on a comparatively small number of officials appointed by either the crown or local lords. Below is a description of the most important state officials in the Kingdom of Jerusalem.

Crown Officers

On the one hand, the Franks brought with them concepts of government from the West. On the other hand, they inherited highly sophisticated systems of raising money and administering their new lands from their Arab and Greek predecessors. The Holy Land had, after all, been administered by the ultimate bureaucracy, the Byzantine Empire, for over 300 years. Successive Muslim regimes had been too reliant on the existing apparatus for their revenue to make major changes in the four-and-a-half centuries of their control.

At the pinnacle, the royal courts were 'Western' in character. Vassals did not prostrate themselves before the king, and kings did not surround themselves with slave or mercenary bodyguards. Women were present, recognised as political and legal beings with rights and a public role as queens, consorts and lords in their own right; they were not sequestered, veiled, muzzled or discounted. The crown's most important officers were not viziers, emirs, caesars or trierarchs, but constables, seneschals, chancellors, chamberlains and marshals. The offices of the crown in the Kingdom of Jerusalem retained their functions throughout the life of the kingdom, unlike in the West, where many of these offices became hereditary yet empty titles held by an eminent baronial family but devoid of meaningful substance. Although the office holders were drawn from the highest ranks of the nobility, i.e. the barons and magnates of the realm, the offices themselves never became hereditary. The other crusader states, particularly Cyprus but also the lesser states and grand baronies had similar administrative structures and officers.

The most important crown officers in the Latin East were the constable and seneschal. The constable appears to have enjoyed somewhat

The 'Ideal Feudal State'

more prestige in these highly militarised societies. The constable was responsible for deploying troops (unless overruled by the king) and held supreme command in the king's absence. He also headed all court martials while on campaign, regardless of whether the offender was a knight, sergeant, squire or turcopole. He carried the royal banner in the coronation ceremony and held the king's horse when he mounted and dismounted during the coronation.

The seneschal, more powerful than his Western counterparts, served as the kingdom's chief financial administrator and fulfilled ceremonial functions familiar from the West. He presided over an institution known as the 'secrète', a body inherited from the Byzantine 'σεκρετον', which was found in both Jerusalem and Cyprus. The 'secrète' was the government department that kept records of land ownership and taxes and evolved into the central financial office responsible for revenue collection and government expenditure. The seneschal appointed, oversaw and dismissed, as necessary, the large staff of treasury baillies and clerks that ran the 'secrète' on a daily basis. In addition, the seneschal could convene the High Court and preside over it in the absence or incapacitation of the king. At the coronation, he carried the scepter.

The chancellor, in contrast, was far less influential than the officers cited above or his contemporaries in the West. At a time when the Western European chancelleries were developing the bureaucratic core of more centralised governments, the chancelleries in the Latin East remained comparably weak. They had no judicial function as an appellate court, for example. They did, however, serve as the central archive, where all charters of the kingdom were drafted, recorded and retained. These charters included some documents that might have been classified differently elsewhere (such as treaties with the Italian city-states). The chancellors were always leading churchmen, and the language of the royal chancelleries in both Jerusalem and Cyprus was Latin in the twelfth century and French in the thirteenth.

The chamberlain in Jerusalem was the king's personal financial manager, responsible for the household accounts. He also administered the oaths of homage, dressed the king for his coronation and headed the coronation procession.

The marshal was the constable's deputy and held his office from the constable rather than directly from the king. He had particular responsibility for mercenaries, taking their oaths and ensuring they were paid. Before a battle, he inspected arms, equipment and horses. The latter was important because if a horse was killed or disabled during a campaign, the crown was responsible for replacing it, a custom known as 'restor'. During a battle, the marshal carried the royal standard and commanded the troop directly before the king, whereas the vanguard was led by the baron in whose territory a battle was fought. After a battle, the marshal took charge of captured horses and redistributed them to anyone who had lost their horse while serving the king. Anyone who disobeyed a command of the marshal lost the right to 'restor'.

Administrative Backbone: Viscounts, Ra'is, Dragomen and More
Below these chief officers of the crown came the thirty-seven viscounts of the kingdom. Viscounties were offices, not hereditary titles, and were drawn from the lower nobility and knights. There were four royal viscounts appointed by the crown to Jerusalem, Acre, Nablus and Darum, and their duties were roughly equivalent to those of English sheriffs. They presided over the 'cours des bourgeois'. The remaining thirty-three viscounts were appointed by the barons who had fiefs with 'cours de bourgeois'.

On Cyprus, in addition to the 'secrète', the Franks adopted wholesale the institution of the 'κομμερκιον', or the 'commercium', a royal department responsible for duties on imports, exports and the sale of merchandise in public markets. During the transition to Lusignan rule, this institution was manned seamlessly by Greek bureaucrats, as was the 'secrète' on Cyprus. Nor was this reliance on Greek bureaucrats a temporary measure, as it continued for the duration of Lusignan rule in Cyprus. Furthermore, the 'commercium' appears to have been headed merely by a 'baillie', presumably one of these native bureaucrats, rather than a crown officer drawn from the higher nobility.

At the village level, there was a local and resident 'Head Man' known as the 'ra'is' (also rays). He was a tenant, usually with a bigger house and somewhat more profitable land, such as olive orchards or vineyards, and he spoke the same language and shared the religion of the other inhabitants of the village. Often, he was the descendent of the 'ra'is', who had been there before the Franks came. The 'ra'is' was an intermediary between the lord and his tenants and represented the interests of the community to the lord.

On the other side, the lord employed a dragoman and a scribe to represent his interests and enforce his laws in the community.

The dragoman had similar duties to a deputy-sheriff or modern police chief; he was responsible for law and order, capturing outlaws and criminals and carrying out the sentence of the manorial court. The scribe, far from being a mere note-taker, was responsible for collecting local taxes, rents and fees, and recording their collection so no one would be taxed twice. These two positions were often held by Franks of the 'sergeant' class (free burgesses), but also by natives. Since many native Christians at this time spoke Arabic and used Arabic names, we do not know if the native inhabitants entrusted with these essential offices were Muslim, Orthodox Christians or converts to Catholicism.

Finally, in the urban centres and ports, large customs houses were staffed by a bevy of customs officials who kept records of all ships, passengers and cargoes moving in and out of the port and collected customs duties. There were customs officials at the city gates as well. Still other officials were responsible for monitoring and checking on the weights and measures used in the markets. Others oversaw the removal of refuse. Some enforced rules on the use and operation of wells, bakeries and bathhouses, while others patrolled the streets to keep order, especially at night. Here, the Frankish states relied heavily on the native population to actively participate in the support and maintenance of their rule.

Sources of Revenue: Taxes, Customs and So Much More

One consistent characteristic of the Frankish kingdoms was their affluence compared to kingdoms in the West. Contemporary accounts from pilgrims often express amazement bordering on envy at the luxurious, even decadent, lifestyle of the residents of Outremer. This was partially an illusion. Items considered outrageously expensive luxuries in the West, such as silk, spices, opium and sugar, were readily available and comparatively cheap in the East. At the state level, however, there is little doubt that the Kingdoms of Jerusalem and Cyprus enjoyed exceptionally diverse and lucrative sources of revenue. This made them remarkably wealthy for their size, despite being periodically bankrupt due to the disruptions caused by warfare.

Raids and invasions were hugely destructive of economic resources, often leaving entire swaths of countryside depopulated and in smoking ruins. Offensive campaigns were an equally exhaustive drain on the royal treasury since the crown was required to pay mercenary salaries, 'restor' (replacement of horses) and cover the cost of supplies and provisions. Thus, while trade and tourism enriched the Italian mercantile communities and the urban middle class, the crown and the feudal nobility collected enormous revenue, yet at the same time needed to expend a substantial portion of it on the collective defence of the realm.

In 1183, the rising threat of Saladin led to the imposition of a comprehensive wealth tax on all subjects: the Church and the feudal lords, the non-feudal Franks, native Christians, Muslims, Jews and (exceptionally) the Italians. It may qualify as the first such national tax recorded in Western history and was viewed as unique at the time because taxpayers assessed and declared their own property value. The proceeds of this tax could be spent on defense only.

In periods of peace, the taxes assessed across the crusader states were based on taxes of the Muslim population predating the First Crusade, which appear to have been comparatively reasonable by contemporary standards. Richard the Lionheart won support during his conquest of Cyprus by promising to restore the tax regime operative in the reign of Manuel I Comnenus, something evidently seen as an improvement over the gouging taxes of the renegade Isaac Comnenus. On the mainland, we know that peasants were free of feudal services, and the rural rents were set intentionally low to attract settlers. Christian peasants paid no more than one-quarter to one-third of their harvest to their lords. In Cyprus, the rents for free peasants could be as low as one-fifth and did not exceed one-quarter. Even serfs in Cyprus paid only one-third of their crop but were also liable for other feudal fees and services, increasing the overall burden. Notably, the Muslim rural population was not heavily taxed if we are to believe the account of the Muslim pilgrim Ibn Jubayr. The latter remarked that Muslim peasants had been 'seduced' by the comparative 'ease and comfort' of their lives when compared to the burdens placed on Muslim peasants in Muslim territory.

Ultimately, the moderate rates of rural taxation were financed through tax revenue generated from commercial and maritime rather than agricultural activities. The Franks, like their predecessors, enriched their treasury by taxing:

- Mills for grinding grain into flour
- Olive and wine presses
- Sugar factories

The 'Ideal Feudal State'

- Ovens (which were usually communal as it took a great deal of scarce wood to heat one and it was more efficient to do this for large quantities of bread)
- Garden produce and orchards
- Bathhouses
- Traffic passing through city gates
- Sales taxes at markets
- Head taxes on the passengers and crew of arriving ships
- Exit taxes for foreigners departing by ship

In addition to these taxes, state revenue was derived from:

- Rights of salvage
- Anchorage and harbour fees
- Import and export duties
- Rents for store-frontage
- Fees assessed by the courts on people found guilty of crimes and misdemeanors.

In Cyprus, the crown also maintained a monopoly on salt, highway tolls and minting coins.

Overall, in the Kingdom of Jerusalem, revenue derived from trade and commerce outweighed income from agriculture – at least in the thirteenth century, after the Kingdom of Jerusalem had become more urban. In Cyprus, the situation was reversed, and taxes on agriculture – including many high-value products such as sugar, honey and wine – outstripped revenue obtained from commercial activities. Over time, however, the taxes on trade and finance undoubtedly increased as a proportion of the total.

The structures for collecting revenue were largely inherited from the Byzantines, namely the previously mentioned 'secrète' and 'commercium'. Here, an army of clerks and scribes employed sophisticated accounting methods not only to collect and record taxes, duties and customs but to pay revenue to the holders of money-fiefs and their rear-vassals if they had any. They also paid alms and covered debts incurred by recipients, rather like a payroll tax deducted at the source nowadays. Pilgrims noted with surprise that the customs clerks were multilingual and able to converse in French, Latin and Arabic fluently.

Most of these employees in Cyprus, and probably in Jerusalem, were native Christians rather than Latin immigrants, although in later years they may have increasingly been 'poulains'.

Defence of the Realm

With the wisdom of hindsight, it is easy to dismiss the crusader states as inherently 'indefensible'. Yet, in the nearly 200 years of their existence, the crusader states were more often on the offensive than the defense. Even the most catastrophic defeats – Hattin and La Forbie – were not militarily inevitable. The demise of the crusader states had complex geopolitical causes, while the Latin East's military institutions were more remarkable for their effectiveness than the reverse.

Very early on, the Franks developed and employed a remarkably simple but effective strategy to counter the 'jihadist' and numerically superior forces arrayed against them. This strategy was built on three components: (1) static defences capable of withstanding assault and siege, (2) mobile forces capable of relieving and attacking, and (3) naval forces capable of breaking blockades and resupplying by sea. In practice, the civilian population took refuge behind the walls of the nearest defensible structure – whether city or castle, where a citizen garrison (in cities) or professional garrison (in castles) fended off assaults until the feudal field army could lift the siege. In coastal cities, command of the sea offered an additional line of defence: relief by sea from the West.

The destruction of the field army at the Battle of Hattin made resistance in the castles and cities hopeless. Most garrisons opted to surrender on terms rather than face slaughter and slavery. Those cities that chose defiance, with the exception of Jerusalem itself, were coastal cities that could hope for relief by sea. Without this naval support, Tyre and Tripoli would also have fallen to Saladin in 1187–88. Finally, once the coast of the Levant was lost, it was the absence of a fortified city to act as a bridgehead for new conquests that discouraged new crusades. Critical to an understanding of this defensive strategy is remembering that borders were meaningless. The Franks never attempted to defend specific territorial borders. Instead, the strategy focused on defending the population and, with it, the ability to re-establish control over the economic resources from which they thrived once the enemy had been defeated.

Static Defence: Walled Cities and Crusader Castles

The great walled cities of the Levant – Antioch, Tripoli, Beirut, Tyre, Acre, Caesarea, Jaffa, Ascalon and Jerusalem itself – were the anchors of the Frankish defence network. Cities that could withstand extended sieges, particularly coastal cities that could be resupplied by sea, were invulnerable to any but the most tenacious opponents. Throughout most of Outremer's history, the armies opposing the Franks were too transient to sustain lengthy sieges and frequently disintegrated or withdrew at the mere approach of the Frankish field army.

The eminent cities and smaller walled towns in the interior such as Hebron, Bethlehem, Tiberias and Nazareth were supported and reinforced by castles great and small. The most famous castles are the large concentric ones that represented the pinnacle of military architectural development of the period, such as the now-famous Crac de Chevaliers, Montfort (Starkenburg) and Kerak. However, most crusader castles were much simpler and smaller, often little more than a tower or a perimeter wall. Altogether roughly 100 Frankish castles have been identified.

For centuries, it was presumed the Franks mostly adapted existing defensive structures in already-established population centres. Archaeological surveys of the last quarter-century, however, prove that nearly half the castles built in the twelfth century were constructed in rural and remote areas of the country near Oriental Christian monasteries or settlements. There is 'almost no correlation between the location of the castles and areas of military confrontation'.[7] In short, the purpose of many castles was not so much defence as administration; they were first and foremost symbols of power and presence and only secondarily places of refuge in an emergency.

Because of the speed with which the Frankish army could mobilise, castles of the pre-Saladin era needed to be capable of holding out no more than one week. Only in the later twelfth century did the Franks start constructing the massive castles we associate with the term 'crusader castles'. In part, this was a response to the threat posed by Saladin and, in part, necessary to compensate for improvements in Saracen siege equipment and tactics. This dictated the construction of thicker and higher walls as well as multiple lines of defence, resulting in concentric castles, such as Crac de Chevaliers.

Immense fortifications, however, required ample garrisons of trained fighting men. Records tend to mention only the number of knights assigned to a garrison because contemporaries knew that for every knight, there were also sergeants, archers, squires and servants or roughly nine men per knight. Thus, castles garrisoned by, say, forty knights were not defended by forty men but by 400 men, 10 per cent of which were knights.

Furthermore, these new castles were extremely expensive to build and maintain. Based on thirteenth-century Templar records for the reconstruction of the castle at Safed, castle construction cost approximately 1 million Saracen bezants; in modern terms, roughly £1 billion. The modern equivalent of the annual maintenance costs comes to roughly forty million pounds. In the twilight of the crusader states, it was as much the inability to finance such expenses as the decline in manpower reserves that doomed the Frankish kingdom. Furthermore, the great concentric castles of the thirteenth century may have had the negative side effect of encouraging more passive tactics, even though offensive operations had served the kingdom so well in the past.

Mobile Defence: An Army of Many Parts with Tactical Innovations

During the first century of Frankish presence in the Holy Land, the field army rather than its castles had been the Frank's greatest military asset. This was the weapon that had enabled five crusader states to be carved out of hostile territory and spearheaded the expansion of Frankish-controlled territory beyond the Jordan and down to the Red Sea.

The field army of the crusader states differed significantly and in various ways from the contemporary feudal armies of Europe. In Western Europe, hilly and forested terrain cut by frequent streams and cultivated valleys made the deployment of large military forces difficult, while the fragmented nature of the political landscape made them largely unnecessary. Furthermore, large feudal armies composed of vassals called up for military service were notoriously unwieldy, undisciplined and ineffective. The men in a feudal levy were essentially farmers and farm managers (the knights), whose service could not exceed forty days, making them worthless for sustained warfare. For such a mediocre and temporary host, kings were usually reluctant to disrupt the economy, as happened when a feudal host was mustered.

Instead, Western leaders of the crusader era preferred to employ smaller, professional forces composed of two elements: on the one hand, the personal retinue or household of the king and his closest associates and, on the other, mercenaries. The former was primarily knights, and the latter were sergeants or men-at-arms and archers along with some siege specialists. Mercenaries were notoriously expensive, inhibiting the number of such men who could be engaged at any one time. This reinforced the overall tendency to conduct offensive military operations with small units of mostly mounted men and to withdraw inside stout walls when on the defensive.

Lastly, many conflicts in Europe of this period were subnational, between magnates, barons or local lords. Even bigger conflicts, such as that between the Plantagenets and Capets, were usually conducted in the form of short raids or surgical strikes directed against the enemy's economic or strategic assets by small troops of professional soldiers. This kind of warfare between small bands of professionals fostered 'an individualistic ethos which valued bravery and comradeship within the group, rather than discipline'.[8] In close combat, men fought one-on-one and face-to-face. These military factors ultimately led to an important social change: the emergence of the knight as a distinct social class, and with it, the cult of chivalry. The latter reinforced pride in individual prowess and class-consciousness at the expense of the infantry.

Fighting in the Near East looked completely different. The topography of the Near East was more open, flatter and less cultivated. At the same time, the enemies of the Franks were centralised states with vast resources that could deploy forces numbering in the tens of thousands. The Franks, in contrast, could rarely deploy more than a few hundred knights at any one time and needed to develop tactics to compensate for this numerical disadvantage.

Modern calculations of the size of Frankish armies are based primarily on a list of fiefs and their military obligations put together in the mid-thirteenth century by John d'Ibelin, Count of Jaffa. It allegedly catalogued the feudal obligations of vassals pre-Hattin and was presumably based on fragmentary documentation and contemporary memory. While it is a remarkable document, it is incomplete and not entirely consistent. Furthermore, in addition to the knights owing feudal service, most lords would have had household knights who would have mustered and fought with them. The ratio of retained knights to fief knights varied between 1:2 and 3:2. Due to vacancies, illness, injuries and minorities, however, it would never have been possible to field 100 per cent of the fief knights. Altogether, the fief knights of the kingdom numbered roughly 700, and a further 300 retained knights could be postulated. In addition, the County of Tripoli had 100 knights and Antioch another 700. However, the knights of Antioch rarely fought with those of Jerusalem, so the maximum effective force the Kingdom of Jerusalem could field with the support of Tripoli was 1,100 knights.

Yet, knights were only one component of the armies of the crusader states. Yuval Harari has demonstrated that mounted archers, on average, made up 50 per cent of the Frankish cavalry and sometimes as much as 80 per cent.[9] This combat arm, unknown in the West, was recruited primarily from the native Christian elites, notably the Armenian and Maronite landowning class. It was deployed, for example, for reconnaissance, to make lightning raids against supply and relief columns of the enemy and to lend greater weight to a charge.

In addition, some fiefs were 'sergeantries', and cities and monasteries often owed sergeant service in specified numbers. Based on the list of John of Jaffa, the total number of sergeants that could be called up was 5,025. These men were well-trained, well-disciplined and well-equipped. Sergeants were deployed as mounted troops and as infantry. They were not serfs, but invariably free men, drawn from the Latin and Orthodox Christian yeomanry in rural areas and tradesmen and craftsmen in urban areas. Arab sources testify to the fact that, like the knights, they could withstand substantial quantities of enemy fire without sustaining injury, much less casualties, which demonstrates they had effective armour. They were also capable of carrying out complicated maneuvers while under fire, including fighting while walking backwards, and opening ranks simultaneously to permit the knights of the army to charge.

In an emergency, the king could also issue the 'arrière ban', a form of 'levee en masse', which drafted every able-bodied man into the army. Such troops, like the peasants of Western feudal armies, were generally of limited military value. Similarly, armed pilgrims, who arrived from the West in unpredictable numbers and remained for uncertain periods, often participated in military campaigns. They swelled the numbers but given their unfamiliarity with the enemy's tactics, the terrain and climate, their value would have been uneven at best.

Naturally, the Frankish kings could also hire mercenaries; these were often crossbowmen from the Italian mercantile states. Yet, they could also be knights. Henry II deposited 30,000 silver marks with both the Templars and Hospitallers to support a future crusade, and the Templar portion was used to hire 'English knights'. Finally, as will be discussed in more detail below, the Franks could count on the support of the militant orders.

Altogether, at the large, confrontational battles during the height of Jerusalem's power, such as Le Forbelet and Hattin, the Franks fielded an estimated 3,000 cavalry and 15,000 infantry. However, in most engagements, from the early battles at Ramla to Montgisard, the numbers of knights involved were closer to 300, 400 and 500. Almost always, the Saracens outnumbered the Franks by two or three – and sometimes ten to one.

Survival as the outnumbered force required sophisticated tactics. Rather than fighting as they had in the West, the Franks adopted two tactical innovations that contributed to their success: the fighting box and mounted archers. The fighting box was a formation in which the most vulnerable components of an army (baggage train, sick and wounded) were placed in the centre, surrounded by mounted knights, who were in turn surrounded by infantry with shields, pikes and bows. All of whom were protected by a screen of mounted archers. The main advantage of the fighting box was that it could defend stationary positions or move as a square across long distances in either advance or retreat. In a retreat, the Franks would take the dead, giving the enemy the impression there were no casualties at all. When holding firm positions, fighting strength could be maintained by rotating the front-line units, giving men a chance to rest and quench their thirst. There are also examples of fighting boxes being used to evacuate civilians from vulnerable territory.

However, the fighting box was not exclusively a defensive tactic. It was also the platform from which the Franks launched their greatest offensive weapon. The primary purpose of the fighting box was to protect the knights' horses from attrition and thus enable them to be used in a cavalry charge at the appropriate time. When the commander judged that a charge could be effective, the infantry opened gaps through which the cavalry charged the enemy.

A charge of Frankish cavalry could destroy the enemy – but only if it was well-timed, well-led and coordinated. Given the enemy's numerical advantage, small charges were worthless and a dangerous waste of precious resources. Only a massive charge had a chance of unbalancing, shattering or scattering the enemy. Critically, like a modern missile, a charge could only be used once. Once released, the knights became embroiled in close combat, dispersed, cut off from command structures and practically uncontrollable.

The salient feature of this tactic is that it required discipline from all participants. Marching and fighting simultaneously are not easy. To be effective, the fighting box had to work as a single unit. Gaps between the ranks had to be prevented and progress maintained without tiring the infantry. It was important for the infantry to keep their shields locked together – more like a Spartan phalanx than anything common in medieval Europe. The fact that armies of the crusader states repeatedly used the fighting box throughout their history testifies to the remarkable discipline of these armies. The tactic both contributed to and reflected respect for infantry and the burgesses that comprised it. However, when the discipline necessary for effective use of this tactic broke down due to poor leadership, the result was utter obliteration – as at the Battle of Hattin.

The other key Frankish innovation was the deployment of mounted archers, something completely unknown in Europe at the time. The crusaders encountered the superb horse-archers of the Turks as soon as they crossed into Asia, and they not only learned to respect them, they imitated them. Neither heavy cavalry nor infantry was suited to conducting reconnaissance, carrying out hit-and-run raids, providing a protective screen for their 'fighting box' or carrying urgent messages. Frankish horses, bred to carry fully-armoured knights, could not – one on one – escape the faster, lighter horses of the Turks. Heavy cavalry deployed on reconnaissance was more likely to be ambushed and eliminated than return with the intelligence needed. Light cavalry was also more effective in hit-and-run raids against enemy camps or territory because the faster, native horses carrying lightly-armoured riders armed with bows were more likely to surprise the enemy – and escape again; they were also more likely to succeed as couriers. Lastly, light cavalry wearing similar armour and weapons as the enemy with a fluent/native command of Arabic was invaluable for intelligence gathering.

The first references in the primary sources to Frankish mounted archers date from 1109. From that point forward, they played an increasingly prominent role in the Frankish military, in some cases operating independently, and in other cases in support of the infantry and heavy cavalry. Frankish mounted archers were misleadingly but consistently referred to as 'turcopoles' in the primary sources of the period. This designation has led to confusion and a common misconception that they were Muslim troops, Muslim converts or the children of mixed marriages. In his lengthy analysis of Frankish turcopoles, Yuval Harari demonstrates that all three assumptions are false. In the Frankish context, the term 'turcopole' simply designated a military arm – mounted archers – without any ethnic connotations. Most turcopoles were native (Orthodox) Christians. This explains why they performed poorly in early engagements before the native Christian elites had developed the necessary skills after centuries of 'dhimmitude', but performed highly effectively after several decades of Frankish rule enabled them to develop the required cavalry and archery skills.

Although primarily deployed in light cavalry functions, turcopoles had two additional functions when accompanying the Frankish army on campaign. During the march/deployment, Frankish armies were almost always harassed by Turkish mounted archers that concentrated on the van and the rear in an attempt to (1) bring the column to a halt, (2) force the rearguard to slow down until a gap developed for exploitation or (3) provoke an ill-timed charge that could be destroyed. Frankish turcopoles could neutralise Saracen archers by acting as a screen around the fighting box, forcing the Saracens out of bow-shot range. Finally, in a set-piece battle, the turcopoles were folded into the heavy cavalry and provided additional weight and numbers to the charge.

Naval Warfare
Despite the critical importance of sea power to the survival of the crusader states, there has not, to date, been a naval history of the crusades. This is astonishing when one considers that reinforcements and supplies brought by sea were instrumental in enabling the crusaders to take Antioch in 1098 and that all the early conquests along the coast of the Levant were won with massive naval support. It was the timely arrival of the Sicilian fleet that saved Tripoli from Saladin in 1188, and without maritime supremacy, it would have been impossible for Tyre to survive between 1187 and 1191. It was the arrival of the French and English fleets that doomed Saladin's hold on Acre at the start of the Third Crusade. Throughout the thirteenth century, control of the Eastern Mediterranean was vital to trade with Europe and was the economic lifeline of the crusader states. In short, the crusader states would not have been sustainable without maritime power.

Yet, the Frankish kingdoms did not maintain naval forces. Instead, control of the sea lanes, so critical to their prosperity and survival, was delegated to the Italian maritime powers. Above all, the fleets of Venice, Genoa and Pisa contained Saracen sea power and protected Western shipping. These bitter rivals collectively maintained maritime supremacy in the Eastern Mediterranean throughout the crusading era while occasionally engaging in bitter naval battles among themselves. After the fall of Acre, the Knights Hospitaller transformed itself into a naval organisation and continued the war with the Saracens at sea as the Knights of Rhodes and then of Malta. It was not until the rise of the Ottomans in the sixteenth century that Western dominance of the Mediterranean broke down. A detailed history of this maritime chapter in history is sorely missed.

The Military Orders

No description of the defensive structures in the crusader states would be complete without mention of the militant orders: the Knights Templar, Knights Hospitaller, the Teutonic Knights and the Knights of St Lazarus. John France goes so far as to describe these institutions as 'the greatest military innovations of the Latins'.[10]

These institutions, all founded in the Kingdom of Jerusalem, were revolutionary in a variety of ways. For example, they were fighting monks, and they offered free professional medical care and pioneered with international financial services.[11] Their relevance to the defence of the crusader kingdoms was based on just two factors: their professionalism and international character. Some historians have gone so far as to claim they were the only 'standing armies' of the period.[12] Certainly, the fighting men in the military orders – sergeants and turcopoles, no less than the knights – trained intensely, received standardised equipment and wore what were, in effect, uniforms that identified them as members of their organisation. Their discipline was exceptional in this age of individualism and chivalric display. Furthermore, as monks, the knights had taken vows of obedience and were schooled to follow orders unquestioningly, an exceptional attitude in an age where kings and lords always 'took council' before making major decisions and no secular knight felt compelled to obey.

From the Second Crusade onwards, the military orders demonstrated the value of these tightly organised, uniformly equipped, disciplined and dedicated fighting men. They were increasingly entrusted with the most challenging tasks and took on the roles we associate today with elite units. They were especially valuable for offensive operations as there were complex limits on feudal obligations and, as a rule, secular knights were not compelled to participate in offensive campaigns.

Equally notable was the international character of the large orders and the financial resources that went with their extensive support infrastructure in the West. Although the three foremost militant orders were founded in the Kingdom of Jerusalem, they drew their wealth and recruits from across Europe. The Templars and Hospitallers had thousands of properties from Scotland to Sicily and from Prussia to Portugal. Sources speak of 9,000 Templar and as many 19,000 Hospitaller houses. These were often little more than a manor or a village, but profits from the various properties were pooled to support their expensive commitments in the Holy Land. Although the Hospital's function was primarily providing health care and social services, it was also entrusted with castles and maintained about 300 knights capable of contributing to the armies of Jerusalem. The Knights of St Lazarus and the Teutonic Knights, likewise started as hospitals, but soon branched out into the business of defence. From their inception, the Templars had a strictly military role and a contingent of knights (an estimated 500) stationed in the Holy Land; they also maintained key castles.

The critical feature of these numbers is that they remained stable, regardless of casualties, because the militant orders had vast recruiting networks associated with their properties in the West, ensuring a steady flow of replacements for the men killed, captured or incapacitated in the Holy Land. This made them better able to sustain losses of both men and material. By the mid-thirteenth century, the costs of maintaining and garrisoning large concentric castles far exceeded the means of most secular lords drawing their income from their fiefs alone. In consequence, the barons of Outremer gradually followed the example of Raymond of Tripoli, who already in 1144 transferred castles and territories to the Knights Hospitaller when he found himself financially embarrassed by ransom payments. As the crusader states faced Mongol and Mamluk threats under a monarchy gutted by absenteeism and civil war, the military orders became the only real bulwark against invasion. They collected men, money and supplies from supporters across Europe and funneled it to the Holy Land. What had once been 'ideal feudal states' based on secular defensive structures gradually became enclaves of mercantile communities protected by professional armies of fighting monks.

Religious Institutions

The Roman Catholic Church has been blamed for the crusades ever since the Reformation, and the popular image today remains one of a Latin church hostile to and hated by the Orthodox churches of the Near East. Indeed, the highly influential history of the crusades written by Sir Simon Runciman in the middle of the last century alleged that Franks were worse than Muslims because they 'interfered in the religious practices of the local churches'.[13] Yet, modern scholars such as Ye'or, Kedar and MacEvitt have documented the reverse: that Muslim regimes systematically oppressed Eastern Christianity, while the Franks gave the Orthodox churches a short but quantifiable period of protection and restoration. Accounts by contemporary clerics of the Armenian and Jacobite churches reflect not only amicable relations but admiration for the piety and fairness of the Franks. In short, the relationship between the Latin and Orthodox churches was more complex and nuanced than the simplistic rhetoric of Protestant reformers or modern atheists suggest.

Syria and Palestine

The First Crusade was undertaken in an atmosphere of co-operation between Rome and Constantinople. Not only did Constantinople request assistance from the West via the pope, Pope Urban II pursued a policy of reconciliation with Constantinople and instructed his legate, Bishop Adhemar, to 'scrupulously respect the rights of the Orthodox hierarchy'.[14] Indeed, Pope Urban expected the crusade to end the persecution of the Greek church in the Holy Land and restore the Greek Orthodox Patriarch Symeon to his see in Jerusalem. Symeon, it should be noted, had been driven into exile in Cyprus by the Fatimids.

Urban's representative on the crusade, Bishop Adhemar, was careful not to displace any existing Orthodox bishops in the territories conquered by the crusaders. Likewise, the Orthodox patriarch in Antioch was recognised as the legitimate ecclesiastical leader of both Latins and Orthodox after the crusaders' conquest of Antioch. In return, Symeon materially and actively supported the First Crusade, sending desperately needed supplies to the crusaders during their sieges of Antioch and Jerusalem. Indeed, Symeon and Adhemar issued joint communiqués, a striking example of cooperation between their respective churches.

The 'Ideal Feudal State'

Yet when Jerusalem finally fell to the crusaders in July 1099, Pope Urban, Patriarch Symeon and Bishop Adhemar were dead. The men who captured Jerusalem from the Fatimids were practical fighting men who had fought their way to the Holy City at great cost in lives and fortune. It is unlikely they understood papal policy towards Orthodox Christianity; they certainly didn't have time to ask. So, they improvised. Since the patriarchate was vacant, they appointed one of their own (Latin) priests to the post – despite having no suitable candidate and although more senior Orthodox clergy were present in the city.

Meanwhile, Daimbert, Archbishop of Pisa, had been appointed papal legate to replace the deceased Adhemar. On his arrival in Jerusalem, Daimbert promptly dismissed the priest selected by the fighting men and made himself the patriarch of Jerusalem. Daimbert sought to exert power over the secular rulers demanding their homage to him in an effort to turn the nascent kingdom into a papal state. His ambitions were facilitated by the presence of a Pisan fleet, an asset vital to the capture of the coastal cities essential to a viable state. Daimbert ran roughshod over the Orthodox establishment, appointing Latin clerics to all vacant sees – including those that came under the jurisdiction of the patriarch of Antioch. His greed, however, was his undoing. He was caught embezzling funds sent from the West for the defence of Jerusalem and was deposed by the new papal legate – a man from rival Genoa. Despite some complex intrigues to regain his position, Daimbert was eventually replaced by a patriarch dedicated to supporting rather than undermining the king of Jerusalem. For the remainder of the twelfth century, 'patriarchs tended to be pious servants of the crown notable for conventional rather than spectacular piety and for competence in administration rather than theological learning'.[15]

The papacy, meanwhile, made serious efforts to unify the various Orthodox churches with Rome. The Maronites were unified with Rome in 1181, and the Armenians officially entered a 'union' with Rome in 1198. For the average parishioner, local priests and monks, however, nothing changed. The Jacobite, Maronite, Armenian, Ethiopian and Nestorian clergy continued to minister to their flocks in their own language, using their traditional rites without inhibitions. They also continued to elect their own bishops and archbishops. It was only because the Greek Orthodox Church was viewed as neither heretical nor schematic but already part of the same 'universal' church that tension between Latin and Greek church hierarchies developed. It was not possible to recognise two bishops to the same see of the same church, so Latins and Greeks competed for the most lucrative posts.

Despite this competition between leaders, the Orthodox religious community, as a whole, flourished under Frankish rule. This was mostly because the secular authorities required the active support of the Orthodox population in both the economy and defence of the realm; they did not want the Latin church alienating that population with excessive religious zeal. Michael the Great (aka Michael the Syrian), Patriarch of the Jacobite (or Syriac) Orthodox Church (1166–1199), assessed the Frankish religious policy as follows: 'The Franks never raised any difficulty about matters of doctrine, or tried to formulate it in one way only for Christians of differing race and language, but accepted as a Christian anybody who venerated the cross, without further examination.'[16] In short, the experience of local churches based on their testimony was not one of oppression.

On the contrary, the Orthodox communities flourished. Orthodox bishops returned to Tyre, Caesarea, Sidon, Tiberias, Gaza and Lydda – all sees that had fallen vacant under successive Muslim regimes. Furthermore, Armenian, Syrian, Greek, Coptic, Georgian and Ethiopian monasteries proliferated and prospered, frequently with Frankish patrons and land grants. In the most sacred shrine of Christendom, the Franks undertook a massive reconstruction that consciously – and sensitively – included separate altars for the various denominations under the same literal and metaphorical shared roof. Likewise, village churches in rural areas were often shared by Latin and Orthodox clergy and parishioners, sometimes with two separate aspes to enable services to be held side-by-side and sometimes simply holding services at different times of the day.[17] Altogether, the crusaders revitalised local Christian communities, re-establishing local bishoprics and monasteries, restoring older churches and building new ones.[18]

The situation within the Latin Church, in contrast, has been compared to 'the army of a banana republic' with far too many 'generals' (bishops) for troops. In addition to the patriarchs of Jerusalem and Antioch, there were four archbishops (Caesarea, Tyre, Nazareth and Petra) and ten bishops (Gibelet, Beirut, Sidon, Banyas, Acre, Tiberias, Sabaste, Lydda, Bethlehem and Hebron). The cathedrals were often the only Latin churches in the entire city. In the wake of the territorial losses after Hattin, the situation became even more absurd with the bishops of lost territories such as Banyas, Tiberias, Hebron and Sebaste residing in Acre with their cathedral canons but no flocks.

On the other hand, in the short period of Frankish rule, the Latin Church brought forth new monastic orders: the Templars, Hospitallers, Lazarists, Teutonics, Carmelites and Trinitarians. The latter, while founded in Paris, was founded because of the acute need to ransom captives from Muslim captivity in the wake of the establishment of permanent Latin Christian settlements in the Levant.

It is also notable that in the First Kingdom, a portion of the clergy adhered to a militant Christianity that included taking an active part in armed conflict. For example, in 1119, after the Antiochene nobility and army had been decimated at the Field of Blood, the patriarch of Antioch ordered the clerics to arm themselves and prepare to defend the city until relief came from Jerusalem. A year later, the laws of Jerusalem promulgated at the Council of Nablus in 1120 explicitly recognised the right of clerics to bear arms for the sake of defence, something that might be interpreted as all armed conflict with Saracens. Archbishop Benedict of Edessa was captured at the Battle of Harran in 1104 but was rescued by Tancred. Bishop Gerard of Tripoli was captured in battle in 1132 but later ransomed. Ralph, Bishop of Bethlehem, was severely wounded in battle in 1165 during one of King Amalric's Egyptian campaigns. A canon of the Holy Sepulchre was killed at the Battle of Le Forbelet while actively fighting. Rufinius, Bishop of Acre, was killed at the Battle of Hattin, and Ralph II, another bishop of Bethlehem, was executed by Saladin during the negotiations for the surrender of Jaffa in 1192. Except for Ralph II, who was clearly engaged in diplomatic exchanges consistent with his office, the other clerics were taken on the battlefield. Rufinius and Ralph I were known to be carrying the relic known as the True Cross, but the other clerics appear to have been actively engaged in the fighting.

Yet while religious tolerance was not entirely untypical in the twelfth century, the thirteenth century was characterised by Catholic zealousness. It saw the founding of the Dominicans in a struggle against one of the most popular and successful heresies of the Middle Ages, the Cathars. This new order became the face of a new and infamous spiritual weapon: the Inquisition. Likewise, the Franciscans, founded in the first half of the thirteenth century, were dedicated to converting pagans – especially

Muslims – to Christianity, if by other methods. The Dominican and Franciscan orders both arrived to the Holy Land in the 1220s.

The thirteenth century also saw the rise of a militant papacy. Innocent III and his successors not only invoked 'crusades' to fight a range of enemies, including their political opponents, they saw themselves as leaders of these crusades. In addition, they sought to eradicate deviant thinking (heresies) and impose greater uniformity of thought and practice upon all Christians – including Orthodox Christians.

Initially, the practical clergy in the Frankish East resisted papal pressure for conformity in practice and theology. Local clerics were attuned not only to the sensibilities of the native population but also recognised the risk of losing their own (small) flocks with excessive zeal. The popes attempted to exert more control by appointing men from their inner circle to the position of papal legate. Men such as James de Vitry (Bishop of Acre 1214–1226) came to the East with prejudices against the local Orthodox churches. In sharp contrast to Adhemar, the attitudes and actions of the thirteenth century legates were coloured by arrogance and contempt rather than a desire for cooperation. Yet, the local population was more deeply embedded in the multicultural environment and more heavily interrelated with non-Latins than ever before, leaving the pope and his ecclesiastical envoys isolated and ineffectual as a result.

Cyprus

The situation in Cyprus was even more difficult for the Latin Church. Prior to the arrival of the Franks, local religious authority was neither fragmented nor weakened by centuries of Muslim rule. Instead, the Greek Orthodox Church represented most of the population and enjoyed a privileged status under the Byzantine rulers. Neither Richard the Lionheart nor the Lusignans attempted to undermine its position, although it may have been Templar attempts to seize properties or establish dominance that provoked the revolt that drove them from the island in 1192. After the departure of the Templars, the status quo ante was re-established. Neither Greek churches nor monasteries were closed or confiscated by the Latins during the establishment of Frankish rule, although economic properties were sometimes expropriated by the crown or given to Frankish secular elites.

Recent studies demonstrate that the number of Greek monasteries on the island doubled between 1190 and 1560. In addition, Frankish patronage of Orthodox churches was significant. Although adherents of the Latin rites, the Lusignan kings viewed themselves as the rulers of the entire population regardless of religious affiliation, resulting in numerous instances in which the crown sided with the Orthodox church in disputes with the Latin church. Tombs and paintings of Latin lords and ladies in Orthodox churches and icons inscribed in both Greek and Latin indicate that many members of the Latin feudal elite attended Orthodox churches. Further down the social scale, there were so many marriages between adherents of the different churches that loyalty and identity blurred. It appears that women, especially, tended to orthodoxy.

The Latin Church on the island, in contrast, was both impoverished and weak. It was dependent almost exclusively on royal grants, and the Lusignan kings were not generous. The archbishop of Nicosia, the premier Latin cleric in the realm, was granted a small plot of land to build the cathedral and only two villages as an endowment. Otherwise, the archiepiscopal see of Nicosia was dependent on tithes from the Latin population. Since the Latin community was comparatively small, the tithes were commensurately modest. A particular disadvantage was the fact that land acquired prior to 1215 was explicitly exempt from the tithe – and most Frankish lords had received their fiefs before 1215. These secular lords consistently resisted calls from the church to surrender their tithe-free privileges.

For the Latin church hierarchy, the situation was further aggravated by the proliferation of competing Latin religious institutions on the island. The archbishop and his three suffragan bishops at Paphos, Limassol and Famagusta competed for patronage from the same small Latin population as did the military, mendicant and other monastic orders. The latter were often refugees from Syria. Cistercians and Benedictines seem to have been specifically well represented, but Carmelites and Augustine houses were also present. A surprising number of nunneries, including two Franciscan, two Cistercian and no less than five Benedictine, were located in Cyprus. Yet, the number of Latin parish churches was probably no more than ten or twelve on the entire island.

The weakness of the Latin clergy in Cyprus may explain the attempts by the Latin Church to force the Orthodox clergy to recognise the primacy of the Church of Rome. A series of agreements between the pope and the Cypriot Orthodox hierarchy generates heated debates among religious scholars to this day. The 'Bulla Cypria' issued by Pope Alexander IV in

1260 is viewed by some historians as the complete subjugation of the Greeks, while others argue it was a negotiated compromise. Still other historians suggest that the battle lines were less between Latin and Greek churches than within the Greek clergy itself, with one faction willing to make concessions to the pope to gain ascendency over its rivals.

Yet, while controversial at the time, *Bulla Cypria* ultimately defused the frictions between the Greek and Latin hierarchies, and by the end of the thirteenth century, tolerance had replaced tension. A leading contemporary scholar on Cypriot intellectual and ecclesiastical history in the Middle Ages, Chris Schabel, argues:

> Greek Orthodoxy survived the Frankish period not so much because of a successful national struggle against complete absorption as because ... neither the Franks nor the Latin Church ever attempted Latinisation. The Latin Church required what it thought was the bare minimum from the Greek clergy – nothing from the Greek laymen – and the Greek clergy gave the Latin Church what it required ... . There was no schism, no heresy.[19]

Chapter 7

Foreign Affairs of the Crusader States
Diplomatic Relations

Warfare has always attracted more attention than diplomacy, yet no power on earth would not prefer to obtain its foreign policy objectives without resort to war. Only when diplomatic efforts fail must the weapons speak. For this reason, diplomacy is one of the most critical weapons in any political – or military – leader's arsenal. The traditional focus of historians on the crusades – by definition, a series of military campaigns – has obscured the fact that the crusader states were masters of diplomacy, effectively pursuing their goals vis-a-vis the West, the Byzantine Empire and the Muslim states around them.

Diplomatic Ties with the Latin West

Turning first to ties with the West, two aspects need consideration. First, the claim that the crusader states were mere European 'colonies', and, second, their role as the custodians the Christian shrines in the Holy Land.

A Special – Not a Colonial – Relationship
Efforts to equate the status of the crusader states to that of colonies – as was done (positively) in the heyday of nineteenth-century colonialism and (negatively) in the anti-colonial late-twentieth century – are more misleading than enlightening. Colonies are established by powerful entities (kingdoms, states, cities) in foreign environments to enrich the home country. The colonial power sends governors and administrators to the colony, who identify with the 'mother country' and enforce policies that benefit not the local region/community/population but the distant metropolis.

The crusader states, in contrast, had no single 'metropolis' and were independent political entities represented by independent rulers for most of their existence. Not until the mid-thirteenth century did absentee

Western rulers attempt to impose their will on the kingdoms of Jerusalem and Cyprus. They failed in the case of Cyprus, and in Jerusalem met with local opposition that prevented their effectiveness.

Furthermore, taxes did not flow out of the crusader states into the coffers of distant European kingdoms. No one in the crusader states paid a 'stamp tax' or any other duty to a European ruler. The taxes on goods passing through the crusader kingdoms, import and export duties, and all the various forms of taxation by which governments finance their activities accrued not to a distant European 'colonial power' – but to the crusader states themselves. Indeed, for the most part, the fabled wealth of Outremer remained in Outremer, enriching the local population and elites – with the possible exception of the trading fortunes made by the Italian maritime cities.

Finally, the Europeans never viewed the crusader states as 'underdeveloped' or 'backward', as the colonial powers of the eighteenth, nineteenth and twentieth centuries did their colonies. On the contrary, for nearly 200 years, crusaders and pilgrims from the West were impressed by the superior standards of living enjoyed by the residents of the crusader states. For all these reasons, the 'colonial model' is inapplicable to the crusader states.

Custodians of the Holy Land

Instead of occupying an inferior and subordinate position as do colonies, the crusader states sat at the symbolic centre of Christianity and thus held a place of privilege in the intellectual and spiritual geography of medieval Europe. The crusader states might have been politically and militarily weak, but they were never considered peripheral.

The residents of the Holy Land were recognised as the 'first line of defence' protecting the Christian heartland from Muslim threats. Yet, at the same time, the pope, monarchs and peoples of Europe acknowledged that the defence of the most important shrines of Christendom was the joint responsibility of all Christians. Consequently, the religious and secular leaders of the crusader states felt entitled to demand the support of the entire (Latin) Christian world to defend their territory. Nor were they hesitant to do so. On the contrary, the Frankish leadership engaged in nearly continuous nagging at the courts of Europe for money, men and ships to assist them in their mission of retaining control of the Holy Land.

Appeals to the West for aid have been documented in 1120, 1127, 1145, 1150, 1163, 1164, 1165, 1166, 1167, 1168, 1171, 1173, 1174, 1181 and 1184. Several of these led to papal calls for new crusades, although only that of 1145 resulted in a major expedition to the East, the Second Crusade led by Conrad III and Louis VII of France. Notably, many of these appeals went out when the Kingdom of Jerusalem was expanding. Some appeals explicitly requested aid for planned offensive campaigns: the request for the Venetian fleet to attack the coast of Antioch in 1120, the request for men to assist in an attack on Damascus in 1127 and all the appeals from 1163 to 1171 when King Amalric was engaged in Egypt.

Nevertheless, most of these appeals took on a formulaic quality in which the 'dire condition' of the crusader states was described, threats to the holy places were conjured, and the dangers to pilgrims depicted. These embassies have deceived contemporaries and historians alike. All too often, Western noblemen mortgaged their lands or otherwise incurred debt to rush to the defence of the 'endangered' Holy Land only to discover there was no catastrophic threat to the shrines of Christendom – or worse, there was a truce with the Muslims in effect and no fighting was allowed at all.

Many historians continue to impute near collapse and acute danger based on the language of these pleas, creating a picture of near-permanent catastrophe and weakness that is not consistent with evidence from other sources showing comparative strength and security. Amalric did not invade Egypt five times because his kingdom was on the brink of collapse or at risk of being overrun any moment. Indeed, the Franks did not even recognise the need to build major castles until the 1170s, during the reign of Baldwin IV. Yet, as the threat to the crusader states waxed under the sultan Saladin, the Kingdom of Jerusalem had already cried 'wolf' too often. Indeed, from the Second Crusade onwards, the repeated calls for aid yielded meager responses – until it was too late, and the kingdom had been lost at Hattin.

Yet, while Western responses to calls for support might have been lukewarm, there was no fundamental conflict of interest between the crusader states and the powers of Western Europe. Western powers might prioritise other issues, as King Henry II of England repeatedly did when he promised to crusade to the East only to remain in his kingdom to defend it against his rebellious sons and the king of France. Yet, no Latin ruler questioned the fundamental principle of Frankish rule over the Holy

Land or their obligation as a Christian monarch to bolster such rule. Nor did any Western power pursue foreign policy objectives that undermined the foreign policy or security goals of the Franks. Differences of opinion were tactical rather than strategic in nature.

For example, when resources intended to reinforce the crusader states of the Levant were diverted to the conquest of Constantinople, many in the Kingdom of Jerusalem lamented the misdirection of aid, but the Fourth Crusade did not fundamentally undermine the viability of the crusader states. Likewise, the decades-long conflict between the Holy Roman emperor and the local barons of Outremer had the long-term effect of weakening central power and making the crusader states more vulnerable. Yet the issue was the rule of law and feudal rights of vassals, not foreign policy such as the expediency of truces with the Ayyubids.

A degree of tension between the Franks and their Western allies was also created by the fact that the Franks as a rule had a better understanding of divisions within the Saracen camp and a more nuanced approach to dealing with their Muslim neighbours than their contemporaries in the West. The latter were far more likely to fall victim to their own hyperbolic propaganda against the demonic enemy, employed to whip up crusading fever and bolster recruitment. The Franks, on the other hand, used 'fewer polemics than one would find in ... almost any petty ecclesiastical dispute in Europe'.[1] Yet these were differences of tone, not substance. This meant that, at times, the Franks' practical approach to dealing with the Islamic enemy met with astonishment and even suspicion on the part of Western leaders, yet there was no fundamental conflict of aims.

Diplomatic Relations with the Orthodox Powers of the Mediterranean

In contrast with the fundamental alignment of foreign policy goals between the crusader states and Western powers, tensions with Constantinople existed from the very start. Yet, it is wrong to assume that relations between the Franks and Byzantium were consistently hostile. On the contrary, diplomatic relations between the Christian powers in the Eastern Mediterranean were complex and fluid.

The baseline of these relations was drawn by the Byzantines, who called themselves 'Romans' and viewed anyone not part of their empire as 'barbarians'. To the Byzantine elite, the kings of France and England were no more civilised than the sultans of Damascus and the Atabegs of Aleppo. Even in the twelfth century, during a period of accord between Constantinople and the crusader states, the Byzantine emperor could describe Latin Christians as 'barbarian peoples whose way of life is entirely incompatible with our own. Their gaze is scarcely human, while ours is full of humanity; our speech is agreeable, while theirs is harsh and garbled. They are all armed and ... bloodthirsty ... while we are peaceful and compassionate and refuse to carry weapons needlessly, not being in thrall to Ares.'[2]

In addition to a profound sense of cultural superiority, the Byzantines viewed Constantinople – not Rome or Jerusalem – as the centre of the Christian world. In the eyes of the 'Romans' living in the 'Roman Empire', Constantinople was not only the new Rome, it was also the new Jerusalem since it was here that the emperor, the head of the church, resided and ruled. Because the patriarchs viewed the emperor as the head of the church, the pope's influence in Constantinople was minimal.

To complicate relations further, the concept of Holy War was alien to Greek Orthodox theology.[3] What the Byzantine emperor envisaged when he requested aid from the West in 1097 was several hundred trained knights ready to serve as mercenaries in the Byzantine army. The emperor expected to place these fighting men under the control and command of Byzantine authorities. As described, what he got was tens of thousands of undisciplined 'armed pilgrims' (an oxymoron in Byzantine tradition). The Byzantine government and administration were overwhelmed, baffled and ultimately frightened of the monster they had created.

This had a profound and long-lasting impact on Frankish-Byzantine relations. The failure of the Byzantines to understand crusading, led to the assumption that the 'real' goal of the crusades was the capture of Constantinople. The emperor's daughter Anna Comnena wrote in her history: 'to all appearances, they were on a pilgrimage to Jerusalem; in reality, they planned to dethrone Alexius and seize the capital'.[4] A Byzantine historian writing about the Second Crusade (1147–1159) likewise claimed: 'The whole western array had been set in motion on the handy excuse that they were going to ... fight the Turks ... but [in reality] to gain possession of the Romans' land by assault and trample down everything in front of them.'[5] The fact that the crusaders made no assault on Constantinople and, in fact, continued to the Holy Land was attributed to the brilliance of Byzantine policy. The Byzantine court patted itself on the back for deflecting the crusaders from their evil intentions and successfully diverting their energies to the conquest of Muslim-held territory instead.

The conquest of Jerusalem failed to assuage Byzantine suspicions but instead created new problems. First, Byzantine emperors claimed all the lands conquered by the crusaders since they had once been part of the Eastern Roman Empire. Second, as the heads of the Christian Church (in their eyes), Byzantine emperors claimed to be the protectors of the Holy Sepulchre. Yet the crusaders were understandably unwilling to recognise such claims for conquests won with hard fighting, blood and casualties. Nor did they acknowledge the emperor as head of the church.

In the century after the First Crusade, the main bone of contention was Antioch. This had belonged to Constantinople as recently as 1086 and thus had only been in Seljuk hands twelve years when it fell to the crusaders. Yet the siege of Antioch had been bitter and costly, and the majority of the crusade's leaders refused to recognise Byzantine sovereignty over Antioch. Every new prince of Antioch tried to assert his autonomy, but the perennial Seljuk threat, particularly after the loss of the County of Edessa, eventually forced each Latin prince to turn to Constantinople for aid. As a result, periods of relative Antiochene independence alternated with periods of abject submission to imperial domination.

In contrast, Byzantine claims to the territories composing the Kingdom of Jerusalem were nominal. Palestine had not been under Constantinople's control since 637, and no serious pressure was exerted on the Kings of Jerusalem to do homage for Jerusalem. This made it easier to find common ground. Nevertheless, relations first hit a new low when Reynald de Châtillon invaded Byzantine Cyprus and engaged in an orgy of savagery, including the mutilation of prisoners, extortion, rape, pillage and destruction.

Surprisingly, this incident proved to be a turning point in Frankish-Byzantine relations. Baldwin III came north to meet with the emperor. He was prepared to make symbolic concessions in light of the Second Crusade's failure and the ensuing reluctance of the West to respond to his appeals for aid. Manuel, for whatever reasons, was prepared to meet Baldwin halfway and not press for absolute submission.

What emerged was a thaw in relations between Jerusalem and Constantinople that produced quantifiable benefits for both parties. Not only did the alliance deter Seljuk attacks on Antioch, it put an end to Nur al-Din's rhetorical threats to Jerusalem itself. Furthermore, the Byzantine fleet assisted Amalric in his ambitions in Egypt, while Byzantine gold flowed into the Kingdom of Jerusalem, particularly for projects such as the renovation of the Church of the Nativity in Bethlehem. In exchange for Manuel adopting 'crusader rhetoric' and recognising crusader goals as honest and worthy, he received some vague form of homage from King Amalric of Jerusalem. Although the exact nature of Amalric's submission is not known, he paid a state visit to Constantinople in 1171 and evidently recognised the emperor as his overlord in some unrecorded manner; this was a more symbolic than material submission to the emperor.

The new relationship between Constantinople and Jerusalem was cemented by three strategic, royal marriages: Manuel Comnenus married the Princess Marie of Antioch, and Baldwin III and Amalric both married Byzantine princesses. The period of détente between the two major Christian powers of the eastern Mediterranean lasted almost a quarter-century until Manuel's death in 1180.

Just three years later, however, Andronicus I Comnenus swept into power on the back of fervent anti-Latin feelings. He had exploited anti-Latin riots – which had resulted in the slaughter of the Latin population in Constantinople – to seize power and murder Empress Marie and her lover. He first had himself crowned co-emperor with Manuel's son Alexius, but two months later strangled Alexius and took sole power for himself. His foreign policy consisted fundamentally of repudiating Manuel I's pro-Western policies and alliances with the crusader states.

Significantly, Andronicus had fled to Damascus and Baghdad when out of favour in Constantinople. In June 1185, he sent an envoy to Saladin proposing a treaty of alliance between their empires. The purpose of the proposed pact was the destruction of the crusader states. Before Saladin's ambassadors could reach Constantinople with his official response, Andronicus was savagely torn to pieces by the mob in Constantinople and replaced by Isaac Angelus. The latter, however, readily renewed the treaty with Saladin – sending off alarm bells in Jerusalem and igniting outrage in the West.

By 1189, the situation had changed yet again. The Franks had been obliterated at the Battle of Hattin, but a major crusade to retake the

Holy Land was gathering. Arab accounts suggest that Saladin was especially unsettled by the prospect of the Holy Roman emperor, Frederick Barbarossa, bringing a large army to the Near East. Saladin sent ambassadors to Constantinople to renegotiate the terms of the anti-Western alliance. He expected the Byzantines to prevent – or at a minimum, harass, delay and impede – the passage of any crusading armies transiting Byzantine territory. Isaac happily agreed to the new terms yet singularly failed to live up to them – though not for want of trying.

Thus, by 1191 Saladin recognised that his treaty with Constantinople was worthless. Arab sources summarised the alliance with Constantinople as follows: 'In truth, the Greek king has never succeeded in his enterprises; we gain nothing from his friendship and need fear nothing from his enmity.'[6]

But the damage to Byzantine-Frankish relations had already been done. Although the alliance between Damascus and Constantinople ended in 1192, it left a legacy of bitterness and mistrust. Furthermore, the West, particularly the Holy Roman Empire, viewed the Byzantines as duplicitous traitors to Christianity. This ill-fated alliance, along with the massacres of the Italians in 1177 and again in 1182, laid the foundations for the so-called Fourth Crusade.

In 1204, Constantinople fell to an army of mercenaries in the service of the Doge of Venice. The victors established the Latin Empire of Constantinople, a fragile association of states with Latin rulers that controlled Constantinople and much of what is now Greece, but failed to destroy Byzantine opposition. Instead, Byzantium fractured into several competing states, all claiming to be the rightful successor to the old empire. Already by 1261, Constantinople was again in Orthodox hands, and the restored Byzantine Empire lasted nearly another 200 years.

Relations between the crusader states and the Latin Empire of Constantinople is a topic that has not been adequately investigated by scholars. Perhaps the most important diplomatic trend of this period was the fundamental change in Byzantine attitudes towards the Latin West. Chris Wright, in his fascinating article 'On the Margins of Christendom', argues that the Byzantines could no longer dismiss Western culture and politics as irrelevant. He suggests that while rightly outraged by the attack on Constantinople, Byzantine elites, for the first time, recognised that the earlier crusades had been genuine efforts to liberate the Holy Land. They began to skillfully evoke crusader rhetoric to condemn the pope's self-serving calls for new 'crusades' to defend Latin control of Constantinople.

Unfortunately, no study of the response of the Franks of Outremer to this development has been published. Likewise, the diplomatic relations between the restored Byzantine Empire and the crumbling crusader states in 1261–91 remains an unexplored diplomatic chapter in the history of the Latin East. However, there is evidence that the Lusignan Kings of Cyprus maintained cordial diplomatic ties with the Byzantine emperors-in-exile. Also noteworthy, if inadequately documented in Western literature, was the overall positive diplomatic relationship between the crusader kingdoms and the Armenians, except for the bitter war of Antiochene succession between 1216 and 1233.

Diplomatic Relations with Muslim Powers

Diplomatic relations with the Muslim world were complicated by theological and strategic issues, yet they were a fundamental feature of politics in the Holy Land throughout the crusader era. Indeed, the first diplomatic exchanges between crusaders and Muslims predate the fall of Jerusalem to the armies of the First Crusade, and diplomacy with Muslim powers continued throughout the existence of the crusader states. These relations were characterised by sophistication and nuance, more often resulting in success than failure.

This is surprising when one remembers that while Islam preaches the ideal of peace, the definition of peace is the absolute victory of Islam. To obtain that ideal, Muslim leaders were obliged to wage war against any part of the world not already absorbed into the 'dar al-Islam', the realm of Islam. Indeed, the very term used for regions not governed by Islamic law is 'dar al-harb' – the realm of war. Thus, unlike their Christian counterparts, Muslim leaders needed no justification for bringing war to infidels. Instead, they needed to justify making peace with them. Furthermore, the Muslim theology of this period viewed permanent peace with the 'dar al-harb' as anathema and specified that truces should not extend beyond ten years and ten months. Added to this ideological barrier to peace was the fundamental strategic one that both parties sought control over the same territory, the Holy Land. This meant that long-term foreign policy goals were inherently incompatible and mutually exclusive.

Yet practical considerations served to soften and blunt the seemingly irreconcilable differences and deflect some conflict. Then as now, wars were costly and their outcomes unpredictable, creating a natural reluctance on the part of responsible leaders to risk it. This bias towards peace was reinforced in medieval society by the fact that agriculture was more extensive and vulnerable than it is today and produced less surplus. This meant that if wars destroyed successive harvests or damaged agricultural assets such as irrigation systems, terracing or orchards, it took years to replace them and famine became a serious possibility. Finally, the economic argument for peace was made more compelling in the Near East by the fact that both the Franks and their Muslim neighbours profited enormously from trade and travel (pilgrim) networks that cut across the religious divide. If trade or pilgrim traffic were significantly disrupted, the urban population in both the Christian and Muslim states suffered reductions in their standard of living. Only with the advent of the fanatical Mamluks, who were prepared to do without the revenue generated by trade through the ports of the Levant, did this compelling argument for finding diplomatic accommodations disappear.

The crusader states also gained temporary peace by diplomatically exploiting the incessant wars between the Islamic powers, dynasties and princes. These created countless and nearly continuous opportunities for the Franks to play Muslim rivals against one another. Over time, the Franks exploited the conflicts between Fatimid Egypt and Abbasid Syria, the Zangids and the Ayyubids, and between various princes within these different entities, such as the rivalry between the viziers Shawar and Dirgham, or between al-Kamil in Egypt and his brother al-Muazzam in Damascus. Tellingly, there is only one case in which the Muslims succeeded in driving a wedge between Christian powers, namely the treaty between Saladin and Constantinople discussed above.

The willingness of both sides to deal with one another – at a tactical rather than strategic level – went back to the First Crusade itself. The Fatimid caliphate tried to divert the crusade from Jerusalem towards attacks on their Sunni Seljuk rival in the north. Although the crusaders had no interest in concluding such an agreement with the Fatimid state, they were perfectly willing to come to terms with the many local Fatimid leaders in control of coastal towns and fortresses along the route to Jerusalem. For their part, the semi-autonomous rulers of the region 'were all, when it suited them, prepared to form alliances that cut across the religious divide, rather than submit to suzerainty of a greater [Muslim] power'.[7]

The willingness on both parts to treat with the religious and strategic enemy on a short-term tactical basis meant that de facto peace reigned in the crusader states far more frequently than war. One hundred and twenty treaties between the Franks and their Muslim opponents have been identified in the historical sources, of which 109 were implemented. The initiative for truces varied considerably over time. The Muslims were more likely to seek truces in the early period (1098–1124), and the Franks were desperate for truces after 1250. In the century and a quarter in between, neither side was preponderant in seeking peace, suggesting an overall balance of power.[8] Notably, until the Mamluk period, both sides negotiated in good faith and, for the most part, abided by the terms of the agreements concluded.

While the First Kingdom expanded primarily by force of arms, the Second Kingdom expanded primarily through diplomatic success. The latter was assuredly due primarily to the fact that Saladin's successors were constantly fighting with one another and hence too fragmented to undertake a major campaign against the Franks. Furthermore, these Ayyubid princes were also all enjoying the benefits of trade and not terribly interested in jihad. Nevertheless, it is to the Franks' credit that they effectively exploited the rivalries of their opponents and played upon their love of luxury to obtain one concession after another, more through the threat of force than the use of it.

The incremental growth of the Second Kingdom culminated in the so-called 'Baron's crusade', an absurd campaign ironically characterised by Christian disunity and a single disastrous battle. Yet it was this crusade that resulted in the near complete restoration of the Kingdom of Jerusalem to the borders of pre-Hattin 1187 – including Sidon, Ascalon and Jerusalem itself – by diplomatic means. In short, during the first half of the thirteenth century, the Franks proved themselves masters of diplomacy in dealing with their Muslim neighbours – until they fatally backed the wrong side leading to the disaster at Le Forbie.

Perhaps even more astonishing than these diplomatic successes, however, are the number of instances in which Franks and Saracens concluded alliances across religious borders. The sultan of Damascus countered Zengi's growing strength and efforts to displace him by forming an alliance with King Fulk of Jerusalem in c. 1140. It was this alliance that was broken during the Second Crusade with no positive result.

Yet, the alliance was soon in place again because it served the interests of both sides. Likewise, Frederick Barbarossa, intent on the restoration of Jerusalem to Christian rule at the start of the Third Crusade, had no qualms about concluding a temporary non-aggression pact with the sultanate of Rum. During the War of Antiochene Succession (1201–10), Bohemond sought and received the assistance of Muslim leaders in both Aleppo and Iconium to help him against his (Christian) Armenian rival. The most fateful instance of an interfaith – and offensive – alliance, however, was the disastrous backing of as-Salih Ismail of Damascus and an-Nasir Daud of Transjordan against as-Salih Ayyub of Egypt, which ended in the disastrous defeat at Le Forbie in 1244. What is consistent across all these various treaties, however, is that 'each side dealt with the other as fellow politicians, not devils incarnate'.[9]

Yet there were limits to such dealings. While a head of state might strategically conclude an alliance with a Muslim counterpart, any attempt – and there were several – to pull the Saracens into the crusader states' internal politics was viewed as treason and consistently failed. When Hugh le Puiset, Count of Jaffa, called in Egyptian help for his rebellion against Fulk d'Anjou, he instantly lost the support of his vassals, a fact that led directly to his defeat. Princess Alice of Antioch made the same mistake in 1132, completely alienating her barons by appealing to Zengi for support; they turned at once to the king of Jerusalem to intercede and remove her from power. Likewise, in 1160, Gerard de Grenier, Lord of Sidon and Beaufort, isolated himself and lost his barony when he sought aid from Nur al-Din in a dispute with Baldwin III. The most famous instance of such an alliance between an individual Frankish lord and a formidable Muslim leader was the separate truce Raymond of Tripoli concluded with Saladin after refusing to do homage to Guy de Lusignan in 1186. This move nearly tore the kingdom apart and resulted in a devastating Frankish defeat at the Springs of Cresson. Only Tripoli's remorse and the diplomatic efforts of Balian d'Ibelin enabled the Franks to patch up their differences and face the Saracens united at Hattin a few months later.

Overall, the inter-religious negotiations were similar to truces throughout the West, yet they had some unique features. In the West, for example, there was a well-established custom of meetings directly between leaders. One needs only to think of the frequent meetings between Henry II and Louis VII. But summit diplomacy had no tradition in the East. In the West, gifts were usually symbols of submission and homage; something offered at the end rather than the beginning of negotiations. In the East, in contrast, the exchange of gifts usually signaled the desire to open negotiations and seek a truce.

Such differences in practice led to a number of misunderstandings in the early years. With time, however, both sides learned to read the other better, and rituals evolved that prevented unnecessary confusion. In this sense, the crusades contributed to the professionalisation of diplomacy, including the practice of granting envoys safeguards against harm and retribution, something we know today as 'diplomatic immunity'.

Lastly, unlike the West, where the terms of treaties were mostly concerned with the control of territorial assets such as cities and castles, peace agreements between Franks and Saracens usually contained a human component. The free passage of pilgrims of both religions through territory controlled by the other was an important feature of most treaties. A more important – and poignant – element was the return of captives.

Throughout the crusader era, the Franks and their Orthodox Christian allies faced slavery every time they were taken captive, whether in battle, siege or raid. Only the highest noblemen were excepted, as they could be held for ransom. For every nobleman held for ransom, there were scores of knights, hundreds of turcopoles and sergeants, and thousands of peasants, women and children sold into slavery. The latter were often the victims of small-scale raiding, a perennial phenomenon even during official truces.

At any one time, thousands of Christians, former subjects of the Frankish kings and princes, were held in captivity by the Muslim enemies of the Franks. Some of these were Frankish settlers; more of them were native Christians. Surprisingly, they were not forgotten. On the contrary, in truce after truce, the Franks remembered their captive subjects. The return of captives – not just noble or knightly prisoners – was a component of negotiations with the enemy. There are recorded incidents when the Franks leveraged a Muslim desire for peace to secure the release of thousands of captives. In one instance – viewed as an example of Frankish 'arrogance' – the Arab chronicler Ibn al-Athir records:

> The Franks sent to review those male and female slaves of their people who had been taken from all the Christian lands and bade them choose whether they would stay with their

lords or return to their homelands. Anyone who preferred to stay was left, and anyone who wanted to go home went there.

This clearly refers to women, which highlights the fact that such agreements were not confined to the release of fighting men. Furthermore, this particular agreement was extremely comprehensive as it applied to the entire city of Damascus. Again, thousands of captives must have benefited from the negotiated settlement.

Yet, such agreements were only possible if the Franks held good cards, i.e. if they negotiated from strength. As a result, many captives languished for years in slavery before a change in fortune enabled the Franks to extract concessions from their opponents. The fact that some captives waited a long time for release does not diminish their importance. On the contrary, even years later, relatives, friends and comrades were determined to obtain the release of those they loved. The fact that Frankish negotiators – always members of the Frankish elite – recognised and respected this is to their credit.

In summary, the Franks maintained sophisticated and largely effective diplomatic relations with all the major players in the Eastern Mediterranean. The exact opposite of the religious fanatics depicted in film and fiction, the Franks readily and frequently concluded truces with their Muslim enemies and were also willing to ally themselves with individual Muslim leaders in the pursuit of tactical objectives. Frankish diplomacy was based on respect for their enemies and a profound appreciation of their differences and rivalries, which belies portrayals of the Franks as racist. Although the Franks were not always successful at navigating the tricky waters of shifting Muslim power politics, they were not insensitive to them. Likewise, they understood Byzantine perspectives and prejudices and ultimately found ways to exploit Byzantine vanity to their own advantage. Meanwhile, their relations with the West remained rooted in the common recognition that the crusader states were the guardians of Christianity's most sacred sites. Despite superficial differences in lifestyle, language and tactics, the crusader states retained solid ties with the papacy and the leading Western European powers throughout their existence, ties which they exploited a much as possible to their advantage without ever surrendering their sovereignty.

Chapter 8

The Economy of the Crusader States
Diversity, Prosperity and Technology Transfer

Introduction and Overview

The establishment of the crusader kingdoms along the coast of the Levant resulted in an economic revival of the region. What had been an unimportant backwater to the Ayyubid and Fatimid caliphates, whose religious, administrative and economic centres lay in Damascus and Cairo, respectively, suddenly become the spiritual heart of the entire Latin-Christian world.

The crusaders resettled the Christian Holy Land after its depopulation through conquest and the resulting enslavement and deportation of much of the native population. Investment into infrastructure revitalised the rural economy and enabled the expansion of trading networks. Existing cities grew, and ancient cities such as Caesarea and Ramla, which had gone to ruin, were revived. Indeed, entire new settlements and villages were built. The larger cities, such as Acre, Tyre, Beirut, Tripoli and Antioch, became booming urban centres with larger populations than the capitals of the West. Not until the mid-thirteenth century did Western European cities start to compete in size with the cities of the Latin East.

Key to this economic boom were strategic investments. Some aided an expansion of arable land and an increase in agricultural productivity. Others entailed the introduction of entirely new agricultural products and enabled industrialisation of the production of select commodities resulting in surpluses for export. As a result, the First Kingdom of Jerusalem was a net exporter of agricultural produce. While the Second Kingdom of Jerusalem was not, it retained the fertile coastal plain, critical for producing fruits, vegetables and chief export crops. Collectively, however, the crusader states increased agricultural output and self-sufficiency in foodstuffs in the thirteenth century due to the acquisition of Cyprus.

Yet, the famed wealth of Outremer did not derive from agriculture. The services sector was sizeable, and industry was significant, while trade became the great engine generating economic prosperity. The expansion of trade was made possible by the development and maintenance of infrastructure networks connecting the coastal urban centres with each other and other cities in the region, such as Aleppo, Damascus, Baghdad and Egypt. The roads, of course, had existed under the Romans and Byzantines long before the arrival of the crusaders, but had mostly fallen to ruin. The Franks undertook their reconstruction and built new roads to enable inland cities such as Nazareth, Nablus, Bethlehem and Jerusalem to be readily accessed by pilgrims and supplied with necessities.

Most importantly, the Franks connected the traditional oriental trade routes with the growing, increasingly prosperous and luxury-hungry markets of Western Europe. Trading privileges had been the lure that harnessed Italian maritime power to the crusaders' cause. As soon as the Italians established a foothold on the coast of the Levant, they transformed the coastal cities into major trading hubs. The value of this trade can be illustrated by Acre, which in the latter half of the thirteenth century alone annually generated crown revenues significantly greater than that of all England.[1] These urban centres not only generated tax revenue, they also created enormous employment opportunities for both skilled and unskilled labour.

Only in the twilight years of the second half of the thirteenth century did geopolitical changes begin to threaten the foundations of the Frankish economy. The Mongols had devastated first Baghdad and then Antioch, leaving the traditional trade routes in shambles. Meanwhile, Mongol domination of the entire Asian continent from China to Constantinople opened a land route for the riches of the Far East. The Black Sea and Constantinople gained in importance at the expense of the Eastern Mediterranean. What might have been a slow decline, however, was turned into a catastrophic implosion by the Mamluk conquest of the mainland crusader states. The Mamluk policy of obliteration and depopulation brought an abrupt end to the age of prosperity.

In contrast, the economy of Cyprus was predominantly agricultural. In the 400 years of Muslim domination of the Levant, it did not suffer in equal measure from the damage of conquest, occupation and depopulation as the mainland. Nor did Frankish conquest cause any meaningful disruption in the island's agricultural productivity. Cyprus' population was not decimated, and the system of land tenure was not altered; Frankish landlords simply replaced the absentee Byzantine aristocrats. Imperial lands became royal lands. Feudal obligations were introduced for the large landowners at the pinnacle of the pyramid, but the impact of such customs on the serfs at the bottom was negligible.

Yet, whereas the Byzantine authorities looked to Constantinople as 'the City' and showed no interest in developing Cypriot industry and trade, the Lusignans consciously promoted both. Furthermore, because the Lusignans were not beholden to the Italian maritime states for their conquests, they had no need to grant them exclusive concessions. Instead, the Lusignans fostered competition between the various Italian merchant states while keeping markets open to Armenians, Greeks, French, Syrians and other merchants. Furthermore, the Cypriot crown retained for itself the lion's share of the economic assets: an estimated one-third of rural villages and monopolies on key products such as salt while keeping firm control over tariffs, duties and infrastructure. The quality and purity of commodities such as gold and silver and products such as silk, sugar, wax and honey were carefully supervised. Price controls were introduced as necessary to prevent price-gouging in periods of scarcity. Perhaps most significant, unlike the mainland crusader states in which Byzantine, Syrian, Egyptian and multiple domestic currencies circulated, the Lusignans maintained a monopoly on the minting of coins in Cyprus; foreign coins were melted down and reminted.

In short, without impeding agricultural activities, the Lusignans diversified the Cypriot economy. Besides giving the kingdom a stronger economic base, it increased rural prosperity as the rural population profited from supplying the growing urban centres on the island with food.

Cyprus also avoided the Mamluk juggernaut. Instead, it was flooded with Christian refugees in the last decades of the thirteenth century. These caused short-term economic disruptions such as skyrocketing food prices (until the royal price controls kicked in) and inflation of urban property prices and rents alongside a devaluation of portable valuables such as gold, silver and gemstones. However, the situation soon stabilised, and for nearly 100 years, Famagusta, Limassol and Kyrenia replaced Acre, Tyre and Beirut as the most important trade hubs for the exchange of goods between the Near East and Europe alongside

Alexandria and Constantinople. In consequence, the fourteenth century was one of the most prosperous in the history of Cyprus.

What follows is a closer look at the various factors that contributed to this economic prosperity on the mainland and in Cyprus.

Agriculture

Agriculture under Muslim Rule

The Holy Land is the proverbial land of 'milk and honey', a fertile region with a moderate climate and sufficient rainfall to support ancient and medieval population levels in abundance. When the crusaders first arrived, however, they did not find a garden of Eden but rather an underpopulated region with encroaching deserts.

The decline of the region started with the Arab conquests. Throughout the first 200 years of Muslim expansion, the principal source of wealth in the Muslim states was booty and slaves from conquered regions. Simply to maintain their lifestyle, elites had to continue their conquests. While the victorious Arab armies moved on to new frontiers, they left behind devastated regions, depleted of moveable wealth and inhabited by decimated and dislocated populations.

The Holy Land was no exception. The initial conquests were accompanied by the wholesale slaughter and enslavement of large portions of the rural population. Those natives who could, fled to the walled cities, abandoning their farms and fields, but tens of thousands were not so lucky. Although most cities submitted to the conquerors on the basis of negotiations that enabled the inhabitants to buy their freedom in exchange for subjugation and the perpetual payment of tribute, this did little to restore rural infrastructure.

On the contrary, in the wake of the Muslim armies came Muslim immigrants who expropriated the land, dwellings and entire villages of the native inhabitants for themselves. The bulk of these new residents from the Arabian Peninsula, however, were herders, not farmers. They did not plant the fields they confiscated. Instead, they let their herds graze on them until they were worthless. This meant that they could only maintain themselves by pillaging, extorting money or confiscating more land from the non-Muslim farmers that remained. The perennial conflict between herdsmen and farmers – familiar all over the world – took on the character of religious conflict. Armed with a religion that viewed all non-believers as inferior and unworthy of respect, the nomads felt entitled to 'devastate with impunity a fertile and densely populated province, leaving nothing but ruins [while] carrying away the population into slavery'.[2]

Yet, while the prosperity and numbers of 'dhimmi' peasants decreased, their tax burden increased. On the one hand, as the pace of conquest slowed, the booty and slaves derived became less plentiful, making the state more dependent on taxes and tributes from already subjugated regions. On the other hand, because the Muslim population was mainly tax-exempt, the caliphate had to compensate for lost revenue on land taken over by Muslims by increasing taxes on the remaining 'dhimmis'. Contrary to the popular view of 'dhimmis' being subject only to one additional tax – the 'jizyah'— 'dhimmis' were subject to an array of extra, burdensome taxes. In addition to the 'jizyah', 'dhimmis' paid taxes on land, income and products and were subject to compulsory labour for construction projects in the shipyards and to man the sultan's fleets. The 'dhimmis' paid for the troops that oppressed them, and the subsidies that supported the tribes that expropriated their lands.

Meanwhile, the triumphant Muslim conquerors enjoyed a lavish and luxurious lifestyle in their flourishing urban centres. The Arab 'golden age' produced celebrated works of architecture, literature and science. Just like the accomplishments of the 'Golden Age' of Athens and Rome, these were the products of a slave economy. Unlike ancient Greece and Rome, however, slaves in the Muslim world were not solely a by-product of conquest and the slave trade; treaties of submission diligently included annual payments in human beings as well as gold. The slave tribute was supplemented by periodic raids into local villages populated by non-Muslims. This amounted to an ongoing and perpetual drain on the human capital of the Holy Land, as slaves were siphoned off for sale and service in the Muslim urban areas outside the region, such as Aleppo, Cairo, Damascus, Baghdad and Mosul. Left behind was a dwindling rural population no longer able or motivated to cultivate more land than was necessary for absolute subsistence.

Ironically, the fact that the Muslim conquerors often obtained slaves from more sophisticated civilisations who enjoyed higher levels of education greatly contributed to the Arab intellectual and artistic flourishing of the eighth to tenth centuries. The high qualifications and diverse talents of some slaves enabled them to rise to positions of significant influence. Later generations of local elites, mainly Jacobites who had been oppressed and persecuted by the Byzantines, chose collaboration with the Muslim regimes over rebellion. The most ambitious native elites, whether Christian or Jewish, pragmatically pursued careers and fortunes in the service of their new masters, just as they had served Rome and Constantinople in earlier centuries. The best educated urban inhabitants – scribes, accountants, translators, architects and builders, doctors and lawyers, merchants and bankers – could and did prosper under Muslim rule. They accepted their subordinate status, the humiliations and extra-taxes in exchange for influence and wealth – or they converted to Islam. These 'dhimmi' elites contributed materially to Arab prosperity and to the intellectual, artistic and scientific achievements of the age.

The success of this class of educated Christians, Jews and Zoroastrians that came to prominence in the Arab world has blinded many observers to the fact that most of their co-religionists remained politically disenfranchised and desperately poor. The chronicles of Muslims, Christians and Jews document the disparity between the lifestyle of the urban 'dhimmi' elites and their rural brothers. The chronicles also highlight vividly the discrepancy between the abstract theories of the 'protected' status of 'dhimmis' and the reality for the majority of the 'dhimmi' population. Protection worked for the bureaucrats, diplomats and bankers useful to the Arab ruling class, but not for simple peasants and unskilled labourers, who were despised. While the urban elites collaborated with the regime and were rewarded, the rural population experienced unremitting exploitation, humiliation and abuse.

Under the Abbasids, the local tax collectors attempted to wring ever-larger payments out of their subject peoples, provoking widespread rural flight. Egyptian scholar Bat Ye'or describes the situation vividly:

> Money was extorted by blows, torture, and death – particularly by crucifixion. Sometimes the whole population of a village – Christians, Jews, and Arabs – were kept in a church for several days without food ... until a ransom was paid ... . Over-taxed and tortured by the tax collectors, the villagers fled into hiding or emigrated to the towns.[3]

The result was a further decline in the rural population and an increased loss of agricultural productivity. And then the Seljuks came.

The Seljuks repeated the age-old pattern of conquest, accompanied by widescale destruction, slaughter and the enslavement of captives. On the eve of the crusades in the late twelfth century, the Byzantine historian Anna Comnena described the Near East's once prosperous and fertile regions as a desert inhabited by Turkish nomads. While this was clearly an exaggeration, Arab, Syriac and Armenian sources corroborate the fact that, across the Holy Land, not only churches and synagogues but entire villages and towns had been abandoned. Agricultural productivity had fallen to a minimum, and desertification was on the rise.

Frankish Agriculture
This was the state of affairs when the crusaders arrived at the start of the twelfth century. Perhaps because the Frankish feudal elite derived its wealth from agriculture, it was quick to recognise the agricultural potential of the Holy Land. Certainly, the Franks set about improving the yield of the land by making strategic investments. The large number of ecclesiastical landlords in the crusader states was beneficial because they could draw on substantial capital reserves from their mother institutions. Furthermore, monastic institutions in Western Europe had long been at the cutting edge of agricultural technology and innovation. Yet, it was not church lands alone that benefitted from investment. Crown and baronial lands also enjoyed investment in such features as terracing, aqueducts, the clearing and opening of springs and wells, the filling of water reservoirs and the construction of wind and water-powered mills to pump water into newly laid irrigation canals and ditches. In addition, the Franks built roads for transporting products to market.

Such investment benefitted the native rural population, who could increase productivity on the land they held. Furthermore, the Franks increased the amount of land under cultivation by actively recruiting agricultural labour from the West. As noted above, roughly 140,000 Latin Christians immigrated to the Holy Land in the first eighty years of the twelfth century; a sizeable portion of those appear to have moved to rural communities. The immigrants were attracted by free status, low rents, an almost complete absence of feudal labour services, modern infrastructure and proximity to the holiest sites in Christendom.

Archaeological surveys conducted at the end of the last century demonstrate that the Franks settled predominantly near existing Christian settlements. Notably, unlike the Arab settlers of the previous four centuries, 'the Franks did not evict the local villagers from their homes. Most of the Frankish villages were established in places which had been abandoned before the arrival of the Franks or in places which were outside the boundaries of the previous villages'.[4] In other words, the Franks took over land that had been abandoned, allowed to lie fallow or had become semi-desert due to overgrazing and neglect.

Once in the Holy Land, the rural immigrants integrated with the local Christian population, using the same markets, baths, shops, tradesmen and even churches. Intermarriage with native Christians was common. The typical rural village of this period had between 500 and 600 inhabitants, composed of farmers and skilled craftsmen such as carpenters, metal workers, butchers, bakers and the like.

In some regions, however, the depopulation of previous centuries had been so significant that the land could support the creation of new villages inhabited exclusively by immigrants. These purely Frankish villages demonstrated some unique features such as collective ovens, collective oil and wine presses, large granaries and sometimes sugar factories. Communal ovens and mills were often co-located since the lord of the manor generally held both; instances of baths built to exploit the heat of the ovens also have been found. Exclusively Frankish settlements also differed from older native communities by being planned rather than growing haphazardly. Some villages spread out along a road; others were built in concentric circles around a new manor house, church or other central focal point such as a mill, granary or oil and wine press. The focal point of the latter type of village often served several satellite villages as well. The remains of manor houses, both fortified and unfortified, testify to the presence of the feudal elite in these villages.

Initially, the new settlers must have been highly dependent on the native rural population to adjust to a new environment. They would have had to learn about the Near East's weather patterns, which differed from the soggy, cool climate of France, England and the Holy Roman Empire, whence they had come. They would have been required to adjust their patterns of sowing and harvesting to different growing seasons. They would have needed to become familiar with different breeds of livestock, including goats and camels. They would also have been confronted with unfamiliar crops such as dates, sugar cane, figs, bananas and citrus fruits. Lastly, they would have had to learn to work with old-fashioned, oxen-drawn ploughs rather than the more effective horse-drawn ones long used in Europe. This was because the soil of the Near East was too shallow; a European-type plough would have dried out and killed the crops.

Soon, however, rural Franks were doing more than adapting; they were expanding and diversifying agricultural production. Wine and pork production, both of which had been neglected under Muslim rule, were ramped up, while sugar and olive oil production were industrialised to produce surpluses for export. Other cash crops were rice, cotton, indigo and balsam.

Orchards were another ubiquitous feature of the Frankish countryside, surrounding many of the urban centres. In addition to olive orchards and vineyards, the Franks cultivated almonds, pistachios, dates, figs, bananas, lemons, oranges, apples, pears, cherries, peaches, pomegranates, plums and carob. Vegetables represented another important agricultural product of the region, although these were grown primarily for domestic or household consumption. These included beans, lentils, cabbages, onions, garlic, artichokes, cucumbers, melons and mustard.

A wide variety of livestock thrived in the Near East and was cultivated by the Franks. Most essential for food were sheep, goats, pigs and fowl, while horses, mules, camels and donkeys were raised as beasts of burden. Oxen held an ambidextrous position, used for milk, meat and leather, but also for ploughing. Finally, fish formed an vital part of the medieval diet due to fasting rules that prohibited meat consumption in certain periods. The demand for fresh fish in the booming coastal cities exceeded local capacity to deliver. In addition to Pisan and Genoese fisherman, Jewish fisherman from as far away as Alexandria fished in the waters of the Levant and offloaded cargoes at the Frankish ports.

One form of livestock was particularly valuable: war horses. Despite the development of specialised horse transports, many crusaders and armed pilgrims arrived in the Holy Land without adequate mounts because many horses died of illness or were killed or permanently injured in accidents during the long journey. Even those horses that survived the trip could not always adapt to the Near East's climate and diet. Last but not least, combat took a heavy toll on horses. The demand for replacement mounts was therefore enormous and could only be met by the local market. The horses bred in the surrounding Muslim states could be of exceptional quality for what they were bred for: speed and agility. As a rule, however, they lacked the stamina and strength required of a knight's palfrey or destrier, both of which were expected to carry a man in full armour either for extended periods (the palfrey) or in intensive and rapid charges (the destrier). The Franks of Outremer cultivated the breeding of horses to Western standards in numbers exceeding their needs. It was undoubtedly a lucrative business. Knights arriving in the Holy Land without mounts were prepared to pay exorbitant prices to regain their military capabilities and status, both of which were lost without horses.

Despite the retention of the fertile coastal plain with its orchards, gardens and sugar factories, the thirteenth century saw a shift in agricultural production away from the Kingdom of Jerusalem to the Kingdom of Cyprus. Under the Lusignans, Cyprus exported surplus wheat, wine, oil, pulses, carob and salt to the Frankish states on the mainland instead of to Constantinople as in the Byzantine period. The Cypriot agricultural economy was significantly more diverse than that of the Kingdom of Jerusalem. In addition to the familiar products of wheat, barley, rye, wine, olive oil and sugar, Cyprus exported salted fish, salt, onions, honey, wax and candlesticks, soap, cotton and silk textiles, pine resin and indigo. It produced cheese, timber, flax, cotton and rice for domestic consumption. The primary agricultural exports were wheat, barley, wine, olive oil, salt, fish, sugar and carob, while the other export products were less substantial in quantity, although not necessarily less in value.

A noteworthy feature of agricultural development in Cyprus under the Lusignans was the employment of highly sophisticated and efficient techniques at the cutting edge of medieval technology. Archaeological excavations show that waterpower was used extensively, including horizontal wheels with vertical millstones (a recent innovation) and water recycling from mills for use in irrigation and fishponds.

Religious Tourism and Financial Services

Although the costs of protecting and maintaining the holy shrines of Christianity were enormous in both gold and blood, the existence of so many pilgrimage destinations within its borders contributed to the economic base of the Kingdom of Jerusalem. In an age before the

The Economy of the Crusader States

concept of 'tourism' had evolved, the Kingdom of Jerusalem had a thriving tourism industry, complete with high and low seasons and other characteristics of modern mass tourism.

The news that Jerusalem had returned to Christian control had barely reached Europe before the first ships carrying pilgrims set out. At the start of the twelfth century, these ships were small, taking on average only fifty passengers in addition to cargo. Soon, however, to meet the enormous demand, specialised 'pilgrim' ships with a capacity for 200 passengers were built. By the thirteenth century, pilgrim ships could take as many as 1,500 passengers per voyage.

The Templars and Hospitallers both engaged in this trade. Records show, for example, that the Port of Marseilles restricted the military orders to two large passenger transports twice per year, presumably to ensure that the bulk of the trade went to local shipowners. Undoubtedly, the military orders transported passengers from other ports as well, mainly Messina, Taranto and Brindisi. Assuming the same number of ships per port, the military orders alone would have transported 24,000 pilgrims to the Holy Land each year. Meanwhile, the majority of pilgrims would have travelled aboard commercial ships owned by local shipowners or the Italian maritime powers such as Venice, Pisa and Genoa. The number of Western pilgrims travelling annually to the Holy Land easily topped 50,000. In addition, pilgrims came from the Byzantine Empire, from Egypt and as far away as Ethiopia, if in smaller numbers. In short, in good years the number of tourists must have approached 60,000.

Nor did the tourist trade disappear when the Christians lost control over Jerusalem, Bethlehem, Nazareth and the Jordan River. Throughout the thirteenth century, the pilgrims continued to come, passing through the coastal ports still in Frankish hands like Acre, before embarking on the dangerous journey through Muslim-held territory to reach the holy sites. When such travel became too hazardous – and there are many recorded incidents of pilgrims being killed, kidnapped or robbed while travelling in Muslim territory in the thirteenth century – the church began offering indulgences and remission of temporal punishment for visiting specific sites in Acre and possibly other Frankish cities. In short, throughout its existence, the Kingdom of Jerusalem accommodated massive numbers of tourists compared to the size of the resident population.

The pilgrims arrived in two great waves, one at the end of the stormy season in the spring and the other just before the storms resumed in October. During these peak periods, hundreds of pilgrim ships clogged the harbours of the kingdom, particularly Acre. Like today, the pilgrims differed in the capacity to pay and in their expectations for services. The very wealthy could charter entire ships for themselves, their companions, entourage and servants, ensuring more comfortable accommodation, increased security and higher-quality food. The less affluent but still well-off could take advantage of 'all-inclusive package deals', which included transportation, food, beverage and servants for the duration of the voyage. The poorest were packed together in the bowels or on the open deck of cargo ships and brought their own food with them for a trip that averaged three to six weeks.

The Kingdom of Jerusalem, meanwhile, developed a sophisticated economic sector dedicated to meeting the needs of these tourists on arrival. This included accommodation, food and entertainment, outfitting, livery and transport services, interpreters, guides and security services for visits to the more distant and isolated destinations, and, of course, souvenirs such as reliquaries, icons and religious jewelry, all of which were produced and sold in the kingdom. Meanwhile, the passenger ships needed refitting for the return voyage, and so chandleries and repair yards also flourished. Altogether, the religious tourist industry created thousands of urban jobs.

The diverse origins of the pilgrims meant they also took advantage of another key service sector in the Kingdom of Jerusalem, money exchanges. Nevertheless, it was not until the thirteenth and fourteenth centuries that financial services became a main economic sector in the crusader states – in Cyprus rather than Jerusalem. The Italian banks established representatives in Nicosia, turning it into a centre for lending – much to the outrage of the local archbishop, who railed against usury. Indeed, the archbishop noted a variety of shady practices that had the effect of raising interest rates far above the accepted norms. These included fake sales, i.e. the borrowers purchased fictitious goods and sold them back at a loss, imaginary penalties for fabricated late payments, and making the borrower sign for a larger sum than was received. 'The fact that borrowers were clearly prepared to go along with such subterfuges, however, despite the unethical character and the high rates of interest they had to pay, shows that there was a strong demand for capital that was to be used to finance commercial ventures.'[5]

Industry and Manufacturing

The industrial sector in the crusader states was less well-developed than tourism, but it was far from insignificant. Agro-processing played an important role, while other industries grew out of the tourist trade and the region's religious significance. Many of these industries – at least those we know about today – entailed the production of high-margin luxury products.

One of the oldest industries in the region was shipbuilding, which enjoyed a tradition reaching back to the Phoenicians. It had been neglected during the Arab period, but under the Franks enjoyed a modest revival. Due to the lack of local timber, however, the shipyards of the Levant were never able to compete with chief shipbuilding hubs such as the Italian city-states or the Hansa League. Nevertheless, Acre boasted a major repair yard, with dry-dock slips for the repair and maintenance of six ocean-going vessels at a time. In addition, evidence of smaller yards for the construction of coastal and fishing vessels has been found. The abundance of timber from the Troodos Mountains probably explains the development of significant shipyards in Famagusta in the late-thirteenth and fourteenth centuries, despite the lack of a strong seafaring tradition in Cyprus.

Likewise, although agro-processing had a long tradition in the Levant, the most crucial agro-industry of the crusader kingdoms was a relatively new development: **sugar**. Prior to the arrival of the Franks, preparation of a primitive sweetener from sugar cane was conducted predominantly at the household level. It was the Franks who transformed sugar production into an extensive and highly lucrative industry.

The driving force behind this development may have been the importance of sugar as an ingredient for the medicines of this period. Both the Hospitallers and Teutonic Knights were active producing and refining sugar not for export but for use in their hospitals. Sugar production was capital intensive. It required investment in both plantation-style production and refining. Highly sophisticated irrigation networks were needed that could both feed and starve specific fields successively to ensure a constant and regulated flow of ripe sugar to water-powered factories. Because sugar cannot be transported far after harvesting without losing its sweetness, the Franks built numerous factories close to the cane fields along the coast and in the Jordan Valley.

When the Franks took control of Cyprus, they introduced large-scale sugar manufacturing to Cyprus. In both Jerusalem and Cyprus, the investment paid off handsomely. The West had an insatiable demand for this luxury product, and profit margins were high, making sugar one of the most profitable industries of the crusader states.

Another agro-based industry was **wine**. Wine production was widespread across the crusader states from Antioch and Latakia down the entire coast, in the region around Jerusalem, and Cyprus. Wine presses have been found inside individual houses and in estate centres. Presses were composed of a stone and connected to plaster-lined vats for treading the grapes, which drained via stone pipes into collection tanks. Written records describe pruning methods facilitating the production of three crop yields from a single vine per year. Despite these intensive farming methods, demand appears to have outstripped supply as wine was routinely imported – and not because domestic wine was of lesser quality. On the contrary, travellers to the Holy Land in this period attest to the high quality of the wines produced in the crusader states, particularly around Bethlehem. Cypriot wines were even more coveted. Wildbrand of Oldenburg, who visited Cyprus in 1212, claimed that Cypriot wine was 'so thick and rich as if meant to be consumed like honey on bread'.[6] To this day, 'Commandaria' wine, named after the Hospitaller commandery at Kolossi, is famous as a sweet wine.

Olive-oil manufacturing is another ancient Near East industry that continued and intensified under the Franks. Frankish-age oil presses have been uncovered in urban and rural dwellings, estate centres and castles across the crusader states, including Cyprus. Despite nearly ubiquitous oil production throughout the crusader states, most was consumed domestically rather than exported. This may be, in part, because oil was an essential ingredient of a more lucrative export, namely soap. **Soap** was known to have been produced in Tripoli, Nablus and Acre on the mainland and in Paphos in Cyprus. Soap is a major product of Nablus until this day.

Another cluster of agro-industries was based on livestock, namely **tanning and the production of leather goods**. Tanneries were always located near a water source (and presumably slaughterhouses) on the outskirts and downwind of urban areas. They were complex, with several plaster-lined pools necessary for different stages of the process. One crusader-era tannery has been identified near the Tanner's Gate in Jerusalem. Once tanned, the leather could be fashioned into a variety of products. These were popular because leather was one of the few comparatively flexible waterproof materials available in this era. For example, leather was used for footwear (shoes and boots), gloves, bags and purses, cloaks, saddles and other tack, but also for book covers and parchment.

Pottery has been produced across the Eastern Mediterranean since prehistoric times. In the Crusades era, high-quality pottery was produced in the Byzantine Empire and in Syria and Egypt. While higher quality wares were imported (Chinese porcelain has been recorded among the imports), the domestic pottery production in the mainland crusader states served everyday purposes and was a 'consumable' of comparatively low value. Indeed, pottery was often used as ballast on ships trading regionally. Most pottery produced in the crusader kingdoms was utilitarian and produced by the local population, who were presumably carrying on the crafts of their forefathers.

The most common products were storage vessels for both liquid and dry goods, cooking and eating utensils such as pots, pans, jugs, jars, basins, bowls, mugs and cups. These objects were made of buff or red-coloured clay, and some were decorated with red or brown designs on a pale background. One popular variant of cooking pots and pans was glazed on the inside to prevent food from sticking, the medieval equivalent of Teflon. The Franks introduced pottery production to Cyprus, and from 1220 onwards, kilns operated in Paphos, Lapithos and near Famagusta. Over time, the quality of Cypriot pottery increased and developed distinctive characteristics. Cypriot pottery was glazed and adopted motifs and images drawn from the romances of the period.

Glass manufacturing is another ancient industry that continued under the Franks. Jewish sources indicate that much glass manufacturing was in Jewish hands, but there is no indication that the Jews had a monopoly on this lucrative business. Glass was both blown into vessels and used as glazing for windows. Crusader-era glazing has been found in both religious and secular ruins, including at a farmhouse site, which suggests that its use extended to the gentry class and was probably used in the homes of the wealthy urban population as well. Window glass was either round panes or plate glass and could be clear or stained. Fragments of dark and light purple, blue, turquoise, dark and light green, yellow and brown stained glass have been found. Colourless glass painted with decoration has also been recovered.

Glass was blown to create various vessels, including lamps, bottles, bowls, jars, cups and goblets. The production of glass lamps was traditional from Byzantine and Arab times, and their manufacture represented no break with the past. Some of the lamps were blue or greenish blue, and some had glass handles of a different colour. Bottles with long necks and a decorated, flaring rim appear to have been quite popular with the Franks, possibly for perfume. Cups, beakers and goblets, all for drinking wine, were also produced in significant numbers, some in light-blue and light-green glass. Beirut, on the other hand, was famous for its ruby-red glass.

Glass in this period might also be etched or cut to create decorations. Some vessels were inscribed with names, sayings, warnings or blessings. Other forms of decoration were 'prunting', small protrusions of glass applied to the exterior surface that presumably made it easier to hold – perhaps for chilled wines and sherbets which caused exterior water condensation in hot weather. More elaborate and expensive decoration consisted of enamel decorations on the finished glass object. The production of enameled glass was recorded in Acre. The most common decorations popular with the Franks were heraldic devices, flowers and plants, animals, birds and mythological beasts.

Contemporary accounts testify to the high quality of crusader-era glass, which was extremely transparent. Writing in the early-thirteenth century, the bishop of Tyre, Jacques de Vitry, claimed the glassmakers of both Tyre and Acre made 'the purest glass with cunning workmanship out of the sands of the sea'.[7] Indeed, the famed Venetian glassmaking industry, which lasted well into the eighteenth century, was founded on high-grade ingredients imported from the Levant, mainly beach sand with a high silica content found at both Acre and Tyre, the centres of the crusader-era glassmaking industry.

Textile production was both diverse and plentiful. Despite its fragility, thousands of textile fragments from the crusader era have been discovered, including silk, cotton, linen, felt and wool, as well as cloth woven from goat and camel hair. Many fragments are composed of hybrid fabrics, i.e. material woven together from a warp of one kind of yarn and weft of another, e.g. silk woven with wool, linen or cotton. Written sources also refer to taffeta, buckram and satin.

Although it is impossible to know where the surviving fragments of fabric were produced, written sources attest that Antioch was a centre of silk production, supplying both Byzantium and the Middle East. There is documentary evidence that some 4,000 silk weavers settled and worked in the County of Tripoli. Other hubs of silk weaving were Tyre, Gaza and Ascalon. Tyre was famous for its white silk. Beirut exported silk and cotton textiles, and cotton was grown around Acre, Tiberias and Ramla, presumably for use in local manufacturing. The dyeing industry was closely associated with the textile industry and was mainly in Jewish hands.

In Cyprus, sources note the production of samite and camlets for export to both East and West. Samite is markedly significant as it demonstrates that Cypriot cloth was competitive in price and quality with the more established textile industries of Syria. Cyprus was also famous for patterned silk and silk brocade, fabrics so valuable they found their way to the Vatican and the courts of Europe. Perhaps most intriguing of all are references to a hybrid fabric produced by weaving silk with strands of gold. This valuable luxury good was known as 'siqlatin', that is 'silk-Latin' – presumably because it was manufactured for Latin Christian (Frankish) customers or because it was produced in the Latin (crusader) states.

Except for iron mines near Beirut, the Kingdom of Jerusalem did not have significant metal deposits. Nevertheless, **metalworking** was an important domestic industry based on imports of raw material from outside the region. It ranged from essential, utilitarian tools to weapons and works of art. At the low-end of the scale, workmen in the crusader states produced farm implements (e.g. spades, rakes and hoes), construction tools (e.g. chisels, picks, hammers and nails), household items (e.g. buckles, buttons, knives, scissors and candlesticks) and essential but low-value commodities, such as nails and horseshoes – just as elsewhere in the medieval world. A unique but nevertheless low-grade form of metalwork common in the Kingdom of Jerusalem was the production of cheap amulets and trinkets as souvenirs for pilgrims and ampullae to collect holy water and holy oil as keepsakes. Presumably, arms and armour were also produced domestically, as the crusader states simply could not afford to depend on imports of these materials so essential to their survival. Knights, in particular, required fitted armour, and that meant it was custom-made and locally-produced. Yet, there is no indication that the quality of production was above average.

On the other hand, examples of high-quality metalwork from the Kingdom of Jerusalem include brass bowls and plates with detailed engravings, as well as organ pipes and church bells found in Bethlehem.

More common, however, were religious souvenirs for the wealthiest class of pilgrims: the nobility and princes of the church. These often took the form of reliquaries in gold and silver, often studded with jewels or embellished with enamel. The gold and silversmiths of the crusader states also produced processional crosses and bishop's crosiers. For secular clients, popular items included small cross pendants and rings with seals, coats of arms or religious motifs. The gold and silversmiths had their workshops in the very heart of the city of Jerusalem.

In the thirteenth century, Acre became a centre for producing and exporting high-quality **composite crossbows**. The design of these bows came from the Muslim East, but the Muslim ban against the export of weapons to non-Muslims severely inhibited direct exports to the Latin East, much less Western Europe. However, the necessary raw materials for these effective weapons (glue and horn) could be imported to the Latin East from Damascus, a major weapons manufacturing centre. This enabled Acre's weapons workshops to develop a near-monopoly on the production of these weapons. The crossbows produced in the Levant were considered so superior to comparable arms made in the West that Frederick II made the import of three crossbows mandatory with every shipment of goods – of any kind – from the Kingdom of Jerusalem throughout much of the thirteenth century.

An export even more unique or representative of the Kingdoms of Jerusalem and Cyprus were icons. **Icons** had a long tradition in Orthodox Christianity, but it was not until the crusader era that they became popular with Latin patrons. The Franks of Outremer developed a taste for icons and contributed to the demand already generated by the local Orthodox population for these decorative and devotional objects. Icon artists mass-produced popular images – such as St George and the dragon and the Virgin with Christ – for sale as finished products, as well as creating half-finished products that could be modified by the insertion of customised features such as a name or coat-of-arms. When commissioned, the local artists also created original works of art with distinctive features.

Another exceptional and decidedly 'upmarket' product of the crusader kingdoms was books – **commercially produced books**. Many visitors to the Holy Land purchased and returned with manuscripts manufactured in Jerusalem, Acre and, later, Cyprus. Given most visitors' short stays of six months or less, it would have been impossible to produce these manuscripts from scratch. As with icons, historians suggest popular texts were mass-produced; that is, fashionable works were copied and stored in anticipation of a sale.

Because the largest cost factor in books was illumination, mass-produced books had little or no illumination whatsoever. Such books were affordable objects for the middle classes, such as merchants, lawyers and simple knights of modest means. Only rarely did a wealthy secular or ecclesiastical patron commission a work with extensive illumination. While illuminated pieces were rare, they were more highly treasured and, therefore, better preserved, while the more common, mass-produced unillustrated copies have been mostly lost.

Finally, the crusader kingdoms had a regional monopoly on the production of objects with Christian motifs, regardless of media or context. These might be as simple as the popular fish motif on pottery plates and beakers or crosses on candlesticks and cutlery. Christian symbols could also be etched, sewn, drawn or branded onto objects designed for daily use, such as a belt buckle, scarf or bodice, saddle or pair of shoes. Yet, they could just as easily be worked into such luxury items as jewelry. Christians of this period were on the whole conventionally devout and unashamed to express it symbolically. Objects with Christian motifs were popular throughout this period with the entire Christian community of the Middle East. In the case of Christians still living under Muslim rule, Christian symbols were forbidden in public and could not be produced locally, making products from the Latin East – provided they could be concealed – even more coveted.

Trade

Despite thriving agricultural, manufacturing and service sectors, trade was the most significant engine of economic prosperity in the crusader states. It is easy to conclude, as many historians have written, that geography dictated this fact. That is an oversimplification and ignores the fact that before and after Frankish rule, the coastal ports were provincial backwaters with little role in the international carrying trade. In the pre- and post-crusades eras, Constantinople and Alexandria – not Acre, Tyre or Famagusta – were the principal trading hubs of the Eastern Mediterranean.

Under the Franks, in contrast, trade flourished on a scale unknown under the Arabs or the Turks. Three factors can best explain the blossoming of trade during the era of the crusades: (1) the overall economic revival of the region under the Franks, which included a growing permanent and transient population (pilgrims, crusaders), (2) the development of new industries (e.g. sugar, wine, religious tourism, glass, icons, books), and (3) Christian dominance of the waterways, making trade across the Mediterranean comparatively safe for Western merchants. Together, these factors sparked a commercial 'revolution' that peaked during the crusader era and subsided afterwards. Furthermore, while the principal beneficiaries of this commercial revolution were the crusader states, a revival of trade was felt across the Mediterranean. This was simply because ships of this period needed to make several stops for water and provisioning when travelling long distances.

Before looking more closely at the components of this trade, it is necessary to stress that the 'safety' of shipping in this era was relative rather than absolute. To be sure, from roughly 1123, when the Venetians destroyed a large Fatimid fleet until the rise of the Ottomans, the Mediterranean was dominated by Western naval power. In the twelfth century, the combination of Byzantine, Sicilian and Italian naval power protected Europe's merchant shipping. In later centuries, the Italians (particularly Venice) and the Hospitallers (Knights of Rhodes and Malta) provided this protection. However, rivalries between the various maritime states also led to periodic naval warfare. Although diminished, Egyptian fleets were likewise active from time to time and proved capable of preying upon Christian merchant shipping. Furthermore, the Venetians were more likely to attack the ships of their Christian rivals (as they had attacked Zara and Constantinople on land) than Muslim shipping. Finally, pirates were never eliminated. While the Mediterranean was not 'safe' in the modern sense of the word, it had become sufficiently safe by the standards of the day to enable trade to grow at exponential rates.

In turn, trade sparked significant advances in naval architecture and a reorientation of production across the region. At the end of the eleventh century, ships were small, single-decked, with at most two-masts, and had steering oars instead of central rudders. By the time Acre fell to the Mamluks, three-masted ships with multiple decks and central rudders were standard. Meanwhile, the economies of the Mediterranean basin shifted their focus away from pure domestic demand towards production for export. Within half a century, trade had become so significant and lucrative that economies began to specialise in sectors in which they held a comparative advantage.

Yet while it is easy to see why trade between the Christian states on the littoral of the Mediterranean flourished after the establishment of the crusader states, the more surprising development was the dramatic expansion of trade with the Muslim world – and beyond. Exposure to the 'luxuries of the Orient' sparked demand for those products in the West. Suddenly spices, pharmaceuticals (such as opium), gold, ivory, incense, silk, and other exotic products such as Chinese porcelain, could be purchased in Christian ports.

To be sure, the most adventurous Western merchants had not hesitated to do business in Arab ports, chiefly in Alexandria, before the establishment of the crusader states. Nevertheless, the sheer explosion in trade after the establishment of Frankish control of the ports of the Levant is itself evidence that most Western Christian merchants of this period were more comfortable trading through Christian ports. This was so much the case that Acre came to rival or possibly briefly eclipsed Alexandria as the most vital trading hub in the eastern Mediterranean. The preference of Christian merchants for Christian ports is understandable. Christian merchants enjoyed substantial privileges in the crusader states, and they felt protected in a way impossible in Muslim countries, where they were highly vulnerable to sudden shifts in policy. The crusader states provided merchants with a base in the Middle East, a foothold where they felt safe and from which they could cautiously explore and exploit opportunities further inland.

For Muslim merchants, trade with the West was lucrative enough to justify the comparatively low risk of venturing – usually only for a few days at a time – into Christian-controlled territory. Muslim trade was aided by Islamic teachings of the era that explicitly condoned trade with 'the enemy', provided 'war materials' were not among the items sold. Thus, Muslim merchants were prohibited from selling weapons, armour, slaves and horses to the Christian West but were otherwise free to trade.

Trade was profitable not only for those engaged in it but for the states through which it passed. Both Christians and Muslims taxed the goods exported, imported and transited through their territories. These taxes and duties were so crucial to the revenue of the rulers that Christian and Muslim alike became increasingly reluctant to disrupt trade through warfare. Indeed, hostilities were sometimes carried out without any impact on trade. The Iberian Muslim traveller, Ibn Jubayr, noted while travelling to Mecca via the Kingdom of Jerusalem in 1184:

> Muslim and Christian ... armies may meet ... and yet Muslim and Christian travellers come and go ... without interference. [Even while Saladin was attacking Kerak] the caravans still passed successively from Egypt to Damascus, going through the land of the Franks without impediment from them. In the same way, the Muslims continuously journeyed from Damascus to Acre [through Frankish territory unharmed] .... The soldiers ... engage themselves in their war, while the civilians are at peace.[8]

The trade routes that converged on the ports of the crusader states in the twelfth century reached all the way to China, India, Siberia and Ethiopia. Siberia sent ermine, marten, otter, beaver and wild cat hides to be worked and sold in the long 'Street of the Furriers' in Jerusalem. Ethiopia sent gold, ivory and incense. From India and China came opium, jade, pearls, porcelain, silk and spices such as pepper, cinnamon and ginger. In addition, ship inventories and customs documents attest to trade in perfume, musk, myrrh, balm, aloe, gum and senna. The Arabian Peninsula provided marble and enameled pottery, while Egypt was a source of cotton and flax. Syria sent carpets, textiles, cotton, and damascened copper and steel weapons – despite the religious prohibitions on selling weapons to the 'enemy'. From Western Europe came timber, iron and scrap iron, silver, copper, amber and wool.

Notably, many of the products from the West, such as timber and iron, contributed to Muslim military capability. In consequence, there were sporadic attempts by various popes in the fourteenth century to prohibit the sale of these commodities to Muslim customers. But the greed of merchants always triumphed over their sense of solidarity with Christianity. Even more reprehensibly, the West was a major source of slaves for the slave-markets of the Muslim world. The Italian merchant states specialised in transshipping human beings from the pagan wilds of northeastern Europe and from Constantinople via the crusader states to the Muslim states. Many of those slaves would later become Mamluks and contribute to the downfall of Frankish rule.

The Frankish ports became large warehousing and transshipment centres for goods in transit between regions beyond the borders of the crusader states. Here goods were collected and stored, enabling a rationalisation of transport. For example, a camel caravan from India might bring hundreds of different products in small quantities. These were then stored in Acre until sufficient quantities of each product had been collected to justify a shipment to the West. This reduced freight costs and increased profit margins.

While trade brought revenue to the political elites in both East and West who taxed the import, export, and transshipment of goods, as well as the ships that anchored and the caravans that passed through the gates of the cities, the merchants themselves made the largest profits. In the crusader states, trade was dominated by the Italian city-states, and their contribution remains highly controversial. Some historians, such as Joshua Prawer, argue that too many privileges and monopolies were granted to the Italian maritime powers, resulting in lost income to the crown and a stifling of a native or Frankish merchant class. Other historians, such as Jonathan Riley-Smith, counter that the networks, experience and overall competence of the established Italian mercantile states fostered a faster growth of trade than would otherwise have been possible. In this sense, he suggests their activities contributed substantially to the crusader states' overall economic prosperity, therefore benefitting all.

There can be little doubt that whatever benefits accrued to the crusader states were a by-product rather than the goal of the Italians. Where commercial interests collided with crusader interests, the Italians routinely sacrificed the welfare of the crusades and the crusader states for their own profits and benefits. This was seen most vividly in the so-called Fourth Crusade and the 'War' of St Sabas. Ultimately, regardless of the economic gains of the Italian mercantile presence in the Latin East, it had become a political liability by the mid-thirteenth century. Intensifying rivalries contributed to the growing fragmentation within Frankish society, seriously undermining the viability of the crusader states on the mainland of the Levant. In Cyprus, too, it was the Genoese and Venetians – not the Turks – that ultimately destroyed the Lusignan dynasty and, with it, the independent Latin kingdom.

Technological and Intellectual Exchange

It was not only commodities and manufactured goods that moved between East and West in the era of the crusades; ideas and technology were also exchanged. It has become commonplace to claim that, due to the alleged cultural and intellectual superiority of the Muslim world in the eleventh and twelfth century, knowledge and technology flowed primarily from East to West. This is an oversimplification of the non-material exchange between the Franks and their neighbours.

While Islamic culture undoubtedly experienced a significant flourishing in the centuries immediately preceding the crusades, Western Europe was not trapped in some 'dark age'. On the contrary, Europe enjoyed noteworthy technological and intellectual advancement in the centuries preceding the First Crusade. Professor Rodney Stark claims: 'The so-called Dark Ages were a period of profound enlightenment in both the material and intellectual spheres, which when combined with Christian doctrines of moral equality, created a whole new world based on political, economic, and personal freedom.'[9]

While Stark may be overstating the case, there is no doubt that the learning of the Greeks and Romans was not lost to Western Europe in the years after the fall of Rome but was preserved and translated in centres of learning across Europe. Furthermore, before the First Crusade, the first Western university had been founded; several others followed it in the next century. These were not schools of theology comparable to Islam's madrassas, but institutions dedicated to scientific inquiry. These Western institutions practised critical peer review and were protected by the concept of academic freedom. Other advances of the pre-crusades era were polyphonic music and the invention of the organ and the violin. Clocks, compasses and eyeglasses were other innovations that made their appearance in the West during the crusading era – without input from the Muslim world.

Yet the most profound Western developments in the centuries before the First Crusade were those practical innovations that enabled agricultural productivity to expand to the point where generations of peasants no longer lived on the brink of starvation. The development of a horse-collar for ploughs enabled the introduction of horsepower in agriculture. Horses could plough at twice the speed of oxen, doubling production. Indeed, they made it possible to cultivate more land. Combined with new ploughs that turned the earth – rather than merely scratching the surface of it – the productivity of the land increased dramatically. Peasants were able to move beyond subsistence agriculture to cash crops. Except in periods of exceptional natural or political disruption, they had enough nutritious food to reach their full genetic potential.

Other practical Western inventions in the centuries before the First Crusade were brakes on wagons and swivel axles, both radical innovations at the time. When combined with the development of the horse-collar and the breeding of larger, stronger horses, these enabled the transport of heavy cargoes over land. This was a boon to trade and helped develop the interior, however, heavy transport vehicles also made a significant contribution to warfare by enabling the transportation of siege engines, for example. Indeed, heavy transportation wagons with teams of four or more horses and large siege engines were just two of the technological innovations brought from the West to the Near East rapidly adopted by the crusaders' Muslim opponents.

Throughout the ages, military technology and tactics have been characterised by rapid innovation, imitation and adaptation. In the context of the crusades, the Franks adopted the surcoat and mounted archers (turcopoles), while the Saracens adopted heavy siege equipment and heavy (lance-bearing) cavalry. In military architecture, useful features in castle construction introduced by either party were almost immediately copied by the other. In his outstanding examination of crusader castles, however, Ronnie Ellenblum demonstrates that it was the crusaders who first made significant advances in military architecture with the introduction of key features such as thicker, higher and concentric walls, posterns, vaulted chambers in the 'safe-zones', and massive storage to withstand lengthy sieges.[10] However, the Mamluks learned fast, and later Muslim castles were equal to those of the crusaders.

Nevertheless, the West benefitted enormously, both technologically and intellectually, from exposure to the Muslim East via the crusader states. The most modern means for making paper, for example, was taken back to Europe by clerics who learned about the process in the Latin East. Likewise, the means for making high-quality glass, which the glassmakers of the Levant had already mastered before the arrival of the crusaders, was introduced in Venice in 1277, giving Venice a competitive edge in that sector that lasted to the eighteenth century.

Overall, when assessing which party benefitted most from contact with the other, we should not automatically assume that the culture more open to adaptation was the weaker or more backward. For example, despite the superiority of European naval architecture, the Arabs could not imitate it because they lacked high-quality shipwrights. The chimneys built in the Holy Land by the Franks fell into disrepair and subsequently disappeared from local architecture after the departure of the Franks, not because chimneys were useless or old-fashioned, but due to the inertia of 'tradition'.

An important factor impacting the direction of technology transfer was the environment. The Franks, not their Arab and Turkish opponents, were living in a new environment, which meant they needed to adapt, not the other way around. Significantly, that new environment was one with extremes of heat unknown in their homelands, an environment that was more arid, less forested and more densely populated. It would have been absurd – and stupid – to cling to traditions and technologies unsuited to the Mediterranean, no matter how well-suited those technologies were for, say, agriculture in Scotland or fighting in Prussia.

The adoption of surcoats is an excellent example of this. In the intense heat of the Syrian summer, wearing a loose cloth garment over one's armour made sense. That the Franks rapidly did so, and – even more surprising – that it became fashionable across Western Europe is not evidence of the inferiority of previous forms of dress. The surcoat had a function that was related directly to the physical environment in the Near East. Its later evolution into a means of showing off one's arms and affinity had nothing to do with Arab/Turkish superiority but rather with Western customs of chivalry.

Similarly, the prevalence of stone structures across the Middle East in an era when most construction in Western Europe was still wooden was not the result of a higher level of civilisation in the Arab world. Instead, it was a function of the scarcity of wood in the Near East. To this day, archaeologists can date crusades-era buildings based on the exceptionally high standards of Frankish masonry and the chimneys.

On the other hand, although Western European ploughs were undoubtedly more sophisticated than the ploughs in use in the Holy Land and had contributed considerably to rising standards of living and higher levels of nutrition among the poor in Europe, they were unsuitable for use in the Middle East. Consequently, Frankish settlers abandoned a higher level of technology unsuited to the environment in favour of an 'old-fashioned' technology that did less environmental damage to a fragile ecosystem.

Adaptation from West to East, on the other hand, was inhibited not only by the fact that the environment remained the same for Muslims but also by Muslim presumptions of superiority. The Muslims viewed Franks as fundamentally backwards because they were 'blasphemers worshipping God incorrectly ... or as idolaters worshipping cross-shaped idols'.[11] In the extreme, they shared the attitude expressed by Bahr al-Fava'id, who wrote: 'Anyone who believes that his God came out of a woman's privates is quite mad; he should not be spoken to, and he has neither intelligence nor faith.'[12]

It is to the Franks' credit that regardless of what they thought of Islam as a religion, they did not dismiss its adherents as madmen or idiots. Because of this willingness to separate religion from science and art, the Franks proved remarkably adept at adapting to their new environment and developing a unique hybrid culture.

There is no better example of this than the impact of Arab medicine on the West. Recent scholarship demonstrates that 'medical practice in the armies of the First Crusade was comparable with Byzantine and Islamic practice, both in terms of practical treatment and also the theory behind the origins of disease'.[13] In short, before the establishment of the crusader states, 'Saracens and Christians shared the same conceptual framework for medical science, which they [both] inherited from the classical world.'[14]

However, in the subsequent 200 years, during which the Franks lived amidst Eastern cultures, medicine evolved rapidly. In this period, after the establishment of the crusader states, scholars can trace new influences on Western medicine from the Latin East. The most significant medical innovation to travel from the crusader states to Europe was undoubtedly the concept of an institution staffed by medical professionals (not monks or nuns) and dedicated to curing – not just caring for – the sick and injured, i.e. a hospital. Yet, while the Franks may have learned about hospitals from Muslims, the latter had learned about hospitals from the Byzantines, making this an example of a 'melting pot' innovation.

Likewise, while the regulation of medical practice and practitioners appears to be one aspect of medicine in which Franks learned from the natives of Outremer, the natives in question were not necessarily Muslims.[15] Scholars believe that as many as two-thirds of the medical practitioners in Egypt, for example, were Christians or Jews. In Syria,

Christians, Jews, Samaritans and Zoroastrians all practised medicine. Many of the most famous crusader-era physicians, such as Abu Sulayman Dawud, who treated Baldwin IV for his leprosy, and Ibn Butlan, a leading medical theoretician and author of medical texts, were Orthodox Christians. When contemporary accounts refer to 'Saracen' or 'Eastern' doctors, they did not necessarily mean Muslim doctors. The bulk of the medical personnel employed by the Franks were Jews, Jacobites or other Orthodox Christians. In short, the apparent preference for 'Muslim medicine' attributed to the Franks by many modern writers is based on a misunderstanding of the primary sources.

Scholars have identified several specific examples demonstrating that the 'exchange of medical knowledge was a two-way phenomenon'.[16] Based on extensive research of both texts and archaeological finds, Osteoarchaeologist Piers D. Mitchell concludes that: 'The evidence ... does not support the widely held view that Frankish practitioners from Europe were ignorant and technically inferior to those who learnt their medicine in the East.'[17]

What was happening in Outremer was that highly trained and dedicated medical practitioners of different religions – Orthodox and Latin Christians, Jews, Shia and Sunni Muslims – lived and worked closely with one another. Those without bigotry were willing and anxious to learn from their colleagues, regardless of religious background. They exchanged experiences, techniques, theory and practice. Under Frankish rule, Antioch blossomed into a major centre for the translation and writing of medical texts as well as the study and development of medical theory. Medicine in Outremer is a textbook example of intellectual exchange between different cultures and traditions, stimulating an advancement in knowledge for all.

Chapter 9

Life and Lifestyle in the Crusader States
Architecture, the Arts, Linguistics, Education, the Religious Orders, Health Care, Social Welfare, Cuisine and Fashion

Unlike the early settlers in the Americas and Australia, the Europeans who established the crusader states were confronted with a densely populated region that had been urbanised for thousands of years. Thus, European settlers who came to the Holy Land had to cope not only with an alien climate and unfamiliar geography, but also with a majority population whose language, architecture and social customs were non-European. To their credit, the Franks rapidly adapted to their new environment. Thus, while the roots of Frankish culture were European, the lifestyle of the Franks of Outremer was shaped by elements borrowed from the people and civilisations that surrounded them. The result was a unique and distinctive identity and culture of their own, reflected in their buildings, art, fashion, food and social structures.

Urban Landscapes, Infrastructure and Architecture

The Near East's geography and climate set the parameters for human habitation in the region, ensuring many common features across cultures and centuries. Furthermore, in major urban areas, the Franks occupied cities that had already existed for centuries or, in some cases, thousands of years. In consequence, Frankish influence was subtle and nuanced. Nevertheless, it is possible to speak of 'Frankish cities' and identify some common features that impacted the life and lifestyle of those cities' inhabitants during the era of the crusades.

Urban Landscapes and Infrastructure

A visitor approaching any major Frankish city from any direction but the sea would first encounter a green ring of cultivated, usually irrigated land composed of orchards and utility gardens. These agricultural suburbs evolved to meet the demands of the urban population for fresh produce such as fruits, vegetables, eggs and dairy goods. Thus, the environment immediately surrounding most Frankish cities was green and lush with vegetation.

Inside this soft-shell of cultivated vegetation, many cities were protected by walls. The height, thickness and defensibility of these walls varied greatly, as did the number of towers and gates. Antioch, for example, was famed for having 400 towers; Ascalon had fifty-three. The smaller cities undoubtedly had fewer towers and gates, but the major coastal cities (Sidon, Beirut, Tyre, Caesarea, Arsuf and Jaffa) were all walled. The majority of these had been fortified for generations, if not millennia, and the Franks did little more than repair or modernise the existing defensive structures. The walls of Ascalon, for example, were built by the Romans, expanded and strengthened first by the Byzantines and then by the Fatimids before the Franks gained control of the city in 1153. The latter did little more than effect repairs and make modest additions.

On the other hand, inland cities were conspicuously non-fortified, providing striking evidence of the comparatively peaceful environment that characterised life in the crusader states for most of the period before Hattin. With the exception of Jerusalem, Banias, Tiberias and Caymont, the major inland cities, such as Nablus, Nazareth, Hebron and Ramla, were not fortified.

The size of Frankish cities varied greatly. Jerusalem enclosed seventy-two hectares, Acre sixty, Ascalon fifty, but Sidon, the next largest city, had only fourteen hectares and Caesarea twelve. In terms of population, Antioch, Acre, Tyre and (in the twelfth century) Jerusalem all had populations exceeding 20,000 people. In the thirteenth century, Acre and Tyre are believed to have housed close to 30,000 inhabitants each. Ascalon had an estimated 10,000, but the other cities were smaller, with Caesarea probably home to just under 5,000 inhabitants. The interplay of geographic space and population determined the population density and had a powerful impact on the character of the city.

Jerusalem was so large that despite a significant population, it was known for its many gardens, squares, courtyards and open markets; it was also famous for its clean, healthy air. There were orchards within the city walls as well as gardens, open markets and many pools. Despite butchers and tanners operating within the walls, contemporary accounts indicate the city did not smell.

Acre, on the other hand, had a terrible reputation as overcrowded and polluted. This was particularly pronounced in the thirteenth century when the city was flooded with permanent refugees from the lands lost to Saladin. The gardens and orchards within the city walls were converted to housing to accommodate these new inhabitants, while the courtyards of the older houses were built up. Even the gardens of the royal palace were divided into parcels and sold-off for development between 1257 and 1273. By mid-century, a population 50 per cent larger than Jerusalem lived on a land area 20 per cent smaller. Despite highly sophisticated and extensive infrastructure, the sewage system inevitably became overwhelmed, and the inner harbour became a cesspool known as the 'filthy sea'.

So much was written about Acre by pilgrims passing through the Frankish port that the image of a cramped, overcrowded and polluted city tends to dominate modern portrayals of life in all cities of the Holy Land in the Frankish era. This ignores the fact that Acre was the exception, not the rule. According to Ibn Jubayr, the houses in Tyre were larger and more spacious than in Acre, the roads and streets cleaner, while the conditions of the Muslims living there better, although he does not say in what way. Likewise, Ascalon had a reputation as clean and pleasant, as did the Frankish cities of Cyprus, particularly Nicosia.

Contributing to the overall positive reputation of Frankish cities were sophisticated public infrastructure projects that could be found throughout Frankish Syria, Palestine and Cyprus, namely aqueducts, cisterns, public pools, fountains, bathhouses and underground sewage systems. Securing adequate water supplies was critical in the Middle Eastern climate, and it is striking that the lack of water is never mentioned in any of the accounts of sieges, underlining how effective Frankish infrastructure was in this regard. Caesarea, for example, had no less than three aqueducts. Jerusalem had one aqueduct and several springs, and the fountains of the city were said never to run dry.

Baths were another prominent feature of Frankish cities. Some were inherited, but the Franks built many more. As with Roman baths, the heat was produced in furnaces and distributed as hot air running through vents under the marble floors. Bathhouses were generally spacious and, as in Roman times, popular places to meet and socialise. The Hospitaller Rule prohibited their brothers from eating and sleeping in bathhouses, an indication that both were possible. Bath attendants provided massages and shaves as well. At least one source suggests wives could accompany their husbands to the baths, but separate days or separate spaces for men and women was probably more common.

Open markets for cattle, horses, pigs, poultry and dairy products were features common to Frankish cities. By their nature, loud and smelly, they were generally located on the city's edge, near the gates. However, covered markets or souks, so characteristic of Near Eastern cities, were also found in Frankish ones. Souks consist of covered streets with vaulted roofing flanked by a series of bays formed by vaulted chambers perpendicular to the road. Each bay housed merchants displaying wares. The most famous Frankish souk is a market street in Jerusalem built under Queen Melisende in 1152 that is still in use today. The central passage is 6 metres high and 3 metres wide, while the shops lining it are each 4 metres square. Holes at regular intervals in the roofs of these medieval souks allowed light and fresh air to enter.

Perhaps more surprising to the modern reader, Frankish cities were served by highly sophisticated, public sewage systems. In Acre, the Hospitallers had a latrine block built on several floors offering thirty-five stone seats and a flushing system. We can assume that while differing in scale, the arrangement was standard across Hospitaller structures. Similar features were found in the Lusignan palace. It is reasonable to presume that Templars, Teutonic knights and the Italian 'fundacos' all had like arrangements. The waste from these latrines fed into a city-wide sewage system. Such systems, which have been identified in more than one crusader city, demonstrate centralised planning and infrastructural maintenance. Furthermore, the major canals for drawing the wastewater out of the city could be accessed from individual houses and shops along the length of the stone drainage pipes before emptying outside the walls.

All in all, the Franks converted existing structures or built new ones to create cities with all the conveniences expected in this period: open and covered markets, factories, workshops, hospices, hospitals, churches, foundations, individual residences and palaces. Frankish construction and modifications put a stamp on the face of the cities they occupied, despite older structures underneath. While this imprint has been effaced by centuries of rebuilding and repurposing Frankish structures, we still have a glimpse of what Franks built in an Arab description of Jerusalem, written shortly after Saladin's reconquest in 1187. Ibn-Khallikan wrote:

> The infidel had rebuilt [Jerusalem] with columns and plaques of marble ... with fair fountains where the water never ceased to flow – one saw dwellings as agreeable as gardens and brilliant with the whiteness of marble; the columns with their foliage seemed like trees.[1]

Military Architecture

One of the most impressive and visible legacies of the crusader kingdoms are the castles erected by Latin rulers, Frankish nobleman, and in particular, the military orders. T.E. Lawrence, better known as 'Lawrence of Arabia', famously disparaged the crusader castles as irrelevant and ineffective because these fortifications ultimately proved incapable of preventing the fall of the crusader kingdoms. Such a judgement is facile. Christian defeats in the first 150 years of the crusader kingdoms occurred almost exclusively in the open field, where Muslim leaders could bring their larger forces to bear: the Field of Blood (1119), Hattin, (1187) and La Forbie (1244). By contrast, when the crusaders retreated into their fortified cities or castles, forcing the Saracens to besiege them, they usually survived to fight another day. Outremer was not lost because its castles were irrelevant or ineffective, but due to a variety of causes discussed earlier.

In his excellent work 'Crusader Archaeology: The Material Culture of the Latin East', Adrian Boas identified no less than five basic types of crusader castles. The simplest was the **tower castle**. Similar castles were already known in the West and became popular in, for example, Scotland and Ireland. In the crusader kingdoms, such castles were usually square with a windowless cellar/undercroft used for storage, wells and kitchens, over which were built two floors topped by a crenellated fighting platform on the roof. Access from the outside was usually only at the first-floor level by means of an exterior stair that ended several yards away from the door; the gap was bridged by a wooden drawbridge that could be closed from the interior to cover and reinforce the door. Each floor had two or more barrel or cross-vaulted chambers, which might have been further partitioned by wooden walls or roofs and floors. Outbuildings containing workshops, storerooms, stables and the like were located around the foot of the tower but were not themselves defensible. A splendid, although late, example of a tower castle is the Hospitaller castle at Kolossi on Cyprus.

The second type of crusader castle, the castrum or **enclosure castle**, had its roots in Roman military architecture and evolved from Roman forts via Byzantium into crusader castles consisting of a defensible perimeter with reinforcing towers at the corners. The Muslims had also adapted this type of defensive structure, and on their arrival in the Holy Land, the Franks took over several existing castles of this type. They also built new castles following this fundamental design, notably Coliath in the County of Tripoli and Blanchegarde and Gaza in the Kingdom of Jerusalem. These castles had large, vaulted chambers with walls roughly 3 metres thick running between the corner towers. These chambers housed the various activities necessary to castle life, from kitchens and stables to forges, bakeries and bathhouses. The upper story of the enclosing buildings generally provided accommodations, eating halls and chapels for the garrison. The roofs of the buildings served as fighting platforms facing out in all directions. They were reinforced by the higher corner towers that provided covering fire.

The third type of crusader castle was a combination of the aforementioned types: a strong, roughly **rectangular complex built around a tower or keep**. The enclosing walls, with vaulted chambers and corner towers, formed the first line of defence, and the keep, the second. A surviving example of this kind of castle is Gibelet (Jubayl) in the County of Tripoli and, based on William of Tyre's descriptions, the royal castle at Darum in the Kingdom of Jerusalem was also of this type.

Towards the end of the twelfth century, the Franks started building outer works to provide a line of defence before the castrum itself. These outer works may have originally been intended to provide a modicum of protection to the towns that often grew up around castles, but they soon evolved into what became one of the most distinctive, indeed iconic, type of crusader castles: **the concentric castle**. These were generally the castles of the military orders, built with the vast resources available to them. They were purely devoted to military dominance as opposed to the castles of secular lords or royal castles. These were the castles that inspired Edward I's castles in Wales in the late thirteenth century. In addition to Crak de Chevaliers, undoubtedly the most famous of the crusader castles, a excellent example of this type of castle is Belvoir, overlooking the Jordan Valley.

Boas distinguishes between **hilltop and spur castles**, but both of these castles were essentially castles that took advantage of natural geographic features to strengthen their overall defensibility. The hilltop and mountain spur castles were built atop steep slopes, occupying an entire hilltop or the tip of a longer corniche. They were undoubtedly the most difficult to take by storm. Sitting on bedrock, they were hard to undermine, and built on steep slopes they were almost impossible to assault. Kerak, the castle of Reynald de Châtillon, was a spur castle, which withstood two unsuccessful sieges by Saladin, falling only to disease or demoralisation more than a year after the Battle of Hattin. Other crusader castles of this type were Montfort (or, as the Teutonic Knights called it, Starkenburg), Beaufort/Belfort, Margat and Saone.

A variation on the theme of the spur castle was using the sea rather than sheer mountainsides to provide protection. The Templar Atlit Castle (Castle Pilgrim) and the castle at Tyre were built on peninsulas extending into the sea and only accessible on one side by land. These castles proved almost impossible to capture. Mining was impossible from three sides due to the sea, and assaults from boats were precarious and challenging to implement. As a result, only the landward side was vulnerable to attack, enabling a smaller garrison to mount a successful defence. Tyre became the only city in the Kingdom of Jerusalem that successfully resisted Saladin after the Battle of Hattin and became the base from which the coastal plain was reconquered.

While it is comparatively easy to identify and describe crusader castles, the motivation and inspiration for them are hotly debated. It was long assumed that castles were built primarily as defensive structures forming a protective wall around a kingdom's perimeter to prevent or inhibit invasion. It has even been suggested they were constructed so a signal could be sent via fires on the towers from one end of the kingdom to the other. As logical as this sounds, it does not square with reality. Rather than on the borders, Frankish castles were more likely to be constructed close to monasteries or concentrations of the native Christian population, regions which were, coincidentally, the areas of the most intensive agricultural production.

It is also worth noting that contemporary sources, such as William of Tyre, stress the offensive character of castles. Thus, for example, the castles at Ibelin and Beth Gibelin were intended as bases for assaulting Fatimid-held Ascalon. The current consensus among scholars is that crusader castles first and foremost projected power. Equally important, they served to facilitate the collection of rents and the distribution of farm produce from areas of production to those of consumption. Based on the archaeological evidence, Ronnie Ellenblum concluded: 'In the final tally, the fortresses brought economic prosperity to some of the regions in which they were built and encouraged settlement in previously unpopulated areas.'[2]

Controversy has also long raged over the traditions and inspirations expressed by the crusader castles, such as to the degree to which the castles were more Eastern or Western. Frankish castle construction techniques and design underwent significant changes over time. Neither tower nor enclosure castles were particularly unique or innovative. Only from the late twelfth century onwards did the Franks introduce genuine innovations. These included vaulted chambers behind and reinforcing walls at ground level, moats before walls, towers with overlapping ranges of fire, firing apertures, posterns, massively increased storage capacity for dried goods and water, and finally, the construction of multiple layers of defence.

Together, these features amounted to 'not an improvement of certain components of older castles, but a totally new, all-inclusive approach to castle defence, involving radical alterations to earlier methods of military architecture'.[3] The leading modern crusader archaeologist, Adrian Boas, concludes: 'Frankish castles advanced within a very short period from the most basic, one might say primitive, types to highly complex and remarkably inventive buildings displaying the highest understanding of military architecture. The Franks exhibited a proficiency at borrowing and adapting from others, and a genius at inventing entirely new types.'[4]

Unsurprisingly, these innovations inspired imitation in East and West. Within a century or more, most of the attributes listed above had found their way into castles built in Wales, Spain, Germany and elsewhere. The Mamluks, however, paid the highest compliment by imitating the crusaders so perfectly that, to the eye of the uninitiated, many of their castles are indistinguishable from crusader castles.

Ultimately, however, the most striking characteristic of crusader castles is their diversity. The castles ranged from simple to complex and employed both comparatively primitive and highly sophisticated features. In short, as in Western Europe, crusader castles came in different shapes and sizes, and each was custom-built to exploit natural elements in the landscape. They were also an expression of the wealth and power of their respective patrons, as well as reflecting the evolving purposes of each castle.

Religious Architecture

From its inception, the Kingdom of Jerusalem viewed itself as the guardian of Christianity's holiest shrines. The Frankish rulers understood these heritage sites belonged not to them or the residents of the Holy Land but rather to all of Christendom. Yet, 'guarding' holy sites also entailed preserving and honouring them. After 450 years of Muslim rule, many of the sacred sites were marked by little more than ruins. Most Christian monuments had been damaged, desecrated, or partially – if not totally – destroyed. The rest were in poor repair. The Franks embarked on a massive building programme designed to restore, expand and beautify the shrines of Christianity. In addition, houses of worship were necessary for the Christian population, who had been denied the right to build such structures for more than 400 years. Altogether, more than 400 Frankish ecclesiastical buildings have been identified by archaeological surveys to date.

The costs incurred by this comprehensive programme of restoration and construction were astronomical. Indeed, the financial resources required for these diverse and expensive building projects far exceeded crown revenues, yet, in the absence of other evidence, we can only speculate on how these projects were ultimately financed. The most likely scenario is that wealthy secular and ecclesiastical patrons in the West, possibly supplemented by contributions from small donors raised by the religious orders across Christendom, donated the needed funds.

Beyond their sheer scale and number, one of the most striking features of these various projects was the degree to which the Franks sensitively and respectfully incorporated the remains of earlier buildings into their renovation projects. In sharp contrast to the prevailing view of crusaders as bigoted barbarians, when it came to architecture, the crusaders sought to preserve rather than destroy. This was true of Muslim structures as well as Christian ones. For example, rather than levelling the two great Umayyad mosques on the site of the Jewish Synagogue (The Dome of the Rock and the Al-Aqsa Mosque), the crusaders simply 'repurposed' them. The Dome of the Rock became a Christian church known as the

Temple of God, and the al-Aqsa mosque was first converted into a royal palace and then turned over to the Knights Templar as their headquarters.

Christian ruins were viewed as semi-sacred, so the Franks made no attempt to obliterate the early Christian or Byzantine character of existing shrines but instead enhanced and expanded surviving fragments. For example, the Frankish Church of the Holy Sepulchre preserved both the mount of Golgotha and Christ's tomb in their original state but incorporated them into a larger building. If the resulting structure is less harmonious than the famed Romanesque and Gothic churches of Western Europe, this was not due to incompetence or the absence of architectural vision. Rather, the apparently disjointed plan was a conscious attempt to 'preserve the original building in as complete a way as possible within the new structure'.[5] This was the rule rather than the exception in Frankish ecclesiastical architecture across the Holy Land.

Yet, in many instances, earlier Christian structures had fallen into such disrepair or were so severely defaced that only new construction would serve. In these structures – notably St Anne's in Jerusalem, the Church of the Annunciation in Nazareth, the Cathedrals of Sebaste, Lydda, St George's Ramla, Bellapais Abbey in Cyprus, St Sophia in Nicosia and St Nicholas in Famagusta – Frankish architectural style prevailed. Without a doubt, Frankish architecture was fundamentally Western, namely Romanesque in the twelfth century and Gothic in the thirteenth. The former dominated in the Kingdom of Jerusalem and the latter in the Kingdom of Cyprus. Yet while borrowing the fundamentals of the Western styles, the Franks incorporated local elements using mostly local artisans, who brought their traditions with them.

The architecture of most Frankish churches in Syria was extremely simple. Frankish churches consistently employed a flat rather than a gabled roof, which seems primitive to observers accustomed to the soaring ceilings of Europe's grand cathedrals. Yet, the functional shape of the churches provided a platform for elaborate decoration, including frescos, sculpture and mosaics. Representational art forms offended Muslim sensibilities and were viewed as a form of idolatry, however, resulting in it being rapidly obliterated as soon as Muslim control over an area was restored. Thus, even where Christian structures survived the last 800 years, the frescos have been obliterated, the sculptures smashed and defaced, and the mosaics chipped away. What remains are structures of deceptive austerity.

Crusades archaeologist Adrian Boas has identified five fundamental types of Frankish ecclesiastical architecture. The simplest was **the single nave church** ending in an apse for the altar facing east, a form familiar from Byzantine churches. This simple style was commonly used for small private chapels inside castles and equally suited to smaller or poorer rural communities. It could, however, be modified into something quite grand. For example, the parish church in Atlit had only a single square nave, but the apse was seven-sided with rib-vaulting and stained-glass windows on each side. The pillars were decoratively carved, and the walls painted.

Equally popular, especially for larger structures, was the **basilica**, consisting of a central nave flanked by one, or more commonly, two side aisles. Usually rectangular and built on an east-west axis, basilicas usually ended in three east-facing apses either carved out of the heavy walls or extending beyond. The ceilings were either barrel or groin-vaulted, and the central nave was usually taller than the side aisles. Again, the basilica was a traditional Christian design dating back to the formative years of Christianity and popular among the Byzantines and Franks. It was used in such important churches as the Church of the Annunciation Nazareth, the Cathedral of St Peter in Caesarea, the Cathedral of Notre Dame in Tortosa and St Mary Major, a nunnery in Jerusalem.

A variation on the classical basilica was the **basilica with transepts**. This form, so popular in the West, never caught on in the Holy Land. Existing examples have stubby transepts which do not approach the grandeur and dimensions of transepts familiar from churches in England and France. The best-preserved crusader churches of this kind are St Anne's in Jerusalem, St George in Lydda and St Nicolas in Famagusta, the latter being Gothic rather than Romanesque. Only a small number of Frankish churches have the cruciform plan familiar in the West.

However, Frankish churches sometimes turned the entire east end of the nave into a chevet with ambulatory and radial chapels. Boas believes this plan was copied from Santiago de Compostela; this was the plan used for the Church of the Holy Sepulchre itself. It was ideally suited for pilgrimage churches because it dispersed pilgrims across multiple chapels. Finally, **polygonal churches** built by the Franks in the Holy Land have been found only in the Templar castle at Atlit and the church of the Ascension on the Mount of Olives in Jerusalem.

In summary, the Franks undertook a comprehensive ecclesiastical building programme to ensure the holiest sites of Christendom had appropriate and functional shrines. In so doing, the Franks sought 'to [meet] the needs and predispositions of the pilgrims'.[6] While the quality of the masonry and the craftsmanship displayed in the decorative elements was high, ecclesiastical architecture in the crusader kingdoms – unlike military architecture – was not innovative and had no particular impact on architectural history.

Domestic Architecture

Frankish domestic architecture consisted broadly of two types: that which had been inherited through the occupation of existing structures and new buildings created from scratch during the Frankish era. They were of a distinctly different character as the former followed Eastern traditions of domestic architecture based heavily on Muslim practice, while the latter was based on Western European models.

Muslim architecture in the era of the crusades was remarkably homogeneous. The dominant feature was an inward orientation. Houses were built for maximum privacy, to keep strangers out and keep women in. The entrance, like the gate of a city, was designed to hinder, not facilitate access, and doors on opposite sides of the street are never directly opposite one another. Windows were small and set high in the wall to inhibit the ability of outsiders to see in – and thereby restricted the ability of inhabitants (particularly women) to look out.

The heart of the house was the courtyard, and most of the rooms opening onto the courtyard could be accessed only via the courtyard itself. This had the effect of making each room self-contained and accessible only via one door. Courtyard houses might have rooms along anything from one to four sides of a courtyard, while the homes of the wealthy might enclose two or more courtyards. In rural areas, the courtyard might lie beside the house, enclosed partially by walls rather than rooms. In urban areas, the central courtyard concept was more common. Cooking was usually done in an oven located in the courtyard.

Most Muslim houses were built with comparatively thin walls, less than a metre thick, and supported no upper story, although they might have cellars used either for storage, dwelling or both. The roofs were flat and sometimes supported by wooden columns. Water was collected on the roof and fed through pipes to cisterns. Sewage systems have been found in some Muslim housing in this period, funneling waste into pits, but standard latrines emptying directly into a pit were more common. The poor built their homes of mud or mud-bricks; the rich of stone, marble and mosaic. Interiors were often plastered and whitewashed. Tiles were also occasionally used as flooring.

In contrast to Muslim houses elsewhere, rural houses in the Holy Land had an open-plan design with few internal partitions; many consisted of a single room. This may reflect the fact that most of the rural population in the region was Christian – and far too poor to build large and elaborate homes. To date, only three villages positively identified as native Christian villages have been surveyed. All the dwellings are composed of a single room opening onto an enclosed courtyard. The construction materials were inferior, namely, fieldstone and rubble. Floors were of stone or packed earth. In one village, houses appeared to share a cistern. All these features are more probably indications of poverty rather than preference.

In contrast, Europe in this period offered a great variety of domestic architectural styles. Given the heterogeneous origins of Western settlers in the crusader states, it is hardly surprising that these styles are all found in structures built by settlers and their descendants in the Holy Land. The Franks built hall houses, courtyard houses, tower houses and burgage houses, the latter being a house with a narrow front on the street and a long deep interior, often standing several stories high.

While Frankish architecture drew upon these traditions, it was notably different from contemporary architecture in the West. The differences are perhaps most pronounced when looking at rural architecture. In Western Europe, peasant housing in the twelfth century was still predominantly constructed of mud and timber with pitched roofs set on wooden beams and covered by slate, tiles or thatch. Walls were thin and unsuitable for supporting an upper story. Fireplaces were non-existent, and cooking was done over a central hearth with a vent in the roof to release the smoke. Many houses of this period were divided into two parts: one for humans and one for livestock.

In contrast, Frankish rural housing was constructed of stone, with walls as thick as 2 metres supporting barrel vaulting. Most houses were two stories with stairs sometimes built into the walls. Interior and exterior wooden stairs may also have been standard. Many Frankish rural dwellings also boasted a proper fireplace with hood and chimney. The windows were slender with a rounded top on the ground floor but larger on the upper floors.

Such houses bear a striking resemblance to European twelfth- and thirteenth-century *urban* architecture. The construction of narrow houses with shared walls along a street, for example, is typical of European cities of this period. Stone construction in urban areas likewise became increasingly common across northwestern Europe in the twelfth and thirteenth centuries. As in the Holy Land, urban stone dwellings in Europe were solidly built to support a second and sometimes a third floor. The ground floor was vaulted with narrow windows and believed to have been used primarily for storage. The upper stories, in contrast, had larger, usually two-light windows, and were used for living space.

Increasingly, by the thirteenth century, fireplaces with hoods and chimneys made their appearance in European urban home, located in the living quarters on the upper floors – not in the cellar. Altogether, the comparison has led archaeologists to conclude that 'Frankish street villages in the Latin Kingdom of Jerusalem drew a great deal more on urban architectural patterns of northwestern European towns than they did on those of rural settlement.'[7] This reflects the Frankish rural settlers' higher social and economic status compared to peasants in Europe and Christian peasants under Muslim rule.

Despite occupying and adapting existing structures on arrival, some Frankish construction took place in urban areas. Here, Frankish domestic architecture differed markedly from traditional Muslim housing in being outward-oriented, facing and opening on the street or a shared courtyard. Frankish homes were also multistoried, often three – and in some cases four – stories. The upper floors were reached by either external or internal stairs, the former carved into the thickness of the walls or of wood and the latter of wood.

Frankish shops opened directly onto the street or courtyard; folding tables for selling goods produced in the ground-floor workshops could be lowered from wide windows on the ground floor. Merchants and shopkeepers lived on the upper stories above their shops with large upstairs windows, balconies or loggia looking out over the street or courtyard. The loggia was the result of Italian influence, and there are still several good examples of these visible today. (Loggia are open but covered porches and balconies formed by arches or supported by columns.) Some of the pillars used by the Franks were reclaimed Roman or Byzantine pillars, but the Franks were skilled at producing pillars themselves. The capitals were famous – even among their enemies – for the lifelike quality of their decoration.

Most buildings in the Middle East were crowned, then as now, by flat roofs, which were sometimes decoratively crenellated. The roof provided additional living or workspace in the form of a rooftop terrace that could be shaded from the sun by canvas awnings or a vine arbor. Whether used as a terrace or not, rooftops almost always collected rainwater, drained via clay or stone pipes into a cistern. The water was purified by allowing the sediment to settle to the bottom; water was drawn into the house through a pipe located well above the sludge. Even the humblest and smallest of urban dwellings had cisterns, often several.

Windows and doors opened onto the streets and common courtyards. The main windows and doors – those facing the front – were generally large and either round or slightly pointed; back and internal doors were sometimes square-headed. Windows, too, were often pointed or double-light rounded windows set in an arch. The large windows in formal rooms were probably glazed. Archaeological evidence suggests that Frankish window-glazing consisted either of plate glass or round glass set in plaster (the latter presumably less expensive and more common). Otherwise, windows had grates or shutters to prevent unwanted intrusions.

Exterior walls were usually plastered and whitewashed, although the homes of the wealthy were sometimes faced with marble. Interior walls were likewise either marble-faced or plastered and whitewashed. The plaster walls may have been decorated with frescoes or painted designs or borders. Wall niches, either open or covered with curtains or wooden doors, were commonly used for storage. Plaster benches built directly against the walls of houses were another common feature. Both reduced the need for furnishings.

The floors of poorer dwellings were either beaten earth or cut out of the bedrock, while upper floors were plaster. In wealthier homes, the floors were usually flagstone on the ground floor, marble or mosaic above. Rugs and carpets were readily available, as these were one of the many products that passed through the crusader states on their way West. The use of tapestries and wall hangings was also likely. Courtyards were usually paved with cobbles.

Frankish houses frequently had fireplaces, and the better homes had indoor privies. A house in Caesarea, for example, had ceramic pipes leading from the upper floor to a sewage tank. Likewise, the houses in planned rural settlements had cisterns and elaborate plumbing. This is hardly surprising; similar arrangements for waste using ceramic pipes have been found in many Byzantine houses of roughly the same period. Many contemporary Byzantine homes also had internal water basins plastered on the inside. By the thirteenth century, residences in Western Europe also started to feature water funneled from rooftop cisterns to lavers and from these to latrines.

Finally, no discussion of urban architecture in the crusader states would be complete without reference to gardens and fountains. To the extent possible, Frankish elites oriented their houses, so their (glazed) windows looked out at views, such as the ocean or mountains, or gardens. The Holy Land offered a variety of beautiful vegetation: trees such as palms, olives, lemons and pomegranates, and flowers such as hibiscus and oleander. Many Frankish gardens contained fountains or incorporated other kinds of irrigation to keep them green throughout the summer.

Only scattered fragments of the sophisticated urban architecture of the Franks have survived into the present. These remains have been largely obscured by subsequent changes of style and function, often making the Frankish foundations unrecognisable to the layman. Most frustrating to the historian is the loss of all the major palaces. The Franks built a royal palace in Jerusalem south of the Tower of David sometime between 1143 and 1174 and maintained a royal residence in Acre. The Lusignans had royal palaces in Nicosia and Famagusta. In addition, leading clerics such as the patriarchs, archbishops and bishops maintained palaces. While we have only one surviving description of a baronial palace, that at Beirut, the leading barons of Jerusalem all had residences in their baronies and probably palaces in Jerusalem. The barons of Cyprus had palaces in Nicosia.

Based on written accounts, we know that the Lusignan palace at Nicosia had a loggia overlooking a square and that arcades supported by columns surrounded the great hall. 'Its great throne room, its balconies, its golden ornaments, its tapestries, pictures, organs, and clocks, its baths, gardens and menageries suggest the most sumptuous of medieval residences.'[8] The royal palace in Famagusta included arched arcades around a central courtyard. It also had a large latrine tract that has survived. Undoubtedly, the most evocative description of the palaces of the wealthy in the crusader kingdoms is provided by Wilbrand of Oldenburg, a cannon of Hildesheim, who visited the Holy Land in 1211–12. He describes the palace of the lord of Beirut, John d'Ibelin, as follows:

> ... it was well sited, overlooking on one side the sea and the ships passing to and fro on it, and on another meadows, orchards and most delightful places. It has a delicate marble

pavement, simulating water agitated by a light breeze, so that whoever walks on it imagines himself to be wading, although his footprints have made no impression on the sand represented there. The walls of the house are covereed all over with marble panels, which by the subtlety of their workmanship imitate various curtains. Its vault is painted so particularly the colour of the sky, that there the clouds appear to scurry, there the Zephyr to blow, and there the sun to define the year and months...In all these things Syrians, Saracens, and Greeks glory in their mastery of their arts through a delightful competition of workmanship. In the middle of the hall, at the central spot, is a pool lined with variegated marble, in which the marble is put together from panels of different colours, which do not jar when a thumb is drawn across them. They represent innumerable varieties of flowers.... In the centre a dragon, which seems about to devour the animals depicted there, emits a jet of crystalline water, pouring it forth in such abundant quantity that in hot weather, dissolving on high, it may humify and cool the air, which is let through fair rows of windows on every side. The same water, resonating throughout the pool and being received into the slenderest of channels, lulls to sleep by agreeable murmurings its lords who sit nearby. I would willingly sit by for all my days.[9]

Unfortunately, nothing of this palace remains today, and the archaeological remains of the other palaces are insufficient to allow us to draw the plans, let alone conjure up images.

Frankish Art

Arguably, 'one of the least known aspects about the Crusades is the art that was commissioned by the Crusaders in the Holy Land from the time they took Jerusalem in July 1099, to the time they were pushed into the sea by Mamluks in 1291'.[10] Yet, considering that the Middle Ages and the Middle East are individually renowned for the artistic embellishment of both practical and sacred objects, it is hardly surprising that the crusader states produced a wide variety of decorative art. Artistic creativity was undoubtedly stimulated by the novelty of sights and experiences that Western craftsmen encountered in the Holy Land in the era of the crusades.

Frankish art encompassed a wide array of media: stone and wooden sculpture; painting on wood (icons) and plaster (frescos); mosaics; metalworking in iron, copper, bronze, silver and gold; manuscript illumination; ivory carving; leatherworking; textiles, ceramics and glass. A thousand years of violent history, however, has ravaged the artistic legacy of the Franks. Particularly damaging to the survival of Frankish art was Muslim intolerance for Christian symbols and motifs and indeed any depiction of human figures, a popular component of Frankish art. What remains are only tantalizing remnants and references that demonstrate its diversity, quality and uniqueness.

A Unique Frankish Style

Studies of these surviving remnants indicate that Frankish art was neither an imitation of contemporary Western European art nor an adaptation of contemporary Eastern art. Although Frankish art was strongly influenced by European traditions, notably Romanesque art in the twelfth century and Gothic style in the thirteenth, Byzantine traditions also impacted it heavily. Indeed, Frankish art incorporated elements of Armenian, Coptic and Syrian Orthodox artistic traditions, and, to a lesser extent, Islamic and even Mongol traditions.[11] These were melded together, resulting in a unique and distinctive artistic style.

The two features that most effectively define Frankish art are its 'multicultural' and 'pious' aspects. The multicultural facet originated in the diverse traditions that influenced it, as described above. The pious factor evolved from the location where it was produced. Most Frankish art, particularly in the twelfth century, was intended to embellish Christianity's holy shrines or provide visitors with keepsakes from their pilgrimage. Whether bejeweled reliquaries or tin ampules for poor pilgrims to carry holy sand and holy water home, most early Frankish art had a religious component.

While this was particularly true of objects made for the transient population of crusaders and pilgrims, even items made for daily use by permanent residents – pottery, cutlery, saddles and shoes – often incorporated Christian symbols. Perhaps this was because, for more than 400 years, the native Christians were denied the right to display these symbols and were now proud to do so. Or maybe it was because the settlers who stayed in the Holy Land were particularly devout, an interpretation suggested by estimates that as much as 50 per cent of the immigrant population in the Kingdom of Jerusalem during the early decades was composed of clerics. On the other hand, art historians and archaeologists have categorised objects as Frankish in many cases based on the symbols; those period items lacking Christian, Muslim or Jewish symbols cannot be classified – yet may actually be Frankish. Ultimately, 'the attempts of art historians to ascribe icons and artifacts to a definite ethnic-cultural and geographic setting, namely "Latin", "Byzantine-Orthodox" or "Islamic", has created rigid mental molds and artificial barriers. These obscure the dynamics of artistic creation and their connection with production and consumption patterns.'[12] Art in the Holy Land was dynamic, with techniques and motifs passing fluidly from one community to the next, particularly in the twelfth century.

By the thirteenth century, the pious element in Frankish art – and life generally – had become more diffused; secular art from this period is also more plentiful. For example, while most books produced in the Holy Land in the twelfth century were devotional works (e.g. prayer books, saints' lives, psalters, gospels), by the thirteenth century, romances, histories, travel logs and law books were also being produced. On the one hand, the disproportionately high number of religiously devout residents declined as a proportion of the overall population as the Italian communes and the native 'poulain' population grew. On the other hand, with the loss of the great Christian shrines at Jerusalem, Bethlehem and Nazareth, the focus of the inhabitants appears to have turned more towards commerce, entertainment and luxury.

Architectural Decoration Sculpture, Mosaics and Frescos

The most important remnants of Frankish art dating from the twelfth century are the decorations of the key crusader shrines: the Church of the Holy Sepulchre (Jerusalem), the Church of the Nativity (Bethlehem) and the Church of the Annunciation (Nazareth), as well as lesser crusader structures such as the Church of St Anne, the Baptistry on the Temple Mount and the Templar and Hospitaller Headquarters. The Church of the Holy Sepulchre was dedicated on the fiftieth anniversary of the crusader capture of Jerusalem on

15 July 1149. The decorations which adorned the new structure reflected Roman, early Christian, Byzantine, Romanesque and even Arab decorative motifs along with Franco-Italian imagery. This was achieved by employing artists and craftsmen from the West and East, sculptors, masons, masters of mosaic work, and painters. Altogether, 'it was a magnificent ecumenical statement of East and West unified in this unique Crusader sculptural ensemble'.[13]

The Church of the Nativity, the next spectacular renovation of the Frankish era, exhibits even more Eastern influence primarily because the Byzantine Emperor Manuel I was a joint sponsor of the project along with King Amalric. Here, mosaics dominated the decorative scheme, building on the remnants of the sixth-century church while adding new mosaic panels. The latter were designed and executed under the guidance of a Byzantine master by Frankish, Venetian and Byzantine craftsmen. Texts worked into the mosaics are in Greek, Latin and Syriac. In addition to the extensive mosaics, the columns were painted.

Work on a major church in Nazareth to mark the site of the Annunciation did not begin until after 1170. It was an ambitious project, with a 73-metre nave. The decoration differed dramatically from Bethlehem and Jerusalem, emphasizing sculpture rather than mosaics or frescoes. Work was not completed before Saladin's invasion in 1187, and five of the column capitals intended for the church were buried for safekeeping. These have since been discovered and the outstanding quality of these figures initially led scholars to suspect a sculptor from southern France. Now, however, it is widely accepted that the artist was local – bearing witness to the high standard achieved by local artists in this period. The sculpture in the portals, tragically, have survived only as broken fragments because Baybars razed the church in 1263.

Much of the stonework done for Templar headquarters in Jerusalem, on the other hand, survived through reuse in Islamic structures because human figures were not depicted. It can be seen today, particularly in the Al-Aqsa mosque. In addition, based on sixteenth-century sketches, it appears the tombs of the first seven rulers of Jerusalem were excellent works of art. Unfortunately, the tombs themselves were severely damaged when Jerusalem fell to the Khwarazmians in 1244 and later utterly destroyed in a fire in 1808.

Likewise, nothing remains of the furnishings and decorations of Frankish dwellings. Nevertheless, visitors from the West frequently commented on the interior adornment and paintings of the houses in the Latin East, albeit without providing descriptions precise enough to enable us to visualise them. The account of the hall in Beirut's palace cited earlier informs us that artisans capable of producing everything from water-spewing dragons to polychrome marble that imitated flowers or hanging curtains and paving stones that mimicked ripples in the sand could be found in the crusader states. For those who could not afford polychrome marble, there was glazed and painted ceramics, wood, and plaster. The two latter media could be painted in monochrome colours or with patterns, foliage or entire scenes.

Manuscript Illustration and Illumination

The Church of the Holy Sepulchre's scriptorium was founded in the first decades of the Kingdom of Jerusalem by monks from Europe, who brought their skills and understanding of the medium with them. By 1134, this workshop produced one of the most remarkable works of Frankish art still extant today: Queen Melisende's Psalter. Between two carved ivory covers studded with gems, the psalter contains multiple illustrations, including twenty-four full-page illustrations depicting scenes from the life of Christ and nine page-headers dedicated to individual saints. Six different artists are believed to have worked on this masterpiece, and it included stylistic elements identified as French Romanesque, Byzantino-Romanesque, Italo-Byzantine, Byzantino-Muslim and even Anglo-Saxon. These blend into a harmonious work with a coherent concept relevant to the patron: an Armenian-Frankish queen married to a Frenchman. While this work created for royalty is the finest example of the quality of work performed in Jerusalem's scriptorium, other works show it was no aberration. Altogether, the remaining examples demonstrate that a thriving industry of artisans working in ivory-carving, jewelry, miniatures and silk embroidery already existed by the 1130s. Throughout the half-century that followed, high-quality liturgical books were produced for those who could afford them. All testify to the hybrid artistic culture evolving at this time in which Western artists borrowed native and Byzantine Orthodox techniques, motifs and saints. Unsurprisingly, Byzantine influence was at its height in the latter two decades of this period, when the Kingdom of Jerusalem was allied with the Byzantine Empire, and Byzantine queens resided in the Frankish capital.

The negotiated surrender of Jerusalem in 1187 enabled the canons of the Holy Sepulchre to survive with their skills (and probably most of their unfinished works) intact. After the establishment of the Second Kingdom, the scriptorium was re-established in Acre. Other ateliers grew up around it, making Acre a centre for book production. One of the most outstanding books produced and illustrated in Acre is the 'Arsenal' bible produced for King Louis IX of France. This and other works testify to the continued existence of the Frankish or 'crusader style' of book illustration that incorporated Eastern and Western elements. Surprisingly, many of the existing examples of Acre's manuscript workshops are secular works. William of Tyre's 'History of Deeds Done Beyond the Sea' was evidently popular, and multiple illustrated versions of this history have survived. More unusual is an illustrated version of John of Jaffa's 'Assizes of Jerusalem'.

Astonishingly, manuscript production continued right up to the fall of Acre. In one surviving manuscript, all the illustrations but the last are done in the distinctive Frankish style; the final illustration is distinctively Venetian. One can imagine this manuscript being spirited aboard a Venetian ship in the final days of Acre, while the artist remained behind to fight and die in the Mamluk onslaught.

Icon Painting
It was not merely in the production of miniatures on parchment that Frankish painters excelled. Acre and Frankish Cyprus both developed into centres for icon painting, that is, larger-scale paintings on wood, while Tripoli and Antioch appear to have engaged in icon production on a smaller scale. Cyprus was particularly famous for its 'vita' icons, in which the central image of a saint was surrounded by smaller scenes depicting his or her life. Like Frankish sculpture, Frankish icons fused elements from the artistic heritage of the culturally diverse population of Outremer. Frankish knights and ladies (based on their dress) pray to Eastern saints; dedications were often bilingual in Latin and Greek.

Surviving Frankish icons reveal their high quality and distinctive features. One of their particularly telling features was the popularity of 'soldier saints' – St George, St Theodore, St Demetrios, St Bacchus and St Minas. These were invariably depicted in armour and mounted on high-stepping or rearing horses. Some carry lances, while others – significantly – are armed with bows, suggesting native Christian patronage of substantial means. Another notable feature of Frankish icons is the frequent inclusion of female patrons – a distinctly Western tradition incorporated into an Eastern art form.

These icons highlight the degree to which icons had become popular for private devotion among the Frankish elites and the Italians. The inhabitants of Outremer increasingly wanted to own and hang icons in their homes. Unlike sculptures or frescoes anchored to the buildings they decorated, icons could be packed away, transported or given as gifts. They even made their way to Italy, where the icon evolved into paintings as we know them today – images painted on canvas or wood to be hung on walls.[14]

Other Art Forms

If Byzantium and Armenia heavily influenced miniatures, paintings, mosaics and sculptures in the Frankish East, artistic objects in glass, ceramics and metal borrowed more from Islamic techniques and traditions. Enameling on glass, for example, was first used by Arab craftsmen, although there is nothing inherently Islamic about it. The same is true of 'damascened' metalwork, the art of inlaying silver or gold on iron. Because many Orthodox Christian patrons still spoke Arabic many objects with Christian motifs but Arabic inscriptions have been falsely labelled 'Islamic' for the centuries. In other cases, merely the use of the damascene technique resulted in mislabelling objects 'Islamic' – despite the depiction of Christian symbols and the use of Latin in the inscription. Such errors are only gradually being corrected by the respective managers of collections.

Finally, music and the performing arts are ephemeral art forms that generally elude historical documentation. We know that an early form of drama was part of the cultural life of Outremer's nobility. Performances of episodes from the legend of King Arthur, for example, were part of the festivities surrounding the knighting of the lord of Beirut's eldest sons. We know that music was part of the culture through Novare's tales of singing satirical ballads outside besieged castles. Organs are mentioned in the inventory of the Lusignan palace at Nicosia. Richard the Lionheart wrote songs and allegedly heard a female slave of al-Adil give a musical performance. More generally, this was an age when polyphonic music flourished, music was notated, and musical instruments became more sophisticated. Given the constant pilgrim traffic to the Latin East, musical trends from the West presumably arrived in Outremer with each sailing season. However, Western musical innovations would have confronted powerful native traditions emanating from Constantinople. It is likely Outremer's music was as multifaceted and diverse as its other art forms and was a unique hybrid, drawing on varied musical traditions. Unfortunately, we will never know it, much less enjoy it.

Language, Literacy, and Intellectual Life

Language

Language has a powerful yet often subconscious impact on identity and culture. When the crusaders arrived in the Holy Land, the most spoken languages by the region's natives were Arabic and Syriac. Greek, which had been the official and commercial language for roughly 1,000 years, was also still spoken by some in urban areas, at least as a second language. In the north, particularly in Edessa, Armenian was the dominant language. Despite their diverse backgrounds, the crusaders spoke French as a common language supported by Latin, particularly among the clerics, and French remained the language of the Franks of Outremer for the next 200 years.

While the Franks spoke French well and could communicate with Europeans in this tongue, the spoken French of Outremer developed its own character. The residents of the Holy Land rapidly began 'to use the eloquence and idioms of diverse languages in conversing back and forth [and] words of different languages [became] common property known to each nationality'.[15]

In rural areas, settlers generally moved into existing towns and villages, working the land on the periphery and cultivating land that had lain fallow; they were initially heavily dependent on the help and advice of the natives to cope with an alien climate and unfamiliar crops. In urban areas, too, the local population far outnumbered the Franks, at least in the first half-century. The Franks frequented local shops, employed local craftsmen, drank in taverns and bathed in bathhouses, all run by natives. The Franks' dependence on the native population created an urgent need to communicate and fostered friendships and marriage.

Among the lower classes of the second and third generation, many Franks were the product of mixed marriages; that is, they had mothers who had grown up speaking Armenian, Syriac or Arabic. Fulcher of Chartres, writing before 1130, notes: 'For we who were occidentals have now become orientals .... Some [of us] have taken wives not only of [our] own people but Syrians or Armenians or even Saracens who have obtained the grace of baptism. One has his father-in-law as well as his daughter-in-law living with him, or ... his stepson or stepfather.'[16] Such arrangements fostered bilingualism as children grew up speaking both their mother and father's tongues.

Even among the feudal elite, intermarriage was strikingly common in the First Kingdom. Baldwin I and Baldwin II both married Armenian women, as did Joscelyn I of Edessa. Kings Baldwin III and Amalric took Greek Byzantine brides. Isabella I of Jerusalem, from whom all the thirteenth-century ruling monarchs of the kingdom descended, was one-half Greek, one-quarter Armenian, and only one-quarter Frankish.

While there is no recorded incident of a knight or lord marrying a Saracen (despite what Fulcher of Chartres says about men of lower rank doing so), surprisingly there is substantial, if anecdotal, evidence that many of the ruling feudal elite spoke fluent Arabic. Various chronicles record, usually without comment, how Frankish lords communicated in Arabic. We know that both Humphrey de Toron II and III spoke Arabic, as did Raymond of Tripoli and Hugh of Caesarea. Some of these lords, such as Renard de Sidon and Nicolas of Acre, read Arabic well enough to translate it. Baldwin d'Ibelin translated Arabic poetry into French. William of Tyre wrote a history of Islam based on Arab primary sources. Some historians allege that the Franks of the second and third generation spoke and read Arabic 'better than their European vernaculars', although the basis for this assertion is unclear.[17] Nevertheless, we know that the sons of John of Beirut, who spent at least half their lives in Greek-speaking Cyprus, were sufficiently fluent in Arabic to translate what the Mamluks were saying in Arabic among themselves to Jean de Joinville during the Seventh Crusade. Indeed, some of the Ibelins spoke French, Arabic, Greek and Latin by this point.

The linguistic situation in Cyprus was different. Arabic had never taken hold on the island, and the majority of the native population spoke Greek. Despite the influx of Syriac and Arabic-speaking refugees from the mainland in the latter half of the thirteenth century, Greek remained the dominant language. French was spoken at the Lusignan court and among the Frankish feudal elite, but Greek was used for various administrative purposes, in diplomatic correspondence and to communicate with tenants, peasants, workers and the like. Consequently, the immigrants were forced to learn Greek, and within a few generations, Cyprus had evolved its own Greek dialect with strong influence from French and Italian. Indeed, one thirteenth-century Greek intellectual complained of the 'barbarisation' of Greek and claimed that 'people learned 'Frankish', so that no one knew what their language was any more'.[18]

Literacy

Spoken command of a language is not the same as literacy, whether in one's native language or a foreign one. Although the overall level of literacy in Outremer was not recorded, some indicators suggest that literacy extended down the social scale at least as far as the gentry class and was also high among urban burgesses. Testaments and bequests reveal that otherwise unremarkable knights owned multiple books from different genres, such as devotional works, tour guides and romances. Biographies and memoirs also mention books. In one case, a woman pilgrim retained her psalter even after she was enslaved following the fall of the Kingdom in 1187, highlighting that women, no less than men, owned and read books in this period.

Library inventories show the diversity and quality of texts available to scholars. They include many works 'inherited' from their Arab predecessors, particularly in the case of Antioch. The Arabs had collected books originating in Persia and India, as well as the classical and Arab worlds. Unlike the Mongols, who turned manuscripts into shoes and destroyed all of Baghdad's thirty-six libraries along with their books, the crusaders preserved existing Arab libraries and expanded them. Thus, Frankish libraries were famous for containing books unavailable in the West, as well as housing the usual translations of many classical works, such as Virgil's *Aeneid* and various works by Aristotle, Euclid, Cicero and Ovid (including 'Art of Love' and 'Remedies for Love'). Antioch was also famous as a centre for scholarly research on medicine, and its libraries contained many translations and original works on medical theory. Histories were another genre in high demand in this period, and the libraries of Outremer offered patrons histories of Rome, Thebes, and above all, the crusades themselves.

Particularly popular, and often found in private as well as institutional libraries and collections, were books containing the prose and epic literature of the period. The works of Chretien de Troyes, Walter de

Châtillon's 'Chanson of Alexander', and the chansons of Roland, Antioch, Jerusalem and 'Chétifs' all circulated widely in the Latin East. In his study 'Reading and Writing in Outremer', Anthony Bale concluded that 'books were part of the everyday and fundamental experience of the Latin Christians of the crusader kingdoms'.

Education

A literate population presupposes education in some form. While many noblemen and women would have received education at home from tutors, public schools were necessary to foster a literate clergy. By 1120, the Church of the Holy Sepulchre had established a cathedral school alongside the more famous scriptorium. Other cathedral schools presumably existed, at least in Antioch, Acre, Nazareth and Tyre. None of these schools evolved into a university, and the Latin East did not contribute to the great contemporary debates on theology and philosophy. Nevertheless, as preparatory schools for European universities and as schools preparing secular elites for service in the bureaucracy and courts, the quality of education appears to have been adequate to above average.

Nor was it the Franks alone who had access to higher education. By the thirteenth century, the crusader states had become a centre for both Samaritan and Talmudic studies, while a Jacobite school was founded in Tripoli. Nablus was the heart of Samaritan worship and scholarship, and a large number of Torah scrolls from the crusader era testify to the vitality of the Samaritan intellectual community. Meanwhile, Jewish immigration to the Holy Land, particularly from Catalonia and France, enabled Acre to become a vibrant Jewish intellectual hub with multiple competing schools of Talmudic study. Indeed, prominent Egyptian Jew David ben Joshua Maimonides fled to Acre to avoid persecution from his enemies in Egypt. In roughly the same period, 1246–59, the Syrian Jacobite Gregory bar Hebraeus established a multidisciplinary school in Tripoli. Hebraeus was the author of numerous works, including books on philosophy, rhetoric, cosmology, natural history, psychology and metaphysics.

In Cyprus, village schools continued to provide rudimentary instruction in Greek, but Greeks seeking higher education had to go to Constantinople. For the much smaller Latin population, each of the four bishops established and maintained grammar schools, while the archbishop established a grammar school and a secondary school focused on theology. Again, while unremarkable as an intellectual centre, the grammar schools of Frankish Cyprus enabled 'a broad diffusion of functional literacy'.[19]

Scholarship and Intellectual Life

Despite the absence of a local academic centre, Cyprus' geopolitical and economic position as an interface between the Arab Middle East, Byzantium and Western Europe ensured that intellectual trends reached Cyprus rapidly from these places. Because Cyprus was secure and wealthy, the Lusignan court was free to focus on topics other than survival. Henry IV was famous for inviting leading intellectuals to his court from the West, Constantinople and Egypt, and the quality of intellectual discourse at the Lusignan court was elevated enough to receive positive notice in Constantinople. Indeed, it has been said that 'the literature produced on Cyprus ... up to the reign of Peter I constitutes a flowering that is without parallel before the Renaissance'.[20]

The Frankish residents of the crusader states on the mainland were likewise more than mere 'consumers' of books and literature; they produced them as well. As mentioned in the previous chapter on economics, the production of manuscripts was an economic activity of note, which ensured they were readily available for purchase.

More important than the physical production of books was the amount of content that originated in the Kingdom of Jerusalem. To be sure, the Latin East failed to attract the great abstract thinkers of the age, yet it was far from devoid of intellectual activity and scholarly work. Unsurprisingly, a great number of works were written in the Holy Land concerning the history of the crusades and the Latin East. The most important of these included: Fulcher of Chartres' history, the *Gesta Tancredi* by Raoul of Caen, the *Bella Antiochena* by Walter of Antioch, the *Hierosolymita* by Ekkehard of Aura, the anonymous *Gesta Francorum'*, and, of course, the aforementioned chansons of Antioch, Jerusalem and the Chetifs, the latter being a romance about crusaders captured by Zengi, the atabeg of Mosul, which was commissioned by Prince Raymond of Antioch.

In a class by itself is William of Tyre's *History of Deeds Done Beyond the Sea,* which has been called 'one of the greatest historical works of the Middle Ages'.[21] Even more extraordinary was Tyre's *History of Islam*, a work commissioned by King Amalric. This work is noteworthy on two counts: (1) that a scholar in the Latin East was sufficiently conversant with Arabic and Arab sources to venture such a task, and (2) that a Christian monarch was sufficiently interested in his opponents to want to understand Islam and its roots.

Philip de Novare was another outstanding intellectual and scribe from the Latin East. Like a medieval Leonardo da Vinci, Novare was a man of many talents. As a knight, he actively participated in most of the military campaigns and battles of his age, yet he was also a poet, troubadour, philosopher, historian and lawyer. Among his contemporaries, he was most famous for his legal handbook on the laws of the Kingdoms of Jerusalem and Cyprus, a book full of practical tips for how to 'plea' or argue a case. Today, he is remembered as the author of the only comprehensive narrative describing the baronial resistance to Emperor Frederick II's rule in Outremer.

Strikingly, Novare was a man of obscure and probably bourgeois origins and limited financial resources, yet he rose to a position of influence and enjoyed widespread respect due to his intellectual – rather than his military – capabilities. That says a great deal about the society in which he lived, particularly since he was not alone in following this career path. On the contrary, other men of more obscure origins, such as William de la Tor, Rostain Aimer, Reynald Forson, Paul of Nablus, Philip Lebel, William Raymond, Philip of Baisdoin, Raymond of Conches, Raymond and Nicholas of Antiaumes and James Vidal gained prominence through their skill with the pen rather than the sword.

Collectively, these men and their aristocratic colleagues, such as Ralph of Tiberias, Balian de Sidon, Arneis of Gibelet, John d'Ibelin of Beirut and his nephew John of Jaffa, produced a diverse body of works from legal treatises and histories to romances. Their influence at home was such that by the mid-thirteenth century, interest and understanding of the law had become 'the chief characteristic of a literate and cosmopolitan baronage in Jerusalem and Cyprus'.[22] Nor was their influence confined to the Outremer. On the contrary, their theories on constitutional government profoundly influenced baronial movements across Europe.

To this day, these works are admired. It has been suggested, for example, that 'the greatest monument to the Western settlers in Palestine, finer even than the cathedrals and castles still dominating the landscape, is the law book of John of Jaffa, which ... is one of the great works of thirteenth-century thought'.[23]

Hospitals and Social Welfare

When the First Crusade set off for Jerusalem at the end of the eleventh century, the provision of social welfare services was not a public or state function. Care of the sick, insane, dying, orphans, senile elders, the disabled, the unemployed and the destitute was viewed as the family's responsibility. Only when families had failed did the Church – as a last resort and out of charity – assume responsibility for those in need.

Thus, when the crusader states were established, the Church had not yet institutionalised social services on a large scale. The provision of charity was ad hoc and administered by individual religious houses at the discretion of the respective abbot or bishop based on the resources at their disposal. While this form of charity could be substantial and continued uninterrupted through the Middle Ages, in the era of the crusades, this traditional form of charity was increasingly supplemented by large-scale, organised social welfare. This movement towards institutionalised church social welfare emanated from Jerusalem, and the change was largely the as a result of a single institution – and its imitators – as will be discussed below.

A New Kind of Monastic Order

As the site associated with Christian salvation, Jerusalem inevitably attracted a disproportionate number of people suffering from hardship or crisis. Year after year, countless chronically ill, disabled, destitute and homeless, abandoned and unemployed people undertook a pilgrimage to Jerusalem hoping for a miracle at best, or death in a holy place at worst. Many others who set out in good health became ill, injured, exhausted, destitute or abandoned along the arduous road to Jerusalem. The plight of many pilgrims arriving in Jerusalem was so piteous, that numerous attempts to establish hospices in the Holy City were made over the centuries, all of which proved unsustainable under Muslim rule. In or about 1080, the Benedictines established a hospice in Jerusalem to care for the neediest Christian pilgrims under a monk named Gerard.

Nineteen years later, Jerusalem fell to the forces of the First Crusade. Not only did the trickle of pilgrims to Jerusalem became a flood, thus creating a huge demand for social welfare services, but the political and religious environment was transformed. It became possible to build Christian structures, to openly preach Christianity, and to appeal to Christian patrons for aid and support. Gerard proved a talented, charismatic and exceptional leader. He created an institution which would, in due time, be recognised by the pope as a unique religious order—one of the few not named for its inspired founder. This order was first known as the Hospital of St John in Jerusalem, but its members were later called simply 'the Hospitallers'. During its period of militarisation, the order was known as the Knights of St John or the Knights Hospitaller.

This new order was not dedicated to contemplation, learning and education, or the fight against heresy or even preaching and the purification of souls. Rather, the Hospitallers were dedicated to 'serving the holy poor'. Regardless of their background or social standing in the secular world, members of the order considered themselves 'serfs' – or sometimes 'slaves' – of the poor.[24] Strikingly, this new order made no distinction between the religion of the poor, vowing to serve all, regardless of creed, colour or race. The members of the new order were admonished to 'love your enemies and do good to those who hate you'.[25]

Even after the militarisation of the Hospitallers in the late twelfth century, nursing and caring for the sick and injured remained an obligation of all members of the Order of St John, including the knights. In fact, the hospital's militarisation caused a major internal crisis lasting more than three decades, from 1171 to 1206. Initially, the Hospitallers appear to have employed mercenaries to fulfil duties such as defending their installations or field hospitals. Gradually, however, the Templar model took root inside the Order of St John, and full-fledged monks were allowed to bear arms and engage in combat. Yet, despite the addition of knights and castles to the organisation and warfare to the agenda, charitable and merciful activities – and above all, health care – remained the raison d'être of the Hospitallers.

Over time, other religious orders with similar missions – albeit rarely with mandates as broad or an ethos as humble – were established. These included the German Hospital (that later became the Teutonic Knights), the Hospitallers of St Thomas of Canterbury (providing medical care to English crusaders), the Order of St Lazarus (dedicated to caring for lepers), the Trinitarian Order (dedicated to ransoming prisoners from Muslim captivity and slavery) and the Spanish equivalent, the Mercedarians. Centuries later, the Hospitallers would be imitated by the Salvation Army. Yet none of the medieval orders were as rich, powerful or widespread as the Hospitallers, and none of the others has endured into our own time.

As international organisations, these religious institutions could draw on resources, both material and human, from across Christendom and pool these resources for specific tasks. This allowed them to collect recruits, alms, gifts, grants and patronage wherever available and deploy it in accordance with need. Royal or noble patronage of an institution could be decisive in its success, and truly international orders like the Hospitallers could obtain royal patronage, not from one, but dozens of crowned heads and their magnates – an enormous resource. For example, in one instance, the king of Jerusalem granted half the spoils of a military campaign to the Order of St John. But it was more common to endow the order with land or other sources of income. The location where the money was raised was unrelated to where it was spent. The international charitable orders could not only take from the rich to give to the poor but also take from the West to give to the East. While this sounds self-evident to us today, in the twelfth century, it was a radical innovation.

Social Welfare
Although the Hospitallers started as little more than a hospice, providing care but no cure to those who sought refuge with them, they rapidly assumed other functions. Early on, they took responsibility for burying the dead – initially paupers who could not pay for a burial. Yet, their prestige grew until wealthy patrons paid them for the honour of a Hospitaller burial. The Hospitallers also provided free meals for the hungry, functioning as what we would now call a 'soup kitchen'. They supplied clothes and shoes to the poor, not just cast-off clothes or donations of patrons, but newly-made garments. As their network of houses grew to many thousands across Europe, the Hospitallers soon found themselves obliged (by their rule) to offer food and lodging to travellers, rich and poor, on pilgrimage or not – and often at significant expense to themselves. In times of crisis, the Hospital and its imitators carried the burden of dealing with refugees. After the fall of Edessa, William of Tyre measured the severity of the crisis by noting that refugees were so numerous, they almost overwhelmed the ability of the Hospital and other religious houses to cope.

In addition, the Hospitallers looked after orphans, a function that was a particular responsibility of the Sisters of the Hospital. Unwed or impoverished mothers and the mothers of twins could give their infants to the Hospital, while abandoned children were likewise brought to the Hospital by whoever found them. Although the Hospitallers ran some orphanages, most of the children were put in foster homes. The foster mother received 12 talents a year from the Hospitallers to cover the child's costs. The payment was contingent on proper care, and the Sisters of the Hospital annually checked on each child to ensure they were properly fed and cared for. If not, the child returned to the Hospital's custody until a new foster mother was found. The children raised at the expense of the Hospital were known as 'the children of St John'. On reaching adulthood, they were given the option of joining the Hospital as members of the Order or embracing 'the seductive allurements of the frivolous world'.[26]

These various activities required legions of workers, the bulk of whom were lay associates of whichever religious order furnished services. Only a small percentage of those providing social services were avowed members of the Order of St John or any of the other charitable orders. Most of the lay workers were charity cases themselves. They were people without steady employment, jobs or family. They were failed apprentices, runaway serfs and abandoned wives; they were refugees, beggars and vagabonds. They found work with the charitable orders, which acted as massive employment agencies, absorbing and releasing people in response to the demands of the labour market.

Medical Care
Yet it was with respect to care for the sick that the Hospitallers made their greatest contribution, not only in the crusader states, but to the history of health care itself. It is important to recall that Western Europe did not have hospitals where acutely ill patients received professional medical treatment at the time of the First Crusade. There were, of course, infirmaries in religious houses for the care of ailing members of the community, but they were not established for the benefit of, nor available to, the general public. Furthermore, the infirmarer (the person in charge of an infirmary in a medieval monastery) and his assistants were first and foremost monks and nuns, rather than trained doctors and nurses. There were also almshouses for the infirm and ageing, hospices for the dying, and various charitable institutions to look after the chronically and incurably ill, such as lepers, the blind and the seriously disabled. In general, however, if the rich were sick, they sent for a physician to

treat them in their homes; if the poor got sick, they treated themselves or sought the services of a barber or other informally-trained medical practitioner. Another feature of eleventh-century Western medicine was the emphasis on spiritual healing through prayer. While men and women patients were separated, there was little to no attempt to separate patients based on the type of illness.

The Byzantine tradition was quite different. Already by the seventh century, most hospitals in the Eastern Roman Empire were financially independent. They employed paid, professional staff rather than relying on members of a monastic institution to provide care and treatment to patients. Most Byzantine hospitals were modest in size, ranging from ten to 100 beds. Only the most prestigious hospitals in Constantinople were larger. These employed multiple physicians and surgeons (further specialised by the type of surgery performed), pharmacists, attendants (nurses), instrument sharpeners, priests, cooks and latrine cleaners. The administration of these institutions was in the hands of the senior medical staff, and the patients were housed in wards based on gender and medical condition. Notably, female doctors are recorded working in the women's wards as well as female nurses.

Equally important, the medical staff of Byzantine hospitals were paid only low salaries, and served only for six months of a year; presumably, they earned the bulk of their income from private practice in the six months when they did not work in the hospital. This suggests that Byzantine hospitals, although no longer run by the Church, were nevertheless viewed as charitable institutions accessible to the poor. While most junior doctors earned no salary because they were considered apprentices in their craft, the larger hospitals contained libraries and teaching staff, making these comparable to modern teaching hospitals.

In the Muslim world, the concept of an institution dedicated to healing the sick appears to have been adopted after contact with the Eastern Roman Empire, following the conquest of Syria and the Levant. It soon became a matter of prestige for Muslim rulers to establish and endow hospitals. By the twelfth century, most major cities in the Middle East boasted at least one, if not more, hospitals. The staff of these hospitals was all paid medical professionals and could be drawn from any faith – Muslim, Christian or Jewish. Although nursing staff in the women's wards was female, doctors were invariably male. The famous Adudi hospital in Baghdad (and presumably other hospitals) was also a training institution with a library and a staff that wrote medical texts.

The administration of most hospitals in the Muslim world was in the hands of a bureaucrat appointed by the ruler. In short, even in the age of the crusades, these hospitals were 'public' in the sense of being state-run. The salaries were small, and again, the doctors worked only half of the time (half-days rather than alternating months), enabling them to earn 'real' money with private patients. Hospitals in the Dar al-Islam were large, often having several thousand beds. Patients were separated by sex and condition. Possibly due to the nomadic past of Arab and Turkish Muslims, the Muslim states were extremely progressive regarding the establishment of mobile hospitals. These travelled with the sultan's armies as early as 942. Mobile hospitals also provided care to outlying, rural areas.

The hospitals of the Order of St John drew on Byzantine and Muslim traditions while retaining some features of Western medical care. Unsurprisingly for a religious order, the Hospitallers maintained the Western emphasis on prayer as a means to recovery. The wards were usually situated to enable patients to hear Mass being read in an adjacent chapel or church. Furthermore, patients were expected to confess their sins on admittance to the hospital because it was believed that sin (and God's displeasure) could cause illness. That said, since Muslims and Jews were treated in the hospitals, we must presume that confession was an option as opposed to a requirement.

Breaking with Western tradition, the hospitals run by the Order of St John employed professionally-trained doctors and surgeons by the second half of the twelfth century, at the latest. Jewish doctors were also employed, taking the oath required of doctors on the 'Jewish book' rather than the bible. In contrast to both Byzantium and Muslim practice, the doctors of the Order of St John were well-paid and worked full-time in the hospitals. On the other hand, the attendants or caregivers were predominantly brothers and sisters of the Order of St John, i.e. monks and nuns. As such, they had no formal medical training, although they presumably gained extensive on-the-job training. The male caregivers are listed as 'sergeants' in the order's records, a comparatively high status. The Rule of the Order of St John required the nursing staff (male and female) to serve the sick 'with enthusiasm and devotion as if they were their Lords'.

Like the Muslims, the Order of St John maintained exceptionally large hospitals in major cities, such as Jerusalem, Nablus and Acre. The Hospital in Jerusalem had more than 2,000 beds, for example, and was divided into eleven wards for men and an unknown number of wards for women. (All contemporary accounts were written by male patients, who did not have access to the women's wards.) Patients appear to have been segregated not only by sex but by type of illness, although this may not have been possible at smaller institutions in more provincial towns. The larger hospitals, such as those in Jerusalem, Nablus and Acre, are described as 'palaces' by eyewitnesses, who stress they were built to provide adequate room for patients and personnel to move between beds. Furthermore, they had large windows that let in fresh air and light. Archaeology has brought to light an aqueduct apparently leading to the flagship hospital of the Order in Jerusalem. In addition, no less than five large cisterns provided ready water, and a network of drains made it possible to flush out refuse and human waste.

Diet formed an essential part of the treatment in Hospitaller establishments, possibly because so many patients were pilgrims suffering more from malnutrition than disease. Food poisoning and various forms of dietary problems were common in this period. Furthermore, medieval medicine was based on the premise that illness resulted from an imbalance between the 'humours' (e.g. blood and bile), and that proper diet could restore a healthy 'balance'. Certain foods, notably lentils, beans and cheese, were prohibited in the hospitals of St John, but white bread, meat and wine were daily fare. Patients also benefitted from the wide variety of fruits available in the Holy Land: pomegranates, figs, grapes, plums, pears and apples are all mentioned in Hospitaller records.

Finally, in addition to following the Muslim example of mobile field hospitals, the Hospitallers created the first known ambulance service. The brothers of St John combed the streets for those in need of care and carried them back to their hospitals. Likewise, during a military campaign, the Hospitallers scoured the battlefields for the injured and brought them to their hospital tents. Those who needed further care were transported to an urban hospital – even if the knights of the order had to surrender their warhorses to ensure transport. It is, therefore, particularly appropriate that one of the most active and successful successors of the Hospitallers is St John's Ambulance corps.

Food and Fashion

Frankish Cuisine[27]

Straddling the trade routes from several cultures, residents of crusader states were exposed to and cultivated a range of culinary traditions. The crusader kingdoms inherited the cuisine of earlier Mediterranean civilisations, including invaders from the Arabian Peninsula and the Near Eastern steppes, but they also enjoyed the cooking traditions brought to Outremer by Latin settlers of Northern and Western Europe. These traditions coexisted and probably influenced one another, yet we can no longer recreate the cuisine itself. Nevertheless, much can be surmised based on the ingredients available to the cooks of Outremer.

Before looking more closely at the content of crusader cooking, however, it is worth noting that the crusader states were arguably the inventors of fast food. The large number of pilgrims flooding the Holy City produced a plethora of cheap inns and hostels, places where pilgrims could bed down for the night. But affordable places to sleep, then as now, did not always offer meals, so pilgrims had to eat elsewhere. A general shortage of firewood meant that not only was bread baked centrally in large ovens, usually co-located with flour mills, but that 'cook shops' producing large quantities of food over a single large oven were more practical than everyone cooking for themselves. The result was the medieval equivalent of modern 'food courts' – streets or markets where various shops offered pre-prepared food. The results were probably not all that different from today; the area in Jerusalem where cook shops were concentrated was known as the 'Market of Bad Cooking' – the 'Malquisinat'.

Turning to the ingredients available, the medieval diet's staple was bread derived from grain, and this was true in the Holy Land no less than in England. Milling was a prerogative of the feudal elite, and bakeries were generally co-located with mills in rural areas near the manor and in urban areas well-distributed around the city for convenience. The primary grains popular in the Holy Land were wheat and barley, but millet and rice were also known. Rice would have been consumed directly rather than converted into bread by the native population that retained Arab and Turkish eating habits.

Animal products were the second pillar of the medieval diet, highly valued, and fully exploited from the meat to the innards. Of the large, domesticated animals, sheep and goats were the most common type of livestock in the region, and the Hospitallers recommended lamb and kid for patients in their hospitals. Jerusalem, however, also had cattle and pig markets. While camel meat is considered a delicacy in much of the Middle East, the camels of Outremer were used primarily as beasts of burden.

Of the smaller animals, poultry and fish belonged to the Frankish diet, the latter being particularly important during 'fasting days', when meat was prohibited, such as throughout Advent and Lent and on certain days of the week. In the Second Kingdom, when the population of Outremer was clustered along the coastline, fish from the Mediterranean represented an important component of the diet. This enriched Frankish cuisine with elements virtually unknown in most of continental Europe, such as squid and octopus.

Game was available in the First Kingdom and Cyprus, including gazelles, boars, roe deer, hares, partridge and quail. However, in the Second Kingdom, territorial losses resulted in much greater population density, which restricted habitat for game, and it all but disappeared from the tables of the elite in the mainland states. Cyprus, on the other hand, was still home to much wildlife (including lions), and the Cypriot feudal aristocracy was (in)famous for its large kennels and addiction to the hunt.

Animal products, such as milk, butter, yogurt, and cheese, were consumed in large quantities in the Holy Land in the era of the crusades. Cheese was particularly important because of its comparatively long shelf life and was produced from cattle, sheep, goat and camel milk. Yogurt, a product used heavily in the Middle Eastern diet, would have been known to the Franks, but we cannot measure how readily it was embraced in Frankish cuisine.

Vegetable varieties were limited by modern standards. Legumes were the primary vegetables of the Middle Ages. In the crusader states, the most important vegetables were beans, including broad beans, lentils, peas and chickpeas, as well as cabbage and onions. Fresh cucumbers and melons were native to the Levant and also formed part of the Frankish diet.

Fruits were a key component of Frankish cuisine, and here again, the residents of Outremer had ready access to fruits, such as oranges and lemons, that were considered luxuries in the West. Along with typical and familiar fruits from the West such as apples, pears, plums and cherries, the residents of the crusader states cultivated pomegranates (particularly around Ibelin and Jaffa), figs, dates, carobs and bananas. Arguably the most indispensable of all fruits were grapes, which were eaten fresh and dried (raisins and currants) and were fermented as wine.

Other trees that yielded significant dietary supplements were almonds, pistachios, hazelnuts and, the most essential of all, olives. Olive oil was and is fundamental to Middle Eastern cuisine. It is the primary source of cooking oil, used both as a means of cooking and a supplement for consistency and taste.

Finally, some of the most valuable dietary 'additives' that make such a difference to the taste of food – honey, sugar, herbs and spices – were readily available at affordable prices in the crusader states. A variety of herbs such as rosemary, thyme and oregano grew in abundance. Likewise, many spices only available at exorbitantly high prices in Europe passed through the ports of Outremer. The coastal cities and Jerusalem had spice markets in which these exotic, high-value products were available in quantities and at prices unimaginable in the West. Frankish cuisine was likely greatly enriched by the widespread use of cinnamon, cumin, nutmeg, cloves, saffron and black pepper, among others.

Given the ingredients the cooks of Outremer had to work with and the inspiration they could draw from their Greek, Arab and Turkish neighbours, Frankish cuisine as a whole – despite the presence of some mediocre fast-food joints on the Street of Bad Cooking – was most likely unique and delectable.

Frankish Fashion[28]

The transient nature of clothing inhibits our ability to know precisely what the residents of Outremer wore. Textile and garment fragments, illustrations, and descriptions in contemporary chronicles are our only primary sources to reconstruct Frankish fashion. Broadly speaking, church and military dress was widely standardised. Although military dress underwent significant changes in the 200 years between 1099 and 1291, this evolution of arms, armour and tack was not unique to the Latin East. Despite minor local variations, major innovations that provided substantial advantages in offense or defence were rapidly adopted across Western Christendom by the ruling military elite that proved remarkably mobile and cosmopolitan.

However, one of the innovations in the military dress widely adopted throughout Europe originated in the East. This was the 'surcoat', a cloth garment worn over armour. Because the intense sun of the Middle East made chainmail dangerously hot, the early crusaders rapidly learned to keep it comparatively cool by covering it with a thin, loose and flowing cloth, as the Arabs did. With the surcoat came the opportunity to wear bright colours and distinguishing devices or 'arms'. Hence, the evolution of heraldry goes hand-in-hand with the emergence of the surcoat as an integral part of a knight's battle dress.

Off the battlefield, the Franks may have been tempted to adopt some of the clothing customs of native inhabitants. However, there is little evidence to support this as depictions of barons and knights in manuscripts, sculptures, and on seals consistently show men of the military elite in military regalia, while bishops and priests look just like their counterparts in the West. The one exception is the rulers of the Latin East, who are frequently portrayed in Byzantine attire. Certainly, the Latin emperors of Constantinople affected 'Eastern' dress (meaning Byzantine, not Arab) in the early part of the thirteenth century.

Nevertheless, we have some tantalizing documentary evidence that, off the battlefield, Outremer's feudal elite developed some distinctive fashions. For example, during the Third Crusade, a commentator from the West noted:

> The sleeves of their garments were fastened with gold chains, and they wantonly exposed their waists, which were confined with embroidered belts, and they kept back with their arms their cloaks, which were fastened so that not a wrinkle should be seen in their garments ... and round their necks were collars glittering with jewels.[29]

In short, the Franks of Outremer had adopted or developed some fashions that looked strange – even wanton – to visitors from Western Europe. Based on their practice in other fields from architecture to miniatures, the Frankish knights and nobles probably developed their own hybrid style.

The women of Outremer are represented less frequently in art and when shown are always in conventional Western garb. Contrary to popular fiction and film, we know that they did not adopt the Muslim custom of going about veiled. James of Vitry (Bishop of Acre 1216–1228) describes with disgust the fact that Syrian Christians still 'obliged' their daughters (though notably not their wives) to go completely veiled, so they were unrecognisable. Other Christian women, most especially Vitry's flock of Latin Christians, clearly did not hide under veils.

In addition, Muslim sources rave about (or condemn) the Frankish women for their seductiveness – something not possible if they were hidden behind the same, opaque black garments as their Muslim counterparts, which obscured face and figure. The poet Ibn al-Qaysarani, for example, was so enraptured by Frankish women that he wrote 'effusive poems' praising their – very visible – beauty.[30] Ibn Jubayr likewise gives evidence that Frankish women went unveiled in his detailed description of a bride and her maids-in-waiting, concluding with the remark: 'God protect us from the seduction of the sight'.[31]

That said, it would not be surprising if Frankish women did adopt some means of protecting their skin from the ravages of the Middle Eastern sun. One of the illuminated copies of William of Tyre's *Deeds Done Beyond the Seas*, includes a picture of Queen Melisende wearing a broad-brimmed sun hat – not standard attire in Paris or London. It is also conceivable that transparent veils might have been worn when outdoors.

While the style of clothing worn by Frankish women may not have differed much from the latest fashion in London, Paris and Pisa, the materials used could have made a significant difference to the effect of those clothes. The same cut of a chemise or tunic, the same style of mantle or cloak will fall, fold, billow and sway differently, depending on its fabric. Many of the textiles of Outremer were sheer, translucent or semi-transparent. Depending on how such materials were used, they could have created enticing (or in the eye of clerics and conservatives, vulgar and immodest) garments, all without deviating from Western fashion.

Likewise, a gown that is simple in cut and form can be transformed by silk brocade or a weft of gold into something – depending on your ideology – stunning and luxurious or self-indulgent and extravagant. Archaeologists have uncovered thousands of fabric fragments dating to the crusader era. They include silk, cotton, linen, felt, wool, and cloth woven from goat and camel hair. There were also several hybrid fabrics composed of a warp from one kind of yarn and weft from another, such as silk woven with wool, linen or cotton.

Certainly, some of the finest cloth known to the medieval world originated in the Near East. Familiar words, like damask, gauze and muslin, derive their names from the cities that first produced them in export quantities, namely Damascus, Gaza and Mosul, respectively. Cloth of gold was known in this period as siqlatin, a term that derives from silk-Latin or Latin silk, an indication that this extravagantly expensive and beautiful material was particularly popular with Outremer's Latin elites.

Almost as important as the cloth from which clothes were made were the dyes used to colour them. Here again, the crusader states sat near the source of many materials coveted for dying. Saffron, turmeric and indigo – not to mention the murex snails needed for vivid scarlet and rich purple dye – were more readily available and cheaper in the crusader states than Western Europe. This makes it probable they were used more widely and generously in Outremer, producing much brighter hues than were common in the West.

Finally, decoration contributes to fashion. In the crusader era, weaving with different coloured threads, block printing and embroidery were all popular forms of decoration. Silk brocade and stitching with spun gold were particularly expensive and coveted forms of textile ornamentation known to have been exported from, if not produced in, the crusader states. The late-nineteenth-century historian Claude Reigner Conder claims the Latin ladies wore 'long-trained dresses with long, wide sleeves' (no different from the ladies of the French or Angevin courts in this period), but (perhaps more unusual) they were 'decked in samite and cloth of gold, with pearls and precious stones' – something that sounds distinctly Byzantine.

It was probably the combination of fine fabric and vivid shades of dye with decorations of gold and bejeweled embroidery that made the clothing of Outremer's Latin elites seem exotic to visitors from the West. Crusaders often commented that the lords of Outremer were wealthy and luxury-loving. Part of that reputation undoubtedly originated in the apparent extravagance of dress that came from being able to afford for everyday use textiles that were saved for special occasions in the West. In conclusion, while fashion in crusader states was set more in Paris and Constantinople than Damascus and Cairo, the use of sheer fabrics, bright colors, and expensive and elaborate decoration made it seem more exotic – not to say scandalous – to many a Western observer.

Chapter 10

The Ibelins
An Archetypical Frankish Family

The Ibelin family was one of the most powerful noble families in the crusader states. Sons of the House of Ibelin were at various times lords of Ibelin, Ramla and Mirabel, Nablus, Caymont, Beirut, Arsur, and counts of Jaffa and Ascalon, the last, a traditionally royal domain and title of the heirs to the throne. Ibelins married into the royal families of Constantinople, Jerusalem, Antioch, Cyprus and Armenia. An Ibelin daughter founded the Cypriot royal family, and three other Ibelin women were queens of Cyprus. Ibelins were repeatedly regents, constables, marshals and seneschals of both Jerusalem and Cyprus. They also led a successful revolt against the Holy Roman Emperor Friedrich II.

Yet the Ibelins were not mere politicians. They were respected scholars. One translated Arab poetry into French; another wrote a legal treatise that is not only a goldmine of information about the laws of the crusader kingdoms but admired for its elegance of style and the sophistication of its analysis. The Ibelins built at least one magnificent palace, whose mosaics, fountains, gardens and polychrome marble inspired the admiration of contemporaries. Their display of wealth and panache during the Seventh Crusade awed the nobility of France.

Yet while the Ibelins were undoubtedly exceptionally successful, they were also in many ways typical. They embodied the overall experience, characteristics and ethos of the Franks in the Holy Land. They came from obscure, probably non-noble origins, and the dynasty's founder can be classed as an 'adventurer' and 'crusader'. They rapidly put down roots in the Near East, intermarrying with native Christian and Byzantine elites. They were hardened and cunning fighting men able to deploy arms and tactics unknown to the West and intellectuals who could win wars with words in the courts. They were multilingual, cosmopolitan and luxury-loving, as comfortable in baths as in battles. Perhaps most importantly, they worked closely with turcopoles and sergeants and forged alliances with the merchant communities, reflecting the Latin East's tolerant and fluid social structures. Finally, like the crusader states themselves, they disappeared from history when the last crusader kingdom fell to the greed of the Italian commercial city-states. In short, the story of the Ibelins is a microcosm of the crusader states, and their story gives the history of Outremer a human face.

Obsecure Origins ca. 1110–1150

Barisan, Founder and First Lord of Ibelin

In the fourteenth century, the Ibelins claimed to be descendants of the counts of Chartres, but the claim is patently concocted. Sir Steven Runciman believed the House of Ibelin 'was founded by the younger brother of a certain Guelin, who was deputy viscount of Chartres, that is to say, the count of Blois' representative in Chartres'. He noted that 'such officers in those days did not enjoy hereditary rank but were often drawn from lawyers' families'.[1] Peter Edbury, argued that onomastic evidence points to Tuscan or Ligurian origins instead.

Whatever his place of origin, and whatever he called himself before coming to the Holy Land, the first man to identify himself as an 'Ibelin' was a certain Barisan. His date of birth is unknown, as is the date he arrived in the Holy Land. However, by 1115 he was described as 'Constable of Jaffa', a significant appointment suggesting he had made a name for himself and earned the trust of the king. Since such positions did not go to youths unless they were of high birth, we can assume that Barisan was a mature man at that time.

In 1134, he prominently refused to side with his rebellious lord, Hugh of Puiset, Count of Jaffa, and it may have been for this that Barisan was rewarded with a fief almost a decade later. In about 1142, the new castle and lordship of Ibelin south of Jaffa was bestowed on Barisan. Notably, he became a vassal of the new count of Jaffa rather than a tenant-in-chief of the king. Through hard work and loyal service, Barisan had reached the lowest rung of the feudal ladder, but he was not yet a baron.

Meanwhile, in 1138, he had married a certain Helvis (or Heloise), daughter of Baldwin of Ramla, one of the barons of the Kingdom of Jerusalem. At the time of this marriage, Helvis was not the heiress; she had a younger brother, Renier. So, this marriage was between a man not

The Ibelins

yet raised to the nobility and the daughter of a nobleman. It was a good marriage but not a spectacular one. The situation changed, however, when Renier of Ramla died childless in 1148. Suddenly, Helvis was the heiress of the prestigious and prosperous barony of Ramla and Mirabel. (Despite the two names, this was a single barony.) Through sheer luck, a good marriage had turned into a spectacular one.

Barisan had little time to enjoy his increased status. He died in 1150, probably peacefully in his bed of old age; he was most likely more than 60 years old and could easily have been 70 or older at the time of his death.

The Second Generation ca. 1150–1200

Barisan left behind three sons, Hugh, Baldwin and Balian. This second generation of Ibelins were renowned fighting men, praised by William of Tyre as 'noble men, valiant in arms and vigilant in every respect'.[2] Each contributed to the rise of the family in significant ways.

Historians conventionally assume that all three were the sons of Helvis of Ramla because no other wife was mentioned in the historical record. However, Hugh immediately came into his inheritance in 1150. Since the laws of the Kingdom of Jerusalem designated 15 years as the age of majority, and a boy under that age required a guardian/regent, Hugh must have been at least 15 in 1150, something not physically possible if he were a child of a marriage concluded in 1138. Furthermore, Hugh played a leading role in the siege of Ascalon three years later, again something he could not have done as an unknighted 14-year-old minor. William of Tyre describes the host that gathered for an assault on Ascalon as follows:

> Among the lay princes present were: Hugh d'Ibelin, Philip of Nablus, Humphrey of Toron, Simon of Tiberias, Gerard of Sidon, Guy of Beirut, Maurice of Montreal, Renaud de Châtillon and Walter of St Omer. These last two served the king for pay.[3]

The prominence Tyre gives to Hugh in 1153 strongly suggests that Hugh was not only a grown man but one who had by 1153 already acquired a considerable reputation at arms.

It is also notable that Hugh only very briefly styled himself Lord of Ramla. This was in the period between Helvis of Ramla's death in 1158 and the year when his younger brother Baldwin came of age at 15 in 1160. This is consistent with Hugh being the guardian of his brother after Helvis of Ramla's death (and hence lord of Ramla for his brother) but not entitled to hold the title after his brother came of age.

In short, Hugh was evidently the child of an earlier, unrecorded marriage – either a woman left behind in France (who was not of noble birth since Barisan was not) or, more likely, a local woman of non-Frankish ethnicity. That Barisan, himself of non-noble birth, would have married a local woman before his elevation into the feudal class is consistent with the pattern of most non-noble crusaders. It would explain why this woman is ignored in later sources when the House of Ibelin jealousy guarded its status and carefully avoided mention of anything that might detract from its prestige.

In 1157, Hugh had the misfortune to be one of the 'prominent men' taken captive in an ambush laid by Nur al-Din at Jacob's Ford. King Baldwin III, returning from relieving and fortifying Banyas, was taken completely by surprise. The king barely escaped capture, while Hugh d'Ibelin, along with the Templar master Bertrand of Blancfort and the Templar marshal (and later master) Odo of Saint-Amand, were taken prisoner. Altogether, some eighty-seven Templars and 300 secular knights were killed or captured in this ambush. Nur al-Din paraded his trophies – the heads of the killed Franks and his prisoners roped together – through the streets of Damascus before cheering crowds.

Hugh's captivity came at a pivotal moment in his life. Only shortly before, he had become betrothed to a young woman from the highest echelons of Frankish society, the daughter of Count Joscelyn II of Edessa. At the time of the betrothal, however, the count of Edessa was in a Saracen dungeon after losing most of his county. Agnes was virtually penniless and already a widow. In short, the marriage brought Hugh no material gain.

Fortunately, his stepmother Helvis of Ramla died in 1158. Hugh, at last, became the guardian of his younger brother Baldwin, the heir to Ramla. He therefore temporarily controlled the income of his brother's barony of Ramla and Mirabel and could use it to contribute to his ransom. Even so, Hugh was unable to raise his ransom without help. In 1159 he was in Antioch where he met with the Byzantine emperor to thank him for ransom payments, and in 1160 Hugh made a grant to the canons of the Holy Sepulchre in gratitude for their contributions as well.

Meanwhile, Agnes de Courtenay had married his overlord, the count of Jaffa, Prince Amalric of Jerusalem. At least one account claims that Aimery took Agnes 'by force'. However, there is no indication of animosity between Hugh and Amalric after Hugh's release from captivity. Ostensibly Hugh viewed royal contributions to his ransom as more important than Agnes.

In February 1163, King Baldwin III died unexpectedly. Since his young Byzantine queen had not yet produced an heir, his younger brother Amalric, Count of Jaffa, was the heir apparent. However, the High Court of Jerusalem refused to recognise Amalric as king unless he first set Agnes of Courtney aside. The reason given was that Agnes and Amalric were related within the prohibited degrees, but such an obstacle could easily have been overcome with a papal dispensation. The real reason may have been that the barons of Jerusalem feared Agnes would use her influence to reward her penniless relatives or that her reputation was so sullied she was deemed unsuitable to wear the crown of Jerusalem. Another explanation is that the church, which viewed a betrothal as sacrosanct, considered Agnes' marriage to Amalric bigamous. This explanation is suggested in the 'Lignages d'Outremer', which claims that no sooner had Agnes been set aside, then she went to Hugh and announced she was his wife. Hugh took Agnes back, but the marriage remained childless.

In 1167, Hugh played a prominent role in Amalric's invasion of Egypt. William of Tyre mentions that Hugh was entrusted with constructing a bridge over the Nile and tasked with protecting Cairo. Later in the same campaign, Hugh led an attack on Bilbais, which was under siege. During this engagement his horse fell in the fosse, breaking its neck and Hugh's leg. According to Ibelin family legend, Hugh's life was saved by Philip of Nablus, who came to his aid at the risk of his life.[4] Perhaps it was due to this event that Hugh undertook a pilgrimage to Santiago de Compostela in 1169. Thereafter, he disappears from charters and chronicles and is presumed to have died either on pilgrimage or shortly after returning. By 1171, his younger brother Baldwin was styling himself Lord of Ibelin as well as Lord of Ramla.

William of Tyre consistently praised Hugh d'Ibelin as a man of courage, vigor and diligence. It was probably these attributes that enabled him to marry into the highest rank of Frankish society. While the union appears to have brought Hugh little, it greatly benefitted his younger brothers. Through Hugh's marriage, the younger Ibelin brothers became uncles of the king's only son, the future king, Baldwin IV.

Baldwin of Ramla 1145–1187 (?)

Baldwin, Barisan's second son, was only 5 years old when his father died.[5] His mother remarried the same year, taking the powerful Manassas of Hierges – a close adherent of Queen Melisende – as her second husband. The marriage aroused the ire of Hugh d'Ibelin because, according to William of Tyre, it removed the wealth and prestige of the barony of Ramla from his command. Since Helvis's second marriage would hardly have impinged on Hugh's claim to Ramla had he been Helvis' son, the issue at stake was control of Baldwin, the young heir. Hugh had expected to benefit from the resources of Ramla and Mirabel until Baldwin came of age in 1160. Helvis' marriage removed Baldwin from his control and denied him access to the revenues of Ramla and Mirabel. This caused Hugh to turn against Queen Melisende and support her son Baldwin III in their domestic power struggle.

When Baldwin III outmanoeuvered his mother and became the sole monarch two years later, Manassas of Hierges was sent into exile, never to return. Helvis of Ramla, however, remained in the Kingdom of Jerusalem and in possession of her fief and her son Baldwin. In 1156, at just 11 years of age, Baldwin was married to Richildis of Bethsan, a maiden of noble birth but not an heiress.[6] In 1158, when Baldwin was still two years short of his majority, his mother died, and his brother Hugh at last became his guardian. In 1160, Baldwin turned 15 and so reached legal maturity.

Baldwin (usually referred to by his title of Ramla in the chronicles) first emerges as an important figure for his contribution to the Battle of Montgisard. Based on the most recent analysis of the battle, the Franks manoeuvered Saladin onto swampy terrain, where the sultan's superior numbers could not be brought to bear. This effective use of the topography was possible because the army of Jerusalem was 'led by a local lord, who knew the terrain better than anybody else on the battlefield'.[7] Despite what numerous modern commentators have alleged, that 'local lord' was not Reynald de Châtillon, a Western adventurer who had spent most of the previous fifteen years in a Saracen prison and before that had been prince of Antioch in the north. It was the nobleman in whose lordship the battle was fought and the man who led the vanguard: Baldwin d'Ibelin.

Meanwhile, after the birth of two daughters, Baldwin separated from his first wife, Richildis, sometime before 1175 when he married Elizabeth Gotman, the widow of Hugh of Caesarea. Elizabeth died childless in 1179, leaving Baldwin free to marry again when the heir apparent, Baldwin IV's sister Princess Sibylla, was a 20-year-old widow with an infant son. While the High Court of Jerusalem sent to France for a suitable husband, Ramla courted Princess Sibylla directly with the apparent ambition of becoming king-consort.

According to the contemporary chronicle written by a client of the Ibelin family (Ernoul), Princess Sibylla was not disinclined to Ramla's suit. Unfortunately for Ramla, he was taken captive by the Saracens in June 1179. Saladin demanded the outrageous ransom of 200,000 gold bezants, or twice what was paid for Baldwin II in 1123. The size of the ransom demand, which could never have been raised from Baldwin's small lordship, suggests that Salah al-Din viewed Baldwin as the next king and expected the entire kingdom to pay the ransom – as was customary for a captive king.

Ramla's hopes of gaining a crown through marriage, however, were crushed by Sibylla's hasty marriage to Guy de Lusignan. Ramla had every reason to be disappointed (not to say outraged) by these developments, particularly because Guy was in no way his equal in terms of status or experience. Ramla's feelings would have been further complicated by the fact that Guy was the younger brother of his son-in-law; Baldwin's eldest daughter Eschiva had been married prior to 1180 to Aimery de Lusignan. To add insult to injury, Baldwin IV raised his new brother-in-law Guy to count of Jaffa and Ascalon, thereby effectively demoting Baldwin from tenant-in-chief to 'rear vassal'. Most insulting of all, it made Baldwin a vassal of the very man who had just stolen the heiress he had courted.

There can be little doubt that this embittered the proud Baldwin of Ramla, but it did not make him a rebel. On at least three occasions between 1180 and Baldwin IV's death in 1185, Ramla dutifully mustered with his knights when summoned by the king. Indeed, he played a prominent role, with his brother Balian, in defeating the Saracen forces attempting to take the springs at Tubanie in 1183. As long as Baldwin IV was king and under Baldwin V, Ramla accepted his fate. Meanwhile, he married one last time, Maria of Beirut, by whom he had his only son Thomas after 1181.

Only the elevation of Guy de Lusignan to the crown in the coup d'etat of 1186 proved too much for Ramla to bear. Rather than do homage to Guy de Lusignan, Ramla took the dramatic and unusual step of renouncing his lands and titles in favour of his infant son. 'It was an extraordinary thing to do. It meant giving up his inheritance, jeopardizing the future of his heirs and abdicating the political and social standing that he, the senior member of his family, and his father and elder brother before him, had nurtured for the past three-quarters of a century.'[8] Baldwin took service with the prince of Antioch, but he disappears from the historical record after his departure from the Kingdom of Jerusalem in 1186.

A man who took such a dramatic step was clearly a man of strong emotions. His hatred and resentment of Guy de Lusignan must have been enormous. More baffling, however, is that his outraged pride was more important to him than power and wealth. Equally notable, if less obvious, is that he was a singularly callous husband and father. He had discarded the mother of his two daughters for no better reason than the chance of a better marriage, and he abandoned his third wife and only son to the dubious mercy of Guy de Lusignan. To be sure, he nominally left his wife and son in the care of his younger brother Balian, but this was legally dubious. A vassal who refuses homage forfeits his fief to his overlord, in this case to none other than Guy de Lusignan. It is a forgotten measure of Lusignan's chivalry (or his intelligent appreciation of how precarious his situation was) that he took no action to seize Ramla and Mirabel from Balian d'Ibelin, but instead allowed him to control both until Hattin obliterated all the baronies of the kingdom.

Balian 'of Nablus' 1150–1193 (?)

The youngest of Barisan's sons and his namesake was an infant at the time of his father's death. He was still just 2 years old when his stepfather was exiled, and 8 at his mother's death. He first enters the historical record as the only knight amidst a list of barons credited with a prominent role in the important Christian victory at Montgisard in 1177.

At roughly the same time, Balian made a scandalously brilliant match, marrying the dowager queen of Jerusalem, Maria Comnena. With this marriage, he became a relative of the Byzantine emperor and a stepfather of the king's half-sister Isabella. Possibly as part of the marriage arrangement, Balian was accorded the title of Lord of Ibelin. One presumes his older brother was persuaded to turn this, the smaller

The Ibelins

of his two lordships, over to his younger brother to make him a more suitable match for a dowager queen.

It is important to remember that, as a widow who was not an heiress, the dowager queen could not be forced into a new marriage. She was financially independent with one of the largest feudal armies in the kingdom; she did not need to remarry. Maria Comnena's marriage to Balian d'Ibelin can only have been voluntary.

The dowager queen brought the wealthy and strategically important royal domain of Nablus to her second marriage as a dower portion. As Maria's consort, Balian assumed command of the barony's feudal leveis, including eighty-five knights. Combined with Ibelin's ten knights, this made Balian one of the most powerful feudal lords – with more than twice the troops of his elder brother Baldwin of Ramla. He was frequently referred to as Balian of Nablus in the records of the time, although the title of Ibelin is more common now.

In accordance with his new status, Ibelin took part in every major military campaign of the next decade and was also a member of the High Court of Jerusalem. In 1183, when Baldwin IV decided to crown his nephew during his own lifetime to reduce the risk of a succession crisis, Ibelin was selected – ahead of all the more senior barons in the kingdom – to carry the young king on his shoulders to the Church of the Holy Sepulchre. He also raised Princess Isabella until 1180, when she was forcibly taken from her mother and forced to live with her betrothed, Humphrey de Toron, at the border fortress of Kerak.

When Baldwin V died in the summer of 1186, Ibelin took a leading role in opposing Sibylla's usurpation of the throne and her devious tactics to crown her unpopular second husband, Guy de Lusignan. When efforts to crown Isabella as a rival to Sibylla failed due to Toron's defection, the majority of the barons, including Balian, did homage to Guy and Sibylla. After his brother Baldwin's departure, Balian took control of Ramla's forty knights. These, combined with the 10 Ibelin knights and the 85 Nablus knights (plus unknown numbers of household knights), made Balian the leader of one of the largest contingents of feudal leveis owed to the crown. He used this power to try to reconcile the usurper, Guy de Lusignan, with the only baron more powerful than himself: Raymond, Count of Tripoli. Like his brother, Raymond refused to do homage to Guy, despite the clear and present danger posed by Saladin.

Ibelin was ultimately successful in his reconciliation efforts. Shortly thereafter, he and Tripoli demonstrated their loyalty to the crown by answering the royal summons to muster under the leadership of Guy de Lusignan to stop Saladin's invasion of July 1187. Against the advice of Tripoli, Balian d'Ibelin and others, Guy chose to abandon the Springs of Sephoria and march the Christian army across an arid plateau to the relief of the beleaguered city of Tiberius.

Tripoli commanded the van of this army, King Guy the centre, and Ibelin the rearguard. The latter was savagely attacked throughout the advance on July 3, decimating the ranks of the Templars fighting with Ibelin. As commander of the rearguard, Ibelin was not with the count of Tripoli when the latter broke through the encirclement. However, Arab sources note that towards the end of the battle, the Franks led several charges, one of which endangered Saladin himself. Possibly, one of these broke through the surrounding Saracen army enough to enable Ibelin and some of his knights to escape. All that is certain is that Ibelin was one of only three barons to fight his way off the field at Hattin. Based on the number of survivors, it appears that roughly 3,000 men escaped with him to Tyre.

Ibelin's wife and four children, all under the age of 10, however, were trapped in Jerusalem with some 60,000 other refugees. As Saladin's armies overran the rest of the kingdom and a siege of Jerusalem became inevitable, Balian did a remarkable thing: he approached Saladin and requested safe conduct to ride to Jerusalem and remove his wife and children.

Saladin agreed – on the condition that he ride to Jerusalem unarmed and stay only one night. Ibelin agreed to these conditions but had not reckoned with the reaction of the residents and refugees in Jerusalem. The citizens and patriarch of Jerusalem begged Ibelin to take command of the defence. The patriarch demonstratively absolved him of his oath to Saladin. Ibelin felt he had no choice. He sent word to Saladin of his predicament, and Saladin graciously sent fifty of his personal Mamluks to escort Balian's family to Christian-held territory, while Ibelin remained to defend Jerusalem against overwhelming odds.

And defend Jerusalem he did. After conducting foraging sorties to collect supplies for the population from the surrounding Saracen-held territory, he successfully held off assaults from Saladin's army from September 21-25. Saladin was forced to redeploy his army against a different sector of the wall. On September 29, Saladin's sappers successfully brought down a segment of the northern wall roughly 30 metres long. Jerusalem was no longer defensible.

With Saracen forces pouring over the breach and into the city, their banners flying from one of the nearest towers, Ibelin went to Saladin to negotiate. According to Arab sources, Saladin scoffed: one does not negotiate the surrender of a city that has already fallen. But as he dismissively pointed to his banners on the walls of the city, those banners were thrown down and replaced with those of Jerusalem. Ibelin played his trump card. If the sultan would not give him terms, he and his men would kill the Muslim prisoners along with the inhabitants, desecrate and destroy the temples of all religions in the city – including the Dome of the Rock and the Al Aqsa Mosque – and then sally forth to die a martyr's death, taking as many Saracens as possible with them. Saladin relented.

The Christians were given forty days to raise ransoms of 10 dinars per man, 5 per woman and 2 per child. Although an estimated 15,000 Christians were still marched off to slavery at the end of the forty days, between 45,000 and 60,000 Christians survived as free men and women thanks to Ibelin's skill as a negotiator. Notably, Ibelin offered to stand surety for the ransoms owed by the destitute, while efforts were made to raise their ransoms in the West. Saladin rejected his offer but 'gave' Balian 500 slaves as a personal gift; that is, he freed 500 Christians that would otherwise have gone into slavery.

Ibelin escorted a column consisting of roughly one-third of the refugees from Jerusalem to Tyre, the closest city still in Christian hands. The man commanding Tyre at the time, Conrad de Montferrat, however, could not admit 15,000 additional people to a city about to come under siege. They would have risked starvation if relief did not come from the west. So, while the bulk of the non-combatants continued to Tripoli, Ibelin and other fighting men remained in Tyre to continue the fight against Saladin.

In 1188, when Guy de Lusignan laid siege to the city of Acre, Ibelin – despite his profound disagreements with Guy – joined him there; his determination to regain territory was more important to him than his disagreements with Lusignan. However, when Queen Sibylla of Jerusalem and both her daughters by Guy de Lusignan died in 1190, the situation changed. Guy's claim to the throne was through his wife. With her death, Ibelin's stepdaughter, Isabella, became the legitimate queen. Recognising that the kingdom at this time needed a fighting man as its king, Ibelin and his wife played the deciding role in convincing Isabella to set aside her husband Humphrey de Toron. The grounds for annulment of the marriage were that she had been forced into the marriage against her will before reaching the legal age of consent. Having divorced Toron, Isabella immediately married Conrad de Montferrat.[9]

Thereafter, Ibelin staunchly supported Conrad de Montferrat as king of Jerusalem. This initially put him in direct conflict with Richard I of England, who backed Guy de Lusignan, the latter being the brother of one of his vassals. As a result, during the first year of Richard's presence in the Holy Land, Ibelin remained persona non grata in Richard's court. In fact, he served as an envoy for Conrad de Montferrat to the sultan's court – something Richard's entourage and chroniclers viewed as treason to the Christian cause.

Richard the Lionheart, however, was neither a fool nor a bigot. He recognised that after he went home (as he must), only the barons and knights of Outremer could defend the territories he had recovered during the Third Crusade. He also reluctantly realised that Guy de Lusignan would never be accepted as king by the barons and knights of the kingdom he had led to such a disastrous defeat at Hattin. So, in April 1192, Richard withdrew his support for Lusignan and recognised Isabella and her husband as the rightful rulers of Jerusalem.

Thereafter, Richard employed Ibelin as a negotiator with Saladin, and in August, Ibelin negotiated the truce that ended hostilities and allowed free access to Jerusalem for unarmed Christian pilgrims. Like the surrender of Jerusalem five years earlier, this was not a triumph, but it was far better than what might have been expected under the circumstances. Notably, Ibelin's truce left Ibelin and Ramla in Muslim hands, something he must have negotiated with a heavy heart, despite being compensated later with the barony of Caymont near Acre.[10]

Richard the Lionheart returned to Europe, and Isabella was crowned queen. Ibelin became the foremost nobleman in his stepdaughter's kingdom, but he disappears from the historical record in 1194. It is usually presumed that he died about this time, but it should be noted that there are other reasons for noblemen to cease signing charters. Both of Ibelin's sons disappear from the charters of King John de Brienne, not because they were dead, but because they were active in Cyprus. Balian and his Byzantine wife may also have taken an active role in establishing Frankish rule in Cyprus,[11] or, like his brother Hugh, he might have gone on a pilgrimage to the West or been engaged in diplomatic activities anywhere from Constantinople to Cairo.

From relative obscurity as the youngest and landless son of a rear-vassal, Balian d'Ibelin rose to premier lord of the realm. Yet Balian's most pivotal role was that of a peacemaker – between Tripoli and Lusignan, between Richard the Lionheart and Montferrat and between Richard and Saladin. He was also instrumental in setting aside the ineffectual Humphrey de Toron, paving the way for the re-establishment of a viable monarchy around which the barons could unite. Yet, his moment of greatest glory was when he offered himself as a hostage for 15,000 destitute refugees who could not pay their ransom. Saladin rejected his gesture, but that does not diminish the spirit of compassion and charity that inspired it.

The Daughters of the Second Generation

Barisan is known to have had two daughters by his wife Helvis, Ermengard and Stephanie. Ermengard married William of Bures, Prince of Galilee – an astonishingly good match for the daughter of a parvenu, and Stephanie either died young, became a nun or married outside the nobility, possibly to a native Christian as no marriage is recorded. Two other girls are known to have been 'half-sisters' of Baldwin and Balian. These are Helvis, who married Anseau de Brie, and Isabella, who married Hugh of Mimars. It is usually presumed they were the children of Helvis of Ramla during her two-year marriage with Manassas de Hierges, but they might just as easily have been the daughters of Barisan by his first marriage with Hugh's mother.

The Third Generation 1190–1240

It was in the third generation that the House of Ibelin reached its pinnacle. This was the generation in which the Ibelins assumed quasi-royal status, founding the royal dynasty of Cyprus and exercising executive authority as regents in both Jerusalem and Cyprus.

Eschiva

The eldest Ibelin of this generation was Eschiva, the daughter of Baldwin by his first wife, Richildis. She married Aimery de Lusignan when still a child and when Aimery was nothing but the younger son of a French nobleman. Although Aimery advanced to the position of constable of the kingdom on his merit, it was the spectacular marriage of his younger brother Guy to Princess Sibylla that catapulted Aimery into the highest ranks of society. Aimery supported his younger brother's coup d'etat in 1186, while Eschiva's father opposed Guy to the point of quitting the country. We do not know whether Eschiva sided with her father or husband or simply felt torn apart.

Aimery fought with his brother at Hattin and was taken captive alongside him. Released with Guy in 1188, he took an active part in the siege of Acre and the Third Crusade. He was forced out of the Kingdom of Jerusalem by Henri de Champagne, who accused him (probably unjustly) of favouring a restoration of his brother Guy. As a result, Aimery joined Guy on Cyprus and succeeded him at his death in 1194. Eschiva, meanwhile, had six children by Aimery, three of whom lived to adulthood.

In 1196, Eschiva retired to a coastal estate to regain her health from an illness about which we know nothing. While there, she was kidnapped by pirates along with her young children. The king of Armenia secured her release because, the records tell us, he held her family – the Ibelins – in high regard. Aimery sailed to Armenia to bring her home, but she lived just long enough afterwards to learn that the Holy Roman emperor had recognised her husband as king of Cyprus. Eschiva died shortly before Aimery's formal coronation in the fall of 1197. We do not know how old she was or the cause of her death.

Eschiva was married to a landless adventurer as a child and ended up married to a king without changing husbands. She lived in the very vortex of Frankish politics in the last two decades of the twelfth century, but we have no evidence that she played a political role. Yet historians puzzle over how the Ibelins, inveterate opponents of Guy de Lusignan, could so quickly become entrenched in his brother's kingdom. The answer is at hand: Eschiva was the key. It was this daughter of the House of Ibelin who enabled and encouraged her kin to become the most powerful supporters of the Lusignan dynasty in Cyprus for the next 100 years.

John, Lord of Beirut 1179–1236

The most famous third-generation Ibelin was Balian's eldest son, John (1179–1236). He is the hero of a history written by the thirteenth-century historian, philosopher and jurist, Philip de Novare. While modern historians object to the positive 'spin' Novare placed on the motives and actions of John and his sons, none can deny that the lord of Beirut was a towering figure of the early thirteenth century, a man widely admired for his learning, wisdom and restraint.

John was the eldest son of Balian d'Ibelin and Maria Comnena, the second of their four children. He was 8 years old when the Battle of Hattin destroyed his world and robbed him of his inheritance. He was in Jerusalem on the eve of the siege where he witnessed the flood of refugees, the fear and despair of the Christians, and was escorted to safety by the sultan's Mamluks. He left behind his father to what he must have believed was certain martyrdom.

Just eleven years later, in 1198, John d'Ibelin was named constable of Jerusalem by King Aimery de Lusignan. Sometime between 1198 and 1205, he traded the position of constable for the lordship of Beirut. The important and prosperous port city of Beirut was retaken for Christendom by German crusaders in 1198 but was so severely destroyed in the process (either by the retreating Saracens, the advancing Germans or both) that it was allegedly an uninhabitable ruin. Despite that, it was an immensely valuable prize because of its harbour, the surrounding fertile coastal territory and its proximity to Antioch and Damascus. It was clearly a mark of great favour and trust that the crown granted John d'Ibelin the lordship of Beirut. John resettled the city, rebuilt its fortifications and constructed a palace that won the admiration of visitors for its elegance and luxury. It was as lord of Beirut that John d'Ibelin has gone down in history.

In 1205 at the age of 26, following his half-sister Isabella's death, John was elected regent of Jerusalem, reigning for Marie de Montferrat, his niece, Isabella's eldest daughter. As regent, he arranged a marriage between another of his nieces, Alice of Champagne (Isabella's daughter by her third husband, Henri de Champagne), with Hugh de Lusignan, the heir to the Cypriot throne. He was also instrumental in arranging the marriage of Marie de Montferrat to John de Brienne.

In 1198 or 1199, Beirut married Helvis of Nephin, about whom nothing is known beyond that she gave birth to five sons, all of whom died as infants. Helvis died before 1207, when John married the widowed heiress of Arsur, Melisende. Beirut had another five sons and a single daughter by Melisende, all of whom survived to adulthood.

In 1210, Marie de Montferrat came of age, married John de Brienne, and the couple was crowned queen and king of Jerusalem, ending Beirut's regency. Almost immediately, he disappeared from the kingdom's witness lists, suggesting less than cordial relations with the new king.

After Marie de Montferrat died in childbirth in 1212, leaving an infant daughter heiress to Jerusalem, Brienne continued to call himself king. But Beirut, who was already deemed a constitutional scholar, viewed Brienne as no more than regent for his infant daughter, based on earlier precedents. The breach between Beirut and Brienne led to Beirut and his younger brother Philip shifting their focus to Cyprus. By 1217, Beirut and his younger brother Philip headed the witness lists on all existing charters of King Hugh I of Cyprus, an indication that they held substantial properties there. During the Fifth Crusade, both Ibelins were listed as vassals of the king of Cyprus rather than the king of Jerusalem, even though John retained the lordship of Beirut, one of the most important baronies of Jerusalem. In 1227, Beirut was named regent for the orphaned heir to the Cypriot crown, Henry I.

Only one year later, the Holy Roman emperor, Frederick II Hohenstaufen, arrived at the head of the Fifth Crusade. As described earlier, Beirut and the emperor clashed immediately, with Beirut defending the pre-eminent role of the High Court against the emperor's attempt to impose absolute monarchy. Beirut won two decisive battles against the emperor's forces at Nicosia in 1229 and more decisively at Agridi in 1232, yet his most significant victories were legal. Beirut successfully foiled all attempts by the emperor to impose his will on the Kingdom of Jerusalem by using complex legal arguments to circumvent submission and prevent full recognition of the emperor's appointed deputies. Ultimately, the Hohenstaufen suffered a complete defeat, losing his suzerainty over Cyprus altogether, while neither he nor his heirs were ever able to exercise authority throughout the Kingdom of Jerusalem.

Beirut died from injuries obtained fighting against the Saracens on the eastern border of the Kingdom of Jerusalem in 1236. Despite fifteen years of civil war, he remained an extremely wealthy lord, in full possession of all the fiefs the emperor had unsuccessfully attempted to disseize. After bestowing his various estates upon his heirs, he joined the Knights Templar and died a monk. Thus, although he spent most of his life fighting the tyranny of a fellow Christian, he ended his life as a devout crusader by taking vows – however nominal – to defend the Holy Land for Christendom.

Historians have accused John of defending only the parochial interests of his family and his class. Indeed, his stance undermined central authority in the Kingdom of Jerusalem and ultimately weakened it. Against this argument stands the fact that his rebellion strengthened the position of the king of Cyprus. Critically, Beirut's contemporaries did not see him as self-serving, or they would not have been so loyal to him. He retained the support of most of his peers – even when the chips were down – and won the enthusiastic and tenacious support of the influential portion of the commons. Organised as the Commune of Acre, these were some of his most loyal adherents. His crowning military victory, Agridi, was a battle famed for the role of the infantry, i.e. the support of the native troops. Despite his vastly superior resources and power, the Holy Roman emperor never succeeded in seducing enough of Beirut's peers into his camp for Beirut to be thrown to the wolves. Every attempt to make peace without the lord of Beirut failed, not because of Beirut's intransigence, but because his peers did not desert him.

In short, whether we can relate to it hundreds of years later, Beirut must have been a man with great charisma and charm. He also repeatedly restrained his hot-headed supporters from provocative actions, including an assassination attempt on the emperor. Initially, at least, Beirut gave his enemies the benefit of the doubt. He surrendered hostages, served in Frederick's army, rescued him from the mob and granted amnesty to his defeated enemies in 1230. He emerges from the chronicles as a man of wisdom, restraint and dignity, who was only reluctantly pushed into rebellion. Once convinced he was fighting for justice, however, like a medieval Brutus or a secular Martin Luther he became utterly intransigent.

Philip, Regent of Cyprus 1181(?)–1227

Philip is often lumped together with his brother John, Lord of Beirut, yet this should not mislead us into thinking the brothers were similar. Novare gives us a glimpse of Philip as an individual in his own right – and a tantalizing hint of a man of passion and loyalty.

In 1224, at the days-long tournament to mark the knighting of John of Beirut's two eldest sons, a knight of Philip d'Ibelin's household 'smote' down a certain Cypriot lord, Amaury Barlais. The next day, Barlais and his men waylaid the knight and came near to killing him. At this point, according to Novare, 'Sir Philip, the baillie, was much angered and wished to attack [Sir Amaury] ... My lord of Beirut, his brother, intervened between them and held them apart by force.'[12] In short, Philip was a man who could become enraged to violence out of love and loyalty to a man in his service.

Novare goes on to tell us that Beirut was so set on reconciling his brother with Barlais that he threatened never to speak to him again unless he pardoned Barlais – and Philip relented.[13] In short, Philip loved his brother enough that the threat of a breach made him cave in on a matter that greatly impassioned him. These are the only incidents that put flesh on the skeleton left by history.

Philip was the fourth and youngest child of Balian d'Ibelin and Maria Comnena. His earliest possible date of birth was 1181, although he might have been born a year or two later. Like his siblings, he was trapped in Jerusalem after the disaster at Hattin and would have witnessed his father's dramatic return and benefitted from Saladin's generosity. His subsequent years of childhood were spent in reduced economic circumstances and great uncertainty until stability returned after the Third Crusade. Philip possibly obtained his schooling as page and squire at his sister's court under her last two husbands, Henri de Champagne and Aimery de Lusignan. By the time his brother became regent in 1205, Philip would have been a knight and presumably held land from his brother.

At some point, however, Philip moved to Cyprus. Here he became a friend and confidant of the young King Hugh, Philip's nephew through his cousin Eschiva d'Ibelin, the king's mother. When Hugh of Cyprus came of age in 1210, he accused his regent, Walter de Montbéliard, of embezzlement and drove him out of Cyprus, turning to his Ibelin kin for support.

Eight years later, during the opening phase of the Fifth Crusade, King Hugh quarreled with King John of Jerusalem and left the Kingdom of Jerusalem with the king of Hungary. In Antioch, he died abruptly, possibly in an accident or from an illness like dysentery. Hugh was just 23 years old and left behind two little girls and an 8-month-old son, Henry. Cyprus needed a regent.

According to one of the chronicles of the period, King Hugh, on his deathbed, recommended Philip d'Ibelin to the High Court. Other accounts claim that Hugh's widow Alice of Champagne urged the High Court of Cyprus to select Philip d'Ibelin. A third version refers only to the knights, nobles and people of Cyprus selecting Philip. None of the accounts mentions rivals or opposition to his appointment, which suggests he had gained the trust of the barons of Cyprus and enjoyed widespread support.

However, in 1223 or 1224, Alice fell out with Philip, apparently because she wanted a larger share of the royal revenue for her personal use. When the High Court blocked her attempt to dismiss Philip, she married the prince of Antioch, expecting that he would champion her cause. Because she failed first to obtain the permission of her knights and nobles, the marriage only enraged them further. Rightly or wrongly, they alleged that if the prince of Antioch set foot on Cyprus, King Henry's life would be at risk. Alice's position was further weakened by the pope, who annulled her marriage on the grounds of consanguinity. Alice then appointed the disaffected Sir Amaury Barlais as her baillie. When Barlais appeared before the High Court of Cyprus to present his credentials, rather than being accepted, he was accused of treason (because he had sworn an oath to Philip) and challenged to judicial combat.

Amidst this power struggle, Philip had the young 8-year-old king crowned Henry I. Although the move was probably intended to bind the knights and nobles of Cyprus to Henry by oath to outflank any new husband Alice might select, it aroused the outrage of the Holy Roman emperor, who was technically Cyprus' overlord. When the Holy Roman emperor eventually came east, he was predisposed against Philip and echoed Alice's charges of malfeasance. By then, however, Philip was already dead. Despite being bedridden the last year of his life, the High Court of Cyprus refused his request to be relieved of the burden of government, and he died as regent in 1227.

Historians are quick to point out that Philip clung to power even though the dowager queen no longer wanted him and highlight the allegations of impropriety leveled by the Holy Roman emperor, casting Philip in a dubious light. Yet, the Holy Roman emperor never allowed his charges to go before a court of law, most likely because he knew his charges were entirely fabricated or at best dubious. It is also significant that a large majority of the High Court consistently sided with Philip. Finally, King Henry remained unfailingly loyal to his Ibelin kin, in sharp contrast to his father's treatment of Montbéliard. This latter fact may be a poignant hint of Henry's love for the man who took the place of his father.

The Daughters of Balian

John and Philip had two sisters, Helvis and Margaret, who strengthened the kinship group of the House of Ibelin through their marriages to leading noblemen in the Kingdoms of Jerusalem and France. Both women married twice.

When still a young girl, Helvis married Reginald, Lord of Sidon. Sidon had fought his way off the field at Hattin and evaded capture. He defended his castle of Belfort against Saladin, allegedly pretending an interest in converting to Islam to buy time to build up his defences. He was seized when he came to negotiate and either tortured in sight of the castle (until he ordered the garrison to surrender) or held in captivity in Damascus until the castle surrendered to secure his release. Out of remorse, the chronicles tell us, Saladin restored Sidon to him as an 'iqta' held from the sultan of Damascus rather than a fief of the crown of Jerusalem. This may be the reason Balian d'Ibelin married his still young daughter to the grizzled baron of Sidon: Sidon was the only baron of Jerusalem that still had at least a promise of land from the victor. If so, it was a miscalculation. Sidon did not regain actual control of his fief until it was recaptured from the Saracens by the German crusade of 1197 and reintegrated into the Kingdom of Jerusalem.

In 1202, five years after regaining his barony, Reginal de Sidon died. He was probably close to or more than 70 years of age, and Helvis would have been just 24. She was also the mother of a young son named after her father, Balian. Helvis assumed control of the barony and served as her son's guardian until he came of age in 1213. Balian de Sidon played a prominent role in the conflict between the barons of Jerusalem and the Holy Roman emperor, serving as regent of the kingdom (often jointly with others) for many years during the Hohenstaufen's absence. He also attempted to mediate between the factions.

Helvis married a second time. Since Helvis was not an heiress, she was not required to remarry, and we can assume this second marriage was of her choosing. Her choice was a newcomer to Outremer, a man who had followed the call to the Fourth Crusade but refused to be misused as a Venetian mercenary. Rather than joining in the sack of Zara and then Constantinople, he proceeded in the company of his brother and others of their affinity to the Holy Land, arriving about the time of Reginald de Sidon's death. He was Guy de Montfort, brother of Simon de Montfort the Elder and uncle of the British parliamentary reformer.

Guy was born in 1160, which made him a good eighteen years older than Helvis and already in his early forties when he arrived in the Holy Land. He was widowed and had an adult son and two adult daughters in France. However, he was willing to stay in the Holy Land and was granted the vacant Syrian barony of Toron, presumably by Queen Isabella, before her death in 1205. Since Helvis was Isabella's half-sister, granting an 'appropriate' title to Helvis' new husband would have been in accordance with feudal practice of the time.

Helvis had one son by her new husband, named for her brother Philip, and two daughters, Maria and Petronilla. Helvis died in or shortly after 1210. As she would have been no more than 33 at the time, the probability that she died in childbirth is high. After her death, her husband Guy returned to France to join his brother Simon's crusade against the Albigensians. His young family was taken under the wing of his brother's wife, the vigorous and pious Alice de Montmorency until she died in 1221. During these childhood years, Philip forged close ties with his cousin Simon. Later, Philip returned to the Holy Land, took up the title of Lord of Toron and vigorously supported the Ibelin rebellion against Frederick II.

Balian and Maria's second daughter Margaret married Hugh of Tiberias in her teens. Hugh was the son and heir of the prince of Galilee and a stepson of Raymond de Tripoli. Since Galilee had been lost in the aftermath of Hattin, his title was nominal, but as a staunch supporter of Henri de Champagne, he probably enjoyed royal patronage. When Henri de Champagne died in the autumn of 1198, Hugh proposed his younger brother Ralph as consort for the widowed Queen Isabella of Jerusalem, but the High Court preferred Aimery de Lusignan, King of Cyprus.

When in 1198 Aimery de Lusignan barely escaped an assassination attempt, his suspicions fell on the Tiberias brothers. He seized their properties and ordered them out of the kingdom. Significantly, the barons of Jerusalem, including Margaret's brother John, rallied to the Tiberias brothers. John, then still constable of the kingdom, argued that the king did not have the right to disseize a vassal without the judgement of the High Court. Nevertheless, the Tiberias brothers did not feel safe in Lusignan's kingdom and chose voluntary exile instead.

Margaret and Hugh first went to Tripoli but continued to Constantinople after the establishment of Frankish control there. As the daughter of a Byzantine princess, Margaret may have been the driving force behind this move. Hugh's arrival in the city is the last recorded event of his life. He is believed to have died in Constantinople between 1204 and 1210. The couple had no children.

After her husband's death, Margaret returned to the Kingdom of Jerusalem in 1210 and married Walter, the heir to the lordship of Caesarea. Walter's inheritance was still held by his mother and her second husband, Aymar of Laron, so Walter and Margaret went to Cyprus, where Walter was named constable in 1210.

As constable of Cyprus, Walter led a contingent of 100 Cypriot knights to Egypt for the Fifth Crusade. He was in Egypt when Saracen forces broke through to Caesarea and laid it to waste, effectively ending his interest in regaining control of his hereditary lordship. He was present at the coronation of Yolanda (Isabella II) of Jerusalem at Tyre in 1225 and witnessed the emperor's infamous banquet in Nicosia. After that, Walter was a steadfast supporter of the Ibelins in their struggle against the Holy Roman emperor. He died fighting with the Ibelins at the Battle of Nicosia on 14 July 1229.

Margaret was left a widow with one son and four daughters, all of whom must have been less than 20 years of age. She did not remarry and probably remained in Cyprus, where she held substantial estates. In 1241, the lordship of Ibelin was recovered from the Saracens by treaty. According to Jerusalem's laws, the lordship fell to Margaret, then 60 years old, as the 'nearest' relative of the last lord, her father, Balian. It must have been deeply satisfying to her to regain Ibelin after more than a half-century. One can only hope she died before it was lost once again in 1253, but the date of her death is unrecorded.

The Fourth Generation 1225–1266

By the time Margaret died, the star of Ibelin, like that of the crusader states, was already in decline. The fourth generation of Ibelins was numerous, yet none played the historically decisive roles that their father and grandfather had. Like the Kingdom that gave them birth, a degree of decadence can be detected. The brightest stars of the fourth generation were known for their intellectual accomplishments, their chivalry, and their magnificence rather than their valour and piety. The last remnants of crusader zeal and religious duty that still echoed in the Old Lord of Beirut were obscured by dynastic and personal self-interest in his sons.

Balian, Lord of Beirut, 1207 (?)–1247
Balian, the lord of Beirut's eldest son and heir, first appears in the historical record on the (unnamed) day of his knighting. Significantly, the entire event was held in Cyprus rather than in Balian's future lordship

of Beirut, which suggests he had spent his youth on Cyprus, consistent with the medieval custom of sending adolescents to serve as squires away from home.

At the banquet in Limassol where Frederick II confronted the lord of Beirut, Balian and his younger brother Baldwin were among the twenty hostages turned over to the emperor as guarantors for Beirut's appearance before the High Court. Novare records that Balian and his brother were 'put in pillories, large and exceedingly cruel; there was a cross of iron to which they were bound so that they were able to move neither their arms nor their legs'.[14] Balian and his brother were not released until weeks later. By that time, Novare notes, they 'had endured so long an imprisonment on land and in the galleys at sea and were so miserable that it was pitiful to behold them'.[15] Despite his release, Balian was forced to remain in the emperor's household, in effect still a hostage, albeit under more respectable conditions.

As soon as the emperor sailed from Acre on 1 May 1229, Balian stood at the forefront of the struggle against him. He sailed with his father to Cyprus in June 1229 and took part in the Battle of Nicosia. After his father had been unhorsed and isolated, and his uncle of Caesarea slain, Balian rallied the knights of Ibelin and led a decisive charge that put their enemies to flight. He was active in the siege of St Hilarion; at one point, when a sally from the castle had overrun the Ibelin camp, 'Sir Balian came ... recovered the camp, and, spurring up to the gate of the wall, broke his lance on the iron of the wall gate.'[16] In another instance, when Novare himself was badly wounded before the castle, Balian 'succored him and rescued him most vigorously'.[17] Even considering Novare's bias and affection for his 'compeer', by the age of 22, Beirut's heir had a reputation as an exceptionally bold knight.

At about this time, Balian married Eschiva de Montbèliard, the daughter and heiress of Walter de Montbèliard, the former regent of Cyprus (1205–1210) by his wife, Burgundia de Lusignan. Eschiva was the widow of a knight, who had been killed in the Battle of Nicosia while fighting on the Ibelin side, Gerard de Montaigu. Furthermore, Balian and Eschiva were cousins and needed a papal dispensation to marry; for whatever reason they failed to obtain this in advance. The archbishop of Nicosia took the case to Rome, and the pope excommunicated the couple on 4 March 1232.[18] The news of this excommunication reached Outremer shortly before the Battle of Agridi in June 1232.

Meanwhile, in the fall of 1231, the lord of Beirut entrusted his heir with holding the port of Limassol against the emperor's fleet. Although Balian had only a few troops, Filangieri opted not to force a landing, sailing instead to Syria, where he captured the city of Beirut – but not the citadel. In early 1232, Balian crossed over to Syria with his father and the Cypriot army to relieve the citadel. When it became necessary to smuggle additional fighting men through a sea blockade by night to reinforce the citadel's garrison, Balian volunteered to lead the task force. Much to Balian's outrage, Beirut chose his younger brother John instead – reasoning that young John was expendable, but Balian was not.

Instead, Beirut sent Balian to Tripoli to persuade the prince of Antioch to support the Ibelin cause. Antioch preferred neutrality. Although he did not arrest or harm Balian, he prevented him from returning to his father. Balian's frustration with his enforced inactivity can be measured by the fact that he sought safe conduct from the sultan of Damascus so he might pass through Saracen territory to rejoin his father at Acre.

As fate would have it, before he could make use of his safe conduct, the imperial forces abandoned Beirut and withdrew to Tyre. Coming south from Antioch with just his personal entourage, Balian was the first Ibelin to reach Beirut after the siege was lifted. He found the citadel severely damaged but was received with great joy by the garrison. Because he remained in Beirut, he was not present at the debacle of Casal Imbert, where his brothers Baldwin, Hugh and Guy were humiliated and defeated in a surprise night attack.

When the imperial forces seized Cyprus, Balian's wife was one of the few women of the Ibelin faction who neither sought sanctuary nor suffered imprisoned at the hands of the imperial authorities. Instead, Eschiva de Montbèliard, 'dressed in the robes of a minor brother ... mounted a castle called Buffavento ... [which] she provisioned with food, of which it had none'.[19]

Balian joined King Henry and his father when they led an army back to Cyprus, yet conspicuously played no role in the capture of Famagusta, evidently because news of his excommunication had reached the lord of Beirut. On the eve of the Battle of Agridi, Novare reports that Beirut

> made [Balian] come before him and demanded that he swear to obey the command of the Holy Church, for he was under sentence of excommunication because of his marriage.

The Ibelins

[Balian] replied that he could not accede to this request. The nobleman [Beirut] ... said: 'Balian, I have more faith in God than in your knighthood, and since you do not wish to grant my request, leave the array for, and it please God, an excommunicated man shall never be a leader of our troop.'[20]

Balian disobeyed. As Novare tells us:

He escaped and went to the first rank where were his brother Sir Hugh and Sir Anceau; he gave them advice and showed them that which he knew to be of advantage, and then he left them and placed himself before them to the side. He had but few men who were with him, for at that time there were only five knights who would speak to him, all the others having sworn to respect the command of Holy Church.

When the advance guard of the first company of Langobards [Imperial troops] approached the division of my lord of Beirut and the king, Sir Balian spurred through a most evil place, over rocks and stones, and went to attack the others above the middle of the pass. So much he delayed them and did such feats of arms that no one was able to enter or leave this pass ... Many times was he pressed by so many lances that no one believed that he would ever be able to escape. Those who were below with the king saw him and knew him well by his arms and each of them cried to my lord of Beirut: 'Ah, Sir, let us aid Sir Balian, for we see that he will be killed there above.' [The Lord of Beirut] said to them: 'Leave him alone. Our Lord will aid him, and it please Him, and we shall ride straight forward with all speed, for if we should turn aside, we might lose all.'[21]

The Cypriot forces were eventually victorious and chased the imperial troops up and over the mountain to Kyrenia. Here, the survivors, including the leaders of the imperial faction, first took refuge in the citadel before later sailing to safety. A garrison of imperial loyalists held the castle for almost a year against a bitter siege in which Balian (evidently back in his father's favour) led an assault on the city. After the surrender of the castle at Kyrenia, the lord of Beirut returned to Syria, but Balian remained in Cyprus with King Henry. In March 1236, he was named constable of Cyprus, but his father died in October of the same year. At the age of 29, Balian had become lord of Beirut.

In 1239, Balian resigned the constableship of Cyprus to take part in what has become known as the 'Barons' Crusade', led by Thibaud of Champagne, King of Navarre; and Richard, Duke of Cornwall. Although Sir Balian was not involved in the ill-advised attack on Gaza, the crusade is significant because it brought Balian together with his cousin Philip de Montfort. Balian signed the letter to Emperor Fredrick in which the Ibelins agreed to accept imperial rule if the emperor would name Simon de Montfort his baillie in Jerusalem. One can only speculate on how the history of the crusader states and England might have been different if Frederick II had accepted the proposal.

In April 1242, Conrad Hohenstaufen, the son of Emperor Frederick and Yolanda of Jerusalem, announced that he had come of age (14) and was replacing Riccardo Filangieri with Tomaso of Acerra as his regent. While Filangieri was hated, Acerra had a reputation for brutally enforcing imperial policies on the Sicilian nobility. His appointment amounted to an imperial declaration of war.

It was nearly fourteen years since the emperor's men had tortured Balian because his father had stood up to false accusations, extortion and an attempt to disseize him without due process. For the last ten of those years, the imperial forces held the north of the kingdom, and the rebels occupied the south in an uneasy stalemate. Both sides claimed to have the law on their side; neither side seriously considered a compromise, yet neither side dared attack the other. The threat of a Hohenstaufen king (not just regent) and a new imperial 'baillie' alarmed Balian of Beirut.

When four citizens from Tyre offered to surrender the city to Balian, the temptation was too great. Balian consulted his closest advisors (first and foremost Philip de Montfort) and decided to seize the city. Balian does not appear to have cared much about the legality of his action; this was war. Nevertheless, a legal fig leaf was found, as described earlier.

Tyre was a nearly invincible city that had held out against Saladin twice. However, allies inside the city opened a seaward postern, enabling Balian and some of his knights to enter. Although almost overwhelmed, other sympathisers lowered the harbour chain enabling Venetian galleys to sail into Tyre harbour in time to reinforce Balian and his men. Assisted

The Ibelins

by the many residents who joined in the attack, the Ibelins and their allies captured the city of Tyre.

Lotario Filangieri and the bulk of the imperial mercenaries took refuge in the citadel. Aware that Accera was already on his way with strong imperial reinforcements, they prepared to hold out, but luck favoured the Ibelins. Riccardo Filangieri, who had sailed for Sicily before the Ibelin attack, encountered terrible storms. His ship foundered, and he returned to Tyre in a coastal vessel, unaware that the city had meanwhile fallen to his enemies. Balian of Beirut took personal custody of the imperial marshal and manifestly subjected Filangieri to the same treatment he had suffered at the emperor's hands in 1229. Furthermore, he had the imperial marshal led to a prominent point with a noose around his neck. Riccardo's brother caved in and agreed to surrender the citadel of Tyre. The Filangieris and their men were then allowed to depart with their portable treasure.

Yet while Balian kept his word to the Filangieris, he acted far less honourably towards his 'queen'. Balian flatly refused to hand Tyre over to the queen or her French consort, using a flimsy excuse. The queen's consort 'saw then that he had no power nor command and that he was but a shade. As a result of the disgust and the chagrin which he had over this, he abandoned all, left the queen his wife, and went to his own country.'[22]

It is unimaginable that John of Beirut would have acted with so little regard for the law or respect for his queen. Yet Balian had succeeded where his principled father had failed. He had reduced the last stronghold of the imperialists, expelled the last imperial 'baillie' and ensured that the latter's replacement did not dare set foot in the Kingdom of Jerusalem. Acerra landed in Tripoli and remained there, with no influence in Jerusalem whatsoever.

Four years later, Balian was named baillie of Jerusalem by King Henry I of Cyprus, who the barons of Outremer recognised as regent for the absent Conrad Hohenstaufen at the death of his mother, Queen Alice. Balian died on 4 September 1247 of unknown causes. He would have been roughly 40 years of age. He left behind at least one son, John, who succeeded to the title of Lord of Beirut.

Balian was less admirable than his father. Balian was not prepared to risk arrest and death for the sake of honor and the rule-of-law. He did not trust promises, certainly not from the emperor. Novare never describes him, as he does his father, prostrating himself face down on the earth in prayer. Rather, Balian's life was characterised by deeds of courage, military competence and leadership, and also by undeniable impetuosity and passion. He charged in, regardless of risks. Nor does he appear to have inherited his grandfather's gift for negotiation, and there is not a trace of his father's caution, calm, restraint and reason in the stories told about him. Nearly alone among his generation of peers, he was not famous as a legal scholar, historian, philosopher or troubadour.

There may be a reason. Balian insisted on custody of Filangieri because of what Filangieri had done to Beirut ten years earlier. Likewise, he insisted on the same kind of pillory for Filangieri as the emperor had made for him. This suggests that Balian was traumatised by the experience of being tortured in the emperor's custody. The 21-year-old nobleman had not expected the treatment he received, and he never fully recovered psychologically.

Balian appears to shine as a soldier, a leader of men – and as a husband. He did not give up his Eschiva; he forced first his stubborn, principled, and pious father – and then the pope himself – to recognise the marriage. He did not do it for land, he had more than enough, and there were plenty of other heiresses, including ones with royal blood he could have had. He did it for love. Once Balian gave his heart, nothing would induce him to abandon his lady.

Baldwin, Seneschal of Cyprus 1208(?)–1266

The lord of Beirut's second son Baldwin lived in the shadow of his more prominent father and brother. He was knighted with his brother Balian, shared Balian's fate as a hostage of Emperor Frederick in 1228 and took part in the Battle of Nicosia and the siege of St Hilarion (1229–30). He was also one of three Ibelins surprised by the enemy at Casal Imbert in 1232, a debacle caused by the Ibelin's poor leadership and hubris. Sir Baldwin was wounded in the engagement yet recovered sufficiently to command a division at the Battle of Agridi.

After that, he remained in Cyprus while his elder brother assumed the senior title of Lord of Beirut. For the astonishing stretch of twenty-one years, from 1246 until 1267, he served as seneschal of Cyprus, a hugely influential position and by no means a nominal title. He took part in King Louis' crusade and was taken captive at the Battle of Mansoura. Jean de Joinville reveals in his account of this crusade that Baldwin understood

Arabic well.[23] Sir Baldwin was ransomed along with Joinville, his brother Guy and his cousin Philip de Montfort. He married Alice, the sister of one of his family's bitterest enemies, Amaury de Bethsan. They had many children, one of whom, Philip, married the titular heiress of Galilee and is mentioned as constable of Cyprus in 1302.

Hugh d'Ibelin 1210 (?)–1238

Hugh died without heirs sometime in 1239 and did not attain any prominence in his short life. Nevertheless, he is recorded taking part in the siege of St Hilarion (1229-1230) along with his elder brothers Sirs Balian and Baldwin. He, too, was surprised at Casal Imbert, and his horse was killed under him. He was discovered with a lone companion defending a small house in the town. At the Battle of Agridi, Sir Hugh was given the honour denied his elder brother Balian of leading the first division. Sir Hugh was also prominent in the siege of Kyrenia in the following winter. Hugh was granted estates in Cyprus rather than in Syria at his father's death. He was roughly 28 years old and still single when he died from unknown causes in 1238.

John d'Ibelin, Lord of 'Foggia' and Arsur 1213 (?)–1258

John served in the emperor's household as a squire during the latter's sojourn in Syria from September 1228 to May 1229. Like his elder brother Balian, he was effectively a hostage for his father's good behaviour. Young John, however, appears to have ingratiated himself with the Hohenstaufen. Novare claims Frederick liked him so much he tried to induce him to return to the West, promising him the lordship of Foggia in Apulia.[24] John did not take the emperor's bait and remained in the Holy Land, although his family was said to call him John 'of Foggia' in jest.

John led the Ibelin relief force that ran the imperial sea blockade of the citadel of Beirut in an open boat. With 100 volunteers (knights, sergeants and squires), he successfully scaled the cliffs to the castle to reinforce the garrison. Thereafter, the garrison 'defended themselves more vigorously, made a countermine against the miners ... recaptured the fosse by force ... [and] made many brave sallies and gained somewhat over those without, and burned several engines'.[25] Whether all that can be attributed to the inspiration and leadership of a youth hardly older than 16 or 17 seems doubtful, but evidently he did not disgrace himself.

On the other hand, he does not rate a mention for his deeds at the subsequent Battle of Agridi or the siege of Kyrenia. At his father's death, he succeeded to his mother's lordship of Arsur with the explicit consent of his brothers. The latter suggests that Sirs Balian, Baldwin, Hugh and Guy believed they were adequately endowed with properties and power elsewhere. Notably, except for Sir Balian, all three of John's other brothers held estates exclusively in Cyprus, a reminder of just how plentiful (and wealthy) the Cypriot estates were – despite being mostly invisible in history because they did not bestow the titles used by the chroniclers.

In 1240, John took part in the Barons' Crusade, getting involved in the rout near Gaza, but escaping capture with his cousins Balian de Sidon and Philip de Montfort. In 1241, he commenced fortification of his castle at Arsur, and two years later, was involved in the capture of Tyre.

In 1246, he was named constable of Jerusalem and baillie at Acre. He stepped down on the arrival of King Louis of France, possibly to take part in the Seventh Crusade, but was persuaded to take up the position again roughly a year later. Significantly, he initially succeeded in convincing the warring Pisans and Genoese to conclude a truce but was less successful in the next intra-Italian war. Nevertheless, John retained the respect of his peers and died in 1258, serving once again as Baillie.

John married Alice of Caiphas and had several children, including his son and heir Balian.

Guy, Constable of Cyprus 1216 (?)–1255 (?)

Guy was one of the Ibelins caught (almost literally) with their pants down during a night attack on Casal Imbert in early 1232. Given his age of roughly 16, however, Guy's role in the debacle could hardly have been great. He was possibly still a squire, and even if newly knighted, was not in command. Furthermore, Guy is not recorded at the subsequent battle of Agridi or the siege of Kyrenia, suggesting that he was very young and, perhaps after the fiasco at Casal Imbert, his father felt he needed more training rather than more responsibility.

At his father's death in 1236, like his elder brothers Baldwin and Hugh, he was given properties in Cyprus rather than in Syria. He did not participate in the Barons' Crusade, remaining in Cyprus instead. By 1247, he was constable there, which explains why he commanded a force of 120 knights in the Seventh Crusade. In 1250, he was taken captive with St Louis. One of his fellow prisoners, Jean de Joinville, called him 'one of the most accomplished knights I have ever known' – and more significantly – 'and one who most loved the islanders in his care'.[26]

Joinville also tells of another incident. After the Mamluks had murdered the Ayyubid sultan and cut his heart from his still warm body, the Christian prisoners expected to be slaughtered. Baldwin d'Ibelin translated what the Mamluks were saying among themselves and confirmed they were discussing whether to decapitate the captive crusaders. There was only one priest aboard Joinville's galley, and he was overwhelmed by men seeking to confess. So, Joinville tells us, 'Guy d'Ibelin knelt down beside me, and confessed himself to me. "I absolve you", I said, "with such power as God has given me". However, when I rose to my feet, I could not remember a word of what he told me.'[27]

In the event, the Mamluks found the potential ransoms too tempting to throw away and entered negotiations instead. Guy d'Ibelin was one of the noblemen who witnessed the discussions. King Louis and the Mamluks came to terms, and after many delays and some chicanery, were eventually set free. Guy returned to Cyprus.

Long before this crusade, Guy had married Philippa Barlais, the daughter of the Ibelin's arch-enemy during the civil war. Edbury notes that Barlais' estates were forfeited to the crown for his treason against King Henry in 1232. With this marriage, the Ibelins probably obtained those lands while restoring them to Barlais' daughter, who could not be held responsible for her father's treason. The couple had ten children, and one of their daughters, Isabella, married Hugh de Lusignan, who reigned in Cyprus as Hugh III.

John, Count of Jaffa and Ascalon 1215–1266

Without doubt, the most famous of the fourth generation of Ibelins – and arguably the best-known Ibelin today – was John of Jaffa, the son of Philip. His fame derives not from deeds of arms and high politics, but rather from a book commonly known as the 'Assises of Jerusalem', described as one of the great works of thirteenth-century thought.[28] This was his final legacy, written at the end of an eventful life.

John was born in Cyprus two years before his father became regent, and the first fourteen years of his life were probably ones of wealth and privilege. All that abruptly ended when, in February 1229, Emperor Frederick II sent the Sicilian count of Cotron to lay waste to the Ibelin's lands. In fear for their lives, John's mother, Alice de Montbéliard, fled with her children in a small boat, encountering such storms, they all nearly drowned. Having barely escaped death at sea, John arrived in Syria to find the emperor had already given orders to disseize him of his estates. He had not yet come of age, much less taken any action against the emperor; his crime was simply being an Ibelin.

Unsurprisingly, he became a staunch supporter of his uncle, the lord of Beirut. In 1232, aged seventeen, he was present at the fiasco at Casal Imbert and was wounded in the engagement. The experience did not dull John's ardour for the Ibelin cause; shortly afterwards, he sold properties in Acre to help finance the expedition to Cyprus. He took part in the campaign that ended with the Ibelin victory at Agridi and was tasked by his uncle of Beirut with rounding up the imperial troops still at large.

Throughout the next decade, he was in regular attendance at the High Court of Cyprus, where he was one of the most powerful lords. In 1237, King Henry of Cyprus married the sister of the Armenian King Hethoum, and John married a second sister of Hethoum sometime before 1242. This made John the brother-in-law of both the king of Armenia and the king of Cyprus. For the rest of his life, John moved in exalted circles and was viewed in East and West as a nobleman of the first rank.

Meanwhile, he evolved into a legal scholar. He was probably the author of the proposal, signed by his cousin Balian, naming Simon de Montfort imperial baillie of the Kingdom of Jerusalem. He was active in devising legal justifications for his cousin's attack on Tyre. His account of the incident is a case study in creative legality. He even found 'legal' explanations for his cousin's cynical refusal to surrender Tyre to the regent the Ibelins had created, something Peter Edbury rightly calls 'transparent hypocrisy'. Notably, he played no role in military actions.

When Alice of Champagne died in 1246, John d'Ibelin's sophisticated legal reasoning provided the figleaf for King Henry of Cyprus to become the regent of the still absent Conrad of Hohenstaufen. King Henry, however, could not be treated as a mere figurehead. He had been the reigning monarch of Cyprus for fourteen years. He was 29 years old and brother-in-law of the Armenian king. Henry of Cyprus could not be ignored or dismissed the way Ralph of Soissons had been.

However, King Henry showed no real interest in Jerusalem; he was content to name deputies to rule for him on the mainland. The first of

The Ibelins

these was Balian of Beirut. At about the same time, Henry granted Tyre to Philip de Montfort, made Balian's younger brother John of Arsur the constable of Jerusalem, and enfeoffed his brother-in-law John with the County of Jaffa and Ascalon as well as the traditional Ibelin lordship of Ramla and Mirabel, both of which had been restored to the Kingdom of Jerusalem through treaties concluded with the Ayyubids at the close of the Barons' Crusade.

Henceforth, John took great pride in his title of 'count'. In keeping with the spirit of the times, John engaged in lavish displays of pageantry designed to enhance his honour. King Louis IX's seneschal Jean de Joinville writes of the landing of King Louis' army on the shore before Damietta, noting:

> To left of us, the Comte de Jaffa ... was about to land; he made the finest show of any as he came towards the shore. His galley was covered, both under and above the water, with painted escutcheons bearing his arms, which are or with a cross 'gules patee'. He had at least three hundred rowers in his galley; beside each rower was a small shield with the count's arms upon it, and to each shield was attached a pennon with the same arms worked in gold.
>
> As the galley approached, it seemed as if it flew, so quickly did the rowers urge it onwards with the powerful sweep of their oars; and what with the flapping of the pennons, the booming of the drums, and the screech of Saracen horns onboard the vessel, you would have thought a thunderbolt was falling from the skies. As soon as this galley had been driven into the sand as far as it would go, the count and his knights leapt on shore, well equipped, and came to take their stand beside us.[29]

But for all his fine display, John was soon seriously in debt. The cost of restoring and maintaining the defences of his county – the southernmost in the Kingdom of Jerusalem and a frequent target of Saracen raids – was exorbitant. In the succeeding decades, as the Mongols, Khwarizmians and Mamluks increasingly threatened the Frankish kingdom, other secular lords gave large portions of their lands to the military orders, but John of Jaffa stubbornly hung on to his county.

In the decade after the departure of King Louis, the Count of Jaffa was periodically called to serve as baillie of the kingdom but does not appear to have been terribly keen to hold the position. He took this office in 1255 but surrendered it to his cousin of Arsur in 1258. The War of St Sabas had seriously damaged the fabric of the country, and the Mongols successively attacked the trade routes that fed the kingdom's economy. The count of Jaffa was forced to conclude truces with the resurgent Saracens. Notably, these were private truces for Jaffa alone, a clear indication of the disintegration of central authority noted earlier. In this period, Jaffa's wife and the mother of his six (or possibly nine) children returned to her native Armenia, taking most of her children with her. At about the same time, John was admonished by the pope for carrying on an affair with Cyprus' young dowager queen, Plaisance of Antioch. It is hard to know which of these events was the cause and which the effect.

In the difficult years of 1258–66, Jaffa wrote his opus magnum. We catch a glimpse of the author in the preface:

> I pray the Holy Trinity that I may receive the grace of the Holy Spirit so as to bring this book to such perfection that it will be to the honour of God and to the profit of my soul and the government of the people of the kingdom of Jerusalem… . I pray, entreat and demand in the name of God that they who read should not use anything here falsely so as to deprive anyone of their rights, but that they use it to defend their rights or those of others as need arises.[30]

John died in 1266. He was succeeded very briefly by his son James before Jaffa fell to the Mamluk sultan Baybars in 1268.

The two daughters of this generation, Isabella, the daughter of the lord of Beirut, and Maria, the daughter of Philip, became nuns.

Swansong of the House of Ibelin 1250–1374

From 1259 to the end of the Kingdom of Jerusalem, no Ibelin held the position of baillie or regent, but the family was neither obliterated nor powerless. Balian of Arsur (son of John of Arsur) was constable of the kingdom from 1268 to 1277, and Baldwin d'Ibelin was constable of

Jerusalem in 1286. Although Balian of Beirut's heir, John of Beirut, never played an important role in the kingdom, Jaffa's younger son, Balian of Jaffa, was a chamberlain of the kingdom 1183–85. This, however, was the last known Ibelin to hold an office in the Kingdom of Jerusalem.

In Cyprus, the family remained powerful for considerably longer, while three sons of Jaffa and two of his daughters settled in Armenia. In Cyprus, Ibelins held the post of constable from 1247–56 (Guy d'Ibelin, son of John of Beirut), 1286 (Baldwin d'Ibelin, father unknown) and 1302 (Philip d'Ibelin, and brother of the ruling queen). Jaffa's eldest son James established himself as a legal expert in Cyprus and was extremely successful in pleading cases in the courts, although the legal treatise he wrote is not regarded as highly as his father's work. Philip d'Ibelin, a son of Guy d'Ibelin, held the powerful position of seneschal for Henry II and remained loyal to him during the revolt of 1306. Other Ibelins found themselves on the other side, and the family weathered the dynastic crisis of 1306–10 well.

Meanwhile, the daughters of the house were marrying into the royal family on a nearly regular basis. Isabella d'Ibelin, the daughter of Guy d'Ibelin (the youngest son of John of Beirut), married Hugh III. Eschiva, a granddaughter of Balian of Beirut, married Guy de Lusignan and was the mother of Hugh IV, who himself married first a Marie d'Ibelin, and later, an Alice d'Ibelin.

The Ibelins remained powerful noblemen in Cyprus until the war with the Genoese, 1373–74. The Genoese beheaded the last titular lord of Arsur, a direct descendant of the first Ibelin lord of Arsur, son of John of Beirut. Another Ibelin, Nicholas, probably still a child, was sent as a hostage to Genoa and never heard from again. Although descendants of the House of Ibelin may survive in Armenia or through the female line (and wherever the name Balian surfaces, an Ibelin connection can be suspected), the last male known to bear the name of Ibelin disappeared from the historical record in 1374. And so, like the crusader states themselves, the House of Ibelin faded from prominence and memory to be remembered only occasionally by historians, novelists and filmmakers.

Conclusion

Because of the ignorant or irresponsible misuse of the term 'crusader' and 'crusades' by politicians, journalists and Islamist terrorists, long-discredited theories from the last century have been perpetuated through thoughtless references and careless comparisons. This shallow and sensationalist – not to mention intellectually lazy – commentary drowns out the voices of serious scholars. As a result, most of the public today believes that the crusades and the crusader states were characterised by bigotry, racism and brutality aimed at the oppression and destruction of the native peoples of the Near East.

Yet, the picture of the crusader states that scholars have meticulously pieced together based on contemporary chronicles, data mining and archaeology does not corroborate these popular assumptions. Instead, the historical record provides concrete evidence of Frankish tolerance, adaptability, peaceful co-existence and cooperation with the various peoples inhabiting the Middle East. For example, from the moment they arrived in Antioch, the crusaders preserved, cherished and expanded the Arab libraries they discovered. Rather than destroying mosques and synagogues, the crusaders either repurposed them or allowed them to continue to operate, preserving these architectural monuments for posterity. Furthermore, the crusaders allowed Jews, Samaritans and Muslims to build new houses of worship. They allowed these religious groups to live according to their laws and publicly celebrate their religious festivals without interference.

Likewise, from the First Crusade onwards, the Franks recognised and respected the Orthodox clergy, at times taking Orthodox priests for their confessors and consistently sponsoring the re-establishment and restoration of Orthodox churches and monasteries. As a result, Greek monasteries flourished and expanded, particularly around Jerusalem, in Antioch and Sinai during the period of Frankish rule in the Middle East.

Conclusion

The hospitals of one of the crusading orders, the Knights of St John of Jerusalem, employed doctors of any religion. In the luxurious wards, patients of all religions were treated equally as 'lords' by members of an order that viewed themselves as 'serfs' to their patients.

The courts sought to ensure that anyone accused of a crime was judged by his peers following local custom rather than an alien legal code. Civil and criminal conflicts between members of different ethnic and religious groups were adjudicated in accordance with the law of the defendant.

Absent from the popular image of crusaders and the crusader states are the more than 100 truces and the many alliances across religious borders. Invisible, too, are the native Christians who worked as scribes, customs officials, merchants and manufacturers, forming the administrative backbone of and contributing materially to the economic prosperity of the Holy Land. Erased from popular depictions of the crusader states are the Arabic and Syriac-speaking Christians who fought alongside the Franks as infantry and mounted archers – despite the fact that these native troops made up the bulk of the Frankish armies, and saved the crusader states from destruction on multiple occasions.

The popular picture of the crusader states does not include the icon workshops, mass book production, or a society that rewarded knowledge of the law as assiduously as skill with the sword. Forgotten are the Muslims who sought refuge in the Kingdom of Jerusalem during the Mongol invasion of Syria and the Jews who immigrated to the Kingdom of Jerusalem because it was an oasis of tolerance in an anti-Semitic world. The historical reality of Templars hosting the Ayyubid princes in their Acre headquarters in 1244 and Frankish noblemen translating Arab poetry into French is obscured by Hollywood depictions of Templars shouting for Muslim and Jewish blood and Frankish noblemen slaughtering unarmed Muslims.

Yet, it is not only the need to correct common misconceptions that makes the study of the crusader states rewarding. These kingdoms, sitting on the crossroads of civilisations, were established by newcomers from the West who were compelled to adapt rapidly to their new environment or face extinction. Not only did they adapt, but they evolved into a unique hybrid society that mixed European culture with Near Eastern traditions. This was not a matter of imitating – much less 'stealing' – technology, art or ideas from more sophisticated neighbours. It was a matter of developing new and innovative products, forms and concepts. In doing so, the Franks of Outremer made significant contributions to the evolution of European society, stimulating advancement across a range of fields.

The most obvious innovations came in the field of warfare. From the adoption of surcoats to the construction of concentric castles, the confrontation between the armies of the Middle East and Western Europe led to significant military advances. The Franks pioneered Western use of mounted archers, evolved the fighting box (combined arms warfare), and in the military orders, rediscovered the value of professional and disciplined regular forces. They perfected the massed charge of heavy cavalry yet also effectively exploited light cavalry in reconnaissance and hit-and-run raids. Finally, they deployed archers behind shield walls to good effect, while Frankish crossbows represented cutting-edge technology. In his study of crusader warfare, Steve Tibble concludes that 'warfare in the east was a crucible of innovation for European warfare, leading developments, not typifying or reflecting them'.[1]

The architecture of the Franks was unique and not only with respect to castles. Frankish domestic architecture combined such Western features as outward-oriented multistorey structures, high ceilings, large windows, loges and balconies with Arab and Byzantine artisanry, such as inlaid marble, glazed tiles, running fountains and intricate decoration. The result was gracious and sunlit structures that used local products such as glass windows, glazed tiles and polychrome marble. Frankish houses included fireplaces with hoods that reduced smoke accumulation (a Western feature) and sophisticated plumbing systems of cistern-fed ceramic pipes feeding into centrally-planned sewage systems (an Eastern feature).

As noted earlier, hospitals as institutions for healing the sick and injured evolved in the Holy Land in the crusader era, based on Byzantine and Arab precedents. Along with hospitals came advances in medicine and progress towards the professionalisation of medical practitioners and the protection of patients from malpractice. The Frankish states provided a meeting place for physicians from various cultures, and Antioch became a centre for the study and development of medical theory.

International banking was another field significantly advanced by the Frankish presence in the Levant. The need for cash transfers over enormous distances fostered the evolution of letters of credit, cheques, currency exchange and other financial services previously unknown, at least not on such a scale.

Last but not least, the Franks contributed to constitutional law. Nowhere else in the medieval world was interest in and discussion of the concept of good governance, the rule-of-law and the monarch's role carried to such heights of sophistication or conducted on as wide a scale as in the Kingdom of Jerusalem in the mid-thirteenth century. In no other kingdom did so many noblemen of a single era study and write about the law, let alone serve as advocates in the courts.

The Kingdom of Jerusalem was also exceptional for the number of men of lower social standing who gained prominence through legal expertise. The inclusion of the commons in governing assemblies was equally innovative and progressive, albeit limited. Yet most important was the advocacy and defence of key constitutional concepts such as the monarchs' subordination to the constitution and the right to due process. In defending these principles against the authoritarianism of Frederick II, the rebels of Outremer undoubtedly influenced the English parliamentary reformer, Simon de Montfort. They deserve credit for their steadfast opposition to tyranny.

The Frankish states of the Levant were not paradise. Even if not perpetually on the brink of collapse, they were vulnerable. They were subject to frequent small-scale attacks, periodic invasions and were ultimately destroyed by warfare. In the thirteenth century, they also suffered from absentee monarchs, political intrigue, and factional infighting. Yet, they were neither fragile constructs doomed to failure nor genocidal, apartheid regimes established by barbarians to oppress enlightened natives.

The evidence is overwhelming – preserved in stone and meticulously documented by Arab, Greek, Syrian and Jewish sources no less than in the Latin and French chronicles: the crusader states in the Levant were the home to a rare flourishing of international trade, intellectual and technological exchange, innovation, hybrid art forms and unique architecture, advances in health care and evolution of the constitutional principles of the rule-of-law. They brought forth a vivid, multicultural society in which tolerance outweighed bigotry. As such, the crusader states' contribution to the evolution of European culture deserves more attention and appreciation as we struggle to integrate diverse cultures in our own time.

Recommended Reading

Primary Sources

Anonymous. *Chronicle of the Third Crusade: A Translation of the Itinerarium Peregrinorum et Gesta Regis Ricardi. Crusade Texts in Translation.* Translated by Helen Nicholson, Ashgate Publishing Ltd., 1997
———. *The Conquest of Jerusalem and the Third Crusade: Crusade Texts in Translation.* Translated by Peter W. Edbury, Ashgate Publishing Ltd., 1998
———. *Crusader Syria in the Thirteenth Century: The Rothelin Continuation of the History of William of Tyre with part of the Eracles or Acre Text. Crusades Texts in Translation.* Translated by Janet Shirley. Ashgate Publishing Ltd., 1999
Baha al-Din ibn Shaddad. *The Rare and Excellent History of Saladin.* Translated by D.S. Richards, Ashgate Publishing Ltd. 2002
Gabrieli, Francesco. *Arab Historians of the Crusades.* University of California Press, 1969
Letters from the East: Crusaders, Pilgrims, and Settlers in the 12th and 13th Centuries: Crusade Texts in Translation. Translated by Malcolm Barber and Keith Bate. Ashgate Publishing, 2013
Novare, Philip de. *The Wars of Frederick II Against the Ibelins in Syria and Cyprus.* Translated by John La Monte, Morningside Heights Columbia University Press, 1936
Pilgrimage to Jerusalem and the Holy Land, 1187–1291. Crusades Texts in Translation. Translated by Denys Pringle. Ashgate, 2012
Tyre, William Archbishop of. *A History of Deeds Done Beyond the Sea.* Morningside Heights Columbia University Press, 1943

Secondary Sources

Allen, S.J. and Emilie Amt. *The Crusades: A Reader.* University of Toronto Press, 2014

Recommended Reading

Andrea, Alfred J. and Andrew Holt (eds). *Seven Myths of the Crusades.* Hackett Publishing Co., 2015

Abulafia, David. *Frederick II: A Medieval Emperor.* Oxford University Press, 1988

Bale, Anthony, ed. *The Cambridge Companion to the Literature of the Crusades.* Cambridge University Press, 2019

Barber, Malcolm. *The Crusader States.* Yale University Press, 2012.

———. 'The Career of Philip of Nablus in the Kingdom of Jerusalem'. In *The Experience of Crusading: Defining the Crusader Kingdom.* Peter Edbury and Jonathan Phillips (eds). Cambridge University Press, 2003

———. *The New Knighthood: A History of the Order of the Temple,* Cambridge University Press, 1994

Barber, Richard. *The Knight and Chivalry.* Boydell Press, 1970

Bartlett, W.B. *Downfall of the Crusader Kingdom.* The History Press Ltd, 2010

Brand, Charles M. *Byzantium Confronts the West.* ACLS Humanities E-Book, 2012

Boas, Andrian J. *Crusader Archaeology: The Material Culture of the Latin East.* Routledge, 1999

———. *Domestic Settings: Sources on Domestic Architecture and Day-to-Day Activities in the Crusader States.* Brill, 2010

———, ed. *The Crusader World.* Routledge, 2016

Boulle, Pierre. *Der Denkwuerdige Kreuzzug Kaiser Friedrich II. von Hohenstaufen.* Christian Wegner Verlag, *1970*

Bromiley, Geoffrey N. 'Philip of Novara's Account of the War between Frederick II of Hohenstaufen and the Ibelins'. *Journal of Medieval History* 3 (1977), 325-338

———. 'Philippe de Novare: Another Epic Historian?' *Neophilologus* 82 (1998), 527-541

Christie, Niall. *Muslims and Crusaders: Christianity's Wars in the Middle East, 1095–1382, from the Islamic Sources.* Routledge, 2014

Cleve, Thomas Curtis Van. *The Emperor Frederick II of Hohenstaufen: Immutator Mundi.* Oxford University Press, 1972

Conder, Claude Reignier. *The Latin Kingdom of Jerusalem 1099 to 1291 AD.* Committee of the Palestine Exploration Fund, 1897

Donvito, Filippo. 'Hangman or Gentleman: Saladin's Christian Hostages and Prisoners'. *Medieval Warfare IV-1* (2014), 39-43

Edbury, Peter W. *John of Ibelin and the Kingdom of Jerusalem.* The Boydell Press, 1997

———. *The Kingdom of Cyprus and the Crusades, 1191–1374*. Cambridge University Press, 1991

———. *Law and History in the Latin East*. Ashgate, 2014

———. *The Lusignan Kingdom of Cyprus and Its Muslim Neighbors*. Bank of Cyprus Foundation, 1993

——— and John Gordon Rowe. *William of Tyre: Historian of the Latin East*. Cambridge University Press, 1988

Edge, David and John Miles Paddock. *Arms and Armour of the Medieval Knight*. Saturn Books, 1996

Edington, Susan B. and Helen Nicholson (eds). *Deeds Done Beyond the Sea: Essays on William of Tyre, Cyprus and the Military Orders Presented to Peter Edbury*. Routledge, 2014

Ellenblum, Ronnie. *Frankish Rural Settlement in the Latin Kingdom of Jerusalem*. Cambridge University Press, 1998

———. *Crusader Castles and Modern Histories*. Cambridge University Press, 2007

Ehrenkreutz, Andrew S. *Saladin*. State University of New York Press, 1972

Folda, Jaroslav. *Crusader Art: The Art of the Crusaders in the Holy Land, 1099–1291*. Ashgate Publishing, 2008

France, John. *Hattin*. Oxford University Press, 2015

Friedman, Yvonne. *Encounter between Enemies: Captivity and Ransom in the Latin Kingdom of Jerusalem*. Brill, 2002

Galatariotou, Catia. *The Making of a Saint: The Life, Times and Sanctification of Neophytos the Recluse*. Cambridge University Press, 1991

Gardiner, Robert (ed). *Cogs, Caravels and Galleons: The Sailing Ship 1000–1650*. Conway Maritime Press, 1994

Gillingham, John. *Richard I*. Yale University Press, 1999

Goldman, Brendan. *Arabic-Speaking Jews in Crusader Syria: Conquest, Continuity and Adaptation in the Medieval Mediterranean*. Unpublished PhD dissertation. John Hopkins University. Baltimore, MD. 2018

Hamilton, Bernard. *The Latin Church and the Crusader States*. Routledge, 1980

———. *The Leper King and His Heirs: Baldwin IV and the Crusader Kingdom of Jerusalem*. Cambridge University Press, 2000

———. 'Women in the Crusader States: The Queens of Jerusalem 1100–90'. In *Medieval Women*. Derek Baker (ed.). Basil Blackwell, 1978

Recommended Reading

Harari, Yuval, 'The Military Role of the Frankish Turcopoles: A Reassessment'. *Mediterranean Historical Review*, 12/1 (1997), 75-116

Hazard, Harry W., ed. *A History of the Crusades, Vol. IV: The Art and Architecture of the Crusader States*. Univ. of Wisconsin Press, 1977

Herzog, Annie. *Die Frau auf den Fuerstenthronen der Kreuzfahrerstaaten*. Emil Ebering, 1919

Hill, George. *A History of Cyprus, Vol. 2: The Frankish Period*. Cambridge University Press, 1948

Holt, P.M. *The Crusader States and their Neighbours*. Pearson Education, 2004

Hopkins, Andrea. *Knights: The Complete Story of the Age of Chivalry: From Historical Fact to Tales of Romance and Poetry*. Collins and Brown Ltd, 1990

Jacoby, David, 'Byzantine Culture and the Crusader States'. In *Byzantine Culture: Papers from the Conference 'Byzantine Days of Istanbul'* May 21-23, 2010

———. 'The Kingdom of Jerusalem and the Collapse of Hohenstaufen Power in the Levant'. *Dumbarton Oaks Papers*, 40 (1986), 83-101

———, ed. *Medieval Trade in the Eastern Mediterranean and Beyond*. Routledge, 2018

———. *Studies on the Crusader States and on Venetian Expansion*. Routledge, 2018

Jordan, Erin, 'Corporate Monarchy in the Twelfth-Century Kingdom of Jerusalem'. *Royal Studies Journal*, 6/1 (2019), 1-15

Jotischky, Andrew. *Crusading and the Crusader States*. Pearson Longman, 2004

Kedar, Benjamin Z. *Franks, Muslims and Oriental Christians in the Latin Levant*. Ashgate, 2006

Kostick, Conor (ed). *The Crusades and the Near East*. Routledge, 2011

Laiou, Ageliki. 'Byzantine Trade with Christians and Muslims and the Crusades'. In *The Crusades from the Perspective of Byzantium and the Muslim World*. Angelki Laiou and Roy Parvis Mottahedeh (eds). Dumbarton Oaks Research Library and Collection, 2001, 157-196

La Monte, John L. *Feudal Monarchy in the Latin Kingdom of Jerusalem, 1100 to 1291*. Medieval Academy of America, 1932

———. 'John d'Ibelin: The Old Lord of Beirut, 1177–1236'. *Byzantion*, Vol. 1/2 (1937), 417-448

Lotan, Shlomo, 'The Battle of La Forbie (1244) and its Aftermath: Re-Examination of the Military Orders' Involvement in the Latin Kingdom of Jerusalem in the Mid-Thirteenth Century'. *Ordines Militares*, Vol. XVII (2012), 53-67

Maalouf, Amin. *The Crusades through Arab Eyes*. Schocken Books, 1984

MacEvitt, Christopher. *The Crusades and the Christian World of the East: Rough Tolerance*. University of Pennsylvania Press, 2008

Madden, Thomas. *The Concise History of the Crusades*. Rowman & Littlefield, 2014

Marshall, Christopher. *Warfare in the Latin East 1192–1291*. Cambridge University Press, 1992

Mayer, Hans Eberhard. *Kings and Lords in the Latin Kingdom of Jerusalem*. Ashgate Publishing Ltd., 1994

———. *Probleme des lateinischen Koenigreichs Jerusalem*. Variorum Reprints, 1983

Miller, Peter. *Die Kreuzzuege: Krieg im Namen Gottes*. Bertelsmann, 1988

Miller, David. *Richard the Lionheart: The Mighty Crusader*. Phoenix, 2013

Miller, Timothy S. and John W. Nesbitt. *Walking Corpses: Leprosy in Byzantium and the Medieval West*. Cornell University Press, 2014

Mitchell, Piers D. *Medicine in the Crusades: Warfare, Wounds and the Medieval Surgeon*. Cambridge University Press, 2004

———. 'The Spread of Disease with the Crusades'. In *Between Text and Patient: The Medical Entrprise in Medieval and Early Modern Europe*. Edited by B. Nance and E.F. Glaze. Sismel, 2011, 309-330

Morgan, M.R. *The Chronicle of Ernoul and the Continuations of William of Tyre*. Oxford Historical Monographs. Oxford University Press, 1973

Morton, Nicholas. *The Teutonic Knights in the Holy Land, 1190–1291*. Boydell, 2009

———. 'Weapons of War: Turkish Archers vs. Frankish Heavy Cavalry'. *History Today* (May 2018), 38-49

Mount, Toni. *Medieval Medicine*. Amberley, 2015

Mourad, Suleiman. 'Jerusalem in Early Islam: The Making of the Muslims' Holy City'. In *Routledge Handbook on Jerusalem*. Routledge, 2019, 77-89

Nicholson, *The Knights Templar: A New History*. Sutton Publishing, 2001

Recommended Reading

———. 'Charity and Hospitality in Military Orders'. In *As Ordens Militares. Freires, Guerreiros, Cavaleiros. Actas do VI Encontro sobre Ordens Militares*. Edited by Isabel Cristina Ferreira Fernandes (coord.). Vol 1. Palmela, 2012, 193-206

———. 'The Role of Women in the Military Orders'. *Militiae Christi: Handelingen van de Vereniging voor de Studie over de Tempeliers en de Hospitaalridders vzw*. Year 1 (2010), 210-219

Nicolaou-Konnari, Angel and Chris Schabel. *Cyprus: Society and Culture 1191–1374*. Brill, 2005

Nicolle, David. *Hattin 1187: Saladin's Greatest Victory*. Osprey Military Campaign Series. 1993

Perry, Guy. *John of Brienne: King of Jerusalem, Emperor of Constantinople, c. 1175–1237*. Cambridge University Press, 2013

Phillips, Jonathan. *Defenders of the Holy Land: Relations between the Latin East and West, 1119–1187*. Oxford University Press, 1996

———. *The Life and Legend of the Sultan Saladin*. Yale University Press, 2019

Pringle, Denys. *Secular Buildings in the Crusader Kingdom of Jerusalem: An Archaeological Gazetteer*. Cambridge University Press, 1997

Reynolds, Gordon M. 'Opportunism & Duty: Gendered Perceptions of Women's Involvement in Crusade Negotiation and Mediation (1147–1254)'. *Medieval Feminist Forum*, 5/2 (April 2019), 5-27

Robinson, John J., Dungeon. *Fire and Sword: The Knights Templar in the Crusades*. Michael O'Mara Books, 1991

Roehricht, Reinhold. *Die Geschichte des Koenigreichs Jerusalem (1100–1291)*. Cambridge University Press, 2004

Riley-Smith, Jonathan. *The Crusades: A History*. Bloomsbury Academic, 2014

———. *The Feudal Nobility and the Kingdom of Jerusalem, 1174–1277*. Macmillan, 1973

———. *Hospitallers: The History of the Order of St John*. Hambledon Press, 1999

Riley-Smith, Jonathan, ed. *The Atlas of the Crusades*. Facts on File, 1991

Runciman, Sir Steven. *The Families of Outremer: The Feudal Nobility of the Crusader Kingdom of Jerusalem, 1099–1291*. The Athlone Press, 1960

Smail, R.C. *Crusading Warfare 1097–1193*.

Stark, Rodney. *God's Battalions: The Case for the Crusades.* HarperCollins, 2010

Suhr, Heiko. *Friedrich II von Hohenstaufen: Seine politischen und kulturellen Verbindungen zum Islam.* Grin Verlag, 2008

Tibble, Steve. *The Crusader Armies.* Yale University Press, 2018

Tyerman, Christopher. *How to Plan a Crusade: Reason and Religious War in the Middle Ages.* Allen Lane, 2015

———. *The World of the Crusades: An Illustrated History.* Yale University Press, 2019

Ye'or, Bat. *The Decline of Eastern Christianity under Islam: From Jihad to Dhimmitude.* Fairleigh Dickinson University Press, 1996

Van Cleve, Thomas Curtis. *The Emperor Frederick II of Hohenstaufen: Immutator Mundi.* Oxford University Press, 1972

Zacour, Norman P. and Harry W. Hazard. *A History of the Crusades, Volume V: The Impact of the Crusades on the Near East.* Wisconsin University Press, 1985

Endnotes

Chapter 1: Genesis of the Crusader States

1. Jonathan Riley-Smith, *The Crusades: A History* (London: Bloombury, 2014), 60.

Chapter 2: The First Kingdom

1. Christopher MacEvitt, *The Crusades and the Christian World of the East: Rough Tolerance* (Philadelphia: University of Pennsylvania Press, 2008), 69.
2. Ronnie Ellenblum, *Crusader Castles and Modern Histories* (Cambridge: Cambridge University Press, 2007), 151.
3. Andrew Jotischky, *Crusading and the Crusader States* (Harlow: Pearson Longman, 2004), 85.
4. William of Tyre, *A History of Deeds Done Beyond the Sea*, trans. Emily Atwater Babcock and A.C. Krey (New York: Octagon Books, 1976), Book XIV, Chapter 18, 76.
5. See note 2, Ellenblum, *Crusader Castles and Modern Histories*, 164.
6. See note 4, William of Tyre, *A History of Deeds Done Beyond the Sea*, Book XX, Chapter 31, 394.
7. Malcolm Barber, *The Crusader States* (New Haven: Yale University Press, 2012), 261.
8. Jonathan Philipps, *The Life and Legend of the Sultan Saladin* (New Haven: Yale University Press, 2019), 71.
9. Christopher Tyreman, *The World of the Crusades: An Illustrated History* (New Haven: Yale University Press, 2019), 167.
10. Baha al-Din Ibn Shaddad, *The Rare and Excellent History of Saladin*, trans. D.S. Richards (Routledge: Abingdon, 2002), 28.

11. Francesco Gabrielli, *Arab Historians of the Crusades* (Berkeley: University of California Press, 1957), 101.
12. Michael Ehrlich, 'Saint Catherine's Day Miracle: The Battle of Montgisard', in *Medieval Military History*, Vol. XI (Woodbridge: Boydell, 2013), 105.
13. See note 12, Ehrlich, 'Saint Catherine's Day Miracle', 105.
14. Malcolm Barber, 'Frontier Warfare in the Latin Kingdom of Jerusalem: The Campaign of Jacob's Ford, 1178–1179', in *The Crusades and their Sources*, eds. John France and Wilaim G. Zajac (Farnham: Ashgate, 1998), 14.
15. See note 4, William of Tyre, *A History of Deeds Done Beyond the Sea*, Book XXII, Chapter 27, 498.
16. See note 4, William of Tyre, *A History of Deeds Done Beyond the Sea*, Book XXII, Chapter 27, 501.
17. Anonymous, *The Old French Continuation of William of Tyre*, translated by Peter Edbury as *The Conquest of Jerusalem and the Third Crusade (Crusades Texts in Translation)* (Aldershot: Ashgate, 1998), chapter 105, 96.
18. Anonymous, *Itinerarium Peregrinorum et Gesta Regis Ricardi*, translated by Helen Nicholson as *The Chronicle of the Third Crusade. Crusades Texts in Translation* (Aldershot: Ashgate, 1997), book 1, chapter 63, 122.
19. Hans Eberhard Mayer, 'Henry II of England and the Holy Land', in *Kings and Lords in the Latin Kingdom of Jerusalem* (Farnham: Variorum, 1994), 737.
20. John France, 'Crusading Warfare in the Twelfth Century', in *The Crusader World*, ed. by Adrian Boas (London: Routledge, 2016), 77.
21. See note 17, Anonymous, *The Old French Continuation of William of Tyre*, chapters 49, 55.
22. Imad al-Din, *The Conquest of the Holy City*, translated by Francesco Gabrieli in *Arab Historians of the Crusades* (Berkeley: University of California Press, 1957), 154.
23. Ibn al-Athir, 'The Perfect History', translated by Francesco Gabrieli in *Arab Historians of the Crusades* (Berkeley: University of California Press, 1957), 140.
24. These figures are very rough and involve multiple assumptions about exchange rates. Nevertheless, they represent the best attempt

to estimate wages and cost of living in the Latin East undertaken by leading crusades archaeologist Professor Adrian Boas of the Hebrew University in Jerusalem. See: Adrian Boas, *Domestic Settings: Sources on Domestic Architecture and Day-to-Day Activities in the Crusader States* (Leiden: Brill, 2010), 228.
25. See note 22, Imad al-Din, *The Conquest of the Holy City*, 163.
26. See note 18, Anonymous, *Itinerarium*, chapter 63, 124.

Chapter 3: The Third Crusade and the Restructuring of the Crusader States

1. Christopher Tyreman, *The World of the Crusades*, 210.
2. The exact number of hostages and prisoners to be released is not certain as different accounts give varying numbers. This number is the figure deemed most reasonable based on conditions in Acre and the size of the respective forces.
3. Anonymous, *The Old French Continuation of William of Tyre*, chapters 105, 107.
4. Anonymous, *The Old French Continuation of William of Tyre*, chapters 105, 108.
5. Baha al-Din Ibn Shaddad, *The Rare and Excellent History of Saladin*, 225-226.
6. Imad ad-Din, *The Conquest of the Holy City*, 234.
7. Baha al-Din Ibn Shaddad, *The Rare and Excellent History of Saladin*, 28.
8. Anonymous, *Itinerarium*, book 5, chapter 24, 302-3.
9. See note 8, Anonymous, *Itinerarium*, book 5, chapter 24, 303.
10. Catia Galatariotou, *The Making of a Saint: The Life, Times and Sanctification of Neophytos the Recluse* (Cambridge: University Press, 1991), 42.
11. See note 3, Anonymous, *The Old French Continuation of William of Tyre,* chapter 133, 112.
12. See note 3, Anonymous, *The Old French Continuation of William of Tyre*, chapter 133, 113.
13. See note 10, Galatariotou, *The Making of a Saint*, 220.
14. See note 10, Galatariotou, *The Making of a Saint*, 203.

Chapter 4: The Second Kingdom or the Kingdom of Acre, 1192–1291

1. R. Stephen Humphreys, 'Ayyubids, Mamluks and the Latin East in the Thirteenth Century', *Mamluk Studies Review* 2:10.
2. Heiko Suhr, *Friedrich II von Hohenstaufen: Seine politischen und kulturellen Verbindungen zum Islam* (Norderstedt: GRIN Verlag, 2008), 17.
3. Ibn Wasil, *Arab Historians of the Crusades,* trans. Francesco Gabrieli (Los Angeles: University of California Press, 1957), 271.
4. Thomas F. Madden, *The Concise History of the Crusades* (New York: Rowman and Littlefield, 2014), 155.
5. Philip Novare, *The Wars of Frederick II Against the Iblins in Syria and Cyprus,* trans. John La Monte (New York: Columbia University Press, 1936), xxvii, 79.
6. Andrew Jotischky, *Crusading and the Crusader States*, 101.
7. Jean de Joinville, *The Life of Saint Louis,* trans. M.R.B. Shaw (London: Penguin Classics, 1963), 204.
8. See note 4, Madden, *The Concise History of the Crusades*, 163.
9. See note 6, Jotischky, *Crusading and the Crusader States*, 238.
10. See note 7, Jean de Joinville, *The Life of Saint Louis,* 252.
11. See note 4, Madden, *The Concise History of the Crusades*, 168.
12. Baybars' letter, translated by Francesco Gabrieli in *Arab Historians of the Crusades*, 311.

Chapter 5: A Mediterranean Melting Pot

1. The myth of Muslim tolerance is so embedded and widespread in modern Western views of Middle Eastern history that it cannot be addressed adequately in this book. The documentary evidence of Islamic oppression and religiously-rationalised exploitation, humiliation, enslavement and extermination are, in fact, vast. Readers interested in the topic should start with Bat Ye'or's books such as *The Decline of Eastern Christianity under Islam: From Jihad to Dhimmitude* (Madison, NJ: Fairleigh Dickinson University Press, 1996) for the situation in the Near East or Dario Fernandez-Morera's *The Myth of the Andalusian Paradise: Muslims, Christians,*

Endnotes

    and Jews Under Islamic Rule in Medieval Spain (Intercollegiate Studies Institute, 2016). For specifics on forced conversions, see Ye'or, 88-91. Both books provide ample bibliographies for pursuing further study on the topic.
2. See note 1, Bat Ye'or, *The Decline of Eastern Christianity under Islam: From Jihad to Dhimmitude* (for the situation in the Near East) or Dario Fernandez-Morera's *The Myth of the Andalusian Paradise for Islamic Spain.*
3. Yuval Harari, 'The Military Role of the Frankish Turcopoles: A Reassessment', *Mediterranean Historical Review*, 12:1 (2008), 105.
4. Pope Urban II quoted by Baldric of Dol in *The Crusades: A Reader*, eds. S.J. Allen and Emilie Amt (Toronto: University of Toronto Press, 2003), 37-38.
5. Michael the Syrian quoted in MacEvitt, *The Crusades and the Christian World of the East*, 25.
6. See note 1, Ye'or, *The Decline of Eastern Christianity under Islam*, 52.
7. See note 1, Ye'or, *The Decline of Eastern Christianity under Islam*, 60.
8. See note 1, Ye'or, *The Decline of Eastern Christianity under Islam*, 107.
9. See note 5, MacEvitt, *The Crusades and the Christian World of the East*, 112.
10. Benjamin Z. Kedar, *Franks, Muslims and Oriental Christians in the Latin Levant* (Aldershot: Ashgate, 2006), V-212.
11. See note 3, Harari, 'The Military Role of the Frankish Turcopoles', 115.
12. Steve Tibble, *The Crusader Armies* (New Haven: Yale University Press, 2018), 98.
13. For details, see note 3, Harari, 'The Military Role of the Frankish Turcopoles', 75-116.
14. Ibn Jubayr, 'The Travels of Ibn Jubayr', in Allen and Amt, *The Crusades: A Reader*, 105.
15. See note 1, Ye'or, *The Decline of Eastern Christianity under Islam*, 68, 71, 77-80, and 110-113.
16. Joshua Prawer, 'Social Classes in the Crusader States: The "Minorities"', in *A History of the Crusades, Volume 5: The Impact of the Crusade on the Near East*, eds. Harry M. Hazard and Norman P. Zacour (Madison, University of Wisconsin Press, 1985), 97.
17. See note 16, Prawer, 'Social Classes in the Crusader States', 101.
18. See note 16, Prawer, 'Social Classes in the Crusader States', 174.

19. Denys Pringle, 'Churches and Settlement in Crusader Palestine', in *The Experience of Crusading: Defining the Crusader Kingdom*, eds. Peter Edbury and Jonathan Phillips (Cambridge: Cambridge University Press, 2003), 177.
20. Hans Eberhard Mayer, 'Latins, Muslims and Greeks in the Latin Kingdom of Jerusalem', in *Probleme des lateinischen Koenigreichs Jerusalem* (London: Variorum Reprints, 1983), VI-176.
21. Chris Schabel, 'Religion', in *Cyprus: Society and Culture 1191–1374*, eds. Angel Nicolaou-Konnari and Chris Schabel (Leiden: Brill, 2005), 181.
22. Fulcher of Chartes in Allen and Amt, *The Crusades: A Reader*, 88-89.
23. *The Continuation of William of Tyre* quoted in Peter Edbury, *The Kingdom of Cyprus and the Crusades 1194–1374* (Cambridge: Cambridge University Press, 1991), 16.
24. *A History of the Crusades: The Art and Architecture of the Crusader States*, Vol. 4, ed. Harry W. Hazard (Madison: University of Wisconsin Press, 1977), 175.

Chapter 6: The 'Ideal Feudal State'

1. John of Jaffa, quoted in Riley-Smith, *The Crusades*, 262.
2. John La Monte, *Feudal Monarchy in the Latin Kingdom of Jerusalem, 1100–1291* (New York: The Medieval Academy of America, 1932), xxii.
3. Geoffrey Le Tor, quoted in Jonathan Riley-Smith, *The Feudal Nobility and the Kingdom of Jerusalem, 1174–1277* (London, Macmillan, 1973), 13.
4. See note 2, La Monte, *Feudal Monarchy*, 87.
5. Peter Edbury, *Law and History in the Latin East* (Farnham: Ashgate, 2014), II-53.
6. Edbury, *Law and History in the Latin East*, VI, 236.
7. Ellenblum, *Crusader Castles and Modern Histories*, 172.
8. John France, 'Warfare in the Mediterranean Region in the Age of the Crusades, 1095–1291: A Clash of Contrasts', in *The Crusades and the Near East: Cultural Histories*, ed. Conor Kostick (London: Routledge, 2011), 72.

Endnotes

9. Harari, 'The Military Role of the Frankish Turcopoles', 79. See also: Steve Tibble, *The Crusader Armies*, 117-124.
10. See note 7, France, 'Warfare in the Mediterranean Region', 73.
11. There is a wealth of literature available in the public domain describing these institutions, their history, organisation, structure, ethos and the like. See more under 'Recommended Reading'.
12. See note 7, France, 'Warfare in the Mediterranean Region', 21.
13. Steven Runciman, *History of the Crusades* (Cambridge: Cambridge University Press, 1951), Vol. 3, 474.
14. Bernard Hamilton, *The Latin Church in the Crusader States* (London: Routledge, 2016), 4.
15. Jotischky, *Crusading and the Crusader States*, 136.
16. See note 13, Hamilton, *The Latin Church in the Crusader States*, 190.
17. MacEvitt, *The Crusades and the Christian World of the East*, 126-130.
18. See note 16, MacEvitt, *The Crusades and the Christian World of the East*, 134.
19. Schabel, 'Religion', 210.

Chapter 7: Foreign Affairs of the Crusader States

1. Riley-Smith, *The Crusades*, 255.
2. Manuel Comnenus quoted in Michael Angold, 'The Fall of Jerusalem (1187) as Viewed from Constantinople', *The Crusader World*, ed. Adrian Boas (London: Routledge, 2016), 291.
3. An excellent summary of Orthodox attitudes towards the church militant is provided in: Nikolaos Chrissis, 'Byzantine Crusaders: Holy War and Crusade Rhetoric in Byzantine Contacts with the West (1095–1341)', in *The Crusader World*, ed. Adrian Boas (London: Routledge, 2016), 259-277.
4. Chris Wright, 'On the Margins of Christendom: The Impact of the Crusades on Byzantium', in *The Crusades and the Near East: Cultural Histories*, ed. Conor Kostick (London: Routledge, 2011), 61.
5. See note 4, Wright, 'On the Margins of Christendom', 62.
6. Abu Samah, quoted in Charles Brand, 'The Byzantines and Saladin, 1185–1192: Opponents of the Third Crusade', *Journal of Mediaeval Studies*, Vol. XXXVII, 3, April 1962: 178.
7. Jotischky, *Crusading and the Crusader States*, 106-107.

8. For details, see Yvonne Friedman, 'Peacemaking: Perceptions and Practices in the Medieval Latin East', in *The Crusades and the Near East: Cultural Histories*, ed. Conor Kostick (London: Routledge, 2010), 229-257.
9. Tyreman, *The World of the Crusades*, 222.

Chapter 8: The Economy of the Crusader States

1. Tyreman, *The World of the Crusades*, 260.
2. Bat Ye'or, *The Decline of Eastern Christianity under Islam*, 119.
3. See note 2, Ye'or, *The Decline of Eastern Christianity under Islam*, 74.
4. Ronnie Ellenblum, *Frankish Rural Settlement in the Latin Kingdom of Jerusalem* (Cambridge: Cambridge University Press, 1998), 96.
5. Nicholas Coureas, 'Economy', in Nicolaou-Konnari and Schabel, *Cyprus*, 127.
6. Wildbrand of Oldenburg, quoted in Boas, *Domestic Settings*, 140.
7. James de Vitry sited in Adrian Boas, *Crusader Archaeology: The Material Culture of the Latin East* (London: Routledge, 1999), 151.
8. Ibn Jubayr quoted in Yehoshua Frankel, 'Muslim Responses to the Frankish Dominion of the Near East, 1098–1291', in *The Crusades and the Near East: Cultural Histories*, ed. Conor Kostick (London: Routledge, 2011), 43.
9. Rodney Stark, *The Victory of Reason: How Christianity Led to Freedom, Capitalism, and Western Success* (New York: Random House, 2005), 68.
10. Ellenblum, *Crusader Castles and Modern Histories*, 231-257, 299-301.
11. Niall Christie, *Muslims and Crusaders: Christianity's Wars in the Middle East, 1095–1382, from the Islamic Sources* (London: Routledge, 2014), 78.
12. See note 11, Christie, *Muslims and Crusaders*, 77-78.
13. Piers D. Mitchell, *Medicine in the Crusades: Warfare, Wounds and the Medieval Surgeon* (Cambridge: Cambridge University Press, 2004), 216.
14. Susan B. Edington, 'Oriental and Occidental Medicine in the Crusader States', in *The Crusades and the Near East: Cultural Histories*, ed. Conor Kostick (London: Routledge, 2011), 189.

15. See note 14, Edington, 'Oriental and Occidental Medicine', 205.
16. See note 13, Mitchell, *Medicine in the Crusades*, 217.
17. See note 13, Mitchell, *Medicine in the Crusades*, 239.

Chapter 9: Life and Lifestyle in the Crusader States

1. Ibn-Khallikan, quoted in Hazard, *The Art and Architecture of the Crusader States*, 138.
2. Ellenblum, *Crusader Castles and Modern Histories*, 112.
3. See note 2, Ellenblum, *Crusader Castles and Modern Histories*, 299.
4. Adrian Boas, *Crusader Archaeology: The Material Culture of the Latin East* (London: Routledge, 1999), 92.
5. Juergen Krueger, 'Architecture of the Crusaders in the Holy Land', in *The Crusades and the Near East: Cultural Histories,* ed. Conor Kostick (London: Routledge, 2011), 218.
6. Riley-Smith, *The Crusades*, 82.
7. Elisabeth Yehuda, 'Frankish Street Settlements and the Status of their Inhabitants in the Society of the Latin Kingdom of Jerusalem' (Tel Aviv: Tel Aviv University, Department of Archaeology): 26.
8. T.S.R. Boase, 'The Arts of Cyprus: Ecclesiastical Art', in Hazard, *The Art and Architecture of the Crusader States,* 174.
9. Wilbrand of Oldenburg, 'Journey in the Holy Land (1211–1212)', in *Pilgrimage to Jerusalem and the Holy Land, 1187–1291*, Denys Pringle (editor) (London: Routledge, 2012), 65-66.
10. Jaroslav Folda, *Crusader Art: The Art of the Crusaders in the Holy Land, 1099–1291* (Aldershot: Lund Humphries, 2008), 13.
11. See note 10, Folda, *Crusader Art*, 13.
12. David Jacoby, 'Aspects of Everyday Life in Frankish Acre', Hebrew University of Jerusalem, (undated paper), 96.
13. See note 10, Folda, *Crusader Art*, 44.
14. Jotischky, *Crusading and the Crusader States*, 149.
15. Fulcher of Chartres' History, Book III, quoted in Allen and Amt, *The Crusades: A Reader*, 88-89.
16. Fulcher of Chartres, *A History of the Expedition to Jerusalem, 1095–1127, Book III*, translated by F.R. Ryan (Knoxville: University

of Tennessee Press, 1969), 152. Reproduced in Allen and Amt, *The Crusades: A Reader*, 88.
17. Urban Tignor Holmes, 'Life among the Europeans in Palestine and Syria in the Twelfth and Thirteenth Century', in Hazard, *The Art and Architecture of the Crusader*, 41.
18. Gilles Grivaud, 'Literature', in Nicolaou-Konnari and Schabel, *Cyprus*, 223.
19. See note 18, Grivaud, 'Literature', 226.
20. See note 18, Grivaud, 'Literature', 237.
21. Tyreman, *The World of the Crusades*, 110.
22. Jotischky, *Crusading and the Crusader States*, 227.
23. Riley-Smith, *The Feudal Nobility*, 230.
24. Jonathan Riley-Smith, *Hospitallers: The History of the Order of St John* (London: Hambledon Press, 1999), 21.
25. See note 24, Riley-Smith, *Hospitallers*, 21.
26. Benjamin Kedar, 'The Jerusalem Hospital', in Kedar, *Franks, Muslims and Oriental Christians*, X 6.
27. Helena P. Schrader, 'Crusader Cuisine', www.crusaderkingdoms.com, posted December 2017.
28. Helena P. Schrader, 'The Scandalous Frankish Fashions: Outfitting Outremer', *The Medieval Magazine*, Issue 124, May 2019, 83-89. (The text has been modified slightly.)
29. Jeoffrey de Vinsauf quoted in Claude Reignier Conder, *The Latin Kingdom of Jerusalem, 1099–1291* (London: Committee of the Palestine Exploration Fund, 1897, reproduced by Elibront Classics, 2005), 178.
30. Christie, *Muslims and Crusaders*, 83.
31. Ibn Jubayr, *The Travels of Ibn Jubayr*, trans. R.J.C. Broadhurst (London: Jonathan Cape, 1952); reprinted Allen and Amt, *The Crusades: A Reader*, 106-107.

Chapter 10: The Ibelins

1. Runciman, 'The Families of Outremer', 7.
2. William of Tyre, *A History of Deeds Done Beyond the Sea*, 131.
3. See note 2, William of Tyre, *A History of Deeds Done Beyond the Sea*, 218.

4. Malcolm Barber, 'The Career of Philip of Nablus in the Kingdom of Jerusalem', in *The Experience of Crusading: Defining the Crusader Kingdom*, eds. Peter Edbury and Jonathan Phillips (Cambridge: Cambridge University Press, 2003), 61.
5. For the dates of birth of Baldwin and Balian, I have followed Hans Eberhard Mayer's essay, 'Carving up Crusaders: The Early Ibelins and Ramlas', in Hans Eberhard Mayer, *Kings and*, XV, 101-118.
6. Arab sources allege that, in this same year, Baldwin (a child of 11) was responsible for oppressing Muslim tenants in villages near Nablus, causing forty families to emigrate to Muslim-held Syria. Since Baldwin was neither of age nor ever in possession of the lordship of Nablus, this account is confused. The lord of Nablus in this period was Philip of Nablus, later, master of the Templars. Nablus did not pass to the Ibelins until 1177 when it was part of Maria Comnena's dower. From 1177–1187, it was held by Balian, never by Baldwin d'Ibelin. The 'oppression' allegedly consisted of forcing Muslims to work on Friday. Many Muslim villagers refused to emigrate, showing that hostility to the Christian lord was by no means as great or widespread as the emigrants later alleged.
7. Michael Ehrlich, 'Saint Catherine's Day Miracle', 105.
8. Peter Edbury, *John of Ibelin and the Kingdom of Jerusalem* (Woodbridge: Boydell Press, 1997), 12.
9. This incident is the source of much slander against both Balian and Maria Comnena. For more details, see: 'Abduction of Isabella of Jerusalem', crusaderkingdoms.com.
10. Arab sources cited by Jonathan Philipps that Balian surrendered a daughter as a hostage that became a Saracen sex slave are false. The fate of Balian's daughters is well-recorded, and neither Saladin – who demonstrated his respect for Balian by escorting his wife and all his children to safety in 1187 – nor Balian, who offered to surrender his own person to prevent paupers from slavery, would have negotiated something so inhumane.
11. For more on this see, 'Ibelins on Cyprus', crusaderkingdoms.com.
12. Philip Novare, *The Wars of Frederick II*, 66.
13. Philip Novare, *The Wars of Frederick II*, 66-67.
14. Philip Novare, *The Wars of Frederick II*, 81.
15. Philip Novare, *The Wars of Frederick II*, 87.
16. Philip Novare, *The Wars of Frederick II*, 106.

17. Philip Novare, *The Wars of Frederick II*, 106.
18. The date is often given as 4 March 1231, but at that time, the Kingdom of Cyprus used a calendar in which the new year started on 25 March, so the date corresponds to 4 March 1232.
19. Philip Novare, *The Wars of Frederick II*, 142.
20. Philip Novare, *The Wars of Frederick II*, 151.
21. Philip Novare, *The Wars of Frederick II*, , 153
22. Philip Novare, *The Wars of Frederick II*, 199.
23. Jean de Joinville, *Life of Saint Louis*, 252.
24. Philip Novare, *The Wars of Frederick II*, 87.
25. Philip Novare, *The Wars of Frederick II*, .
26. See note 24, Jean de Joinville, *Life of Saint Louis,* 248.
27. See note 24, Jean de Joinville, *Life of Saint Louis,* 253.
28. Riley-Smith, *The Feudal Nobility*, 230.
29. See note 24, Jean de Joinville, *Life of Saint Louis,* 204.
30. John, Count of Jaffa, quoted in Edbury, *John of Ibelin and the Kingdom of Jerusalem,* 100.

Conclusions

1. Tibble, *The Crusader Armies*, 132.

Index

A

Abbasids, x, 123, 131, 202, 19
absolutism, 100
accountants, 128, 144, 202
Acre, xii, xx, xxi, xxii, xxvi, xxvii, xxviii, xxix, xxxii, xxxiii, 19, 25, 26, 46, 54, 58, 60, 63, 64-66, 68, 69-71, 73, 76, 77, 80, 83-119, 124, 132, 133, 134, 135, 146, 150, 162, 167, 173, 174, 178, 179, 197, 198, 199, 207, 208, 210, 212, 213, 214, 215, 216, 217, 218, 219, 226, 227, 228, 240, 246, 249, 251, 260, 264, 277, 278, 280, 283, 289, 290, 296, 298, 303
Adhemar, Bishop of Puy, xi, 13, 18, 24, 176-177, 180
administrators, 45, 81, 128, 161, 147, 157, 183
Agnes de Courtenay, 35, 152, 270-271
agriculture, 165, 192, 198, 200-206, 220-221
Agridi, Battle of, xxviii, 98, 282-283, 289, 290-291, 294, 295, 296, 298
agro-processing, 209
Ain Jalut, 111
al-Adil, Brother of Saladin, xx, xxiii, xxiv, xxv, 60, 83-84, 86, 88, 247

al-Ashraf, son of al-Adil, xxxii, 101, 115
al-Din Baybars, 111
Al-Jazira, 83
Aleppo, xiii, xiv, xix, xxxi, 24, 27, 28, 29, 30, 43, 46, 51, 83, 108, 109, 187, 194, 198, 201
Alexandria, xvii, 39, 106, 138, 200, 205, 215, 217
Alice de Bethsan, 295
Alice of Champagne, Queen of Cyprus, 99, 194, 281, 284-285, 293, 298
Alice of Caiphas, 296
Alice de Montbéliard, 298
Alice de Montmorency, 287
al-Kamil, son of al-Adil, xxv, xxvi, xxvii, xxviii, 88-89, 91-92, 100, 101, 192
al-Muazzam, son of al-Adil, xxvi, 88, 89, 91-92, 192
alliances, xx, xxi, 25, 29, 20, 22, 37, 46, 51, 85, 103-104, 110, 189-190, 192-194, 267, 303
Alphonse, Count of Poitiers, Brother of Louis IX, 106
Amalric, King of Jerusalem, xvii, xviii, 35-39, 44, 51-52, 54, 152, 155, 179, 185, 189, 244, 249, 252, 271
Anatolia, xxix, 14, 15, 16, 86, 109

Andronicus I Commenus, Byzantine Emperor, xviii, xx, 189, 319
an-Nasir Daud, Ayyubid prince, Sultan of Damascus, 102, 103, 194
Antioch, xi, xii, xiii, xiv, xv, xvi, xvii, xxi, xv, xxxii, xxxiv, 6, 14-19,21, 24, 29-32, 34, 37-38, 41, 47, 53, 56-58, 64, 65, 68, 82, 86, 87, 98, 100, 109, 112, 114, 124, 125-126, 129, 139, 146, 154, 167, 170, 173, 176, 177-179, 185, 188-189, 191, 194, 197, 198, 210, 212-213, 224, 226, 246, 250, 251, 252, 267, 273, 274, 281, 284, 285, 290, 302
aqueducts, 70, 111, 203, 227
Arabs, xxvii, 48, 123, 144, 215, 222, 250, 264
archers, 14, 26, 59, 62, 71, 72, 74, 108, 131, 140, 144, 151, 168, 169, 170-173, 221, 303, 304
architects, 202
architecture,
    Byzantine, 13-14, 234, 235, 238, 239, 242-244, 258, 259, 266, 304
    domestic, 236-241, 304
    military, 216, 221, 222, 229-233
    religious, 233-236
    rural, 140, 236-240
    urban, 140, 225-229, 236-241
    Western, 140, 264, 304
Armenians, 17, 29, 34, 125-126, 131, 135, 142, 146, 177, 191, 199, 249

armour, 14, 71, 152, 170, 172, 206, 213, 217, 222, 246, 263-264
Arsuf, xii, xxii, xxxi, 26, 71, 104, 111, 226
Arsur castle, 296
as-Salih Ayyub, son of al-Kamil, 102, 103, 104, 194
as-Salih Ismael, son of al-Adil, 101, 102
Ascalon, xi, xvi, xx, xxx, 25, 26, 332, 33, 8, 47, 48, 53, 54, 60, 61, 73, 102, 104, 124, 133, 137, 146, 150, 167, 193, 213, 226, 227, 232, 267, 269, 273, 297, 299
assassins, xvi, xxii, xxxi, 76, 109
Atabeg Kerbogha, 16
Athlit (Castle Pilgrim), xxxiii, 94, 116
Augustines, 139, 181
Ayyubid dynasty, 83
Ayyubids, xxix, xxx, 83, 85-87, 88, 92, 101, 103-107, 111, 118-119, 186, 192, 299

B

Baalbek, 83
Baghras castle, 64
Baha al-Din, 44, 72, 74, 75
baillies, xxvii, 95-97, 100, 159, 161
balconies, 84, 238, 240, 304
Baldwin I, King of Jerusalem, xii, xiii, 25, 27, 118, 152, 249,
Baldwin II, King of Jerusalem, xiii, xiv, 27-29, 30, 35, 188, 249, 273

Index

Baldwin III, King of Jerusalem, xiv, xv, xvi, xvii, 33, 35, 37, 188, 249, 270, 271, 272
Baldwin IV, King of Jerusalem, xviii, xix, 44-46, 50-51, 54, 146, 152, 185, 224, 272, 273, 275
Baldwin V, King of Jerusalem, xix, xx, 54, 273, 275
Baldwin of Boulogne, Count of Edessa, xi, 13, 18, 22
bananas, 204, 205, 263
banking and bankers, 128, 202, 206-209, 304
Banyas castle, xiv
barley, 206, 261
basilicas, vii, 2, 235
baths and bathhouses, 41, 163, 165, 227, 228, 230, 248
Baybars, Mamluk sultan of Egypt and Syria, xxxi, xxxii, 111, 112, 114, 244, 300
Beaufort (Belfort) castle, 231, 286
Beaujeu, William de, Templar Master, 115
Bedouins, xxxvii, 48, 54, 153
Beirut, City, xxxiii, xix, xx, xxviii, xxxviii, xxxiii, 19, 25, 56, 60, 64, 74, 80, 84, 96, 116, 124, 132, 167, 178, 197, 199, 213, 213, 226, 240, 245, 267, 295
Belvoir castle, 231
Benedict, Archbishop of Edessa, 179
Benedictines, 139, 181, 254
Berbers, xxxvii
Berengaria of Navarre, Queen of England, 78, 79

Bertrand of Blancfort, Templar Master, 270
Bethgibelin castle, 230
Bethlehem, xii, xxix, 19, 22, 23, 25, 27, 47, 55, 60, 92, 132, 167, 178, 189, 198, 207, 210, 213, 243, 244
bishoprics, 178
Blanchegarde castle, 36, 230
Bohemia, 142
Bohemond I, Prince of Antioch, xii, 13, 14, 16, 18
Bohemond III, Prince of Antioch, xvii, xxi, 37, 38, 53, 64
Bohemond IV, Prince of Antioch, xxv, 194
books and manuscripts, 38, 214, 215-216, 242, 243, 245-246, 250-252, 264, 316
Buffavento castle, 290
builders, 146, 202
Bulgaria, 142
burgesses, 61, 250, 98, 102, 139, 140, 146, 147, 157, 159, 163, 172
Byzantine Emperor, xvi, xviii, xxi, 2, 9-12, 15, 16, 18, 21, 32, 34, 37, 46, 52, 187, 188, 191, 270, 274
Byzantine Empire, xxxvii, 3, 6, 15, 160, 183, 190, 191, 207, 211, 245

C

Caesarea, xii, xxvi, xxxi, 19, 25, 71, 88, 104, 108, 111, 135, 156, 167, 178, 197, 226, 227, 235, 239, 287, 288

327

Cairo, x, xxv, xxvi, xxxi, 27, 38, 39, 40, 41, 42, 43, 58, 57, 60, 78, 83, 88, 89, 103, 104, 105, 107, 197, 201, 266, 271, 278
Carmelites, 139, 179, 181
carob, 205, 206, 263
castles, xxvii, xxix, xxxv, 27-28, 36, 60, 64, 79, 89, 92, 94, 95, 102, 108, 114, 116, 136, 140, 151, 154, 166, 167-174, 175, 185, 195, 210, 221, 229-233, 235, 253, 255, 304
Catalonia, xv, 251
cathedrals, 17, 28, 145, 178, 181, 235, 251, 254, 253
cattle, 228, 262
cavalry, 8, 19, 26, 32, 47, 59, 62, 72, 74, 106, 131, 170, 171-173, 221, 304
clerks, 161, 165
chancellors, 160-161
Charlemagne, King of France, xi, 7
Charles, Count of Anjou, xxxi, xxxii, 114
Charles Martel, King of France, ix
chimneys, 140, 222, 237, 238,
china, 198, 218
Christians, 4, 7, 122, 127, 129, 132, 202, 223, 224
churches, x, xxviii, xxx, xxxiv, xxxv, 4, 9, 17, 23, 28, 99, 103, 112, 114, 127, 129, 132, 139, 141, 176-178, 180-182, 204, 228, 234-235, 302
Cistercians, 139, 181
cisterns, 140, 227, 236, 237, 239-240, 260, 304

cities, xi, xix, 3, 15, 18, 19, 22, 26, 27, 29, 36, 60, 69, 79, 84-86, 92, 111, 114, 117, 118, 124, 133, 136-138, 140, 145, 150, 154, 157, 166-174, 258, 260, 263, 266
climate, 80, 200, 204, 205, 225, 227, 248
clothing, 129, 132, 263-266
Comnenus dynasty, 78
  Alexius I Commenus, Byzantine Emperor, xxiii, xxiv, 6, 9, 10, 12, 13, 14, 17, 18, 187, 189
  Andronicus I, Byzantine Emperor, xviii, xx, 189
  Isaac, Despot of Cyprus, xxii, 78-79, 143, 164
  Manuel I, Byzantine Emperor, xvi, xvii, 37, 39, 164, 188-189, 244, 319
  Maria, Queen of Jerusalem, xvii, 51, 61, 274, 281, 284, 323
  Theodora, Queen of Jerusalem, xvi, 37
Communes, 136-143
Conrad III (Hohenstaufen), King of Jerusalem, xv, xxvi, xxx, 31, 33, 99, 101, 102, 113, 185, 292, 293, 298
Conrad, Marquis de Montferrat, xx, xxii, xxvi, 63-66, 76, 81, 87, 91, 99, 101, 102, 113, 119, 277, 278, 292, 293
constable, 106, 146, 160-161, 267, 268, 279, 281, 287, 288, 292, 295, 296, 299, 300, 301

Index

Constantinople, ix, xi, xvii, xviii, xx, xxiii, xxiv, xxvii, xxviii, xxxi, xxxvii, 2, 3, 6, 7, 10-13, 15, 18, 24, 30, 34, 35-40, 46, 67, 78, 86, 126, 138, 143, 144, 176, 186-192, 198-200, 202, 206, 215, 216, 218, 248, 251, 252, 258, 264, 266, 267, 278, 286, 287
Coptic Christians, 38, 39, 42, 124, 125, 126, 143, 178, 242
cour de la chaine, 157
cour de la fonde, 157
Cour des Bourgeois, 156, 157, 158-159, 162
courtyards and courtyard houses, 79, 226, 227, 236-239, 240
Crac de Chevaliers, 112, 167
Chretien de Troyes, 250
crossbows and crossbow production, 214, 304
crossbowmen, 74, 170
crusaders, xi, xii, xv, xxi, xxi, xxiii, xxiv, xxv, xxvi, xix, xxxiv, xxxvii, xxxviii, 4, 8-9, 12-21, 22-24, 32, 33, 46, 64, 67-68, 69, 70-76, 77, 83-90, 101-102, 105-107, 118, 123, 129, 131, 133-135, 138, 142, 146, 172-173, 176, 178, 184, 187-188, 191, 192, 197-198, 200, 203, 205, 216, 221, 229, 232, 233, 241, 242, 248, 250, 252, 255, 265, 266, 270, 281, 297, 301-303
crusades, xx, xxxii, xxxiv, xxxvi-xxxiv, 9, 17, 20, 34, 68, 80, 85, 105, 111, 130, 133, 143, 166, 173, 176, 180, 183, 185, 187, 190-191, 195, 202, 211, 215-216, 219-221, 225, 234, 236, 241, 250, 252, 254, 259, 262, 302
cuisine and cooking, 211, 236, 237, 261-263
Cyprus, Island, ix, x, xxii, xxiii, xxiv, xxv, xxvi, xxviii, 6, 37, 69, 77-82, 84, 87, 91, 93-98, 104-106, 124-125, 143-148, 176, 180-182, 188, 197-200, 206, 209-210, 211, 213, 214, 227, 230, 234, 246, 249-250, 246-262, 267, 278, 279, 280, 282-283, 284, 278, 280, 282-288, 292, 301
Cyprus, Kingdom, xxii, xxiii, xxiv, xxv, xxvi, xxvii, xxx, xxxi, xxxii, xxxiv, 77-82, 84, 87, 88, 93-98, 104-106, 113-116, 124-125, 143-148, 180-182, 184, 191, 206, 214, 234, 240, 262, 267, 278-279, 280, 282-288, 290-298, 300-301

D

dairy products, 226, 228
Damascus, xii, xvi, xv, xvi, xviii, xxx, xxxi, 26-30, 32, 33, 38, 41, 43, 49, 56, 57, 60, 83, 102, 103, 108, 109, 112, 124, 185, 187, 189, 190, 192-194, 196, 197, 198, 201, 214, 218, 266, 270, 281, 290
Damascus castle, 286
Damietta, xxv, xxvi, xxx, 37, 88, 89, 105-108, 299

Dar al-Harb, 3, 191
Dar al-Islam, 2-6, 6, 43, 191, 259
Darbsak castle, 64
Darum castle, 230
dates, 204, 205, 263
decoration, 211, 212, 234, 238, 243, 244, 266, 304
demography, xxxvi, 122-124
dhimmis, 125, 127, 128, 132, 133, 134, 143, 144, 158, 201, 202
diet, 205, 260, 261, 262
diplomacy, 89, 92, 183, 191, 193-196
diplomats, 128, 160, 202
diplomatic immunity, 128, 138, 195
doctors, 45, 144, 224, 257, 258-259, 303
Dominicans, 13, 139, 179, 180
doors, 229, 236, 239
Dorylaeum, xi, xv, 14, 32
dragomans, 162, 163
dyes and dyeing, 213, 266

E

Edessa, xiv, xv, xxxiv, 15, 24, 25, 30-34, 35, 124, 125, 188, 248, 256
education, 40, 110, 201, 251-252, 255
Edward I, King of England, xxxii, 115, 151, 230
Egypt, ix, x, xvii, xxiv, xxv, xxvi, xxix, xxx, 3, 4, 28, 37-40, 41-43, 46, 47, 85, 86, 88-89, 91, 102, 104, 105, 107-111, 117, 124, 185, 189, 192, 194, 198, 207, 211, 218, 223, 251, 252, 271, 288

Eleanor of Aquitaine, xiv, xv, xvi, xix, xxi, 32, 52, 77
England, x, xxi, xxiv, xxv, xxxi, xxxvi, 54, 68, 74, 77, 79, 102, 142, 151, 152, 154, 155, 157, 185, 187, 198, 204, 235, 261, 292
Eschiva de Montbèliard, 289
Eschiva of Tiberias, 58
Ethiopia, 207, 218
Ethiopians, 123, 126, 135, 143, 177, 178
Eustace, Count of Boulogne, 13
exports, 85, 165, 184, 197, 205, 206, 209, 210, 213-214, 216, 219, 266

F

fabrics and textiles, 206, 212, 218, 265
factories, 164, 204, 206, 209, 228
Famagusta, 79, 80, 97, 117, 181, 199, 209, 215, 234, 235, 240, 290
fashion, 232, 255, 263-266
Fatimids, x, xi, xiii, xvii, 4, 19-21, 23, 26, 27, 29, 36, 38, 39, 41, 42, 47, 123, 131, 176, 177, 192, 192, 216, 226, 232
feudal class, 76, 270
feudal elite, 9, 96, 127, 138, 145, 156, 157, 158, 159, 181, 203, 204, 249, 261, 264
feudal obligations, 150, 151, 153, 154, 169, 175, 199
feudal services, 139, 151, 153, 156, 164, 169, 226
feudalism, 149-150
Field of Blood, xiii, 29, 179, 229

Index

fighting box, 70, 171-173, 304
figs, 204, 205, 260, 263
fireplaces, 140, 237, 238, 239, 304
fish and fishing, 87, 205, 206, 209, 215, 262,
fleets, ix, xiii, xvii, xxi, xii, xxiv, xxvii, xxx, 20, 25, 27, 29, 33, 36, 39, 40, 47, 64, 69, 70, 79, 80, 95, 97, 106, 107, 113, 137, 173, 174, 177, 185, 189, 201, 216, 290
floors, 137, 228, 229, 237-239
food, 8, 15, 70, 87, 106, 199, 202, 205, 208, 211, 221, 225, 256, 260, 261-263, 290
fortifications, 16, 27, 89, 103, 114, 141, 156, 167, 229, 281
fountains, 148, 227, 229, 240, 267, 304
France, xiv, xviii, xxiv, xxxi, 3, 11, 52, 54, 68, 69, 77, 87, 91, 105, 106, 107, 134, 138, 142, 14, 185, 187, 204, 235, 244, 251, 267, 270, 273, 280, 286, 287
Franciscans, 139, 179, 180, 181
Frederick I Barbarossa, Holy Roman Emperor, xvi, xxi, xxiii, 67, 68, 190
Frederick II (Hohenstaufen), Holy Roman Emperor, xxiv, xxv, xxvi, xxvii, xxix, xxx, 88, 89, 90-103, 105, 108, 113, 118, 253, 267, 282, 283, 287, 289, 292, 294, 295, 297, 305
frescos, xxxv, 234, 239, 242, 243-244
fruits, 80, 197, 204, 226, 260, 262-263

Fulcher of Chartres, 22, 142, 248, 249, 252
furs, 218

G

gardens, 70, 148, 206, 226-227, 229, 240, 267
Gaza, xvii, xxix, xxxvi, 25, 36, 48, 60, 101, 102, 104, 178, 213, 230, 266, 292, 296
Genoa, 301, 137, 174, 177, 207
geography, 215, 225
Gerard, Bishop of Tripoli, 179
Gerard Rideford, Templar Master, 55
Gerard de Montaigu, 289
Gerard de Grenier, Lord of Sidon and Beaufort, 194, 269
Gibelet (Jubayl) castle, 230
glass, glass manufacturing and glazing, 211-212, 216, 221, 235, 239, 242, 247, 304
Godfrey of Bouillon, Duke of Lower Lorraine, Protector of the Holy Sepulchre, xi, xii, 13, 19, 20, 21, 23, 24, 138, 150
governors, 5, 78, 133, 183
grain, 27, 80, 105, 164, 261
grapes, 210, 260, 263
Greek Orthodox, 17, 82, 86, 126, 145, 176, 177, 180, 182, 187

H

Hama, 83
Harran, Battle of, xii, 179
Hattin, Battle of, xx, 48, 50, 59, 60, 61, 63, 72, 104, 149,

166, 169, 171, 172, 179, 185, 189, 193, 194, 226, 229, 231, 274, 276, 278, 280, 281, 284, 286, 287
Helvis of Nephin, 281
Helvis of Ramala, 279, 268, 269-270, 272
Henri, Count of Champagne, xxii, xxiii, 76-77, 84, 138, 280, 281, 284, 287
Henry VI, Holy Roman Emperor, xxiii, 83, 84
Henry I, King of Cyprus, xxvi, xxxi, 113, 282, 285, 293
Henry II, King of Cyprus, 114, 170, 301
Henry I, King of England, 35
Henry II, King of England, xv, xix, xxi, xxxi, 46, 58, 63, 67, 68, 151, 185
Henry III, King of France, xxviii, xxix, 102, 103
Henry VI (Hohenstaufen), Holy Roman Emperor, xxxiii, 83, 84
Herakleios, Byzantine Emperor, 2
herbs and spices, 163, 263, 217
High Court, xxv, 36, 44, 51, 54, 55, 76, 81, 87, 92, 94, 95, 96, 98, 100, 101, 145, 149-156, 271, 273, 275, 282, 284-285, 287, 289, 298
Holy Roman Empire, xxiii, 84, 135, 138, 144, 190, 204
Homs, xii, xiv, xxxii, 26, 30, 83, 112
honey, 165, 199, 200, 206, 210, 263

horses, 15, 17, 70, 71, 75, 96, 105, 106, 109, 129, 132, 152, 155, 162, 163, 171, 172, 205-206, 217, 220, 221, 228, 246
hospices, 228, 254, 257
hospitals, 41, 109, 175, 209, 223, 254, 255, 257-260, 262, 228, 303, 304
Hugh, Duke of Burgundy, 52
Hugh le Puiset, Count of Jaffa, 194, 268
Hugh of Caesarea, 249, 273
Hugh of Tiberias, 287
Hugh of Vermandois, 13
Hugh I, King of Cyprus, xxiv, xxv, xxxi, 87, 282, 284
Hugh II, King of Cyprus, xxxi, xxxii, 87, 113
Hugh III, King of Cyprus, 114, 301
Hugh IV, King of Cyprus, 301
Hugh V, King of Cyprus, xxv
humours, 206
Hungary, 142

I

Ibelin dynsasty, 279
  Alice, 301
  Baldwin, 249, 295, 296, 297, 300, 323
  Baldwin of Ramla, 53, 268, 272-274, 275
  Baldwin, Seneschal of Cyprus, 294-295
  Balian, Lord of Beirut, xxviii, 56, 61, 75, 99, 102, 103, 104, 155, 156, 247,

Index

300, 288-294, 295, 296, 298-299, 301, 323
Balian of Nablus, 274-279, 280, 281, 284, 285-288
Barisan, First Lord of Ibelin, 268-272, 274, 279
Eschiva, 58, 273, 279-280, 284, 289, 290, 294, 301
Guy, Constable of Cyprus, 106, 296-297, 301
Helvis, 285, 286-287
Hugh, Lord of Ramla, 269-272, 278, 290
Hugh, son of John Lord of Beirut, 295-296
Isabella, daughter of John of Beirut, 300
John, Count of Jaffa, 148, 156, 169, 170, 246, 253, 290, 293, 295-300
John, Lord of Arsur, 295-296, 301
John, Lord of Beirut, xxiv, xxv, xxvi, xxviii, 87, 93-101, 104, 156, 240, 249, 253, 280-283, 285, 288, 293, 300, 301
John, Lord of Beirut, son of Balian of Beirut, 87, 301
Margaret d'Ibelin, 285
Maria, 287, 300
Marie, 301
Petronilla, 287, 300
Philip, Regent of Cyprus, xxvi, 282, 283-285, 297, 300, 301
Ibn al-Athir, 62, 72, 195
Ibn Jubayr, 13, 164, 218, 227, 265

icons and icon production, xxxv, 145, 181, 208, 214, 216, 242, 243, 246-247, 303
illustration and illumination, 214, 243, 245-246
Imad al-Din, xiii, xiv, 30, 40, 61, 63, 75, 194
immigrants, xxxiv, 82, 124, 125, 138, 142, 147, 148, 158, 204, 238, 241, 242, 243, 250
imports, 162, 165, 184, 214, 219, 211, 213
India, 218, 219, 250
industry and manufacturing, 198, 199, 207, 209-214, 215, 245
infantry, 8, 14, 26, 29, 32, 57, 59, 64, 70, 71, 72, 98, 115, 131, 140, 147, 169, 170-173, 283, 303
infrastructure, xvi, xxxv, 23, 28, 72, 111, 123, 125, 175, 197, 198, 199, 200, 203, 225-240
intellectual life and exchange, 184, 201-202, 220-224, 248, 251, 252-253, 288, 305
irrigation, 28, 125, 141, 192, 203, 206, 209, 240
Isabella, Queen of Cyprus, 301, 297
Isabella I, Queen of Jerusalem, xxii, xxiii, xxiv, 51, 54-56, 65, 66, 76-77, 87, 249, 275, 277-279, 286, 287
Isabella II, Queen of Jerusalem, *see* Yolanda
Isabella of England (Plantagenet), xxviii, 101, 102
Italian city-states, 39, 86, 89, 119, 135, 161, 209, 219

333

J

Jabala, xxi, 64, 124, 132
Jacob's Ford castle, xviii, 49
Jacobites, 41, 125, 126, 143, 176, 177, 178, 202, 224, 251
Jacques de Vitry, Archbishop of Tyre, 212
Jaffa, xii, xiii, xx, xxii, xxiii, xxiv, xxxii, 19, 20, 25, 60, 70, 71, 72, 74, 77, 84, 87, 92, 104, 150, 167, 179, 226, 263, 267, 268
Jaffa, Count of, John d'Ibelin, 169, 170, 246, 253, 297-300, 301
Jaffa, Treaty of (aka Treaty of Ramla), xxiii
James de Vitry, Archbishop of Acre, 180, 264
Jerusalem, City, viii, ix-xv, xvii-xx, xxii-xxvii, xxix-xxx, 2-8, 10, 11-21, 22-29, 30, 33, 34, 35, 37-40, 43, 44, 46-50, 53-67, 75-76, 83-93, 95, 122, 124, 125, 130, 133-137, 139, 155, 156, 161, 166, 167, 170, 176, 177, 179, 184, 187, 188-189, 191-192, 194, 198, 210, 213-214, 218, 226-231, 233-235, 240-241, 243-244, 246, 251, 252, 254-256, 260-262, 267, 268, 271-273, 275-282, 284, 292, 297-303
Jerusalem, Kingdom, xxxii, xxxiv, xxxvi, 22-29, 36, 38, 39, 40, 44, 46, 47, 50, 56, 57, 58, 63, 70, 75-77, 93, 95, 98-102, 103-121, 125, 126, 140, 150, 151, 152, 154, 157, 160, 162, 165, 174, 175, 185, 186, 188, 189, 193, 197, 206-208, 233, 238, 243, 245, 252-253, 269, 271-272, 274, 279, 282, 285-288, 293, 296, 297-303, 305
Jews, xi, xxxiv, 4, 5, 7, 11, 20, 32, 42, 122, 127, 129, 132, 133-135, 164, 202, 211, 259, 302, 303
Jihad, 2-6, 40-44, 57, 85, 104, 111, 118, 127, 193
Joscelyn I, Count of Edessa, 249
Joscelyn II, Count of Edessa, 30, 270
Jubail, xii, 25
Just War, Theory of, 7

K

Kerak castle, xvi, xix, 36, 42, 231
Khwarazmians, xxx, 244
Kilij Arslan, 14
knights, xx, xxviii, xxix, 7, 9-16, 20, 22, 24-27, 29, 32, 47, 48, 50, 56, 57, 59, 60, 61-64, 67, 70-72, 74, 76, 80, 81, 86-88, 91, 94, 96-98, 102, 104, 105, 108, 115, 127, 130, 136, 138-140, 146, 147-149, 151-155, 162, 168-172, 174, 175, 187, 195, 206, 213, 215, 228, 246, 250, 255, 260, 264, 270, 273, 275, 276, 278, 284, 285, 288, 289, 292, 295-297
Knights Hospitallers, xiii, xx, 27, 39, 57, 63, 71-73, 92, 98, 104, 112, 114, 115, 1116, 30, 136, 170, 174-175, 179, 207,

Index

209, 210, 216, 228, 230, 243, 255-260, 262
Knights Templar, xiii, xiv, xxxi, 27, 48, 49, 55, 57, 58, 80, 81, 94, 98, 104, 111, 115, 116, 168, 170, 174-175, 180, 231, 234, 235, 243-244, 255, 270, 282
Kolossi castle, 230
Kurds, xxxviii, 39, 41
Kyrenia, 80, 199
Kyrenia castle, 291

L

La Forbelet, Battle of, xix, 50, 171, 179
labour, 35, 123, 128, 198, 201, 203, 257
landlords, 144, 145, 159, 199, 203
landowners, 27, 133, 137, 144, 145, 159, 199, 203
Latakia, xxi, xxxii, 19, 64, 74, 114, 124, 132, 210
Latin Church, 37, 82, 126, 129, 139, 144, 148, 176, 178, 179, 180-182
latrines and privies, 228, 236, 239, 240, 258
lawyers, 144, 159, 202, 215, 253, 268
Lazarists, 179
leather and leather goods, 205, 210-211
legal scholars, 100, 155
lepers, 45
leprosy, 45, 51, 224
Lewes, Battle of, xxxi
Limassol, 199

literacy, 248-252
literature, 9, 45, 131, 191, 201, 250, 252,
livestock, 4, 42, 111, 204, 149, 204-206, 210, 262
Louis VII, King of France, xi, xiv, xv, 31-33, 52, 77, 185, 194
Louis IX, King of France, xxx, xxxi, xxxii, 93, 105, 108, 246
Lotario Filangieri, 293
Lusignan dynasty, 82, 87, 145, 219, 280
    Aimery de Lusignan, King of Cyprus, King of Jerusalem, xxiii, 82, 84, 87, 273, 279, 281, 84, 287
    Burgundia de Lusignan, 87, 289
    Geoffrey de Lusignan, Count of Jaffa, 35, 52
    Guy de Lusignan, King of Jerusalem, xviii, xix, xx, xxi, xxiii, 52-56, 58, 59, 61, 64, 65, 75, 81-82, 119, 146, 148, 152, 156, 194, 273, 275, 275-280
    Hugh de Lusignan, 95-97, 281
    Hugh IV, 301
    Hugh VII, xvii
    Hugh VIII, 38
    Ralph, 287
luxury goods, 209, 210, 213, 215,

M

Mamluks, xxx, xxxi, xxxii, xxxiii, 31, 47, 61, 107, 108-118, 123, 147, 192, 216-218, 221, 232, 241, 249, 276, 281, 297, 299
Manassas of Hierges, 272, 279

manor houses, 204
Mansourah, xxx, 107
manufacturers, 303
Manzikert, x, 6
Margat castle, 231
Marie de Montferrat, Queen of Jerusalem, xxvi, xxv, 87, 282
Marie of Antioch, Byzantine Empress, xxxii, 189
Maria of Beirut, 273
maritime power, xxxv, 25, 136, 173, 174, 198, 207, 21
markets, enclosed, *see* souks
Marqab castle, 114
marshals, xxvii, 71, 72, 95, 116, 130, 160, 161-162, 267, 270, 293
masons and masonry, 141,146, 222, 236, 244
medical care, 174, 255, 257, 259
medical theory, 224, 250, 304
medicine, xxxv, 209, 223-224, 250, 258, 260, 304
Melkites, 125, 126, 129
merchants, xxxv, 85, 128, 130, 137, 139, 147, 158, 199, 202, 216-218, 228, 238, 303
metals, 213, 218, 242
metalwork and metalworking, 213, 242, 247
Michael I, Rabo, 41
Michael the Syrian (the Great), 33, 178
militant orders, 33, 57, 113, 136, 139, 171, 174, 175
mills, 28, 141, 164, 203, 204, 206, 261
Mirabel, 37, 52, 267, 269, 270, 272, 274

monasteries, xxxiv, 4, 10, 23, 28, 129, 167, 170, 178, 180, 231, 302
money exchanges, 208
monopolies, 153, 199, 219
Montfort (Starkenburg) castle, 231
Montfort dynasty,
   Eleanor, Countess of Leicester, 102
   Guy, 286-287, 290, 295, 296
   Philip de Montfort, 155, 287, 292, 295, 296, 299
   Simon de Montfort IV, lord of Montfort-l'Amaury, xxix, 119, 286, 287, 292, 298
   Simon de Montfort V, Earl of Leicester, xxxi, 102, 103, 155, 305
Montgisard, Battle of, xxviii, 48-50, 171, 272, 274
Montreal castle, 28
Morphia, Queen of Jerusalem, xiii, 27
mosaics, 234, 242, 243-245, 247, 267
mosques, 9, 41, 42, 44, 109, 132, 233, 302
Mosul, xiii, xx, 16, 30, 43, 51, 86, 201, 252, 266
Muslims, xxxiv, 164, 224, 259, 302

N

Nicaea, xi, xxviii, 13
Nicosia, Archbishop of, 181, 289
Nicosia, Battle of, xxvii, 95, 288, 289, 294

Index

Nicosia, City of, 79, 80, 95, 97, 145, 148, 181, 208, 227, 240, 247, 282, 288
Normandy, 11, 138
Notre Dame Cathedral, Tortosa, 235
Nur al-Din, Sultan of Aleppo, xxx, 34, 37, 38-44, 124, 189, 194, 270
nuts, 263

O

Odo of Saint-Amand, Temple Marshal, 270
olives, olive oil, oil presses, 162, 164, 205, 206, 210, 263
orchards, 71, 111, 162, 165, 192, 205, 206, 226-227, 240
orphanages, 41, 257
ovens and bakeries, 137, 141, 165, 204, 230, 236, 261

P

palaces, 109, 112, 148, 227, 228, 234, 240-241, 245, 247, 260, 267, 281
Palestine, 2, 4, 23, 40, 44, 89, 122, 130, 131, 140, 143, 146, 147, 176-180, 188, 227, 253
paper, 221
patients, 257-260, 262, 303, 304
patriarchs, 139, 117, 178, 187, 240
peasants, 4, 10, 81, 117, 139, 141, 143, 144, 149, 164, 170, 195, 201, 202, 220, 221, 238, 250
People's Crusade, 10
Persia and Persians, viii, ix, 2, 3, 20, 122, 128, 250

Peter the Hermit, xi, 10
pigs, 40, 205, 228, 262
pharmaceuticals, 217
Philip, Count of Flanders, xviii, 46, 68
Philip II (Augustus), King of France, xviii, xxi, xxii, xxv, xxxiii, 67, 68, 69, 73, 75, 151
Philip de Novare, 100, 147, 253, 280
Philip of Nabulus, 269, 271
Philippa Barlais, 297
pilgrimage, 2, 8, 10, 34, 134, 187, 206-208, 235, 242, 254, 256, 271, 278
pilgrims, xix, xxxv, xxxvii, 6, 9-11, 12, 23, 27, 28, 75, 134-136, 138, 150, 163, 165, 170, 184, 185, 187, 195, 198, 205, 206, 207-208, 213, 214, 216, 227, 235, 236, 242, 254, 260, 261, 278
pillars, 235, 238
Pisa, 24, 137, 174, 177, 206, 265
ploughs and ploughing, 205, 220, 222
pollution, 205, 227
Pope Gregory VII, x
Pope Gregory IX, xxvi, 67, 90, 99, 251
Pope Honorius III, xxv, 88
Pope Urban II, xi, 7, 9, 10, 67, 126, 176-177
population, xxxiv-xxxv, 4, 13, 15, 16, 24, 27, 28, 32, 34, 38, 39, 45, 61, 64, 65, 67, 78, 81, 82, 85, 92, 111-112, 115, 122-148, 157, 159, 163, 164, 166, 178,

337

180-182, 189, 192, 197, 199, 200-204, 207, 211, 214, 216, 225-227, 231, 233, 237, 243, 248, 249, 251, 261, 262, 276
pottery and ceramics, xxxv, 211, 215, 218, 242, 245, 247
poultry, 228, 262
precious stones, 218
Premonstratensians, 139
prisoners and captives, xxviii, xix, 29, 37, 57, 60, 62, 69, 70, 89, 102, 104, 108, 110, 118, 127, 128, 149, 188, 195, 196, 203, 255, 270, 277, 297

Q

Qalawun, Mamluk Sultan of Egypt, xxxi, 112, 114
Quran, 5, 41, 122, 127, 128
Qutuz, Mamluk Sultan, xxxi, 111

R

ra'is, 158, 162
raisins and currants, 263
Ralph, Bishop of Bethlehem, 179
Ralph II, Bishop of Bethlehem, 179
Ralph of Soissons
Ralph of Tiberias, 253
Rufinius, Bishop of Acre, 179
Ramla, xii, xxiii, 19, 26, 47, 48, 49, 56, 60, 171, 197, 213, 226, 234, 269, 272, 299
Ramla, Treaty of, *see* Treaty of Jaffa
Raymond, Count of Toulouse, xii, 12, 13, 18, 19, 34, 138
Raymond II of Tripoli, xvi

Raymond III of Tripoli, xvii, xix, xx, 18, 38, 45, 56, 58, 194, 249, 275, 287
Raymond of Poitiers, Prince of Antioch, xiv, xv, 30, 252
religious orders, 28, 233, 255, 257, 259
rents, 139, 140, 163-163, 199, 203, 232
restor, 162, 163
Reynald de Châtillon, 231
Richard I, King of England, xxi, xxii, xxiv, 67-81, 143, 145, 151, 164, 180, 247, 278-279
Richard, Duke of Cornwall, xxix, 95, 103, 292
Richard Filangieri, Imperial Marshal, xxvii, xxviii, xix, 95-99, 290, 292, 293-294
Robert, Count of Artois, 106, 107
Robert II, Count of Flanders, 13, 14, 33, 46-47, 52, 68
Robert, Duke of Normandy, 13
Roland, 251

S

St Hilarion castle, 97
St Mary Major Nunnery, Jerusalem, 235
St Peter Cathedral, Caesarea, 235
St Peter's Cathedral, Rome, ix, 3
Safed castle, 168
sailors, 137, 158
salt, 153, 165, 199, 206
Samaratins, xxxiv, 133-135, 164, 224, 302
Saone castle, 231

Index

Saracens, xviii, xx, 3, 12, 14, 18, 22, 26, 27, 30-34, 36, 48, 49, 50, 57, 58, 59, 61, 64, 65, 69, 70, 71, 72, 74, 80, 85, 88, 89, 92, 104, 106, 107, 109, 116, 132, 140, 142, 167, 168, 171, 173, 174, 179, 186, 193, 195, 221, 223, 224, 229, 241, 249, 270, 272, 273, 276, 277, 281, 282, 288, 290, 299, 300

scholars, xxxiv, xxxv, 3, 5-7, 40, 45, 100, 110, 127, 140, 155, 176, 181, 190, 223, 224, 232, 244, 250, 267, 302

science, 201, 223

scribes, 146, 165, 202, 303

scriptoriums, 245, 246, 251

sculpture, 234, 243, 244, 246

Seljuks, x, xi, xv, xviii, xxi, xxix, 5-7, 13, 15, 16, 17, 23, 26, 28-31, 38, 42, 67, 109, 123, 131, 188, 189, 192, 202, 203

seneschal, 106, 160, 161, 294, 299, 301

serfs, 139, 141, 143, 159, 164, 170, 199, 255, 257, 303

sergeants, 11, 26, 48, 81, 108, 127, 140, 146, 151, 153, 157, 161, 163, 168, 169, 170, 174, 195, 259, 267, 295

settlers, 22, 26, 70, 81, 127, 128, 138-142, 146, 164, 195, 203, 204, 222, 225, 237, 238, 243, 248, 253, 261

sewage and plumbing, 227, 228, 236, 239, 304

Shirkuh, Kurdish general, 39-41

shipbuilding, 209

shipping and ships, xix, xxviii, 16, 20, 36, 47, 50, 64, 69, 74, 78, 79, 80, 95, 96, 97, 105, 106, 107, 113, 135, 163, 165, 174, 184, 207-208, 211, 216, 219, 240

shops, xxxv, 204, 228, 238, 248, 261

Siberia, 218

Sibylla, Queen of Jerusalem, xviii, xx, xxii, 45, 51-56, 61, 65, 69, 273, 275, 277, 279

Sidon, xiii, xx, xvii, xxxiii, 19, 25, 60, 64, 74, 84, 97, 101, 104, 108, 116, 124, 132, 178, 193, 194, 226, 249, 286

siqlatin, 213, 266

slaves and slavery, 2, 20, 31, 32, 48, 60, 63, 110, 111, 123, 128, 129, 148, 166, 195, 196, 200, 201, 217, 218, 227, 255, 277, 323

soap, 206, 210

social welfare, 254-266

souks, 228

South Africa, 142

spices, 163, 217, 218

Stephan, Count of Blois, 13, 16

sugar and plantations, 80, 163, 164, 165, 199, 204-206, 209-210, 216, 263

Sultanate of Rum, xxi, 6, 13, 67, 194

surcoats, 222, 304

synagogues, x, 4, 133, 203, 302

Syria, ix, xiv, xxiv, xxv, xxvi, xxviii, xxxvi, 3, 4, 6, 16,

339

19, 81, 82, 85, 88, 94, 97, 103, 104, 111, 113-119, 130, 131, 140, 143, 144, 146, 147, 176-180, 181, 192, 211, 213, 218, 223, 227, 234, 258, 290, 291, 295, 296, 298, 303

T

Tancred, nephew of the Duke of Taranto, 13, 15, 179
technology, xxxv, 117, 203, 206, 220-224, 303, 304
tenants-in-chief, *see* vassals
Teutonic Knights (Deutsche Ritterorden), xxvi, 94, 98, 104, 112, 115, 174, 175, 179, 209, 228, 231
textiles and textile production, 212-213, 263, 266
theology, 40, 180, 187, 191, 220, 251, 252
Thibaud, King of Navarre, xxix, 101, 102, 292
Tomaso of Acerra, 292
Toron, 84, 94, 102, 104, 286, 287
Tortosa, xii, xxi, 25, 26, 64, 235
Tortosa castle, 116
Toulouse, 11
tourism, 6, 164, 206-215, 216
tourists, xxxv, 135, 207-208
Tours, Battle of, ix, 3
trade and commerce, xxxv, 36, 85, 104, 118, 130, 134, 145, 146, 164, 165, 173, 192, 193, 198, 199, 201, 207, 209, 215, 219-221, 305

trade routes, 198, 218, 261, 300
tradesmen, xxxv, 139, 141, 170, 204
Transjordan, 28, 36, 46, 47, 55, 57, 60, 83, 89, 102, 103, 104, 131, 194
translators, 128, 144
travel, xxxv, 27, 114, 192, 207, 223, 243
treaties and truces, xviii, xix, xxi, xxiii, xxiv, xxvi, xxvii, xxix, xxxii, 19, 38, 46, 50, 57, 64, 74, 75, 77, 84-87, 89, 92, 93, 101, 103, 108, 110, 114, 156, 161, 185, 193, 194, 195, 201, 278, 296, 299
Trinitarians, 179
Tripoli, xii, xvii, xxi, xxv, xxxii, xxxiv, 25, 26, 34, 47, 57, 61, 64, 75, 84, 96, 114, 124, 125, 126, 132, 167, 170, 173, 197, 210, 213, 230, 246, 251, 290, 293
Turan Shah, Sultan of Egypt, xviii, 107, 110, 111
turcoples, *see* archers
Turks, x, xi, xii, xviii, xxi, xxxvii, 14, 15, 39, 68, 123, 172, 187, 215, 219
Tyre, xiii, xx, xxi, xxii, xxvii, xxix, 19, 25, 27, 60, 63-65, 70, 76, 77, 87, 90, 96, 98, 99, 113, 116, 124, 132, 133, 134, 137, 150, 166, 167, 173, 178, 197, 199, 212, 213, 215, 226, 227, 251, 276, 277, 288, 290, 292, 293, 296-297
Tyre castle, 231

Index

U

urbanisation, 125

V

Valania, 64
vassals, 9, 12, 23, 35, 44, 94, 95, 99, 130, 138, 143, 146, 149, 151-157, 160, 165, 168, 169, 186, 194, 278, 282
vegetables, 197, 205, 226, 262
Venice, xxiv, 86, 137, 174, 190, 207, 216, 221
villages,
    Frankish, 22, 133, 139, 141, 152, 181, 197, 199, 204, 238,
    native, 82, 123, 129, 133, 200, 201, 203, 237, 248, 323

W

walls, 13, 15, 19, 29, 47, 49, 54, 62, 63, 92, 114, 115, 116, 140-141, 166, 167, 221, 226-227, 228, 229, 230, 232, 236-239, 241, 247
Walter de Brienne, Lord of Jaffa, 104, 108, 112, 135
Walter de Châtillon, 251
Walter de Montbèliard, xxiv, 87, 284, 287, 288, 289
Walter of Antioch, 252
warehouses and warehousing, 137, 219
waterpower, 206
water reservoirs, 203
William, Archbishop of Tyre, 41
William de Beaujeu, Master, 115
William de la Tor, 253
William, Duke of Aquitaine, 34
William 'Longsword', Marquis de Montferrat, xviii, 46, 52, 53, 76
William Marshal, Earl of Pembroke, 52
William of Bures, Prince of Galilee, 279
William of Tyre, Archbishop of Tyre, 33, 35, 50, 52, 53, 54, 80, 230, 231, 246, 249, 252, 256, 265, 269, 271, 272
William the Conqueror, King of England, 13
windows, 211, 235, 236, 237, 238-40, 260, 304
wine and wine production, 27, 41, 80, 105, 141, 164, 165, 204, 205, 206, 210, 212, 216, 260, 263
wells, 19, 31, 50, 70, 163, 203, 229
wheat, 206, 261
workshops, 214, 228, 230, 238, 246, 303

Y

Yolanda, Queen of Jerusalem, xxv, xxvi, 87, 90, 91, 99, 101, 118, 274, 275, 288, 292

Z

Zengid dynasty, 43
Zoroastrians, 128, 202, 224